Shooter's Bible

GUIDE TO HANDLOADING

Shooter's Bible
GUIDE TO HANDLOADING

WAYNE VAN ZWOLL

SKYHORSE PUBLISHING

Skyhorse Publishing books may be purchased in bulk at special discounts for sales promotion, corporate gifts, fund-raising, or educational purposes. Special editions can also be created to specifications. For details, contact the Special Sales Department, Skyhorse Publishing, 307 West 36th Street, 11th Floor, New York, NY 10018 or info@skyhorsepublishing.com.

Visit our website at www.skyhorsepublishing.com.

10 9 8 7 6 5 4

Library of Congress Cataloging-in-Publication Data

Names: Van Zwoll, Wayne, author.
Title: Shooter's bible guide to handloading : a comprehensive reference for responsible and reliable reloading / Wayne van Zwoll.
Description: New York, NY : Skyhorse Publishing, 2015.
Identifiers: LCCN 2015033790 | ISBN 9781632202871 (paperback)
Subjects: LCSH: Handloading of ammunition--Handbooks, manuals, etc. | BISAC: SPORTS & RECREATION / Shooting. | SPORTS & RECREATION / Hunting. | SPORTS & RECREATION / Outdoor Skills.
Classification: LCC TS538.3 .V36 2015 | DDC 683.4/06--dc23
LC record available at http://lccn.loc.gov/2015033790

Cover design by Brian Peterson

Print ISBN: 978-1-63220-287-1
Ebook ISBN: 978-1-63450-971-8

Printed in China

CONTENTS

AUTHOR'S NOTES AND ACKNOWLEDGMENTS vii

INTRODUCTION: HANDLOADING ix

CHAPTER 1: PIONEERS IN HANDLOADING 1

CHAPTER 2: HANDLOADING, SIMPLY 23

CHAPTER 3: HANDLOADING TOOLS 43

CHAPTER 4: HEADSPACE IS NOT IQ 53

CHAPTER 5: PRESSURE 57

CHAPTER 6: GIDDY-UP! 63

CHAPTER 7: TESTING HANDLOADS 73

CHAPTER 8: BORN IN THE BARRACKS 83

CHAPTER 9: WILDCATS 95

CHAPTER 10: FAST-STEPPERS GONE FACTORY 105

CHAPTER 11: THE SHIFT TO SHORT 119

CHAPTER 12: HANDLOADING THE OLD-FASHIONED WAY 125

CHAPTER 13: COLONIAL LOADS 131

CHAPTER 14: MORE ON BULLETS 143

CHAPTER 15: BULLETS FOR BIG GAME 157

SHOOTING SECTION 171

CHAPTER 16: HOW TO HEAR WHEN YOU'RE OLD 173

CHAPTER 17: SOFTER SHOOTING ISN'T FOR SISSIES 179

CHAPTER 18: SHOOTING WELL IN WIND 183

APPENDIX 1: HANDLOADS FROM WAYNE'S BENCH 189

APPENDIX 2: PRODUCT DIRECTORY FOR HANDLOADERS 209

APPENDIX 3: HELPS FOR HANDLOADERS 215

AUTHOR'S NOTES AND ACKNOWLEDGMENTS

Producing this book kept me from having fun for many, many months. If the effort justified such deprivation, it should be apparent. You should find this book both entertaining and useful, and find that it cuts across the brands to which all handloading manuals are slaves. You should find here the best techniques, tools, and components, from a sweep of industry sources. You'll revisit handloading pioneers now gone and look over the shoulders of ballisticians who run sophisticated laboratories that yield current data. The text owes much to veteran hunters and competitive marksmen—and women—who routinely put several bullets through one hole in paper. You should come away, too, with ideas for better ammunition to ring steel targets bent by mirage in a distant zip code.

If the words and photos fail to deliver, it's my fault. To the extent they make this book a good buy and, eventually, one of the most-consulted tomes in your library, it's because many people contributed. I can't name them all, so I won't bore you with a list. Some are identified in the text, but countless others have taught me much about handloading and shooting. This is indeed an industry rich in both history and talent—and full of selfless souls willing to share their expertise. I thank them all most sincerely.

Of course, I'm indebted to Earl Wickman, who gave generously of his coaching when, pretzeled over the iron aperture of a Remington 40x, I made every youthful blunder possible in my halting progress toward competence behind a trigger. And I owe Alice, who warned me repeatedly that writing this book would make me surly, unreasonable and fat. She was right.

—**Wayne van Zwoll**

INTRODUCTION: HANDLOADING

Handloading saves you money. I wondered about that four decades ago, my fist tight around the $15 demanded by Herters for its iron "C" press. Heavy enough to anchor a light destroyer, it crowded the counter of the 28-foot mobile home I occupied during graduate school. A 50-pound keg of surplus H4831 came my way for $150. With barely enough cash left for primers, bullets, tomato soup, and the month's rent, I plunged into handloading. In my .270, a reworked Mauser, a 130-grain Sierra pushed by 59 grains sent mule deer to the Great Beyond. I shot my first elk with a 180-grain Speer over 69 grains in a .300 H&H, another rebarreled 98.

Whether you handload for rifles, handguns or shotguns, you get real value for your efforts. While many concepts and practices transfer from metallic cartridges to shotshells, this book treats rifle (mainly) and pistol loads.

BEYOND ECONOMICS

Handloading wrings potential from cartridges neglected or hamstrung by factories with an eye to profits and litigation. My recipe for 87-grain Sierras in the .250 Savage produces half-minute groups—three times the precision of commercial loads. IMR 7828 powers Noslers from my .264 Winchester 300 fps faster than chart speed. Handloading the .45 Colt—factory-loaded to squib speeds for the gaggle of old and cheap revolvers so chambered—gives it muscle in stout handguns like those by Freedom Arms.

Want more reasons to handload? It's fun. It's a personal investment that hikes the satisfaction you get from each shot. And it pulls you away from the television screen, where people who know nothing about ammunition march in lockstep with the equally ignorant on crusades to disarm you. Handloading calms you, reminds you that the Second Amendment still

▲ The author has long handloaded the 7x57. He killed this Oregon buck in the 1970s with a 145-grain Speer.

matters to the legions of fellow enthusiasts who built your press, machined your dies, punched the flash-holes in those cases, and turned the cannelures on your bullets—and to many millions more who share your passion for shooting, collecting and studying the history and mechanics of firearms. Handloading imbeds you ever more deeply in this clan (women included!), while distinguishing you from the great unwashed who simply pull triggers on commercial ammunition.

In my 40 years at the bench, the growing market power of handloaders has produced a cornucopia of hardware and components. The last couple of decades alone have yielded hundreds more bullets and powders in cartridges only the clairvoyant among wildcatters might have imagined in my youth.

Now, cursed be the scalawag who dismisses the factory load as fodder for infidels. I shoot a lot of it. And over my shooting career, it's been much improved. Bullet velocities once viable only with primer-flattening handloads now grace shop shelves. Bullet types range from the varmint-vaporizing to cohesive champs that drive laser-straight through the muscle and bone of creatures the size of chest freezers, with enough leftover romp to sever an oak limb and lace a Peterbuilt engine block.

Handloading requires your time and a bit of study. You have the time—the regulation 24 hours everyone gets each day. Study is simply an extension of passion. You *are* a shooter, aren't you?

Like racing motorcycles, skydiving and snorkeling with sharks, handloading is not as dangergous as it might appear to the uninitiated. But because hand-loading puts you close to things that could impair or abbreviate your life, you're smart to mind these caveats:

YES, YOU CAN TRY THIS AT HOME. BUT . . .

Handload only if you can honestly claim a reasonable level of intelligence, proof of which is your willingness to read all caveats twice, take them to heart, and admit in all humility that, no matter how long you've been shooting or how many times you've pumped a press handle, you do not know all there is to know about handloading. And won't. Ever.

At the bench, focus on the job, not the clock. Hurry-up handloading results in sloppy work and substandard ammunition. It can cause mistakes that ruin costly rifles and leave you thoroughly bandaged when you'd as soon look unblemished. Store components only in original containers. No, you will *not* remember you put 4198 in that empty 4831 canister. You will *not* tell at a glance the difference between 140-grain .270 spitzers and the 140 7mms you dumped in the .270 box. Mix-ups are embarrassing at best; they can be lethal.

Keep an organized bench. Working up starter loads for a new cartridge, you'll likely charge only a few cases between changes in powder type. Permit just one canister on the bench at a time. Finishing with that propellant, dump all remaining powder from the measure (or, if you adopt my habits, the plastic pepper shaker) into the original canister. Close it. Put it away. Ditto the bullets.

If a cartridge won't chamber easily, extract it and check the bullet for rifling marks, the hull for overall length. A bullet seated into the rifling, or a case mouth jammed up against the chamber mouth so tight it bites into the bullet can bump pressures to uncomfortable levels. A snug fit at shoulder or rim (a condition of minimum headspace) isn't dangerous. But before you lean on that bolt handle to close it, figure out what's tight.

Keep your loading room secure. Priming compound is an explosive. Smokeless powder is a fuel that burns so fast most people think it explodes. Both are best kept from the hands of young innocents and dull adults. Of course, you'll not allow an ignition source in that room. Electric heaters and wood stoves can be as hazardous as cigarettes.

Label all loads prominently, with age-resistant ink, on ammo boxes. Working up loads three at a time (as I often do to start) consider marking each cartridge on primer or case head with a grease pencil or Magic Marker. Color-code them, and record the code in a notebook.

Discard cases showing incipient separation—typically a white line just in front of the extractor groove, where the web gets thin enough to allow brass to flow forward upon firing. You'll get stretch here with each shot, more with belted cases in generous chambers.

Firing "work-hardens" brass. Brittle brass wants to break. When it does, escaping gas can wreck your rifle and your looks. Annealing brass restores its ductility. Still, it's poor economy to use tired brass or hulls stretched too far or repeatedly.

When testing handloads, wear glasses as well as ear protection. I forego both when hunting, and would rather fire without glasses at the bench. But I don them anyway, enduring fogged and smudged lenses and the discomfort of ear hooks under my muffs. Metal particles, even gas from a blown primer or case rupture, can destroy your eye.

Do not fire someone else's handloads. You can't know if the in-law who assembled a box of 7mm Magnum cartridges knows the difference between IMR 4198 and IMR 4831, or why maximum charges for 150-grain bullets can be hellish behind 200s. Unless you want more quality time with your attorney, do not sell, trade or donate your handloads to anyone else. Those 7mm-08 cartridges that neatly dispatch deer become bombs when the unwitting thumb them into a .25-06.

Most importantly, *think*. Neither handloading nor chronographing require a high IQ. The logic of a plow horse will do. Lose your concentration, though, and you can imperil your shooting career.

Working press and powder measure demands focus. So, too, does chronographing, especially if you're trying to shoot tight groups at the same time. Add rifles and loads, and you have that many more reasons to do the job alone. Onlookers drain your focus. Make a point of denying yourself the company of curious people who don't know you can't afford distraction.

Once, on the range with a fellow who'd just bought a lovely .270 from me, I heard an oddly harsh report. A quavering moan ensued. I raced over to find the rifle torn asunder, its French walnut stock split in three pieces, the extractor gone, the bolt frozen. My amigo was bleeding around his shooting glasses. "Those handloads of yours . . ." He winced as he wiped his brow. Convinced he was not seriously hurt, I examined the box of .270 ammo. I had charged those cartridges with H4831, a slow, bulky powder. It's hard to get enough H4831 in a .270 case to blow up a 98 Mauser. Indeed, it's downright impossible. I was sure I could have carded powder at the case mouths and seated 130-grain bullets without exceeding safe pressures. The box of suspect loads *did* wear my hand-written label. It dawned on me suddenly, however, that the box was also full. I mentioned this and asked where the delinquent cartridge had come from. Still dazed, my friend nodded toward another box. A glance told me it held .308 rounds—for the fellow's other rifle. In haste he had grabbed that ammunition by mistake. In a .270 rifle, the .308 cartridge is poison. Its case is shorter, so the larger bullet doesn't quite reach the chamber's neck. The Mauser extractor holds the hull against the bolt face. Ignition is certain. But forcing a .308 bullet through a .277 bore hikes pressures to obscene levels. My partner was lucky the bolt held.

More recently, on the bench with a borrowed lever rifle and chatting with its owner, I turned back to the target, aimed, thumbed the hammer, and squeezed. Clack. I waited several seconds before opening the action—standard procedure to control the muzzle in the event of a hang-fire. When I dropped the lever, an empty case tumbled out. First thought: "I must have forgotten to cycle." So I chambered another round and settled the rifle again on the bags.

Then an angel tapped me gently on the shoulder. I considered other possibilities. Flipping open the action, I looked into the muzzle. Dark. The first .348 Improved round I'd chambered had been sized and primed. But the handloader had neglected to include powder before seating the bullet. When I pulled the trigger, the primer fired, pushing the 200-grain softnose into the bore, where it lodged just ahead of the throat. The primer's report couldn't escape the case or the bore, and was further muffled by the heavy hammer fall. Had I fired a second round, the results would have been jarring. The lodged bullet would have interrupted the forward travel of the one behind just as gas pressure was peaking. This catastrophic event would most probably have shredded the rifle and my left hand—or caused even greater mayhem.

Assumptions can scuttle your shooting career. Thinking is always a good idea.

Enough cautions. Properly conducted, handloading is fun. And it's a safe pursuit. I've endured no more pain at the bench than I have at the dinner table or watching television. Enthusiasts who seated their first

▲ This primer is seated sideways. Soak it in oil to de-activate before removing with a decapping pin!

bullets in caves littered with dinosaur bones have enjoyed long, rewarding lives, wearing out many sets of trim dies before other ills pulled them from the powder scale. I suspect you'll find handloading as engaging, instructive and useful as they have.

TO ERR IS HUMAN

Handloading is a safe practice, provided you pay attention to what you're doing. Multitasking is a bad idea. Avoid, too, handloading under the press of deadlines. Historically, stress has proven inimical to safe, accurate loads. A Navy report in the wake of our Civil War noted that of 25,476 muzzle-loading rifles found on battlefields, "at least 24,000" were loaded. "Half of these contained two loads each, one fourth from three to ten loads each. . . . In many of these guns, from two to six balls have been found with only one charge of powder. In some, the balls [were] at the bottom of the bore with the charge of powder on top. . . . Twenty-three loads were found in one Springfield."

And that was with just one ball, one cap, and one charge of powder to assemble at a time.

A SENSE OF WHAT WORKS

This book is not a manual—not a compendium of specific loads. Before you handload, you'd be smart to get several manuals. I've listed what I consider the best in this book, with contact information. Cross-referencing is a big help in developing loads. Stiff charges in one manual may be listed as mid-range in another. Powders used by one manufacturer may not appear in another's manual, though they're excellent propellants for the task. Check enough manuals, and you'll get a feel for what should serve a cartridge well. While no substitute for data, that sense of what *should* work speeds up load development and helps you fashion useful starting loads for wildcat rounds not listed in manuals. It's also a good first step to safe loads for rifles with short throats and other bore anomalies.

▲ New propellants give traditional cartridges new life. Hodgdon offers Hornady's powder to handloaders.

Chapter 1: Pioneers in Handloading

The middle of the twentieth century delivered some of the best big game hunting this country would ever see. It brought the best of Winchester's bolt rifles and ranks of new, short belted magnum cartridges. Before the Ford Mustang, Jack Kennedy, Sputnik, and Elvis Presley, shooters found headline news in the start-up of companies promising more and better ammunition. Handloaders, especially, benefited from the efforts of pioneers like Joyce Hornady, Bruce Hodgdon, Fred Huntington, Roy Weatherby, and Dick and Vernon Speer. But their work built on the efforts of wildcatters in the early days of smokeless powder.

CHARLES NEWTON

Born in Delevan, New York, January 8, 1870, Charles Newton worked on his father's farm until finishing school at age 16. After a two-year stint teaching, he applied his quick mind to the study of law and was admitted to the state bar. But his passion was not for courtrooms. He spent six years in the New York National Guard, then began developing cartridges with then-new smokeless propellants. Eventually, in association with Fred Adolph, he turned his hand to designing firearms.

A talented German gunsmith, Adolph immigrated to the United States in 1908 and established a shop in Genoa, New York. By 1914, he had published a catalog of rifles, shotguns, and combination guns. Some were imported; others he built. Adolph distinguished his business by chambering high-velocity big game cartridges, among them nearly a dozen by Charles Newton. The smallest but perhaps best known was the .22 High-Power. A 1905 development on the .25-35 case, it pushed 70-grain .228 bullets at 2,800

▲ Many handloading pioneers chased higher velocities with small-bore rifles, for game like coyotes.

fps. The "Imp" built a bigger-than-life reputation on animals as formidable as tigers. More realistically, it proved a deadly deer cartridge. And it inspired shooters to think of reaching beyond range limits imposed by blunt bullets and iron sights.

In 1912, the talented Newton necked the .30-06 to .257 and called it the .25 Newton Special. His 7mm Special foreshadowed the .280 Remington by half a century (as did the 7x64 Brenneke developed in Germany about the same time). Also in 1912, Newton delivered to Savage a short, rimless .250 cartridge that followed the .22 High-Power as a new chambering for the 1899 lever rifle. Newton suggested a 100-grain bullet, but Savage hawked instead an 87-grain missile at 3,000 fps—lightning speed in those days. The .250-3000 moniker derives from that initial load. Newton's work with short cases helped bring the .300 Savage to market. Its hull measured 1.87 inches but packaged 10 percent more power than a .30-30.

▲ In 1912, Newton developed the .250 Savage (left), here with the .257 Roberts (1934), .25-06 (1969).

Newton came up with a .22 Long Range pistol cartridge by shortening and necking down the .28-30 Stevens. The bullet was the same .228 jacketed spitzer loaded in the .22 High-Power. He fashioned his .22 Newton from the 7x57 hull, driving a 90-grain bullet at 3,100 fps from a barrel with fast 1-in-8 twist. The .22 Special on .30-40 Krag brass launched a 68-grain bullet at nearly 3,300.

A single-shot enthusiast, Charles Newton experimented with big-rimmed cases like Winchester's .405, necking it to 7mm, even .25. He designed .30, 8mm and .35 Express rounds from 3 ¼ -inch Sharps hulls. His rimless .30 Newton had the profile of modern belted magnums and approached them across the chronograph. It delivered more punch than hunters considered necessary for North American game then. Inspired by the .404 Jeffery hull, Newton's .35 and a handful of other big rimless and rebated cartridges appeared around 1910. One of his most celebrated efforts was the .256 Newton. Ballistically similar to the .257 Roberts Improved, it fired a .264 bullet, not a .257. Charles preferred it to the .25-06 for two reasons. First, .25-06 chambers of that time varied in dimensions, and as tight chambers hiked pressures; Newton didn't want his name linked to rifles that fell apart. Secondly, Mauser produced 6.5mm barrels.

Early in his cartridge-designing days, Newton had dreamed of building his own rifles. In 1914, he formed the Newton Arms Company in Buffalo, New York. With a factory under construction, he traveled to Germany to seek a supply of rifle actions from Mauser and J.P. Sauer & Sohn. He intended to restock them, then barrel them to .256 Newton and .30 Adolph Express. A flier advertised .256 Newton barrels "of the best Krupp steel" with raised, matted ribs and sight slots—for $17! In March 1915, the first Newton rifles appeared in a catalog. The 1898 Mauser actions wore barrels in .256, .30 and .35 Newton. Hunting-style stocks by Fred Adolph and California gunsmith Ludwig Wundhammer gave them a sporting look. Available in three grades, they were priced from $42.50 to $80.

Alas, Newton's timing could hardly have been worse! The first two dozen Mauser rifles were to arrive 15 August 1914. Germany went to war the fourteenth. With international conflict nixing his promised Mauser rifles, Charles Newton tapped the Marlin Firearms Company for barrels in .256 Newton, threaded for 1903 Springfields. He planned to sell them for $12.50 as replacements to hunters pining for something other than a .30-06. He would fit them with Springfield sporter stocks. But rifles and components were in short supply. All arms factories were up to their eyeballs in lucrative government contracts.

Charles Newton had to sit on his hands, but he didn't stop thinking. By 1916, he had incorporated desirable features of the Mauser and Springfield designs into a rifle whose only non-original part was the mainspring. He hired lengendary barrel-maker Harry Pope to oversee barrel production and claimed that Pope had helped him develop segmented rifling in Newton barrels.

The first of Newton's new rifles went on sale January 1, 1917. They got favorable press. But once again the timing was wrong. The United States entered the war April 6, the government assuming control of all ammunition production. Though Newton loaded his own cartridges, he depended on Remington for cases. Early in 1918, ammo was coming off the line. But the banks supporting his firm sent it into receivership, and by year's end, the Newton Arms Company was no more. About 2,400 rifles had been built. Another 1,600 were completed by Bert Holmes, who acquired all assets. Holmes sold more than 1,000 rifles for $5 each before giving up trying to run the plant himself.

In April 1919, New York machinery dealers Lamberg, Schwartz and Land formed the Newton Arms Corporation. Their plan was to market as genuine Newtons several bin-loads of poor-quality rifles they had bought from Bert Holmes. Charles Newton filed suit and won a delayed settlement. Marshaling assets, he then launched the Chas. Newton Rifle Corporation (April 19, 1919). Evidently the plan was to equip a new factory with surplus tooling from Eddystone Arsenal.

Nothing came of the Eddystone deal. The only rifles sold by the Chas. Newton Rifle Corporation were commercial Mausers. They had butterknife bolt handles, double-set triggers, triple-leaf sights. Some featured parabolic rifling, some a cloverleaf of muzzle grooves—ostensibly to vent gas in such a way as to prevent bullet tipping. Riflemen liked these actions and Newton's stocks. He got roughly 1,000 orders. But Germany's overheated postwar economy couldn't supply that many rifles under the contract terms. Only 100 or so arrived Stateside. Ever optimistic, Charles Newton started another venture in 1923, with Arthur Dayton and Dayton Evans, who had helped him bankroll his 1919 venture. The Buffalo Newton Rifle Corporation, founded in Buffalo, soon moved to New Haven, Connecticut, where the first Buffalo Newton rifles shipped in 1924. They had interrupted-thread lock-up and four-groove nickel-steel barrels chambered to .30-06 and four Newton rounds: .256, .280, .30, and .35. Walnut stocks featured a crossbolt behind the magazine, but no receiver lug to arrest recoil! Many stocks split. Western Cartridge Company, which had begun supplying Newton rounds in 1921, listed Buffalo Newton ammunition.

Once again money had become scarce for Charles Newton. After borrowing on his life insurance, he pleaded with Marlin's Frank Kenna to build his rifles under contract. The astute, conservative Kenna demurred—despite Newton's claim that his company was on the brink of success, and that, at the rate of 1,000 rifles a month, Marlin could build rifles for $8 each. Buffalo Newtons then retailed for $60.

In 1929, the Buffalo Newton Rifle Corporation folded, after producing around 1,500 rifles. With characteristic zeal, Charles Newton applied himself to another action design and came up with the New Newton Straight Pull Rifle. Its two-lug bolt and Springfield cocking piece suggested bolt-rifle ancestry; but Newton had also borrowed from the straight-pull Lee Navy and Winchester lever-action designs. In fact, Newton renamed the rifle the "Leverbolt." If Marlin produced the rifle, implored Newton to Frank Kenna, he'd split profits down the middle. When Kenna required proof of demand, Newton published a flyer soliciting a $25 down payment for each Leverbolt rifle. The remaining $35 would be due when the rifle was delivered. Sadly, even this offer failed to bring the necessary 500 orders.

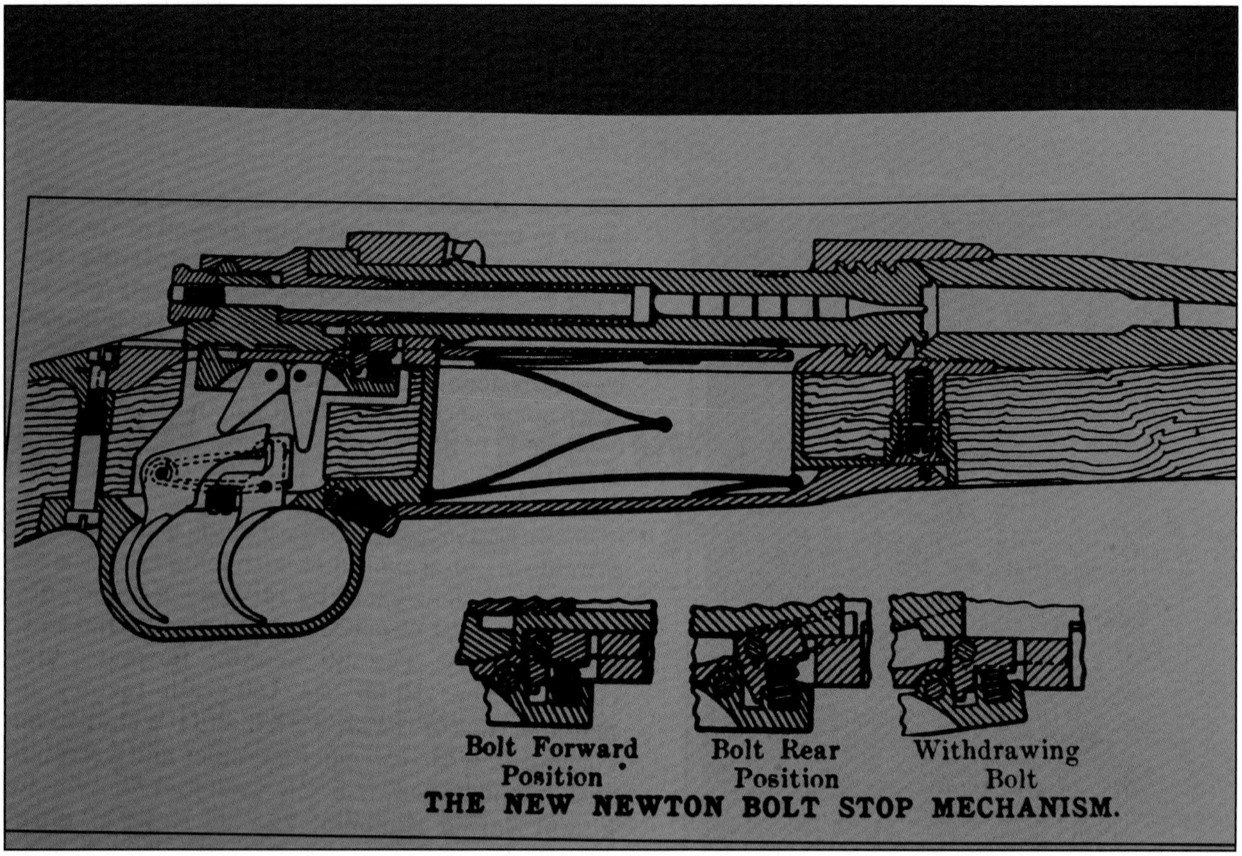

▲ Charles Newton was an able wildcatter and rifle designer—and, alas, a frustrated entrepreneur.

In October, Wall Street collapsed, dashing the dreams of many Americans, including Newton's. His irrepressible spirit succumbed at last to the Depression. He died in New Haven, March 9, 1932, age 62.

Most certainly, Charles Newton's work with high-performance cartridges prepared the way for the post-World War II debut of short belted magnums. It also inspired other wildcatters and designs. While the .25-06 is generally credited to Neidner, it may well have appeared on Newton's bench first. A generation before Roy Weatherby, Newton had game bullets clocking over 3,000 fps. His interrupted-thread locking lugs predated the Weatherby Mark V bolt by 30 years. His three-position safety appeared 20 years before Winchester's. This lawyer-turned-inventor also fashioned a partitioned game bullet in 1915.

It's a shame Charles Newton's brilliant cartridge designs—and his perseverance in bringing superb rifles and high-performance loads to shooters—earned him few rewards.

JOYCE HORNADY

At his birth in 1907, Joyce Hornady's parents named him after a Methodist bishop. During World War II, Joyce taught marksmanship in a Guard Training Unit. Not long after the war and a short stint at Nebraska's Cornhusker Army Ammunition Plant, he partnered with Vernon Speer in a bullet-making enterprise. The union soon dissolved, however. Speer went to Idaho, while Hornady moved from Lincoln to Grand Island, Nebraska. In 1949, he set about making hunting bullets. The business earned $10,000 its first year and triple that figure by its third. A 150-grain Spire Point bullet Joyce Hornady fashioned for the .30-06 remains, six decades later, one of the company's top sellers!

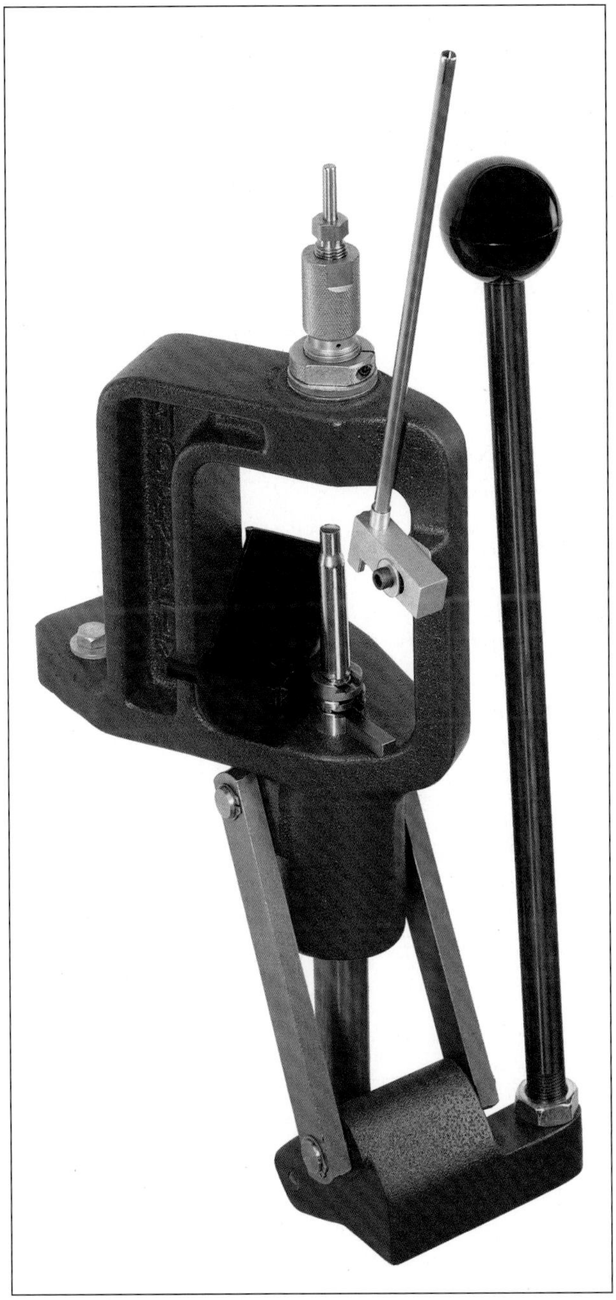

▲ Joyce Hornady started out making bullets with Vernon Speer. Hornady now lists many loading tools.

The Korean War prompted Hornady to suspend sporting-bullet production to manufacture other hard goods. In 1958, brisk demand for bullets justified construction of an 8,000-square-foot plant. A 200-yard shooting tunnel followed. Then Hornady Bullets announced a bullet nose designed for flatter flight and better accuracy. The Secant Ogive profile has since distinguished Hornady's pointed softpoints.

In 1964, Joyce Hornady began loading ammunition under the Frontier label. He employed canister powders, once-fired cases, and his own bullets—first in .243, .270, .308 and .30-06. Vietnam's unrest reduced access to fired cases, so Hornady began buying new brass in 1972. About that time, his son Steve moved back to Grand Island. Born the same year as the business, Steve had tried his wings at Pacific Tool Company, a manufacturer of handloading hardware in Lincoln. As the Pacific products seemed a natural extension of his bullet business, Joyce bought the company and moved its tooling in-house. He broadened Hornady's base during the 1970s with the acquisition of West Coast Shot Company. The Reno, Nevada enterprise became Hornady Magnum Shot, but was later sold back to its original owner.

Steve recalls his father as a supremely talented mechanic. "He could make anything run," Steve said, "but he had no formal training in metallurgy, so a lot of our early growth was by trial and error." A visionary, Joyce was ever keen to improve Hornady products and increase the company's market share. Tragically, the founder of Hornady Bullets perished in a plane crash in 1981, en route to the SHOT (Shooting, Hunting and Outdoor Trade) Show in New Orleans with employees Ed Heers and Jim Barber. Steve Hornady took the company reins as president. His sister, Margaret Hornady-David, and her husband, Don David, moved to Grand Island to become vice-president and chief engineer respectively.

At that time, the InterLock feature in Hornady bullets was only four years old. The company offered Spire Point, Flat Point, Round Nose, Super Explosive, Hollow Point, Boat Tail Hollow Point, as well as conventional pistol bullets for handloaders, and basic muzzleloader projectiles. The line would soon grow to include XTP Pistol bullets, plus polymer-tipped rifle and muzzleloader bullets like the A-MAX, V-MAX, SST and InterBond bullets.

In 1983, under family management, Hornady Bullets was absorbed into a newly formed Hornady Manufacturing Company. The other divisions, Frontier Ammunition and Pacific Tool Company,

▲ Hornady's Nebraska-based bullet firm has become a major supplier and innovator of sporting ammo.

became Hornady Custom Ammunition and Hornady Reloading Tools. A year after that, the firm was making its own cartridge cases and loading them. "We became an integrated company," said Steve. "Our ability to design and supply both cases and bullets ensured a degree of flexibility and autonomy. We've since been blessed by terrific talent. This company is really run from the bottom up."

Under Steve's leadership, Hornady has aggressively pursued new products, from bullets to rifle cartridges and handloading items. But each project gets thorough vetting. "We supplied bullets to Mike Bussard at Federal Cartridge when that company was experimenting with a .17 rimfire. But we weren't then ready to invest in a round we weren't equipped to load. Later our chief engineer, Dave Emary, applied new powders. I wasn't very receptive; but Dave persisted. When I joined him at the range, we had fun! I figured shooting that was fun for us would be fun for others. When I called Darrell Inman at CCI to see about loading a .17 rimfire, he told me I had to order five million cartridges—and buy the tooling!" Steve took the gamble. It paid off. Within weeks of announcing the .17 HMR, Hornady doubled its order for cartridges. "In no time, we were back-ordered 12 million rounds!"

New centerfire rounds followed. Hornady fashioned .308 and .338 Marlin Express rounds for the Models 336 and 1895 lever rifles, with the FlexTip bullets it loads in LEVERevolution ammunition. The soft, resilient polymer tip allows for a pointed profile without the hazard imposed by hard conical tips contacting primers in a tube magazine. LEVERevolution cartridges in .30-30, .32 Special, .35 Remington and .45-70 breathed new life into traditional lever rifles. The stable included modern rounds like the .444 Marlin, .44 and .357 Magnums, and the .450 Marlin, developed at Hornady. The firm's FTX bullet is now cataloged as a component. Its 14 configurations range in diameter from .30 to .50 (including .348, for owners of the iconic but discontinued Winchester 71), and in weights from 140 to 325 grains.

Bolt rifles have also benefitted from Grand Island's bullet-and-ammunition maker. The .300 and .338 Ruger Compact Magnum rounds feature a series of propellants Dave Emary helped develop to wring magnum velocities from carbine-length barrels. Powders with the same properties have since become available to handloaders. Hornady approached Ruger with the idea for a .204 cartridge, then produced it. The .376 Steyr had its start in Grand Island. After Ruger's Steve Sanetti suggested a .30-06-length .375. Hornady developed it and the subsequent .416 Ruger on the same fat, rimless case. The company supplies brass for John Lazzeroni's cartridges, and bullets for other ammunition companies.

Hornady headlines in this current decade include GMX lead-free hunting bullets, Critical Defense handgun ammunition that plows deep, broad channels behind heavy clothing, and a Dangerous Game line of ammo that offers solid-bullet options for new and classic rounds, 9.3x74 to .500 Nitro Express. There's TAP rifle and handgun ammo for law enforcement. Superformance cartridges with special powders bring the firm's Light Magnum ballistic performance up to date without compressed charges. There are loads and components for hard-to-find numbers like the .404 Jeffery, .405 Winchester and .45 Schofield.

An aggressive R&D lab keeps Hornady's inventory cycling at headlong pace. Stiff demand for ammunition and handloading tools during 2013 stacked back-orders industry-wide. But Hornady has worked hard to match output to demand. One Hornady press on the 108,000-square-foot factory now turns out more bullets in a day than Joyce Hornady's company did during its first year! Lock-N-Load handloading hardware has been hard for dealers to keep in stock, as shooters who've grown up with Hornady ammunition look to the firm when equipping their benches.

The firm is still a family-run affair, with Steve at the helm. In 2006, Jason Hornady, Steve's son, joined the firm after 15 years as a shooting sports industry representative. Jason is now director of sales and company vice president. Marval (Mrs. Joyce) Hornady helped with the business into her eighties. Daughter Margie has retired from it; son Robert passed away in mid-2008. Hornady Manufacturing is a member of Sporting Arms and Ammunition Manufactuer's Institute (SAAMI), the National Shooting Sports Foundation (NSSF), and other industry groups – and a founding member of the Shooting Sports Heritage Foundation, which Steve helped organize. He's quick to credit others for the company's success. "Our biggest asset is our workforce," Steve reminds me. It now numbers nearly 300.

"Ten bullets through one hole." Joyce Hornady's standard for accuracy still applies at the Grand Island plant that bears his name. From bullets and handloading tools to ammunition, the company serves shooters with high expectations for precision.

TOUGH TESTS TO TOP!

During one of my early visits to the Hornady factory in Grand Island, Nebraska, I asked the plant supervisor how the company ensured that all batches coming off the line are uniformly accurate. "Every bullet run is tested at 100,000-unit intervals," he said. "Rifle bullets for accuracy, pistol bullets for upset." Wide velocity spreads make mushrooming difficult to control in handgun bullets. "Our .38s and .45s are tested at 750 fps and 1,500, those for the .454 Casull at 1,000 and 1,600. Those velocities work for black powder rifles, too." Some pistol bullets serve double duty as sabot projectiles in muzzleloaders. My host showed me a ragged one-hole group. "We shoot four five-shot groups with rifle bullets for accuracy. The *average* must meet our standards. For .30s that's .600 at 100 yards, for .17s it's .400. The 6mms come in at .450, the .338s at .750. Those are *hunting* bullets. More stringent standards apply to match bullets: .350 for .22 match. We check those more often too: every 30,000 units." Hornady's 30-bore match bullets are tested at 200 yards, where they must shoot inside .800.

BRUCE HODGDON

Brewster E. Hodgdon, born in 1910 in Joplin, Missouri, grew up to apprentice under his father, a civil engineer. But one wintry day, in the back of an open 1917 Buick en route to a farm survey, Bruce chose another path. He studied business at Pittsburg State College, then attended Washburn. Shortly after testing his salesmanship peddling gas appliances, he married Amy Skipworth in 1934. Soon Bruce and Amy had a house with a garage on two acres, plus a chicken coop and a small orchard.

His success in sales only fueled Bruce's dream to *own* a business. Surplus gunpowder would give him that chance. Huge stocks of powder had been jettisoned at sea following World War I, just to get rid of it. A handloader even during his Navy service in the 1940s, Bruce set out to buy as much powder as he could from military depots, then peddle it to handloaders. He bought his first 25 tons with cash borrowed against his life insurance policy. It was 4895, ideal for the popular .30-06. He stored that powder in a derelict boxcar in a rented pasture. A one-inch ad in *The American Rifleman* summoned buyers, who got 150 pounds for $30!

Bruce's son, J.B., recalls shipping that powder. "The first cans were metal" he said. "My brother, Bob, and I glued on the labels and built shipping boxes from orange crates. On our way to school, we drove tons of 4895 to REA and Merriam Frisco terminals in the trunk of a 1940 Ford." When copper-lined kegs gave way to cardboard, "we sold the salvaged copper for more than those first batches of powder." Soon mail orders included other reloading components, eventually rifles and ammunition. Meanwhile, Amy had put her talents to use as the Hodgdons' bookkeeper.

In 1952, brisk powder sales prompted Bruce to quit his appliance job in Kansas City to focus on his nascent powder business, B.E. Hodgdon, Incorporated. J.B. and Bob joined him after finishing school in 1959 and 1961. Ted Curtis, Homer Clark and Dave Wolfe (founder, Wolfe Publishing) helped Bruce lobby the

Interstate Commerce Commission to downgrade the classification of certain kinds of smokeless powder to "Flammable Solid"—so containers of under eight pounds each, in shipments totaling less than 100 pounds, could be sent by common carrier. In 1966, the family split the powder enterprise from the firearms business to form Hodgdon Powder Company. Its headquarters would come to include powder magazines and packaging facilities on 160 acres six miles west of the company office at 6231 Robinson, in Overland Park, Kansas. From there, Bruce Hodgdon would sell about four million pounds of powder.

A top seller, largely because of its availability, was H4831. Developed for use in 20mm cannons, H4831 also suited the belted magnum cartridges then beginning to snatch market share from the .30-06. "We got some surplus H4831 fresh," J.B. remembers. "Some came from disassembled ammo. To move it quickly, we included primers in a bargain package. Primers weren't easy for handloaders to find. One of Dad's packages included a 150-pound keg and 15,000 primers for $49.95." Or you could settle for a 50-pound keg with 10,000 primers, or a 20-pound keg with 5,000. "Bob and I screened that powder with a double-mesh drum cranked by hand. Big debris, such as wadding from 20mm cannon shells, stayed in the middle. Fines sifted through to the floor. There were no SAAMI specs for performance, or practical ways to measure pressure. We tested powder uniformity with a crude electric chronograph and generated data by measuring the heads of fired cases. Half a thousandth was too much expansion." He grins. "Crude, all right. But that powder pushed a lot of bullets into bullseyes and kept a nation of hunters in venison!" J.B. tells me H4831 was the most uniform of surplus powders. "Dad first picked that up in 1949, as I recall," says J.B., "a couple of years after his first 4895."

Ron Reiber has worked at Hodgdon for more than 20 years. He knows the origins of other popular surplus powders. "H335 was first designated WC 844, a powder for the 55-grain .223 load for the M16. It followed BL-C2, developed as WC 846 for 147-grain hardball in the .308." Powder that began as WC852 took on a new moniker when Bruce found it excelled in his .22-250. "He used 38 grains behind a 50-grain bullet for 3,800 fps," Ron tells me. "The powder became H380. H870 was fuel for the .50 BMG."

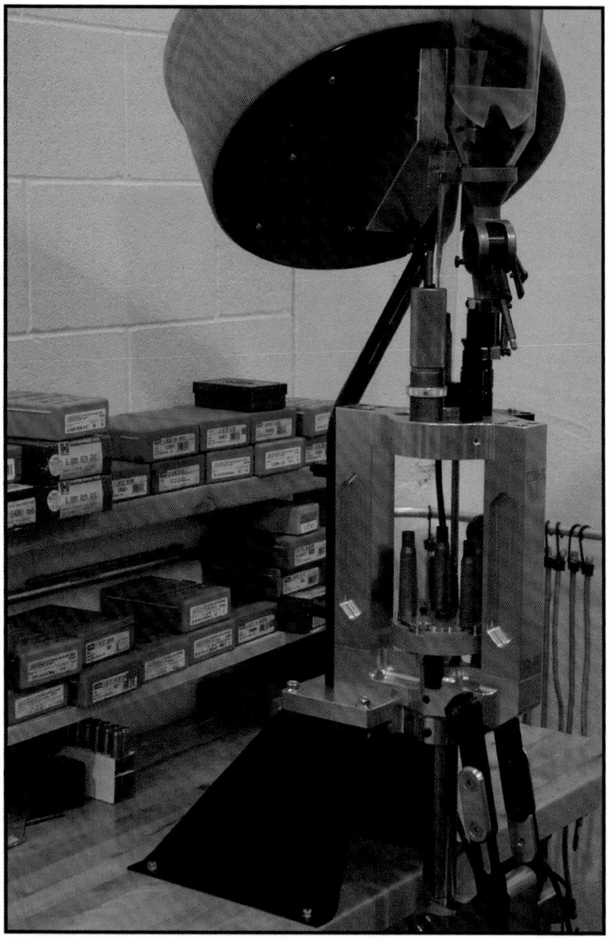

▲ Pioneering ammo firms like Black Hills have well-equipped loading benches, as did their forebears.

By 1959 surplus powder stocks had so diminished, the Hodgdons looked for commercial sources. Before and during World War II, the U.S. government had subsidized Olin and DuPont in the United States. The French-owned Australian Thales plant (which currently manufactures Hodgdon's extruded powders) also got its start as a US-funded project. "Following the war," says J.B., "countries transferred ownership to commercial interests. One of our first non-military sources was a plant in Scotland established to supply powder to the British."

The Hodgdon enterprise bought spherical powder, pioneered by John Olin in 1933, from the Olin Corp. At first Bruce called it ball powder. "But we soon learned Olin had registered that name," says J.B., "so we changed our designation to spherical." At this writing, Olin's Winchester powder is made by St. Mark's, an industry supplier owned by General Dynamics and operated at a Florida location. Since 2005, Hodgdon has marketed Winchester canister powders under licensing agreement. IMR (Improved Military Rifle) powders are manufactured at a factory near Montreal. DuPont chose not to sell extruded powders to Hodgdon in the 1960s. Ironically, Hodgdon now owns DuPont's IMR business! "We distribute Finland's Vihtavuori line, too," adds J.B. He stresses that Hodgdon is not a powder manufacturer. "However, we do engineer powders with our suppliers. For instance, we developed Trail Boss with a high-bulk density for Cowboy Action loads. That bulk won't let handloaders inadvertently double-charge a case."

Hodgdon now markets about 120 kinds of propellants, which account for 70 percent of consumer sales of rifle, handgun and shotgun powders. This is according to Chris Hodgdon, who now handles much of the public relations work for his family's company.

Bruce Hodgdon died in 1997. It's unlikely that, in his youth, borrowing on his life insurance for a mountain of surplus rifle powder, he foresaw today's crowded field of sporting cartridges. Or that he predicted the spate of new fuels and bullets to ride the belted-magnum revolution of the 1950s and early 1960s. Then again, his keen eye saw value in what others considered waste. He followed his instincts, and without manufacturing a single pound of powder, his family established the Hodgdon name as the best-known supplier of propellants in the industry.

It remains so. Handloaders who tap the Hodgdon line still come up with a wide choice of powders for every purpose.

P. O. ACKLEY

One of the best-known wildcatters in the post-war age of wildcatting was Parker Otto Ackley. He is most celebrated for his "Improved" cartridges—commercial rounds whose cases he altered to increase their powder capacities and reduce bolt thrust. This he accomplished by fire-forming factory ammunition

▲ P. O. Ackley "improved" cartridges (here the .35 Whelen) by steepening the shoulder to 40 degrees.

in Improved chambers, bored with less taper and a sharper (typically 40-degree) shoulder. Headspacing was unchanged, both for rimmed and rimless rounds. Ackley used the original datum line on the shoulder of the latter to save a step in case forming and permit riflemen to safely and effectively fire factory-loaded rounds in Improved chambers.

Among the best descriptions of Ackley and his cartridge designs appears in the well-researched and exceedingly useful book, *Wildcat Cartridges*, by Fred Zeglin, himself an accomplished gunsmith and rifle-builder. I've here excerpted part of that review, with permission and light editing for space:

"A native of Granville, N.Y., Ackley graduated from Syracuse University, *magna cum laude*, in

1927. Following his marriage to Winnefred Ross in 1928, the couple established a farm and a trucking business. She stopped teaching to raise a family. . . .

During the Great Depression, they moved to Roseburg, Oregon, where, in 1936, Parker started a gunsmithing and barrel-making business. The enterprise flourished there until 1942, when Ackley went to work for the Small Arms Division of the Ogden Arsenal. . . . Leaving the Arsenal in 1944, they moved to Cimarron, New Mexico, for a year, where Parker re-established his gun business. In 1945, Mr. Ackley brought that business to Trinidad, Colorado. From 1946 to 1951, he taught gun-making theory and metallurgy at Trinidad State Junior College. Here he performed many of his storied experiments with rifle actions and case design.

In 1951, Ackley sold his gun business in Trinidad and moved his family to Salt Lake City, Utah. His wife, Winn, opened a branch of Tandy Leather Co. The first female in that company's management, she retired in 1968."

P. O. Ackley was a regular contributor to *Guns & Ammo* and *Shooting Times* magazines. He soon developed a reputation for telling the truth. His magazine articles contributed greatly to Ackley's fame in the firearms industry and helped build his business. His *Handbook for Shooters & Reloaders, Volume I* appeared in 1962. *Volume II* followed in 1966.

Ackley's scientific approach to testing cartridges, barrels, and actions set him apart. He carefully recorded test results, using them as empirical evidence to verify or trash longstanding assumptions. For example, to prove his points concerning case design and bolt thrust, Ackley described tests with a Savage 99 and a Winchester 94. Creating a condition of grossly excessive headspace in the 94 action, he proved three major points:

1. Minimum case taper transfers more pressure to the chamber walls, minimizing bolt thrust.
2. An oily chamber or cartridge increases bolt thrust.
3. While the chamber and bolt bottle much of the gas pressure, the case itself contains some.

"To further illustrate the value of Improved case design, Ackley reported his tests with a Savage 99, originally in .250-3000. He started with a load of HiVel #2 and a 100 gr. bullet that delivered 2,900 fps and peak pressure of 52,000 psi. Cases extracted easily. He increased the powder charged until the action locked up upon firing. He then rechambered the Model 99 to his Improved .250-3000, fire-forming brass to fit, then boosting powder charges. When the load that had frozen the rifle's action was fired in the Improved chamber, the lever swung open with little effort. Extraction and ejection were normal.

In 1938, Ackley announced his first wildcat, the .219 Zipper Improved. He made three versions before he was satisfied with the design, eventually recommending use of .30-30 brass (instead of .25-35) to form the cartridge. A small-bore enthusiast, Ackley pioneered .17-caliber centerfire rounds during the 1940s and '50s. The .17 Ackley Bee, first called the .17 Ackley Pee Wee, was one of the first.

In a forthright assessment of shoulder angles, Ackley wrote, "Most of our own .22 cases, such as the .228 Ackleys, the Improved Zippers, the .17 caliber [have a] 28-degree shoulder. We have tried the 45-degree shoulder but did not like the results; we can see no increase in efficiency. . . . [This squares with findings] by Ashurst, Gipson and Lovell; they all agree that 28-degree and 30-degree shoulder slopes are the best. . . ."

Ackley is credited with 62 wildcats; more than 40 of these are Improved cartridges. But by all accounts he did not jump to claim credit for his work. He recognized the efforts of Harvey Donaldson, Vernor Gipson, Lyle Kilbourn, Art Mashburn and Hervey Lovell—fellow post-Depression wildcatters.

Oddly enough, P. O. Ackley did not approve the label of "Improved" for blown-out cases, writing that it was

"an unfortunate selection because any 'Improved' cartridge has little relation to its commercial counterpart except for the fact that the 'Improved' chamber will accept factory ammunition without

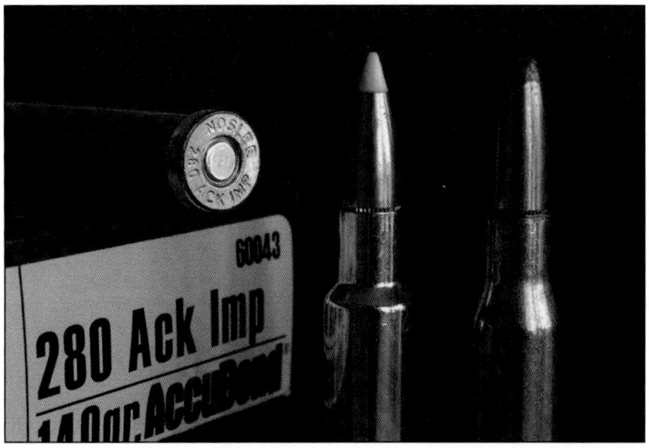

▲ P. O. Ackley hiked case capacity by forming 40-degree "Improved" shoulders. No headspace change.

> any danger to the shooter. Cases for an 'Improved' cartridge [can be fashioned without] using forming dies, which are required for a pure wildcat."

Mr. Ackley died in 1989 at the age of 86.

FRED HUNTINGTON

Fred Huntington's father (also named Fred) was an Illinois native who worked as a salesman. In 1906 he moved west with his wife to Oroville, in northern California. There the elder Huntington opened a laundry and dry-cleaning service—a business he accepted in lieu of repayment of a $5,000 loan. Young Fred, born December 5, 1912, grew up a well-adjusted lad who took a shine to shooting. Although his father preferred fishing over hunting and was usually too busy with the laundry for either, the young Huntington indulged his passion for shooting through high school. After graduating, and a year studying the laundry business, he put down roots in Oroville tending the family enterprise.

But as time and money allowed, and almost without design, Fred turned a hobby into a profitable venture that would wrest him from the laundry. "I started shooting seriously around 1937," he recalled. "Not just pulling the trigger, but handloading and competing. And, of course, hunting." In 1941 Fred came across a book by W. F. Vickery. *Advanced Gunsmithing* is well known among shooting enthusiasts—at least, those with a few gray hairs. Beyond gunsmithing, it has a section on fashioning .22-caliber bullets. As the United States entered the Second World War, ammunition and components became scarce. Bullet-making was an imperative for shooters with a high-volume habit. Fred wrote to Vickery, who took an interest in the young man and sent him a set of .22 bullet dies. In the rear of the laundry, Fred had already turned out a few bullets on an old Seneca Falls lathe. He swaged .22 rimfire cases to form jackets for some of his early missiles. Vickery's dies added a new dimension to his work. Perhap, thought Huntington, *he* could manufacture not only bullets, but dies!

Soon Fred struck upon the idea of making bullet-forming dies to function with the Pacific press built in San Francisco. He brought the resulting product to Frank Stratinsky, then chief tool-and-die man for Pacific. Stratinsky introduced Fred to Captain Grosvenor Wotkyns, who'd contributed to development of cartridges like the .22 Hornet. Wotkyns admired Huntington's work and snapped up a set of dies. He also bought another for a friend. The tooling got a warm reception among local riflemen and generated more orders for Huntington dies. But they needed, said Wotkyns, a distinctive name. "Why not call them Rock Chucker Bullet Swages?" A tad unwieldy, that label *was* descriptive. Many, if not most of the .22 bullets from those dies saw use in heavy-barreled rifles fired at yellow-bellied marmots—rockchucks, in local parlance. Fred reduced Wotkyns' mouthful to RCBS.

In 1943, Fred Huntington, Jr., founded RCBS to manufacture handloading hardware in Oroville.

By 1948, the business was growing steadily, but the shop was still modest: a 20x20 room crammed with energy, ideas and steel. To build the enterprise, Fred gathered good people around him. Al Swift and Jack Ellis helped with die work, as the shop grew to include gunsmithing services. Frank Stratinsky joined the team as well. Huntington had already earned a patent for his bullet-forming die. Another patent followed. With Al Swift, he designed a loading press. The New Leverage System Model A RCBS Reloading Press would influence subsequent press designs industry-wide. The tool drew criticism at first. "But when the patent ran out," chuckled Fred, "Two firms agreed to pay royalties to use that design!"

Don Tucker and Bill Keyes came to the Huntington shop with little training but a lot of ambition. They

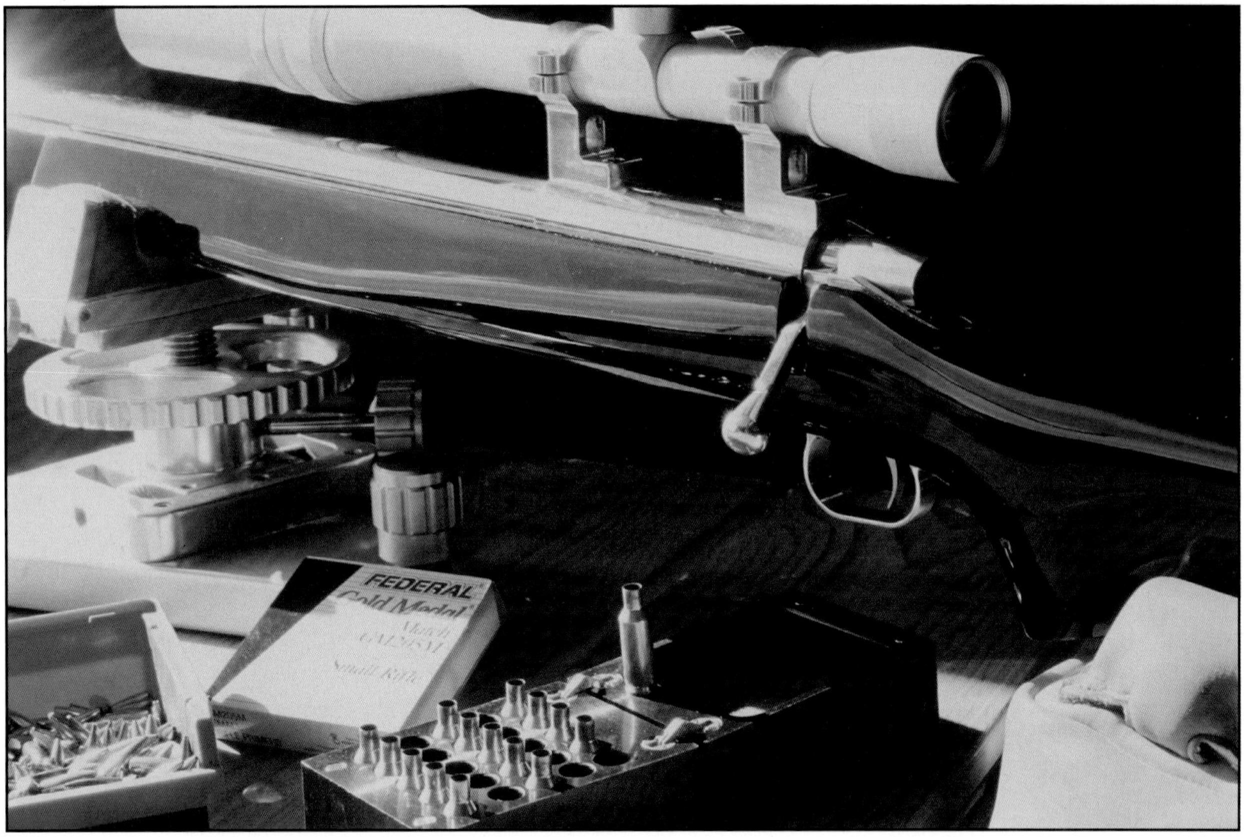

▲ Handloaders owe much to the benchrest game. This left-bolt benchrest rifle has a right-side port.

both soon learned to produce superior tooling. Meanwhile, Fred was coming up with new products. As the green Rockchucker Press became an industry standard, the RCBS "Reloader's Special" kit brought thousands of shooters into handloading.

In 1952, Fred's father offered to help Fred take over the family dry-cleaning business, or grow it. But Fred wanted nothing to do with laundry. Instead, he expanded his handloading-tool enterprise into his own garage to gain more space. In 1954, Fred built a larger shop, 30 by 60 feet, next to the old one. Four years later he finished a 7,500-square-foot factory. It soon grew to 50,000 square feet.

In 1976, with 250 employees at RCBS, Fred sold his business to Omark Industries. He remained to supervise production. Fred's two sons also stayed with the enterprise. Charles "Buzz" Huntington became general manager for Huntington Die Specialties. Buzz was the face of the Huntington family at the annual SHOT Show until his passing in 2013.

Fred's long hunting career included many prairie dog shoots in Wyoming with Bill Matheny. He also hunted with W. F. Vickery and with Jack O'Connor, who wrote up their 30-day Yukon adventure (1956) for *Outdoor Life*. Fred accompanied Warren Page and Pete Brown (shooting editors for *Field & Stream* and *Sports Afield*) on big-game hunts. The Oroville RCBS store displays more than 100 of Fred's mounted animals.

Fred Huntington passed away in 2013.

VERNON SPEER

Vernon Speer was born in 1901 in Cedar Falls, Iowa. At age 21, after serving in the U.S. Navy during the Great War, he built his own aircraft engine, installed it in a biplane, and took to the sky in a test flight. Work as a tool foreman for John Deere grounded him until 1941, when he became chief ground instructor at a flying school in Lincoln, Nebraska. There he also

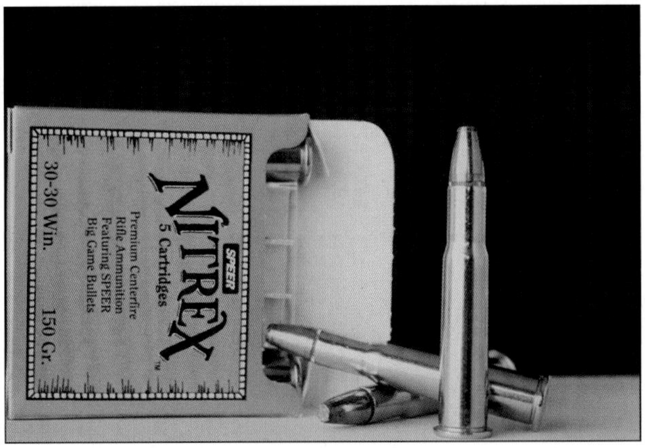

▲ Vernon Speer's cartridge company gave old and new cartridges shelf appeal in Nitrex ammunition.

started making bullets. Handloading was in its infancy, and jacketed bullets had yet to become widely available as components. With the war effort causing shortages in brass and copper, Vernon Speer struck upon the idea of using spent .22 rimfire cases for bullet jackets. He built a machine to iron out the rims and draw the hulls to proper dimensions for .224 jackets. A brief partnership with Joyce Hornady ended in 1944, when Speer left Hornady and Nebraska to establish his own business in Lewiston, Idaho. For two years he sold jacketed .224 bullets in paper bags, while laying the groundwork for a new bullet manufacturing plant on the banks of the Snake River.

Armistice renewed the flow of gilding metal to commercial ammo production. Speer took quick advantage by expanding his line of bullets to include more popular types, weights and diameters. His son, Ray, joined the growing firm in 1952. Two years later Ray produced the first Speer Reloading Manual. Ever the experimenter, Vernon developed his Hot-Cor process to ensure better marriage of the bullet's core and jacket. He realized early on the advantages of re-usable packaging and bought injection-molding equipment to make sturdy plastic boxes for Speer products. In 1969, he began loading bullets in handgun cartridges, introducing the Lawman line of ammo. Gold Dot bonded pistol bullets appeared in the catalog in 1994. They and subsequent Gold Dot ammunition have since become popular among law enforcement officers. Speer remained a family-owned business until 1975, four years before Vernon Speer's death.

While Vernon's name is widely known among shooters, his brother, Dick, (14 years younger) also contributed a great deal to the growth of handloading. A machinist at Boeing Aircraft in Seattle, Dick moved to Lewiston after Speer's bullet factory began operations. He soon tooled up to produce specialty cartridge cases. Shooters keen to brew handoads for discontinued, proprietary or wildcat rounds took note. First selling the hulls under the label "Forged From Solid," Dick named his part of the business Speer Cartridge Works. While his extrusion processes were sound, the quality of raw stock varied widely in those days. Consequently, so did case quality. A high rejection rate, combined with the limited demand for specialty brass, scuttled Dick's enterprise.

Undeterred, Dick looked to handloaders for inspiration. They confirmed that ammo companies couldn't (or wouldn't) ensure a reliable supply of component primers. Speer seized on this failing as an opportunity. In 1951 he committed to primer production and hired explosives expert Dr. Victor Jasaitis from Lithuania to come up with new percussive compounds. His first primers were FA-70s to fill various government contracts. Later Jasaitis would develop non-corrosive primers for sporting cartridges. To differentiate his business from Speer Bullets, Dick and partner Arvid Nelson changed the firm's name to Cascade Cartridge, Inc. Now known universally as CCI, it soon outgrew its cramped corner in Vernon Speer's bullet plant. Dick bought a 17-acre chicken farm a short distance upriver, near the Lewiston Gun Club. There, in a converted coop under a tar-paper roof, he continued producing rifle and pistol primers.

Dick eventually bought that property, and in 1957 expanded operations to include the manufacture of shotshell primers. Two years later he started making "power loads"—rimfire cartridges for nail guns and other industrial tools. Rimfire rifle ammunition was the natural sequel, in 1963. CCI Mini-Mag .22 ammo sold briskly, as did subsequent rimfire lines from the Lewiston plant. Four years after its industry debut, Dick Speer sold CCI to Omark.

A strong, profitable operation, CCI continues to employ a host of Idahoans near the mouth of the

Snake River Canyon. It has improved its centerfire primers to give handloaders lower seating pressures and easier ignition. In 1991 it opened a new primer facility in Lewiston and became a major supplier of cannon primers to the U.S. armed forces.

JOHN NOSLER

A decade before the Great War, few in California contemplated archdukes or European treaties. Turning a dollar here and there, in real estate and hardware sales and delivering fresh milk, Byrd Nosler moved his family to Pomona, then to a ranch near Huntington Beach. "I was seven," recalled son John. "The next year, Dad took in an old Dort that needed service. I tinkered with it, got it running, and sold it. What I wanted was a Model T. So I rode my bicycle around until I saw one behind an old house. I went to the door and asked the lady there if she'd like a bicycle." The derelict Model T had evidently over-stayed its welcome—or she had a soft spot for enterprising young boys. She agreed to an even swap. John used his father's mules to drag the car home. It was the start of a long love affair with cars.

Western Auto Supply became John's source for automobile parts. Eventually, he started building overhead-valve engines. "I learned to see problems as opportunities in disguise," he said—a perspective that would fuel his later work with big game bullets.

John was a gun enthusiast from an early age. He traded a set of Model T connecting rods for his first deer rifle, a .25-35 Winchester lever-action. But he had little money to fund more than an occasional hunting trip. In fact, the Depression forced him from high school. John went to work as clean-up boy at a Ford dealership in Chino for fifteen cents an hour. It proved a good place to indulge his passion for fast cars. "A pal and I souped up a Model A with a B engine, adding counterweights to the B's crank." Reportedly, that hotrod purred at speeds to 100 mph! Ford Motor Company must have picked up on those sprints, as it adopted Nosler's crankshaft design.

In 1933, John Nosler married Louise Booz. The couple moved to Reedsport, Oregon, where John managed a Ford dealership. Union activity in the timber industry shut many sawmill operations and had a devastating effect on local economies. Automobile sales nose-dived. John scrambled to replace his lost income, trucking produce from California to southern Oregon. "I drove one of the first Peterbilts on the road," he recalled. "It could haul 20 tons, three times as much as a Ford!" Though it wrung only six miles from a gallon of diesel, that much fuel cost John just five cents. After a stint trucking for the war effort, he returned to servicing civilian markets.

By this time, John had begun shooting competitively. In 1946, Louise gave birth to a son. That fall, John went moose-hunting in Canada and faced a problem that would redirect his life.

Coming upon a mud-caked bull-moose, John fired repeatedly into the beast with his .300 H&H Magnum. The bull absorbed the hits without the expected collapse. Eventually, the damage proved fatal, and John was quick with an autopsy. His bullets had come apart on the thick, encrusted hide. He decided to build a better softpoint, one that would penetrate tough targets reliably.

Back home in Oregon, John built a press and bought a screw machine. He drilled out both ends of 5/16 copper billets, turned them to bore-size, and inserted lead cores. Fred Huntington of RCBS donated tooling to finish the dual-core bullets, which John called Partitions. The dam of jacket material separating the core, fore and aft, permitted the front end to act like an ordinary softpoint, while it protected the heel.

Noses from Partitions typically endured some fragmentation, but the heels drove on like solids, ensuring deep penetration. Result: the vitals of big game struck by Partitions were shredded by the expanding nose. If heavy muscle or bone turned it to shards, the heel bored through.

The first Partitions weren't very accurate, but on their maiden hunt two moose fell to John's new bullet. Big bones that would have shattered ordinary softpoints were themselves splintered. Nosler's pals quickly asked him for bullets. So began Nosler, Inc.

Over the next decade, John came up with other ideas for bullets, including the Zipedo, introduced in 1965. Five years later, he adapted to Partition bullets the impact extrusion process used to form Zipedo jackets. This change, and modern tooling, yielded more concentric jackets and better accuracy. The

▲ John Nosler started his firm with a bullet. Nosler's custom ammo now rivals the best of handloads!

Solid Base bullet came in 1972. Shortly thereafter, Federal Cartridge became the first ammunition company to load Nosler bullets. By this time, the Bend, Oregon firm had changed its name from The Nosler Partition Bullet Company to Nosler Bullets.

Ballistic Tip bullets, unveiled in 1984, gave the family-owned business a big boost. "We were the second North American firm to use a polymer bullet tip," says John's son, Bob Nosler, now CEO. While Canada's Dominion brand had the Saber Tip first, that company has expired. Legion bullet makers have since adopted the pointed polymer nose. It looks supersonic standing still! The accuracy and flat flight of Nosler Ballistic Tips have made the design hugely popular among hunters. Nosler used it in 2002 on its first bonded bullet, the AccuBond, and on the lead-free E-Tip in 2008.

"Along the way we developed target bullets, handgun bullets, and brass solids for heavy African game," Bob adds. "Combined Technology bullets in Winchester loads were designed mainly by Nosler."

In 2009 Nosler began offering loaded cartridges with its own headstamp. Weight-sorted brass has trued necks, chamfered case mouths and de-burred primer pockets. A broad range of chamberings, .204 Ruger to .416 Weatherby Magnum, includes the .280 Ackley Improved, a favorite of the Noslers since John's hunting days. Trophy Grade ammo delivers all but the hand-finishing of Custom cases, at a lower price. Handgun ammunition has followed.

John Nosler died in 2010, age 97. But Bob and his son, John, have since grown Nosler's line with new products, including Varmageddon bullets and Long Range AccuBonds. Ballistic coefficients for the latter, with extended boat-tails, start at .561, the 210-grain .308 reaching .730! Dark-gray polymer tips distinguish these bullets and LR ammunition. New heavy-game loads include safari cartridges with solid and softnose options.

ROY WEATHERBY

Among the best-known wildcatters of the early postwar era was Roy Weatherby. Born in 1910 to a Kansas sharecropper, Roy knew poverty. His parents had 10 children, but no automobile, no electrical service, no indoor plumbing. Roy recalled walking behind an aging plow horse, watching enviously as a neighbor pulled five bottoms three times as fast with a Fordson tractor.

In 1923, Roy's father, George, opened a one-pump filling station in Salina. Then the family moved to Florida, "nine of us in a four-passenger Dodge, camping in a tent along the way." George laid bricks, while Roy hauled mortar. Growing up, the young man peddled garden seed to neighbors for the money to buy a BB gun. He would later clerk in a music store, sell washing machines, and drive a bread truck. Back in Kansas, Roy was determined to further his education. Southwestern Bell employed him while he took night classes at the University of Wichita. There he met Camilla Jackson. They married in 1936, and the following year, they left the nation's breadbasket for the glitter of the Golden State. Like legions of others, Roy felt the pulse of promise on Route 66.

The couple wound up in San Diego. Employed by a local utility, then the Automobile Club of Southern California, Roy was soon making good money: $200 a month. A lathe and a drill press from Sears found their way into his basement shop. Soon Roy was building rifles on commercial and military surplus actions. He fashioned his own cartridges, too—fast-stepping rounds that gave hunters additional reach and killing power. The .220 Rocket, an improved .220 Swift, appeared in 1943. It has been widely acknowledged as the first high-velocity Weatherby.

Roy had a reason for wildcatting cartridges. On a deer hunt in Utah in 1942, "I wounded a buck with the .30-06, and after following the blood trail until dark, I finally had to give up. I had a sad feeling for that animal. . . . That's when I started thinking about getting a bullet to travel fast enough so it would disintegrate inside the animal's body, and the shock would cause instant death even though [the hit] was not in a particularly vital area." The animal, he pointed out, would not suffer, and the hunter "wouldn't be wounding one and taking another."

This reasoning, no doubt, nettled .30-06 aficionados. Obliquely, it blamed the bullet for the failings of the shooter. But the incident set Roy on a mission that would bring huge benefits to all riflemen, no matter their taste in big-game cartridges. While Weatherby's legendary salesmanship would later propel his company to success, Roy's early case designs owe much to fellow wildcatter R. W. Miller. In 1940, Miller was experimenting in his California shop with the .300 Hoffman, a powerful round dropped from Western Cartridge Company's line seven years earlier. Miller employed radiused shoulder junctures to smooth gas flow and keep a lid on pressures. E. Baden Powell from *The American Rifleman* suggested that Miller reduce bolt thrust by reducing case taper. The resulting cartridge was called the PMVF: Powell Miller Venturi Freebore. In 1944, the two men went into business; but they ran short of cash and in 1945 sold out to Hollywood Tool and Die.

About this time, Roy Weatherby carried a .270 PMVF on a deer hunt. He admired the design. But Miller demurred when Roy asked him to put a radiused shoulder on Weatherby cartridges. George Fuller, a machinist friend who had fashioned the reamer for Weatherby's .220 Rocket, agreed to produce that radius. Shortly thereafter, business partner Bill Wittman and Texas oil baron Herb Klein would commit funds to help the ebullient Weatherby take his wildcatting another step.

Roy was still a part-time gun-maker; but he knew a fork in the road when he saw one. To pursue his wildcatting—and to build enough rifles to satisfy steadily increasing demand—he would have to quit selling for the Automobile Club, his employer now for eight years. It was a tough decision. He liked his boss, J.L. Magee; and Roy's $600 monthly salary was quite a sum in that day. Also, he and Camilla had just started building a new home in Downey, California. Leaving the security of a rewarding job to strike out on his own entailed huge risk. But on August 21, 1945, Roy wrote his letter of resignation. The young man's character came through more clearly than any trepidation he might have felt.

> ". . . I will remain your employee until such time as you find someone suitable to take my place. . . . During this time I will continue to do my job to the best of my ability, keeping the interest of you and the Automobile Club in mind. . . . I want to thank you, Mr. Magee, for hiring me back in 1937. You have been the finest boss I have ever had. . . ."

Magee wrote him back to wish him well.

A co-worker at the Automobile Club had already fueled Roy's optimism by offering to rent him shop space for one hundred dollars a month. The building was at the junction of Long Beach and Firestone boulevards in Southgate. Roy outfitted it with a big neon sign. He had to borrow from friends to equip it. He opened the shop, complete with a retail sporting goods store, on the first of September, 1945. All told, he'd sunk less than $5,000 into the new venture; but that must have seemed a fortune then. Over the next five years, the business grew slowly. Roy plowed almost all its profits back.

He was heartened when a letter he wrote to *Sports Afield* magazine, rebutting a January article by Charles Askins, brought kudos from readers. Other shooters, too, were keen to open the throttle on bullets!

Roy's enterprise was so linked to that crusade, he would earn the moniker, "high priest of high velocity."

As the Weatherby gun shop outgrew its 25x70-foot space, Roy looked for alternatives. A plot of ground with 240 feet of road frontage lay just around the block on Firestone Boulevard. Reluctantly, but with no other path, Roy tapped his friend and Weatherby stockholder Herb Klein, who wrote a check for the property. Herb also funded a new building. By April 1951, Roy had vacated the shop at 8823 Long Beach Boulevard and moved into a 20,000-square-foot facility that would remain Weatherby's base for more than four decades. Roy put down roots there, established his name and branded his business there. Firestone Boulevard gave Weatherby its corporate image. Glossy, full-color catalogs showing Weatherby rifles also pictured Roy, nattily dressed, courting business tycoons and entertainment celebrities, hosting war heroes and politicians. A huge mural of the East African plain became the trademark background for photos of Roy at work in his office, or meeting with important clients.

Roy's first rifles were built on the most-available bolt-action mechanisms: the 1898 Mauser, 1903 Springfield, and 1917 Enfield. He also used Model 70 Winchesters and other actions supplied by customers. Roy imported FN Mausers beginning in 1949. Charter chamberings included the .220 Rocket and the .228 Weatherby Magnum. Neither became a commercial offering. But the .270 Magnum that followed, a high-velocity round, trimmed to fit .30-06-length actions, endured. It became a favorite of Roy and, later, his son, Ed. The .270, with the .257 and 7mm Weatherby Magnums that appeared about the same time, set the stage for a spate of short belted rounds from other makers. The .300 Weatherby, with its full-length 2.85-inch case, arrived in 1945. It drove a bullet nearly 300 fps faster than the .300

▲ Globe-trotting hunters put Weatherby's rifles and cartridges to the test where reliability mattered!

H&H Magnum from which it was formed. Roy demonstrated the .300's power on film, severing a thick tree branch with a single shot and a straight face.

In those days, Roy shaped his own stocks and deep-hole-drilled and contoured his own barrels. He installed Jaeger triggers. Roy and Maynard Buehler were friends, with a shared interest in restoring and collecting vintage automobiles—so Buehler safeties and scope mounts were standard on Weatherby rifles. In 1954, Weatherby introduced its Imperial scope, with two adjustments on top of the tube. One was a focusing knob; the other incorporated both windage and elevation dials. The scope was made by Hertel and Reuse. In 1955, Weatherby contracted with Timken for its barrel steel, after failed experiments with chromed bores. A shrewd businessman, Roy rebarreled completed rifles to keep his warehouse stock in synch with demand.

By 1954, post-war inflation threatened to push the price of Weatherby rifles to levels well beyond the $150 to $165 he'd been asking for his custom bolt guns. Tooling costs and wages had all but erased profits. He decided having rifles produced elsewhere to his specifications, then imported. In Europe, he and Maynard Buehler traveled to BSA, then on to Schultz & Larsen, about one hundred miles out of Copenhagen. Mr. Larsen trotted out a new rifle he'd made up for Roy, from specifications sent earlier. Its rear-locking action was large enough and stout enough for the .378 Weatherby Magnum cartridge just introduced. The .378 was not only longer than the .300 Weatherby; it was bigger in diameter (.603 compared to .532 at the belt). Roy evidently had little enthusiasm for the S&L's pot-bellied profile, a result of the single-column magazine. But his 1953 safari, which featured the .378, had already drawn orders. So he asked Mr. Larsen for a small shipment of rifles. Eventually S&L would deliver a modified action with staggered magazine.

A visit to the Sako plant in Finland confirmed that Firearms International had exclusive rights to US distribution, but that Sako might still supply a new Weatherby rifle. The actions would be from FN in Belgium—traditional Mausers. Roy ordered 1,000. He and Maynard Buehler cancelled a planned stop at Husqvarna in Sweden. This manufacturer also had a US distributor (Tradewinds) and was up to its neck in orders. In Berlin, the Heym people welcomed their visitors, but required that Weatherby provide all tooling for a new rifle. Roy dismissed that idea out of hand.

Subsequent dealings with Steyr, Sako, and BSA convinced Roy he needed to design and build his own rifle action. He and a talented company engineer, Fred Jennie, went to work.

While Roy admired the Mauser action and its derivatives, he knew most were built to bottle about 70,000 copper units of pressure (CUP). He wanted this rifle to handle 200,000! Of course, Weatherby cartridges didn't generate that much, but they *did* operate at a higher level than the .270 Winchester and other "high-intensity" rounds of that day. And handloaders commonly tested their velocity limits. Besides, Roy wanted a rifle that would stand up to handloading *mistakes* that tore other actions apart. He envisioned a countersunk bolt face and breech face, completing enclosing and supporting the case. A trio of vents in the bolt body would direct gas away from the shooter's face, in the event of case rupture. Instead of two big locking lugs, Roy chose three rows of three small lugs—an interrupted-thread design. Bolt lift would be reduced to 54 degrees, an advantage under scopes. A full-diameter bolt body would mitigate the "Mauser wobble" at full retraction.

Roy took a prototype of the new action to the 1955 NRA meetings. Two years later he showed a production-ready rifle to world-renowned sportsman, Elgin Gates. "We don't have a name for it yet," Roy admitted. "And it's our fifth rendition!" After a moment, Gates replied: "How about the Mark V?"

The Weatherby Mark V rifle quickly came to define the company. Its angular profile, stunning Claro walnut, high-gloss finish and powerful, flat-shooting Weatherby Magnum chamberings infused a futuristic flavor, which Roy appropriated in the slogan, "Tomorrow's Rifles Today." As new even more potent cartridges evolved, Roy stocked some rifles with dense-grained European walnut and tough, heavy mesquite from our Desert Southwest. By the late 1970s, Weatherby had established a fine relationship with Calico, a walnut supplier in California. At this writing Calico still furnishes most of Weatherby's wood.

The first Weatherby Mark V receivers were manufactured by Pacific Foundry International in California from sand castings. Shortly, high failure rate drove Roy to the forged receivers of J.P. Sauer in Germany. Production would later shift to Japan, where high quality could be maintained at modest cost. Mark V rifles are now, again, built in the United States.

As handloading couldn't provide the growing demand for Weatherby cartridges, Roy looked hard for a commercial supplier. By 1948, he was contracting for factory loads. In the early 1950s, Norma began producing Weatherby Magnum ammo. This Swedish firm is still the source of Weatherby-brand ammo.

During the 1940s and 1950s, Roy actively sought out new ways to market rifles. In 1950, he got a van for travel to dealers. The side-panel illustrating Weatherby rifles would hardly make sense in urban L.A. today! Roy also had a Buick wagon outfitted with a built-in walnut gun vault. Pull-out drawers held scoped rifles. A super-salesman, he insisted on a mobile, aggressive sales force. Personal contacts earned Roy a lot of business. For years after postage costs made it a questionable business practice, he mailed Christmas cards to everyone who bought a Weatherby rifle.

While he spent less time afield with his rifles than promoting them, Roy did make the obligatory safari. Two, in fact. On both he carefully recorded the performance of his rifles and cartrides. After more than a month in Africa in 1948, he concluded, ". . . there is no substitute for velocity and one thing sure, it isn't bullet weight." He favored lighter bullets than are recommended now, and were surely anomalous then. "I am convinced the 130-grain .270 bullet is superior [to the 150-grain Core-Lokt]. . . . The 87-grain bullet [in .257 Magnum] seems to have more killing power at 100 yards than does the 100-grain bullet."

Roy's detailed field notes described not just shots that downed game instantly, but hits that didn't have the desired or expected effect: ". . . I killed a zebra at 335 yards with a 150-grain Peters belted bullet in my .270 Magnum—dead with one shot—still I shot a topi at 100 yards with the 300-grain Silvertip in my .375 Magnum—he fell down, got up, and never stopped running. So—where are we?"

Few so-called "controlled expansion" bullets were available anywhere in 1948. John Nosler was still experimenting with his two-part partitioned design. Bullet cores and jackets designed for the .30-06 and its ilk commonly came apart on impact when wildcatters like Weatherby hiked velocities above 3,100 fps. On that first safari, Roy had loaded some .300 Magnum ammunition with Remington Bronze Points. He wrote of stoking them to 3,600 fps! His .257 spat 87-grain softpoints at a claimed 3,900 fps! Hornady Spire Point and Winchester Silvertip bullets fired on this expedition wouldn't pass muster in penetration and retained-weight trials now; but Roy preferred grenade-like upset. The only heavy bullets I recall him recommending were the 220-grain full-patch (solid) missiles he carried in his .300 Magnum for elephant. When he got his chance, one shot through the brain felled the great beast.

These days, Norma's Weatherby ammunition features a variety of flat-shooting, deep-penetrating missiles like the Barnes TSX and Nosler AccuBond. With a dozen factory loads for the .300 Weatherby alone, handloaders must look harder now to trump Norma's offerings. Still, the brass is among the best available, and Roy would be the first to approve loads finished, one at a time, on a basement bench!

Herb Klein's guiding hand and ready funding were crucial to Weatherby's survival in the early years. In 1956, Klein received the first Weatherby Award, a trophy still presented annually to hunters of extraordinary achievement. But those two men didn't always see eye-to-eye. The relationship was strained when Herb installed his comptrollers at Weatherby—then a hunting crony and a nephew. Roy proposed a buyout of Herb's half-interest in the company. Klein demanded $125,000 return over his investment. Roy agreed, but then found other partners in J.P. Sauer and Dynamit-Nobel, the German companies each getting 25 percent of Weatherby. Their tenure lasted just four years. In 1966, Roy's friend and NASCO Industries owner Leo Roethe gave $500,000 for those shares—$187,000 less than the Germans had paid!

Roy Weatherby and Herb Klein remained good friends until Herb's death in 1974. Meanwhile, the

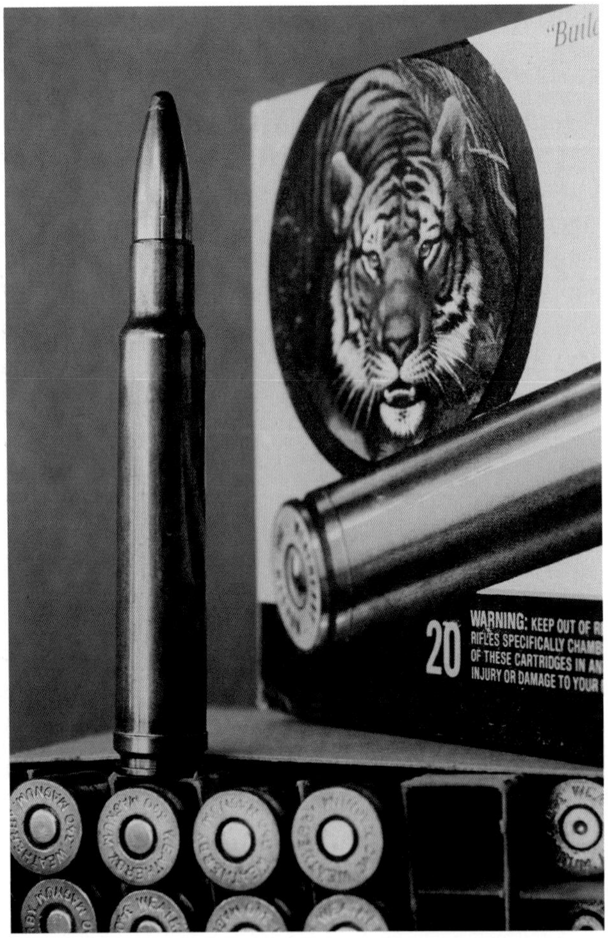

▲ A latecomer to Roy Weatherby's line of magnums, the potent, flat-shooting .340 arrived in 1962.

company kept growing. By the time the Mark V rifle had been in production 20 years, Weatherby had introduced most of its current line of cartridges. In 1962, it announced the .340, a necked-up .300. In 1968, the .240 arrived—a belted round but on its own .30-06-size hull. The loud, hard-kicking .30-378 came in 1998. This fire-breather followed a request from Alabama's Redstone Arsenal for a load that would kick a bullet downrange at 6,000 fps. In 1959! Shooters loved it the .30-378. It's still a top seller.

In 1981 Elgin Gates, who'd been shooting special handguns at long range, urged Roy to build a bolt-action pistol for the petite .224 Weatherby. The Japanese built it until they decided they couldn't in good conscience ship a rifle whose barrel was going to be lopped on arrival to produce a pistol!

▲ Fifty years after Roy Weatherby fashioned his first belted magnums, Don Allen had his own line of cartridges on the rimless .404 Jeffery. He and wife, Norma, founded Dakota Arms to build rifles for them.

During his final decade, as his son, Ed, and others took the helm at Weatherby, Roy indulged his passion for fine cars. He owned a 1930 Franklin, but never managed to snare the Deusenberg he coveted. He collected Lincolns and Packards, and owned a Clipper and a Patrician. The pump shotgun introduced as the Weatherby Patrician years later owes its name to that car. New Weatherby shotguns and rifles have profiles and finishes aimed at a younger market. "Tomorrow's Rifles Today" has given way to new slogans, but remains a focus at the company's Paso Robles headquarters. A stable of Mark Vs, with affordable but sleek, accurate Vanguard rifles on Howa actions, carry on the tradition that has long made a Weatherby the dream of every riflemen.

ROCKY GIBBS

During a March snowstorm in 1955, rifle-maker Rocky Gibbs moved from Richmond, California, to Viola, Idaho, where he'd bought a 35-acre tract laid out to accommodate a 500-yard rifle range. In his shop, Rocky re-established Gibbs Rifle Products and expanded a line of cartridges on the .30-06 hull, with the shoulders moved forward. Fashioning a Gibbs case, handloaders had to create a false shoulder (with dies and fire-forming) to maintain headspace. Or they could spring for the Rocky Gibbs Wildcat Case Forming Tool, a hydraulic press that operated without

Hercules Unique and Cream of Wheat (small charge of fast powder and a filler to fire-form cases).

Even before his Idaho move, Rocky had hot-rodded his Remington 721 in .270, dismissing P. O. Ackley's 40-degree shoulder. A Keith Francis reamer that cut a long chamber with a 35-degree shoulder and a .250 neck resulted in the .270 Gibbs. Reportedly, Rocky Gibbs set a record with his new cartridge at a Richmond match. That was in 1953; a year later, Rocky would put six more cartridges in a proprietary stable that would change little over the years.

The .240 Gibbs, most easily formed from .25-06 brass, is among the most enduring of the Gibbs wildcats—though Rocky made relatively few rifles so chambered. He recorded over 3,600 fps with 75-grain bullets, 3,500 with 85-grain bullets and 3,250 with 105-grain Speers. Rocky described the .25 Gibbs as the only wildcat that shot flatter than his .240 and compared it with the .257 Weatherby. His records showed 3,900 fps from 75-grain bullets and nearly 3,550 with 100-grain spitzers.

▲ Lazzeroni's 8.59 Galaxy, Dakota's .330 are rimless magnums after the tradition of early wildcatters.

Rocky claimed his .270 Gibbs was "the best all-around cartridge for a handloader." Even Jack O'Connor acknowledged its merits in *Outdoor Life*: "As far as I can tell, Brother Gibbs doesn't do it with mirrors." By Gibbs' reckoning, his .270 kicked 130-grain bullets downrange at 3,430 fps, in front of 63 grains IMR 4350, placing the round in league with the .270 Weatherby Magnum and tall rungs above the .270 Winchester. While Rocky also championed his 7mm, and claimed 3,300 fps with a 139-grain bullet, this wildcat never sold particularly well.

The .30 Gibbs earned some notoriety as a poor man's magnum. Francis Sell wrote about it in his excellent book on deer hunting. Rocky massaged 3,000 fps from that .30 with 180-grain bullets, a match for the modern .300 Winchester Magnum and .300 WSM. Certainly the .30 was much more popular than the 8mm Gibbs, which Rocky thought a good way to salvage 8x57 Mausers that made their way Stateside on the heels of the Second World War. The .338 Gibbs joined Rocky's line sometime after 1958. But that was the year Winchester announced its .338 Magnum.

Gibbs had a flair for the dramatic and was openly concerned about his data being pirated. He kept his test records secret, instructing his wife to burn them just before his death from leukemia at age 58 in 1973. Listed bullet speeds for Gibbs wildcats are best approached with caution.

Manolis Aamoen Gibbs was a man for his time. His work included publication of a booklet titled "Front Ignition Loading Technique," which detailed duplex charges developed by Charlie O'Neil, Elmer Keith and Don Hopkins of OKH fame. But the Gibbs legacy really comes from the loading bench. With surplus infantry rifles and cartridges formed from GI hulls, Rocky helped shooters push bullets very fast, to kill game farther along their arc.

Chapter 2: Handloading, Simply

Verily, handloading is easier to do than it is to explain. Describing tools, components, and techniques separately—a reasonable tack to indulge the inexperienced—is to court verbosity. Many words make for dull text. At a well-equipped bench, under the tutelage of a savvy shooter, you'll soon get the hang of it.

Without bench or mentor, and even if you have both, reading can save time and money and help you produce better ammunition.

As handloading starts with the cartridge case, so will I.

CARTRIDGE CASES

The metallic cartridge dates to the late 1800s, and rimfire cases. Still used for small .17- and .22-caliber cartridges, the rimfire hull carries its priming in a folded rim that also stops the cartridge at the rifle chamber's lip. The cartridge fires when the rifle's hammer or striker dents the thin brass, crushing the priming at that point in the rim, held in place by the barrel steel. The spark inside the case ignites the powder charge. The burning powder produces gas that expands rapidly to push the bullet out the barrel. Like modern .22 ammunition, the first rimfire cartridges held little powder. They generated modest pressures. Rimfire rounds cannot be handloaded.

Centerfire priming became practical between our Civil War and the advent of smokeless powder in the 1890s. It comprises a pellet of priming compound in a metal cup with an internal anvil. Seated in its pocket in the middle of the thick brass head of the case, the primer is detonated as in a rimfire cartridge: by a blow from the hammer or striker. The pellet is crushed against the anvil and explodes; flame jets through a flash-hole (or twin flash-holes) in the case to ignite the powder. Centerfire cartridges can be

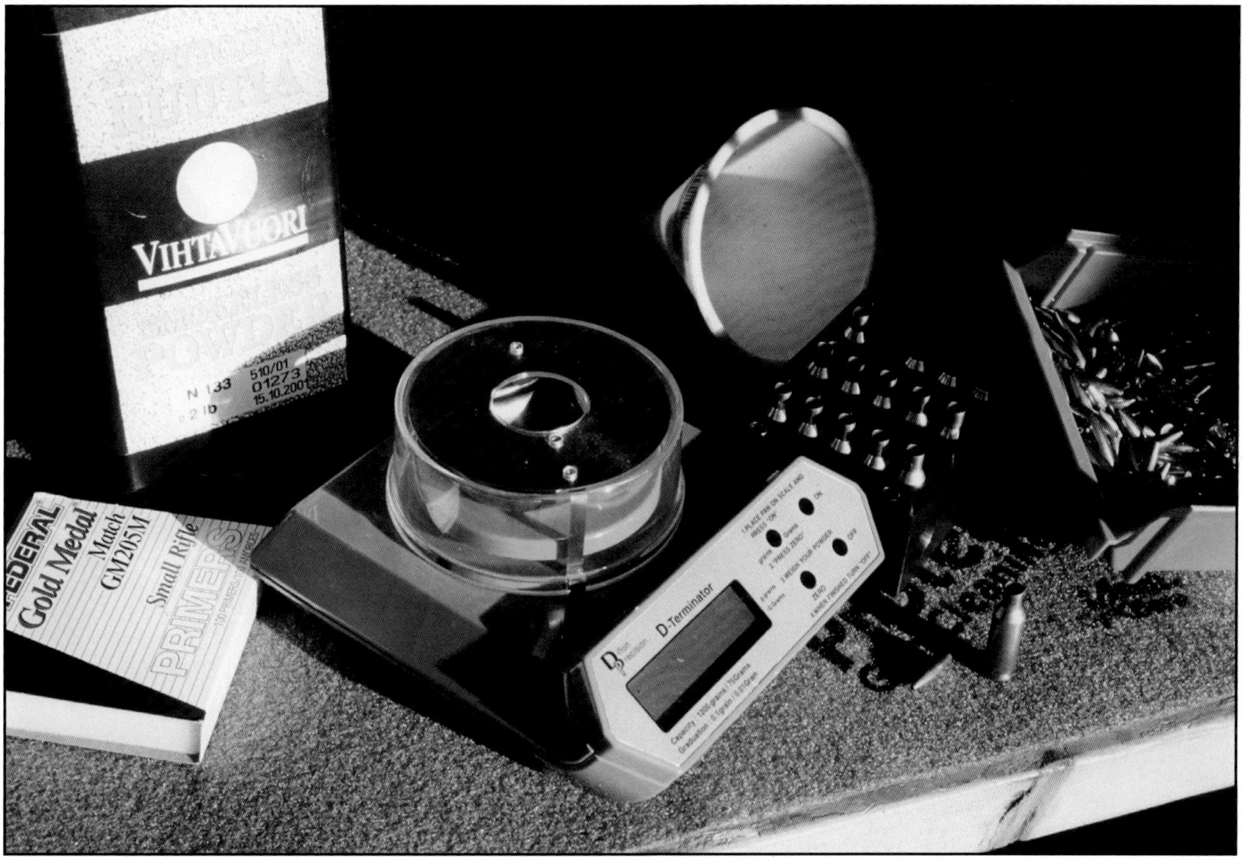

▲ The quality of tools and components matters more than does the number of gadgets on your bench.

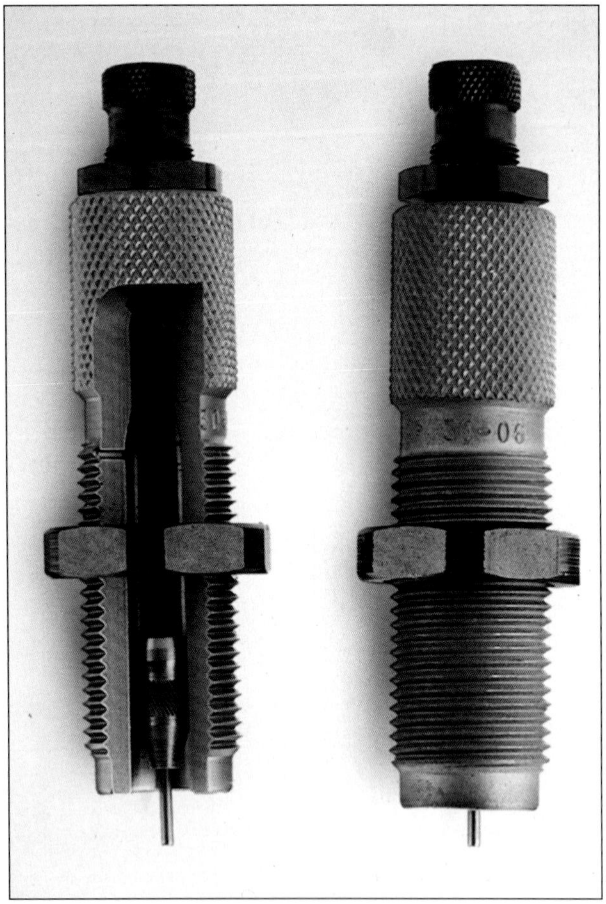

▲ This cutaway view of a sizing die shows the expander ball above the decapping pin. Keep interiors grit-free!

handloaded after the spent primer is driven out and the case, expanded to chamber dimensions by the gas of firing, is squeezed in a die back to its original size.

Whether new or fired, brass cases should be run through a sizing die to bring them to uniform and desired dimensions. Clean them first, in a tumbler with walnut-shell or other polishing media. Grit, even dust, can damage dies. Check after tumbling to ensure hulls are free of walnut chips or other debris.

Some cases, typically loaded with cheap bullets for practice with military small arms, are of steel. They're not suitable for handloading. Ditto aluminum hulls used for mild pistol ammo.

You're smart to use cases from the same maker and preferably the same lot. If a Winchester case has a thinner wall than a Remington, it probably has greater powder capacity. Variations in capacity mean variations in pressure and velocity, thus greater shot dispersion than if you'd used uniform cases. If you're finicky about accuracy, you'll weigh cases, too, batching them for uniformity. Set aside hulls more than .5 grain over or under the mean. Prepare one hundred cases at a time so you can cull severely and still have enough ammunition for load development. If you're popping prairie dogs or shooting competitively, big batches make sense even after you've settled on a load.

Measure your cases, base to mouth. Cases stretch as they're used, and periodic trimming may be required. You shouldn't need to trim fresh or once-fired hulls. But if you detect variation, set your case trimmer to take half a millimeter from the mouth of a case exactly the specified length for the cartridge. Then run all cases through the trimmer. Within practical limits, case length doesn't matter as long as all the cases are of the same length and short enough that the case mouth doesn't contact the chamber mouth. Hulls too long and pinched by the chamber apply an unintentioned crimp, hiking pressures during bullet release and impairing accuracy. There's nothing wrong with trimming bottleneck cases a tad short. That way you can get several firings before having to trim again. Of course, you'll avoid trimming short those cases that headspace on the mouth, like the .45 ACP.

Deburr the case mouth inside and out with a deburring tool. A tapered lip eases bullet seating and chambering and helps ensure uniform neck tension. Don't remove a lot of metal; a couple of twists may be enough. Again, remember that the .45 ACP and other pistol rounds headspacing up front function best with a clean, square leading edge.

To ensure *truly* uniform cases, measure neck wall thickness with a ball micrometer, or a Sinclair wall thickness gauge. Measure four points around the neck's perimeter. Neck wall variations may reflect case wall variations, which can't be so easily gauged. Disparities of .0015 or greater in the measurements of *one* case means you'll want to outside-turn the neck to make wall thickness uniform.

The Sinclair outside-turning tool I use has a mandrel that slips inside the neck, centering it and establishing a gap for the blade, which is backed off enough to allow the neck to slip onto the spud easily. The next step is to tighten the cutter down until, as you spin

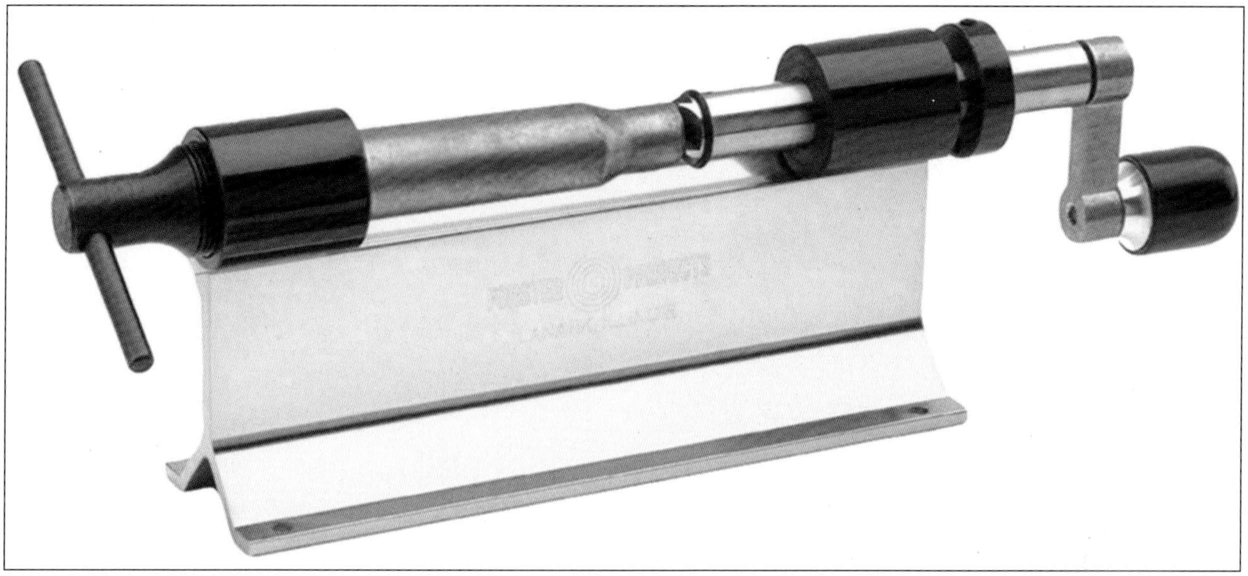

▲ A hand-spun trimmer like this Forster is easy to use, keeps cases proper length. Deburr before using.

the case, it barely contacts the "high spots," or thick sections of the neck. Rotate the case as you nudge it forward on the spud. Shaved spots appear bright. Now ease the blade incrementally closer to the spud, so subsequent rotations gobble more brass. Stop as soon as the neck is uniformly bright, or just before. Wall thickness exactly the same at every point around the neck ensures the bullet will be gripped with uniform tension and cleanly released. Concentric cases orient themselves more uniformly in ordinary chambers and more easily enter "tight" or "match" (minimum-dimension) chambers that can produce superior accuracy. A hull with no wall variation also collapses uniformly in the sizing die.

Inside-turning is another option. You'll need a different tool. This operation removes "donuts," as well as brass shoved forward by repeated firings and by case forming.

The head of each case also needs attention. Check flash-hole diameter in the primer pocket. Most centerfire rifle flash-holes are punched to .082. Check them with a #45 wire size drill bit. Some hulls, like the PPCs, the 6mm BR and .223 Remington target cases, have .060 flash-holes. While you're at it, select cases with visibly off-center flash-holes.

Deburr each flash-hole with a flash-hole deburring tool inserted from the case mouth. Punched holes are commonly ragged on the inside, where you can't see. But primer flame is affected by that rim of jagged metal, and so is ignition. You don't want to remove material from the web, just that excess brass protruding inside the case. A depth gauge, set on the case mouth, helps with this operation. Use caution. Take

▲ Turning necks ensures concentricity, easy feeding in tight chambers, consistent bullet orientation.

▲ You can neck-size with any die. Benchresters make it a practice; cases last for dozens of loadings.

▲ The coloring on these Black Hills cases results from annealing, to ensure ductile brass up front.

just the burr; don't cut into the web. Some cases, like match-grade hulls from Norma and Lapua, feature machined heads with drilled flash-holes. They tend to be more closely matched by weight and are less apt to show ragged flash-hole edges.

Primers in ammunition loaded for military use have historically been crimped in. Before trying to seat new primers in pockets with a crimp, you must first chamfer the pocket's protruding rim or iron it out with a steel plug in your press.

Brass that has been fired a few times gets "work-hardened" and brittle. Annealing will bring back the necessary ductility to the front of the hull. Oddly enough, heating, then quenching brass makes it more pliable, while that process tempers steel, making it harder! The easiest way I've found to anneal cartridge cases is to set them, base down, in a cake pan filled with water to a level about halfway up the case. Big pans allow me to set up twenty cases at a time, spaced so I can tip over each without felling others. Then, with a butane torch, I heat the neck and shoulder of the first hull gradually and as uniformly as I can until the neck is cherry red. Tipping the case into the water anneals it, and then I'm on to the next hull.

Annealed brass commonly takes on a blue or white tinge; you'll notice a color shift on each case where it met the water surface. Annealing is the main source of color on "two-tone" military 5.56 and 7.62 hulls. Don't anneal the rear half of your brass; it doesn't stretch as much as the front. Web and head are thick because they must be strong; they needn't be as ductile as neck and shoulder. Once annealed, a bottleneck case should be good for several more firings, its life depending largely on how hot your loads. Yes, you can anneal a second time; but it's generally best to discard cases twice hardened.

DIES AND SIZING

A sizing die is fashioned of hard steel and machined precisely to bring fired cases back to original dimensions—those set by SAAMI (the Sporting Arms and Ammunition Manufacturers' Institute)—for each cartridge. "Small-base" die sets are available for rifles with modest camming power (namely, pumps and autoloaders). Such dies squeeze cases down a tad more than do standard dies, to ensure easy chambering.

The die determines how far you can reduce case dimensions. But the relationship of the die and the shellholder (that slotted steel disk, specific to the case head, you insert in the press ram) also matters. Adjusted in the press for full-length sizing, the die will "kiss" the shellholder firmly when you lower the press handle. With or without a case in the shellholder, you'll feel a pop in the handle as the ram comes to its topmost position.

Before easing even one hull into your sizing die, you'll want to adjust its decapping pin. It should protrude just far enough that the spent primer just clears the case head as it tumbles free. You don't want the pin assembly to contact the inside of the case, or the pin to extend so far that it's prone to breakage.

With the sizing die threaded to its lock ring finger-snug in the press, loosen the smaller lock ring on the decapping stem at the top of the die. Adjust the decapping pin so it protrudes about .3 inch below the die mouth. With the proper shellholder in the press ram, let the ram come to its topmost position, loosen the die lock ring, then screw the die down until it kisses the shellholder. You're ready to resize.

But wait. There's an alternative! If you'll be using the next handloads in the rifle from which you retrieved this lot of brass, you may wish to neck-size only. There's no sense putting the full squeeze on a case, work-hardening the brass from base to mouth, when you need only bring the neck down a bit to hold another bullet firmly. Assuming the chamber is round, the case should re-enter it as easily as it exited on ejection. Neck-sizing prolongs case life. The procedure is simple: With the die lock ring loose and the die contacting the shellholder, back the die off the thickness of a penny. Now the die will squeeze the neck down, and the expander button will open it for bullet seating; but the case won't enter the die far enough to compress the body.

A problem with neck-sizing only is that if your chamber is slightly egg-shaped (some are!), the cartridge may not seat easily unless you happen to orient it the way it was oriented before. Also, a skin-snug fit allows no room for dirt, and if you load a warm case into a cold barrel, dimensional differences caused by the temperature can make for hard bolt closure. In the field, you'll want cartridges to chamber easily, without even an occasional hitch. That's why handloading manuals recommend hunting ammo be full-length resized. If you're developing loads for more than one rifle, neck-sizing will almost certainly bring you grief, because chambers dimensions do vary. Cases "fire-formed" in one rifle will not enter a smaller chamber, unless you reduce the case body to fit.

Once your cases are prepped, and you've decided whether to full-length or neck-size, tighten the die's lock ring against the press. I use only my fingers on lock rings, including those on the decapping assembly. You can impose a small end wrench on hex nuts, if you like, but keep pliers away from lock rings. They mar the knurling and are unnecessary. If you must loosen the overly tight rings on new dies (an irritating condition all too common), swath the rings with

▲ Lubing cases by rolling them on a lube-impregnated pad ensures easy travel through the resizing die.

▲ Forget lube, and you'll stick cases. Get in a hurry seating bullets, and you may ruin necks like this.

▲ To ease passage of the expander ball in case sizing, lube the inside of necks with graphite on a brush.

heavy cloth folded double and grip it firmly with those pliers.

You're now almost ready to run those hulls through your press. But first you must lubricate them, or they'll stick in the die. A bare brass case can be well and truly stuck with a single stroke of the press handle. At that point, you'll rue your failure to lube it. If, with Herculean effort, you manage to move the ram without bending or breaking something on your press, you'll pull the case in two. Then you'll order a stuck case remover from RCBS and wait until FedEx delivers it before you return to the bench.

To prevent such aggravation, pour or rub a little case lube onto a pad designed for that purpose. Distribute the lube gently with your fingers. Rotate the case body on the pad to give the brass a thin film on the surface of the neck, shoulder, and body. Don't overdo it. Too much lube, and you'll get hydraulic dents in the shoulder. Use a nylon brush to treat the inside of the case neck to ease passage of the expander ball in the die. I prefer dry graphite lube to oil inside the necks. In oil form, case lube can adversely affect the powder. When using oil, I swab case necks dry after sizing. But a dry swab makes sense even if you apply graphite, to ensure the lube doesn't limit necessary neck tension on the finished cartridge. (It's important, after sizing, to wipe the outside of the case dry, too, so there's no lube to pick up grit or interfere with the case gripping the chamber wall as it expands upon firing.)

Slip the lubed case into the shellholder until it stops, then carefully lower the press handle so the ram brings the case into the die. Go slowly. The case should be centered by the shellholder, but it should also have enough "slop" to center itself perfectly. If you feel the case bind, lower the press handle, then hold the case near the head with your fingers, and give it a slight spin as you ease it up into the die.

After removing a sized, de-primed case from the shellholder, inspect its primer pocket. Don't fret if there's a shadow of residue; but dirty pockets need touch-up with a pocket-cleaning tool or a brush. The flash-hole must be open. Discard cases with off-center flash-holes. Accuracy buffs use a special hand tool to make flash-holes uniform in diameter, deburring them afterward and surfacing the primer pockets with another tool to give each exactly the same depth. In

▲ Wax can be used in lieu of grease for lubricating cases. It's cleaner to handle, if not as quick to apply.

my view, you needn't go to those lengths for hunting ammo. On the other hand, anything you can do to increase uniformity is good.

PRIMING

The primer is the spark plug of every cartridge, the only truly explosive component. Small, but full of energy, the primer releases its energy suddenly when struck a sharp blow.

Igniting powder was not so easy in early firearms. Crude black powder quickly set alight in open-air resisted ignition in the chamber that bottled expanding gas to launch a ball. The first guns, developed in Europe a century and a half before Columbus sailed for the New World, were heavy tubes. The Swiss called these firearms culverins. They required two attendants. A culveriner held the tube, while his partner, the "gougat," lit a priming charge with a smoldering stick or rope. Culverins were clumsy and inaccurate and often misfired. Still, the noise and smoke they generated could unnerve an enemy armed with spears and pikes. Culverin muzzles fitted with ax heads could save the day when ignition failed. Eventually, these weapons were modified so one soldier could load and fire unassisted.

Stationary guns aimed at a wall or a massed adversary didn't require short lock time—the interval between starting a firing sequence and the exit of ejecta—because gun and target had a fixed relation-

BEWARE THE WHITE RING!

As a paper clip will break if repeatedly bent back and forth, a cartridge case will fail if subjected to repeated expansion (firing) and compression (sizing). Full-length sizing eventually leaves a white ring in front of the case web. This is where the forward part of the case becomes just thick enough that it does not expand tight to the chamber wall during firing. If the chamber is generous enough to let the cartridge move forward at the striker's blow, gas pressure from the burning powder will iron the ductile front of the case to the chamber while pushing the head back against the bolt face. This tug-of-war yields a thinning of the brass at the leading edge of the web. You'll see it as a white ring. Belted cartridges can display this ring in a couple of firings. Ignore it, and you could get a split, even case separation. Vented gas will score the chamber and can find its way through the action to damage other parts or injure you. The cure: Neck-size only if you're using the case in the same rifle. Even belted hulls will then headspace on the shoulder, limiting stretch. A snug fit not only yields longer case life, but helps the round center itself in the chamber for better accuracy.

▲ Neck-size to save unnecessary working of brass, and so cartridges fit more closely in the same rifle.

▲ Competitive shooters test loads to choose primers. Accuracy depends on uniform spark and burn.

ship. But soldiers on the move could ill-afford to wait for a rope to smolder through to the charge. They needed instant ignition. The first lock was a crude lever by which a long wick was lowered to the touch-hole in the barrel. A shorter (faster) wick evolved, to be replaced by a match assisted by a cord kept smoldering atop the barrel. The shooter eased a serpentine device, holding the match, onto the cord until the match caught fire. Then he moved it to the side and to the touch-hole with a trigger adapted from the crossbow. Guns with this crude mechanism became known as matchlocks. The Spanish arquebus was one.

On their belts, arquebusiers carried extra wicks smoldering in perforated metal boxes. But these hardly ensured reliable discharges. In 1636, during the battle at Kuisyingen, a soldier evidently managed only seven shots in eight hours! To eliminate the capricious wick, sixteenth-century Germans developed the "monk's gun" with a spring-loaded jaw that held a piece of pyrite (flint) against a serrated bar. To fire, the shooter pulled a ring to scoot the bar across the pyrite. Sparks fell in a pan, whose trail of fine gunpowder brought flame to the touch-hole. Improvements resulted in the wheellock, around 1515, in Nuremberg. The wheellock's sprocket, wound with a spanner under spring tension and latched, was released by the trigger to spin against a shard of pyrite secured by another spring. A pan caught the sparks. Wheellocks were less affected by moisture than were matchlocks. They were faster to set and gave quicker ignition.

Roles of pyrite and steel were reversed in the Lock a la Miquelet, named after Spanish miquelitos (marauders) in the Pyrenees. Oddly, this mechanism appears to have Dutch origins. It would later evolve into the flintlock, whose spring-loaded cock swung in an arc when released. The flint in the jaws of the cock hit a pan cover or hammer, moving it off the primed pan, which received sparks from the flint-on-steel contact.

The cock later became known as a hammer, the hammer a frizzen. Flintlock guns were less expensive to build than were wheellocks, and in time proved more dependable.

A common weakness of matchlock, wheellock, and flintlock mechanisms was exposed priming. Moisture could quickly render it inert, and the firearm useless. A weak spark might fail to ignite even dry priming. Flame there might not reach the main charge, yielding only a "flash in the pan." Generating fire inside the gun became possible in the early 1900s, with the discovery of fulminates. Chemists found that fulminic acid (an isomer of cyanic acid) produced shock-sensitive salts. A blow caused them to release their energy immediately, and more reliably than flint generated sparks. In 1774, a physician to Louis XV wrote about the explosiveness of mercury fulminate. Adding saltpeter to fulminates of mercury produced a shock-sensitive but stable explosive. Called "Howard's powder" after Englishman E.C. Howard, who discovered it in 1799, this compound may have figured into experiments by Scottish clergyman Alexander John Forsythe. In 1806, Forsythe became the first man on record to ignite a spark in the chamber of a gun. Two years later, Swiss gunmaker Johannes Pauly built a breech-loading gun that fired a cartridge with a paper percussion cap on its base. A spring-loaded needle pierced the cap, detonating the fulminate.

The advent of internal combustion drew enormous interest from military and civilian circles. New ammunition and the guns to fire it were developed simultaneously by legions of inventors. In 1818 Joseph Manton, an Englishman, fashioned a spring-loaded catch that held a tiny tube of fulminate against the side of the barrel over the touch-hole. The hammer crushed the fulminate, and breech pressure blew the tube to the side. The Merrill gun, 14,500 of which went to the British government, had this mechanism. In 1821, the London firm of Westley Richards designed a flintlock-style pan for fulminate primers that detonated when pierced by the hammer's sharp nose. Two years later, American physician Samuel Guthrie made a more convenient fulminate pellet.

Many inventors have claimed credit for developing the percussion cap, but it is most commonly attributed to sea captain Joshua Shaw of Philadelphia. In 1814, Shaw was denied a patent for a steel cap because he was British-born and not yet a US citizen. He persevered with a disposable pewter cap, then one of copper and, in 1822, his own lock. Twenty-four years later, Congress awarded the inventor (then 70) an honorarium for his brilliant work.

The percussion cap didn't succeed on its own. A hollow nipple funneled the fire to the powder—a faster path than a trail of powder in a pan, and nearly weatherproof. But despite the clear superiority of the cap over flint, percussion rifles were slow to earn public approval. They were rumored to kick harder, while delivering a weaker blow to the target. Also, in the early nineteenth century, chemistry was still viewed with suspicion by many, and the erratic performance of early primers made governments slow to replace pyrite. British firearms authority Colonel Hawker qualified his endorsement of percussion ignition: "For killing single shots at wildfowl rapidly flying, and particularly by night, [I certainly favor] the detonating system, as its trifling inferiority to the flint gun is tenfold repaid by the wonderful accuracy it gives in so readily obeying the eye. But in firing a heavy charge among a large flock of birds the flint has the decided advantage." Short years later, flint ignition would become all but obsolete.

Modern centerfire primers derive from Shaw's percussion cap. Drawn-brass, solid-head cartridge cases have no anvil (a solid surface to replace the nipple, against which the firing pin strikes to ignite the priming powder). Since 1880 in the United States, primer cups with internal anvils have been used in cases with a central flash-hole. These Boxer-style primers come in two sizes for rifle cartridges, two for handguns. The large and small rifle primers are of the same diameter as large and small pistol primers, respectively; but the primer pellets differ. A Large Rifle primer weighs 5.4 grains with .6 grain of priming compound.

European cartridge designers followed a slightly different path, choosing to incorporate the anvil in the case and punch two flash-holes in the pocket, one either side of the anvil. This Berdan primer has a couple of advantages over the Boxer: There's more room in it for priming compound, and the flame can go straight through the holes rather than having to scoot around the anvil and its braces. The Boxer primer owes its popularity largely to handloaders, who can punch out old primers with a de-capping pin while sizing the case in a die. Berdan primers must be pried out with a special hook or forced free by hydraulic pressure. In an odd twist, Edward Boxer, namesake of American-style primers, was British. Europeans named their primer after Hyram Berdan—an American! Both men were military officers.

Early Boxer primers ignited black powder easily but sometimes failed to fire smokeless. When more fulminate was added to the priming mix, cases began to crack. Blame fell on the propellant, but the culprit was really mercury residue from the primer. This residue, which had been largely absorbed by the fouling of black powder, accumulated in hulls using smokeless. It attacked the zinc in the metal, causing the hulls to split. The first successful non-mercuric primer was the military H-48, developed in 1898 for the .30-40 Krag. Its main detonating component: potassium chlorate, whose corrosive salts didn't damage cases but could ruin bores by attracting water. Vigorous cleaning with hot water and ammonia, followed by oiling, kept rifling shiny. Still, even short-term neglect could result in pitted bores.

In 1901, the German Company Rheinisch-Westphalische Sprengstoff (RWS) announced a new primer, with barium nitrate and picric acid instead of potassium chlorate. These compounds did not cause rust. Ten years later the Swiss had a non-corrosive primer, while German rimfire ammunition featured *Rostfrei* (rust-free) priming. Rostfrei contained neither potassium chlorate nor ground glass, the common element used to generate friction when the striker hit. This solution proved imperfect, because barium oxide turned up as a residue, scouring the barrel as aggressively as had the glass. Glass was purged from American military primers before World War I, when the FH-42 supplanted the H-48. Wartime primer production overloaded drying houses in the United States, causing sulfuric acid to build up in the priming mix. Misfires resulted. The FH-42 gave way to the Winchester 35-NF primer, later known as the FA-70. This reliable but corrosive primer remained in military service through World War II.

Remington was the first company in the United States to announce non-corrosive priming. Its "Kleanbore" debuted in 1927. Winchester followed with "Staynles," and Peters with "Rustless." All contained mercury fulminate. German chemists Rathburg and Von Hersz managed to remove both potassium chlorate and mercury fulminate from primers. Stateside, Remington beat competitors to a non-corrosive, non-mercuric primer. The main ingredient was lead trinitroresorcinate, or lead styphnate. Then comprising up to 45 percent of the priming mix, lead styphnate remains an important component in small arms primers today. The US Army adopted non-corrosive, non-mercuric primers in 1948.

Development of bigger hunting cartridges and extra-slow-burning powders in the 1940s prompted research into primers with a stronger flame. More priming compound wasn't the answer; the blast could shatter powder directly in front of the flash-hole, causing erratic pressures. Dick Speer and Victor Jasaitis, a chemist from Speer Cartridge Works, came up with a better idea: the addition of boron and aluminum to the lead styphnate base to enable primers to burn longer. The result would be more heat, more complete ignition before primer fade. This first successful magnum primer was just what Roy Weatherby needed for his magnum cartridges. Other munitions firms followed suit. Speer primers, still made in Lewiston, Idaho, now wear the CCI (Cascade Cartridge Industries) label.

Shotshell manufacture was plagued with the same primer problems visited on the production of rifle and pistol cartridges, and it came by the same salvation. But the shotshell cup assembly is different. A deep battery cup holds the anvil and a smaller cup containing the detonating material. As with rifle and pistol primers, a foil cover protects the pellet. But the primer pocket of a shotshell has no bottom; hence, the flash-hole is in the battery cup. Made of thin, folded brass like old balloon-head rifle cases, shotshell heads are reinforced with a dense paper base wad or a thick section of hull plastic. Battery cups seal the deep hole in the base wad.

Primer manufacture is much the same now as at the outbreak of the Second World War. Enormous batches of primer cups are still punched and drawn from thin sheet metal and indexed on large perforated metal trays. A second perforated plate is smeared with wet,

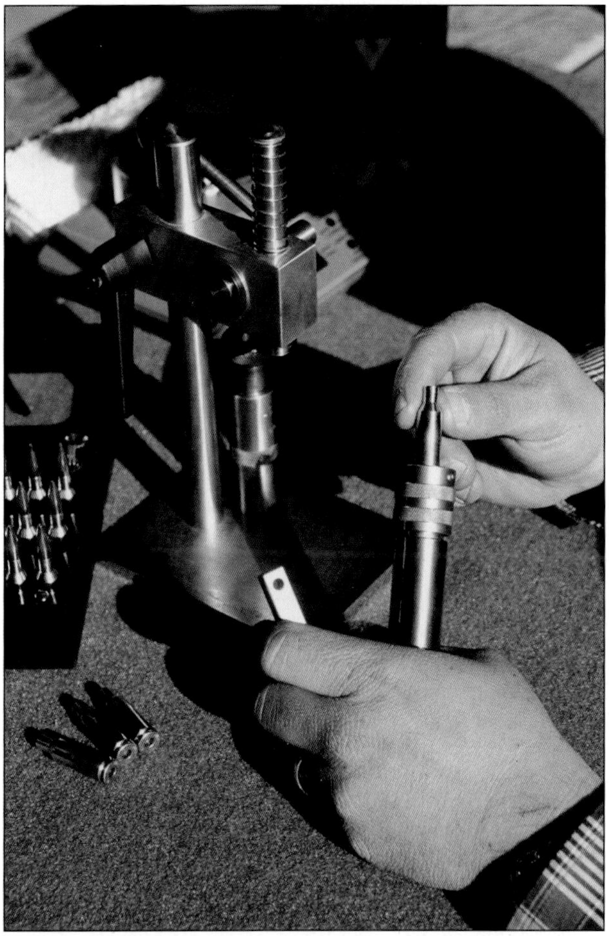

▲ Priming with a hand tool helps you feel for uniform seating. Discard cases with loose primer pockets.

dough-like priming compound and positioned precisely on top of the first so the dabs in the holes can be pressed down into the open-faced cups. Or the cups are filled by a worker brushing the compound across the face of the table. Next comes a foil disc (or a shellacked paper cover). Anvils, punched from another metal sheet, are then inserted.

Priming mix is stable when wet, but extremely hazardous to work with when dry. No mix is ever allowed to dry as a lump in a primer room. Walls separating this sanctum from the rest of an ammunition factory are bombproof, because an accidental explosion here can be catastrophic. The room's roof and outside walls are typically flimsy, to ensure easy release of pressure in event of an explosion and to limit the force directed toward the factory and its powder stocks. Survivors of primer room blow-ups are few.

Primer choice can influence pressure, velocity, and accuracy. In rifles, I stick with standard Large Rifle primers until powder charges exceed 65 grains. That's about where belted magnums like the 7mm Remington and .300 Winchester part company with the .30-06 family, and where charges of the slowest powders become useful in capacious cartridges. The longer-burning Magnum primers more consistently ignite big charges of slow powders. They're also useful in cold weather or with powders particularly hard to unite.

For decades, I would prime cases in my press, loading primers one at a time onto the primer arm, then pushing the arm into the slot in the ram. Easing the ram, with the deprimed case in the shellholder, onto the primer arm inserted the new primer. There's nothing wrong with this method, but you'll prime faster and get a better feel of the seating if you use a hand tool by Lee or RCBS. Each of these inexpensive units has a primer tray with grooves that, with a little shaking, orient the primers you've dumped onto it. Then all you do is slip a cartridge case into the tool's shellholder and squeeze the grip. Remove the primed hull, insert another, and you're ready to go again. Tubes on progressive presses speed priming even more.

A primer must "bottom" in the pocket to support the anvil firmly a uniform distance from the bolt face, so the primer can't move and the striker hits with the same force each time. Correct depth for large rifle

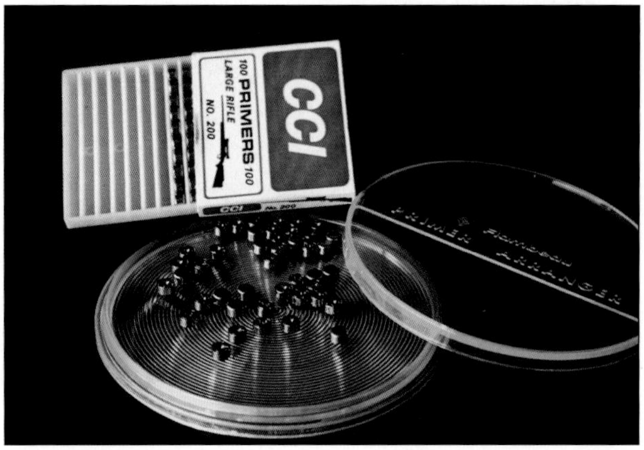

▲ Gentle shaking on ribbed trays orients primers. Keep primers in original boxes, away from heat, oil.

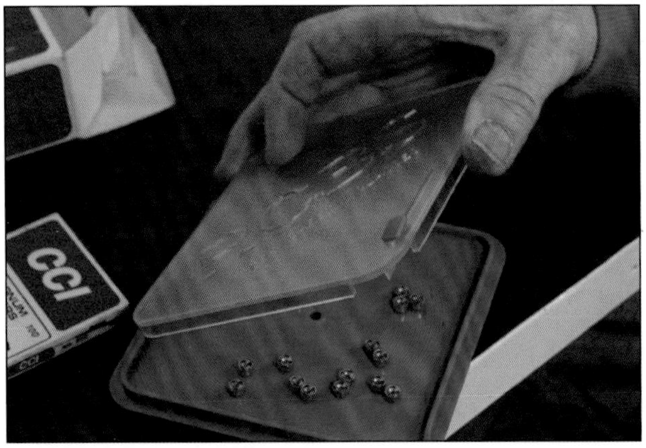

▲ Hand-priming tools like RCBS's have ribbed trays to orient primers, then held upright by the cover.

primers is .128 to .132. Small Rifle primers, and Small and Large pistol primers, require a depth of .118 to .122. Don't fret about pocket diameter unless primer fit is so tight that you crumple primers trying to seat them—or if the primer slides in with almost no friction. Behind full-power loads, primer pockets can swell, eventually becoming too big to hold primers securely. High breech pressures can split primers, expanding the pocket at the same time. A pocket that won't hold a primer is a death knell for that case. Throw it away.

Cleaning tight pockets should enable them to accept primers more readily. Removing brass from the pocket wall is another option, but can shorten the useful life of the case. While primer diameters must hew to specific dimensions, I've found diameters can differ

▲ Fastidious handloaders insist on new brass from the best sources. Then they check, sort and prep it.

slightly. If primers routinely seat too easily or require excessive effort with a carefully prepared batch of cases, try another brand.

POWDER

In the nascent days of gunpowder, described by English friar Roger Bacon in 1249, launching missiles with it seemed a novel idea. Crude firearms eventually crawled from the primordial muck, the first of them about a century and a half before Columbus sailed for the New World.

From its first use as fuel in the fourteenth century until the middle of the nineteenth, black powder generated the gas that hurled balls and bullets. "Black" is essentially a blend of fuels and oxidants.

▲ Ideally suited to rimmed cases, modern hinged-breech guns (here a Steyr Duett) also accept rimless.

▲ Ball powder is Winchester-trademarked spherical. DuPont's extruded IMR series dates to the 1920s.

Nitroglycerine, discovered in 1846 by Ascanio Subrero in Italy, promised higher performance. A clear liquid comprising nitric and sulphuric acids plus glycerin, "nitro" is an oxygen-rich compound eager to rearrange itself into more stable gases. It doesn't need a spark to make this change; a jolt will do. With age, nitro becomes less predictable and more dangerous. In 1863, Swedish chemist Emmanuel Nobel and his son Alfred learned how to put this touchy substance in cans—which made it easier to handle but no less hazardous. After the Nobel factory in Germany blew up, Alfred rendered the chemical less sensitive to shock in a porous earth called *Kieselguhr.* Dynamite followed in 1875.

Meanwhile, Swiss chemist Christian Schoenbein discovered that cotton treated with sulfuric and nitric acids formed a compound that burned so fast the cotton became ash without igniting black powder on top of it! John Hall and Sons built a guncotton plant in Faversham, England. It blew up. So did most other guncotton plants. Chemists concluded this frisky substance had little use as a propellant because it burned too fast and lacked stability. In 1869, German immigrant Carl Dittmar built a plant to treat sawdust with nitroglycerin. He called the product "Dualin," and followed it with his "New Sporting Powder." By 1878, Dittmar was building a mill in Binghampton, New York. It blew up, taking much of the city with it.

Eventually nitroglycerin would be added to nitrocellulose (single-base) powders. These double-base propellants have more energy. Nearly all smokeless powders incorporate a stabilizer—commonly, diphenylamine—to prevent decomposition. A graphite coating limits the hazard of static electricity and makes handling easier. A flame retardant reduces muzzle flash.

After the transition from black to smokeless powders near the close of the nineteenth century, an "MR" label began appearing on cans of DuPont powders. It meant "military rifle." The IMR line of "improved military rifle" powders came along in the 1920s, when four-digit numbers replaced two-digit numbers in DuPont designations. MR 10 and kin were supplanted by IMR fuels, beginning with 4198. The first had relatively fast burn rates, for the small medium-bore cartridges of the day. In 1934, DuPont came up with IMR 4227, followed by IMR 4895 in the early 1940s, specifically for the .30-06 in the M1 Garand. About that time the first "magnum" IMR propellant made its debut. Developed for 20mm cannons, 4831 would become one of the signature fuels for big, high-velocity hunting rounds.

Incidentally, powder numbers have nothing to do with burning rate. According to Larry Werner, an expert in the industry, powder from DuPont is labeled chronologically. High numbers indicate recent propellants. Those under development have traditionally been tagged "EX" for "experimental." Larry, whose experience dates to the 1950s, observed that "almost always, firearm design precedes cartridge design. Powder selection comes last. We'd start with a cookbook formula, then tweak the mix until we had it right. Once the customer was satisfied and committed to, say, 5,000 pounds of propellant, the EX fell from the designation, and commercial labeling replaced it. Powders made expressly for military use had no prefix."

Powder charts by DuPont and other companies help handloaders compare burning rates so they can choose an efficient powder for a given cartridge. "Closed bomb" tests are used to measure burn rate. A charge of powder ignited in a chamber of known volume produces a pressure curve that's compared to the curves from other propellants. But a powder's behavior relative to that of its kin can change, not only with changes in case capacity and bore diameter, but bullet weight. IMR powders were assigned Relative

Quickness values. Larry Werner said IMR 4350 has an arbitrary value of 100, fast-burning IMR 4227 an RQ of 180. IMR 4198 comes in at 165, IMR 3031 at 135. IMR 4064, 4320 and 4895 are listed at 120, 115 and 110, though some manuals show a slightly different order. Savvy handloaders try several propellants with similar burn rates to come up with a top load.

DuPont's old MR line included single-base and double-base powders. "All commercial spherical propellants are double-base," Larry Werner told me. "Nitro delivers more energy per grain. It also reduces the tendency for grains to draw moisture. Its main drawback is residue. Double-base powders don't burn as clean." He said that to get nitroglycerine's full effect, you need 8 to 12 percent in the mix. VihtaVuori 500-series powders have up to 25 percent nitroglycerin. But many powders hawked as double-base have less. The extra oomph of double-base powders makes them logical picks where case capacity is limited.

Powder grains vary in shape. Spherical propellants like the Winchester-trademarked Ball series also include flattened, platter-shaped grains, though flake powders define another category. Spherical and flake propellants whose grain surface area diminishes during the burn are called regressive. Extruded or "stick" powders resemble little tubes. The hole in the center helps control the burn rate and the pressure curve. Powders whose grain surface stays about the same size as it burns rank as neutral. A single-hole extruded powder falls into this category because, as flame eats away at the outer surface, it also consumes the tube from inside out. The burn inside increases surface area as the hole becomes bigger, while outside combustion reduces diameter. Eventually the tube burns through between the hole and the outer surface. At that final point of gas release, of course, the grain shrinks rapidly. Large extruded grains may have multiple holes that enable them to burn progressively. The opening of these holes more than offsets the reduction in outside surface during initial phases of the burn, so until all material between holes burns through, grain surface area increases as the powder is consumed.

"Extruded powders are usually more consistent over temperature ranges than spherical powders," Chris Hodgdon points out. "The margin is slight,

◀ Extruded, flake and spherical powders are formulated for specific tasks in rifles, pistols, shotguns.

▲ Double-base spherical powders pack lots of punch in short-action cases, across a range of burn rates.

▲ These slow-burning powders excel with heavy bullets in big, necked-down magnum rifle cartridges.

averaging 4 percent. New spherical fuels have shown great consistency." He adds that Hodgdon's Extreme line, introduced with Varget in 1996, shows the least variation of any powder in the company's stable.

Quick-burning propellants are suited to small, wide-mouthed cases and short, lightweight bullets. Building pressure quickly behind long, heavy bullets with lots of bearing surface can induce a pressure spike because bore friction and mass keep those bullets from accelerating fast enough to dissipate the rise in pressure. Watch a tennis pro deliver a ferocious forehand serve, and you'll see the ball jet across the net. Eye-blink response. If the same athlete tried that with a cannon ball, he or she would ruin the racquet, and the ball would fall within spitting distance. It's not that a cannon ball can't move fast. But it has much more inertia than a tennis ball.

Long, heavy rifle bullets mightily resist the push of powder gases. Their weight may only equal that of a shorter, big-bore pistol bullet, but the greater bore friction set up by the longer rifle bullet—along with its smaller base—begs a slow, progressive powder. Pistol bullets (and shotgun slugs and muzzleloader bullets of similar profile) give the propellant a big base against which to spread pressure. The short shank limits friction. A bore that's generous in diameter, relative to the weight and length of the powder column and friction imposed by the bullet, offers gas a big cavity that grows fast as the projectile moves. Slow powder paired with a pistol bullet will disappoint, as the bullet outruns expanding gas. A short barrel exacerbates this failing, dumping pressure at the muzzle before it has transferred all its energy to the bullet.

The best propellants in pistols (with traditional handgun cartridges) are those that build pressure quickly, but whose pressure peaks don't equal those of rifle powders in stout actions. A rifle's long barrel gives slow propellants time and space to accelerate heavy, friction-bound missiles. Progressive extruded powders are intuitively those you'd pick for sustained thrust in fixed-breech rifles, but spherical powders can work in this arena, too. Additives take the place of grain structure to throttle burn rate and gas release.

Gas-operated sporting rifles work best with propellants near the middle on burn-rate charts. It's unlikely you'll get proper cycling with super-slow fuels that fill cases. Pressure curves must match rifle design so the proper level and duration of thrust is delivered through the barrel port.

As with cartridge cases, you're smart to buy as much powder as practical of a single lot. Burning characteristics can vary between lots. They also change with age. You'll likely try several powders and loads to get the one that performs best. I prefer powders in the middle of the burn-rate range for the round. Ideally, the powder column fills a bottleneck case to the shoulder. Slight compaction is fine during bullet seating, but I prefer not to crush powder. For hunting, I typically approach the maximum levels in loading manuals. Those maximums, I've found, are generally conservative, with a margin of safety. Adjusting powder charges 1 or 2 grains at a time makes sense for big

▲ Wayne uses a small plastic pepper shaker to tap powder onto the pan of a balance-beam scale.

rifle cases, but as you approach maximums, you may find smaller adjustments produce significant change in pressure, velocity, and accuracy.

There can be a difference in burn-rate between IMR and Hodgdon powders of the same number. The Improved Military Rifle series has been around since the 1920s. Hodgdon bought the IMR line in 2003 but marketed its "H"-prefix powders for decades before that transaction. Differences in blending distinguish H4831 and IMR 4831. Same goes for 4350 and a few others. "Load data for H4831 and IMR 4831differs," Chris Hodgdon points out in an example. "The disparity isn't great, but typically IMR 4831 is faster by a slim margin. When not specified, you can assume the powder is IMR." Ditto for some other extruded powders that bear both prefixes. In magnum cases, with charges of 70 to 80 grains, I've found IMR 4831 faster than H4831 by the equivalent of 2 or 3 grains in the load. The "Short Cut" version of H4831 behaves like its forebear. IMR 4227 and H4227 are essentially identical in burn rate.

▲ Don't pour powder from can to scale. Use a measure, or a small handheld container like this.

You're smart to weigh each powder charge for rifle handloads. Powder measures throw uniform charges of spherical propellants, and make sense for high-volume pistol loads on progressive presses in which cases march, at each stroke of the press handle, about a central spindle. But stick powders don't meter well. You'll have more confidence in any load when you've weighed the fuel. Both balance-beam and electronic scales deliver accuracy to .1 grain. Use a powder trickler to add final grains in controlled increments—or, as I do, tap them out from a small cup or shaker to finish the charge.

The uninitiated may cringe at the thought of crushing powder as they seat bullets; but compressed loads may be necessary with certain powders in some cases. Consider, for example, the .338 Winchester Magnum. Heavy-bullet loads require slow powder, but this case is of modest size, and the mouth (bullet base) is pretty generous. So it's hard to get enough, say, H4831, inside the hull to push these big bullets fast. Three tricks will help. First, neck-size only. You'll gain a little powder space by not compressing the front of the case. Secondly, introduce powder slowly, tipping and tapping the case on its rim as you rotate it. Grains will settle more tightly. Third, use a drop tube—a metal or plastic column beneath your funnel. Grains will enter the case in a thin stream, jostling to fill air space.

Mild compression of extruded powder by the bullet heel won't impair performance. But extreme compression can break extruded grains and flakes, changing their burning behavior. Seating bullets with a long-handled press on cases full to the mouth with powder, you can shatter the propellant, or even imprint it on bullet bases. I have a Nosler Partition pulled from a case stuffed with H4831. Its lead base is cobble-stoned by the indentations of powder grains with no place to go. Too much compression, in my view. In extreme cases, the press of the powder can even cause bullet creep in the rifle's magazine during recoil.

My rule of thumb is to compress no more than a neck-full of extruded powder. If the bullet must be seated deeper, I turn to faster propellant. Usually that's different fuel altogether; but sometimes you'll get a slightly faster burn (and slightly shorter powder column) from powder with the same numbers but a different prefix. Ball powders don't compress well. Trying to squeeze H380 from the neck into the body of a hull is like trying to push marbles into a soup can that's already full of them.

While many propellants that date to the military-surplus era still belong on every handloader's bench, new powders have shouldered others aside. Hodgdon, for example, now sells Superformance and LEVERevolution powders. These derive from Hornady's efforts to develop high-octane factory ammo for specific cartridge classes. The LEVERevolution series announced a few years ago incorporates what are now called Flex-Tip bullets—spitzers with resilient plastic tips that deliver flat arcs without the danger of magazine detonation that historically scotched use of pointed bullets. Innovative powders, from formulas Hornady's Dave Emary helped concoct at St. Marks, drives those bullets at high speed without exceeding sane pressure limits. The .300 and .338 RCM use them to wring fast exits from short barrels.

Chris Hodgdon concedes it would have been impractical for Hodgdon to list a propellant specific to each Hornady load. "But our LEVERevolution works exceedingly well across a range of popular lever-rifle rounds, from the .25-35 to the .338 Marlin Express. Some speeds have jumped dramatically—a 300-fps increase with 150-grain .30-30 bullets." The Superformance powder Hornady trotted out in 2009 was a direct result of the LEVERevolution project. "It's mainly for bolt-rifle rounds," Chris explains. "In a burn-rate chart, I'd put it between H4831 and H4350. But it's more versatile than either, and out-shines both in short barrels. We've had great results with it in the .22-250, .243, 6mm and .300 RCM. It's also a fine propellant for Winchester Super Short Magnums."

When using older powders, you'd be smart to examine the grains before charging any cases. Red dust signals deterioration that can result from poor storage but also, I'm told, from improper finishing in production. Powder so afflicted is best flushed down the toilet, with any damaged or "dud" primers. To prolong the useful life of gunpowder, keep it tightly capped in its original container in a cool, dry place. Don't subject it to hard freezes, which can affect grain structure.

When you're developing loads, be aware that powder can deliver misleading signs of pressure. For example, muzzle flash may seem to indicate too much propellant, when in fact it results from low-pressure loads. Black residue on case necks is no harbinger of doom; it tells you instead that the load does not generate enough pressure to seal the case neck against the chamber wall upon bullet release, and some blowback is occurring.

No matter what kind of powder you put in your handloads, or how much, only about a 30 percent of

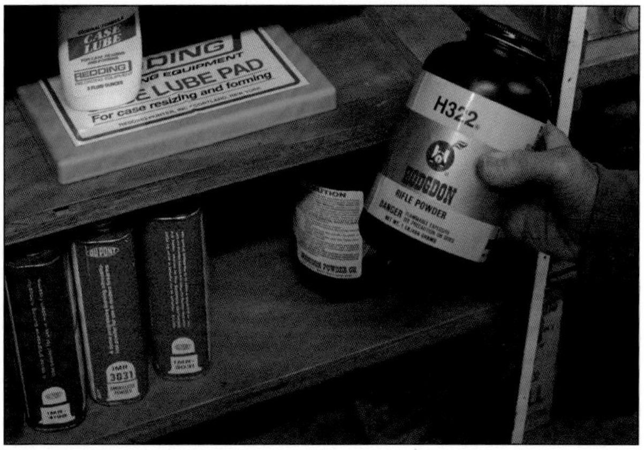

▲ Keep only one can of powder on the bench at a time. Store others beneath or on a separate shelf.

DETONATION DANGER!

Few slow powders work well in reduced charges. Such loads can even be hazardous. Detonation has occurred with some types—presumably when primer flame shoots across the top of the partial charge, starting the burn from front and back of the powder column at the same time. Replicating this event has been problematic, but speculation has it that pressure waves result. It's best to avoid reduced loads with slow extruded and ball powders. A case should be full enough that when horizontal the powder covers the flash-hole. While corn meal and synthetic fillers have a long history keeping powder at the rear of the hull behind cast bullets, such loads typically feature fast propellants. If you plan to throttle back more than 10 percent from starter loads, proceed with caution.

NO RULES FOR POWDERS?

Some years ago, I embarked on a righteous crusade to produce a comprehensive table on powder burn rates. I telephoned chemists, ballisticians and veteran handloaders, then tapped the wisest of trolls at powder companies to reconcile discrepancies in existing charts. Unanimously and diplomatically, these sages told me I was full of prunes. "Different *lots* of powder can burn at different rates," they explained, "so rates can overlap or change places. Also, burn rates don't respond uniformly to changes in case shape and capacity, or bullet weight. A powder that burns faster than another in a small case might burn slower in a big hull." I abandoned my project. Burn-rate charts in loading manuals are useful but still just guides. To try a powder absent in data, use a published starting charge of a propellant of similar burn-rate.

its energy stays in harness behind the bullet. About the same amount is lost as heat inside the case and the barrel. Nearly 40 percent becomes useless exhaust at the muzzle!

BULLETS

Your choice of bullets for rifles and handguns hinges on their intended use and your own personal preferences. Bullet weight and shape affect velocity, energy, and trajectory—also accuracy. You may not want the most accurate bullet, if an alternative design gives you the best terminal performance in tough game with vitals the size of a beach ball. But upset and penetration matter not at all when your object is a tight group or high X-count in a match.

There's so much to contemplate in bullet design, I'll save *that* for later. Back to the bench . . .

After charging a batch of cases, spin the seating die into your press so the die mouth is a penny's thickness off the top of the shellholder. Loosen the seating stem and turn it out so when you insert a bullet into an empty case with a stroke of the press handle you barely stick the bullet in the case mouth. From that point, you can turn the seating stem down incrementally between strokes until you reach the desired seating depth and overall cartridge length.

It's important to seat bullets to clear the magazine box and the rifling. The Neanderthal method is to seat the bullet so it just clears the magazine, then chamber the cartridge. If it chambers easily, and no land marks appear on the bullet after extraction, the cartridge is as long as practical. Of course, there must be enough shank inside the neck for a firm grip. An old rule of thumb: Neck contact should at least equal caliber designation, so a .270 needs .270-neck contact with the bullet shank. If seating is too shallow, or if you can't chamber the round, or if chambering leaves land marks on the bullet, you must adjust the die deeper. There's now clever tooling that helps you seat bullets precisely for best performance without this trial and error.

Crimping is an option if the bullets you're using have cannelures for that purpose. Crimping isn't necessary for most loads and introduces another variable that can affect accuracy; however, it adds grip to the case neck, preventing bullet-creep in powerful and tube-fed rifles. Heavy recoil can cause bullets in a magazine or cylinder to pull away from their cases. It's an inertia issue: The heavy bullet wants to stay as the lighter hull jumps immediately to the tug of the rifle or handgun.

So-called "safari" rounds—say, the .416s and up—jolt the rifle so hard that cartridges in reserve (in barrel or magazine) endure severe pull. The heavier the bullet, the more violent the force. That's why a 500-grain solid in a .458 Winchester is best crimped, while a 140-grain softpoint in a 7mm Remington need not be. The 7mm Magnum's case is essentially the .458's, necked down, but the cartridges are quite different. The .458's bullet, three and a half times as heavy, delivers terrific recoil as it accelerates from zero to 2,000 fps almost instantly. Meanwhile, the 500-grain bullets in the stack are yanked violently back by their case necks. A friction-only grip may not be enough to prevent bullet-creep. Result: The cartridges may bind as they "bridge" between front and back of the magazine box. They fail to feed, and the buffalo that resents your intrusion puts hoof-prints on your safari shirt.

The 7mm's lighter bullet sets up less recoil, and those in the box don't tug as hard on case necks.

Crimping is a tradition for bullets in tube magazines as well. There spring tension is pushing the bullets *into* the cases. Powerful handgun cartridges merit crimps partly because the contact area between bullet and case is relatively small compared to that of long rifle bullets in bottleneck hulls. Example: The .44 Magnum's 300-grain bullet has a great deal of inertia relative to the friction bond between it and the thin-mouthed pistol brass. Also, a .44 Magnum revolver weighs roughly half as much as a centerfire rifle of comparable power, and is decidedly frisky in recoil. The pull on bullets in the cylinder is sudden and strong. Crimps ensure bullet creep won't "tie up" the cylinder and make the gun inoperable.

Special crimping dies are available for cartridges commonly crimped. But you can crimp almost any cannelured bullet with a standard seating die. With a bullet seated to proper depth, insert the cartridge in your shellholder, and run the ram to its topmost position. With the seating die's stem spun out so it does not engage the bullet, turn the die down until it stops. The inside of the die should now bear against the mouth of the case. Lower the ram, then screw the die in another quarter turn. Run the ram up; you'll press the case mouth against the die's tapered suface, which forces the mouth into the bullet's cannelure.

Want more crimp? Screw the die in incrementally until you're satisifed. Then lower the stem so when you seat the next bullet, it stops with the cannelure at the case mouth as the mouth contacts the crimping rim inside the die.

Remember that anything impeding easy bullet release affects pressure curves. Crimping can hike pressures pending bullet release, but not dangerously, provided you use your noggin when setting the die. Modest crimps are also easier to apply uniformly, and they deform the bullet less than tight crimps—both factors that help you retain accuracy while ensuring against bullet creep. For some pistol loads, crimping actually improves accuracy, as it boosts the pressure needed to pop bullets free, for cleaner, more uniform release. Many crimped factory loads—rifle and pistol—deliver fine accuracy. Benchrest shooters and other riflemen whose sole measure of success is one-hole precision do not crimp.

Lee's crimping tool gives you more control than a seating die adjusted to pinch the case mouth onto the bullet. Never crimp except into a crimping groove or cannelure! And crimp lightly to start!

When not crimping, you're free to seat bullets farther out than cannelures indicate—within limits imposed by your magazine and throat. Cartridges must fit comfortably in your magazine, and when you chamber one, the bullet's shank must lie shy of the rifling. Seating a bullet so far out that the rifling grips the bullet is usually a bad idea. Expanding gas must build higher pressure to push it into the lands than to start it in the throat. Also, if the rifling engraves far enough onto the shank, you may pull the case from the bullet when you try to extract the loaded round, spilling powder into your magazine while leaving the bullet stuck in the bore.

HOW CLOSE TO THE LANDS?

Bullets seated against the lands when chambered must overcome the engraving force at the same time they're breaking free of the neck. Generally, I set dies for .1 bullet-land clearance—close enough to ensure a straight start for the bullet while allowing it to easily break its friction bond with the case. Solid-copper bullets are less malleable than jacketed lead-core missiles, so may require a longer run to the lands to keep pressures in check. Barnes recommends its X-Bullets be seated .050 shy of the lands. Full-throttle handloads with lead-free bullets seated out are best approached with extra caution.

To check throat length, seat a series of bullets progressively farther out until you feel one contact the rifling. Check for the marks. (Smoking a bullet with a match before chambering, you'll see the rifling marks more clearly.) Then set your seating die to ensure land clearance.

▲ Use properly sized loading blocks at the bench to avoid mix-ups, spills. Buy enough. They're cheap.

HOW MANY LOADS?

For any new cartridge—especially those for which limited data is available and wildcats of your own making—load conservatively at first, and keep those lots small. (I often charge only five or six cases to start.) As you narrow powder and bullet choices and boost velocities, you'll shoot more of each load, eventually winding up with a few recipes that merit extensive testing. Then you may wish to fire ten shots per trial to get more accurate data and check consistency. Slowly increasing the number of cartridges per loading session as results eliminate certain components gets you most quickly from useless ammunition to loads you'll want to take on safari or to important rifle matches.

▲ Superior handloads and a careful 410-yard shot put a smile on this Wyoming hunter's face.

Chapter 3: Handloading Tools

The handloading industry began as a circle of small shops set up by shooters to supply tooling for themselves and friends. As it grew, so did the shops, to be joined by larger companies established to make other items.

Good tools produce good loads. Forster, RCBS, and Redding catalogs belong in your files. Lyman, too. Hornady was late to the game, but now markets many fine handloading tools. You don't need *every* device, or the Cadillac model for each step. I've loaded for years on a $15 Herter's press; an inexpensive Lee hand tool suffices for priming. Manual case trimmers work as well as electric versions, and unless you handload for a brigade of hunters, should suffice. Electronic scales have all but supplanted balance beams and may be worth the extra cost. They're more accurate and can be faster. Carbide and titanium nitride-treated dies speed the sizing of straight-walled hulls. Digital micrometers make sense if your eyes have been with you more than 40 years. Stuck case removers rescue the unthinking . . .

I didn't have all this stuff at first. Just press, dies, and lube pad. If you're picking up Junior's bill at college and saving to fund national health care, you might have to equip that bench piecemeal, as I did.

You can also save money with kits like the Partner package offered by RCBS. It includes a press of that name, with other items you need to start handloading: a balance-beam scale, lube pad and lube, neck brushes, a deburring tool and powder funnel, plus a case block to hold your cartridges and the latest Speer Reloading Manual. List price at this writing is about $250. Or choose the RCBS Reloader Special 5 kit, an upgraded package with that press and 5-0-5 scale, a version of which has served me for 40 years!

▲ A bullet puller uses inertia to yank a bullet free, unscathed, and saves the powder. You'll want one.

▲ Not all useful tools are complex or costly. Here a simple brass brush cleans residue from case necks.

If you have special needs, shop one tool at a time. Loading cartridges as voluminous as the .30-378 Weatherby—and surely the .50 BMG—you'll need a press with a long stroke and a wide maw. Plan to load in quantity? Consider a turret press, whose multi-station head can hold all the tooling you need to complete loading one cartridge. Install sizing and seating dies and powder measure, so with successive strokes of the ram, and a fingertip turn of the turret, you get a complete cartridge pronto. Or leave the turret in one position and run it like a single-stage press, sizing a batch of cases before you advance the turret to the next station. Redding's seven-station T-7 press and the RCBS six-station turret press each accommodate primer tubes. True progressive tools, like Dillon's, use a rotating base to advance the case through a series of stations. That plate turns at each ram stroke automatically. So a finished round pops out at every cycle, without further action on your part. These and all single-stage presses accept 7/8-14 dies. That thread is an industry standard.

The number of accessories you can buy for a handloading bench are legion. Some you'll find less useful than others. While measuring breech pressures may be impractical, minding case head expansion is a

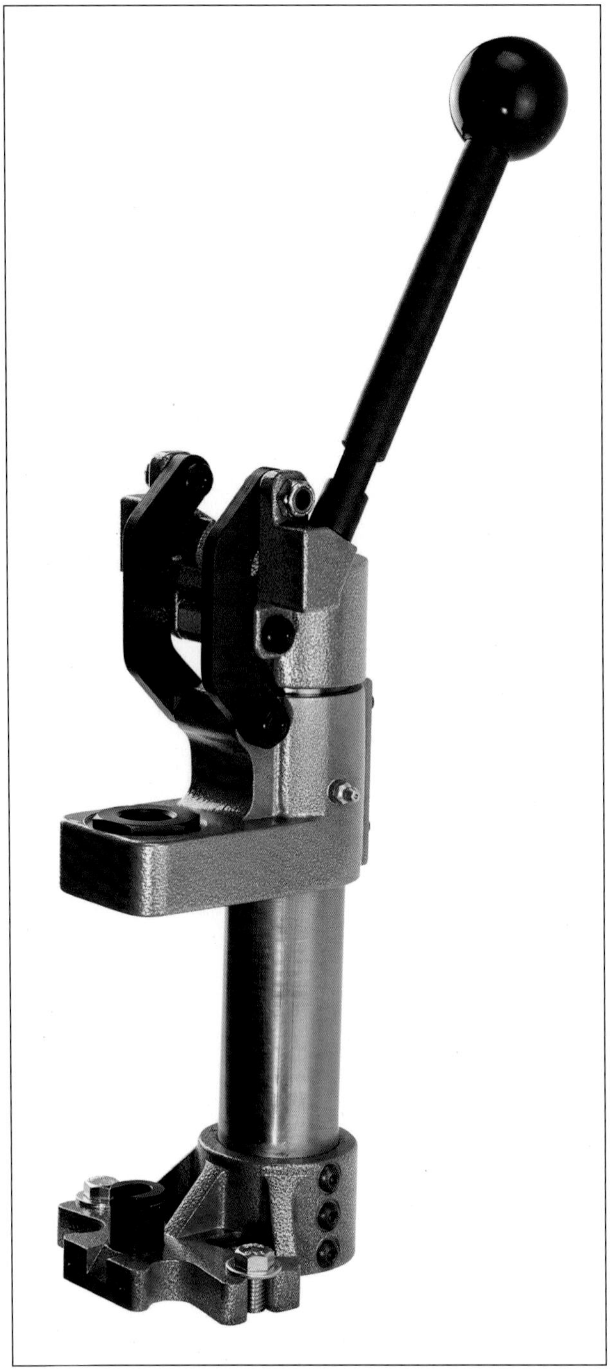

▲ RCBS (Rock Chucker Bullet Swage) lists a huge array of handloading tools, including special presses.

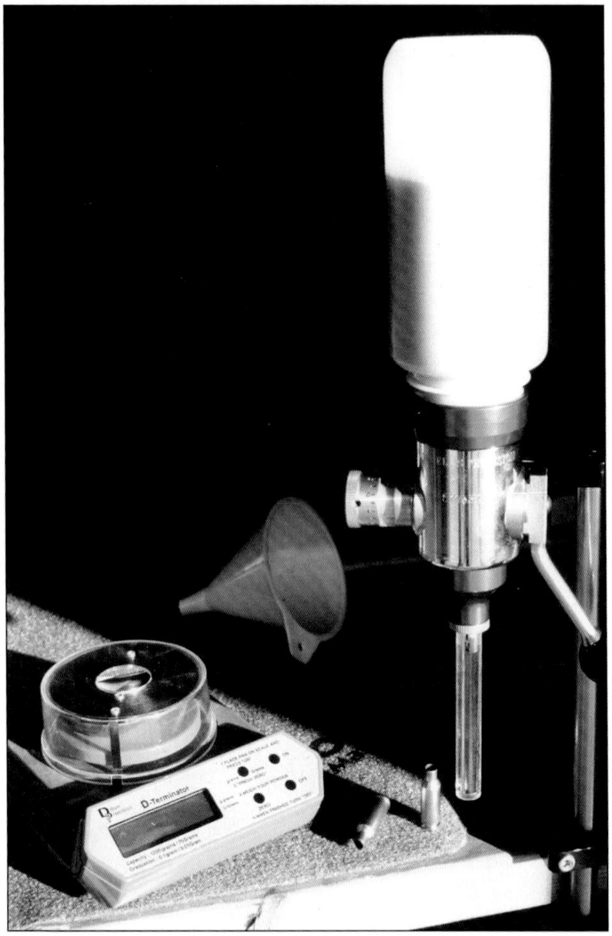

▲ Use a powder measure with a balance beam or electronic scale to run periodic checks on the charges.

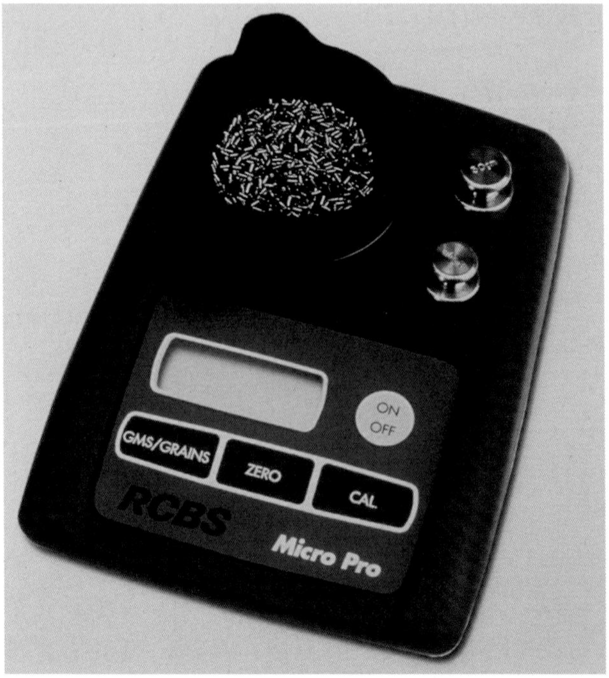

▲ Electronic scales can be faster to use and easier to read than balance beam scales—if not more accurate.

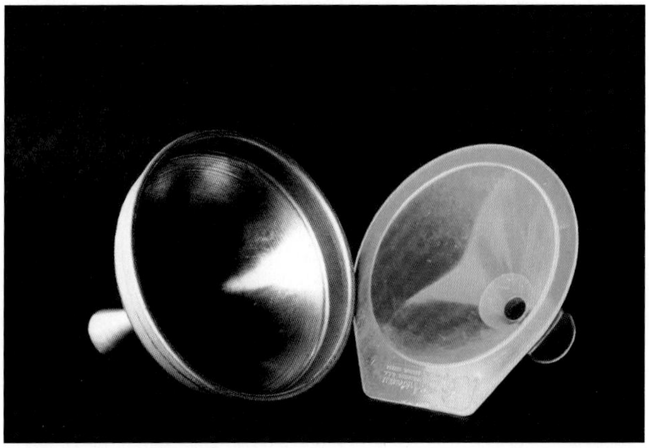

▲ Alloy and plastic both funnel powder—and both prefer spherical! Keep funnels free of case lube.

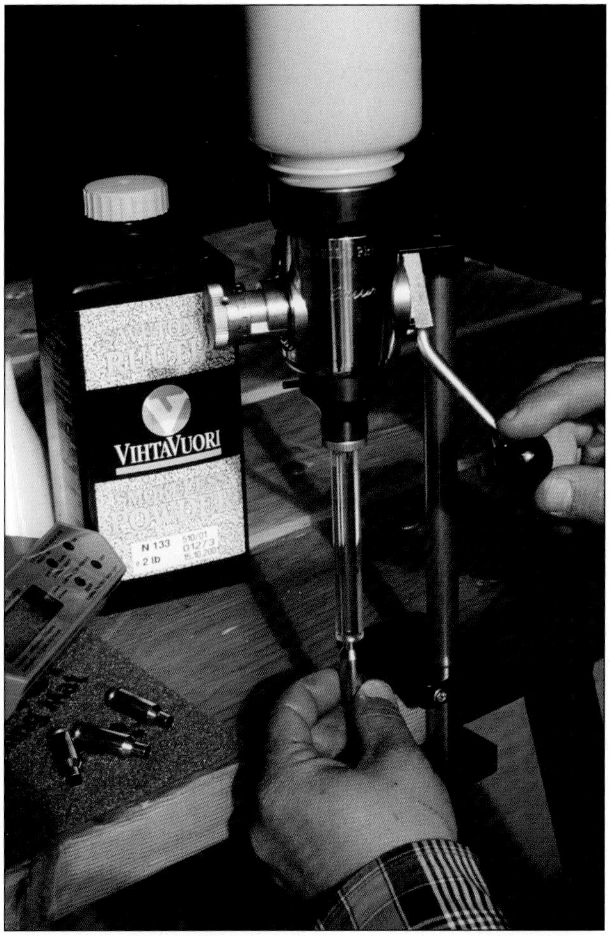

▲ A well-made measure delivers powder in identical doses. A drop tube helps sift full-case charges.

must. You'll need an accurate caliper (and micrometer). Both digital models and the old-fashioned type with a swinging needle provide requisite precision.

Before you accumulate items that become clutter, load a few cartridges with basic tools. You'll soon learn what you need and what's someone else's notion of a gadget worth pitching.

Standouts among companies focused from the start on handloading include Redding Reloading, of Cortland, New York. Eons ago, when I was new to wildcatting, company president Richard Beebe shared his data for the .270 Redding, an outstanding deer cartridge on the .308 case. This was before the debut of the 7mm-08. The Redding shop has since grown aggressively, and come up with some of the finest tools and measuring instrument to grace a workbench. I've reported on some. The Redding catalog is a must-have for handloaders. It offers tooling for beginners as well as for veterans.

Redding Competition Seating Dies bring a spring-loaded seating stem into contact with a bullet's ogive early in the up-stroke of the press ram. The stem's inside taper and close fit to the die body ensure precise alignment. A bell-shaped die mouth eases case and bullet entry in progressive presses. Redding sells separate dies for crimping. To size a cartridge for close fit in a minimum or match chamber, (or in a wildcat chamber) try Competition Neck Sizing Dies with bushings. The bushings, machined to .001 size increments from .185 to .365, self-center on the case, held in perfect alignment with the die in a spring-loaded sliding sleeve. Of course, Redding lists standard die sets—some with carbide sizing bodies—for a wide range of popular cartridges. The firm also catalogs case-forming dies and bullet-making hardware, including SAECO bullet molds and SAECO's Lubri-Sizer and Lead Hardness Tester. I like the Redding Match-Grade 3R powder measure, with micrometer lock screw to hold the setting precisely. For loaded ammo there's the Instant Indicator comparator, which checks headspace and seating depth to .001.

Another company with top-quality tooling is Forster, of Lanark, Illinois. Originally known as the Bonanza, Forster's Co-Ax press has dual guide rods instead of a single ram. Co-axial movement of the ram with the die, courtesy those beefy rods, is this unique tool's

◀ Like RCBS and Redding, Forster lists a wide variety of dies and accessories for serious handloaders.

◀ Most die sets for bottleneck rifle rounds include sizing (left) and seating dies. These are from RCBS.

◀ Straight cases like the .45-70 merit three-die sets. RCBS offers this one for Cowboy Action shooters.

selling point. Its long handle, on a yoke, gives you three times the leverage of an ordinary C-type press, claims Forster. The snap-in die receptacle makes the Co-Ax a delight to use. Cartridge access is second to none. A primer seater with just .001 radial clearance protrudes .005 below the level of the case head, ensuring uniform primer depth. The Co-Ax is neither a new press nor a cheap one. It's a very *good* press, with a permanent place on my bench.

▲ Forster's "Bonanza" co-axial press is strong, but compact and convenient, big enough for long hulls.

▲ A yoked handle, big case opening and quick-change die holder make Forster's press one of the best!

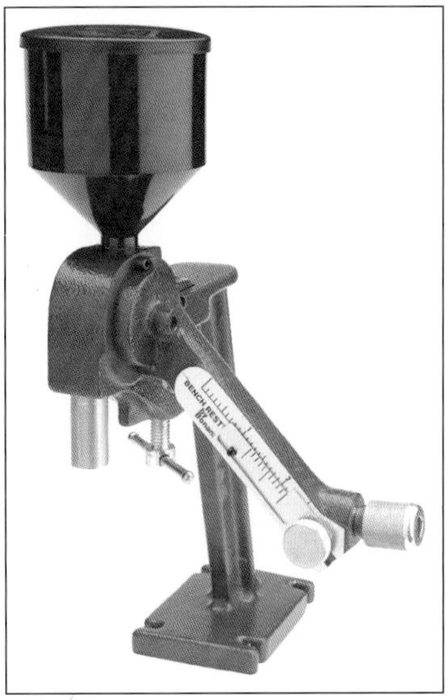

◀ Forster's Benchrest powder measure speeds handloading, but ensures a precise charge in every hull.

▲ Graphite-coated neck brushes, like these from Forster, prep cases after sizing for easy bullet seating.

Forster also manufactures standard and competition dies, bullet pullers, headspace gauges, a 3-in-1 Case Mouth Cutter that "cuts length square." Forster's Case Trimmer System trims, turns the outside of necks and reams them, *and* refines primer pockets. The firm's stuck case remover is one device you can't fully appreciate until you need it. A neck-turning tool with carbide cutter comes with pilots for just about any case you can imagine.

▲ An alternative to the inertia bullet puller, this one is designed for use in a press. Forster has it.

If you're keen on making your own lead bullets for handguns and reduced rifle loads, you'll want the Lyman Products catalog. Now the brand includes shooting accessories, like handgun grips and shotgun magazine extensions, cleaning products, target throwers, and even flashlights. But Lyman hasn't abandoned its bread-and-butter handloading items: presses and dies, case trimmers and tumblers, and the like. The Middletown, Connecticut, firm is *the* primary source for bullet molds and casting hardware. Lyman's Cast Bullet Handbook remains "the only complete source for cast bullet data." Established in 1878, Lyman has one of the longest histories of any firm still serving shooters.

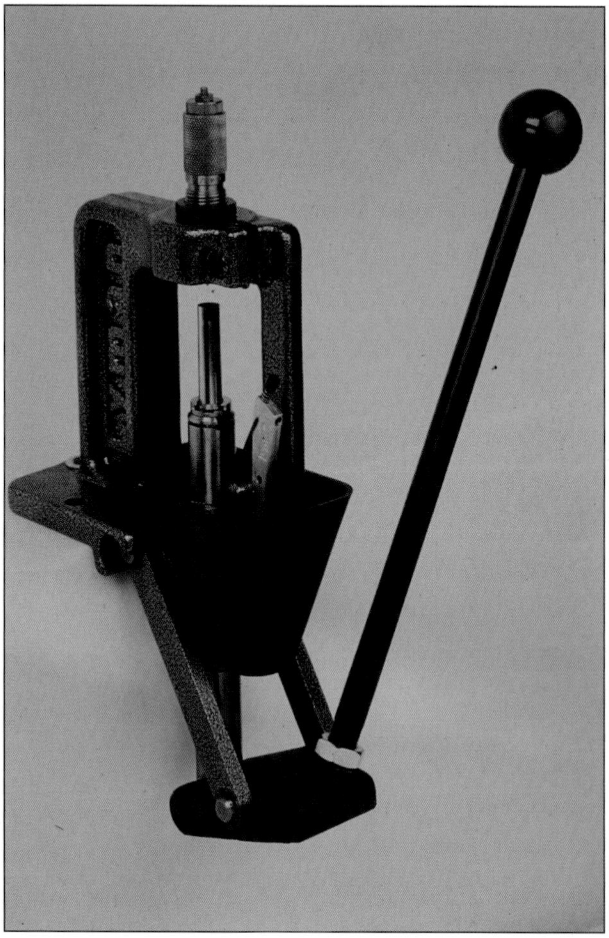

▲ This Lyman press is of sturdy, accessible "O" design. Dual toggles add stability. Note primer apron.

The tonnage of handloading hardware competing for a place on your bench includes basic tools and specialty items from names like Wilson (dies), Harrell/Culver (powder measures), MTM (molded cartridge blocks and boxes), Starrett (calipers) and Dillon (progressive presses). Sinclair and Brownells, both now of Montezuma, Iowa, list their own products and other brands for advanced handloaders. If you don't have current Sinclair and Brownells books, you don't know what your bench is missing! More importantly, you can't compare features and capabilities among the tooling and accessories you'll want.

▲ A neck-turning tool ensures cases are concentric, neck tension uniform. Better accuracy results.

◀ A powder trickler helps you add those final grains quickly without adding too much. A time-saver!

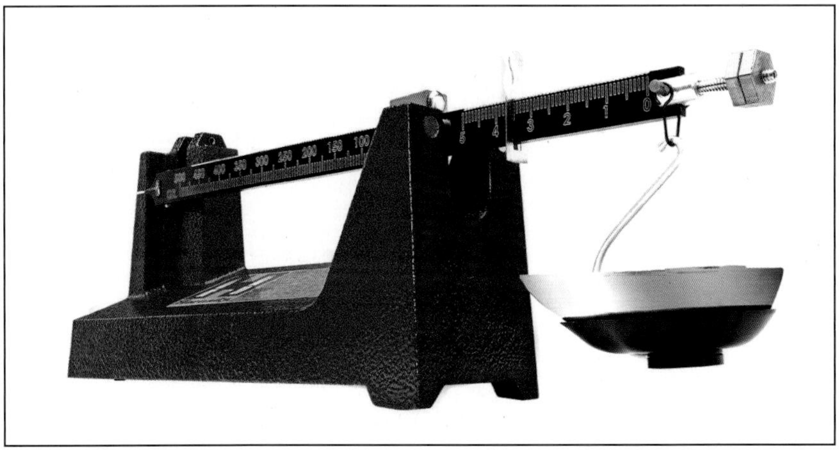

◀ Beam scales should be dismantled and kept covered when not in use to protect bearing surfaces.

You surely won't need all the tools employed in the commercial production of ammunition—or more than a corner of the garage—to turn out superior handloads. One of the savviest handloaders I know still cranks super-accurate rifle and pistol loads (and even casts his own bullets) in an 8x10 cubicle. With his two gun safes and an ammo cabinet, it's hardly wheelchair accessible. A box of cartridges has a hard time finding a landing zone on the bench. But everything's in easy reach!

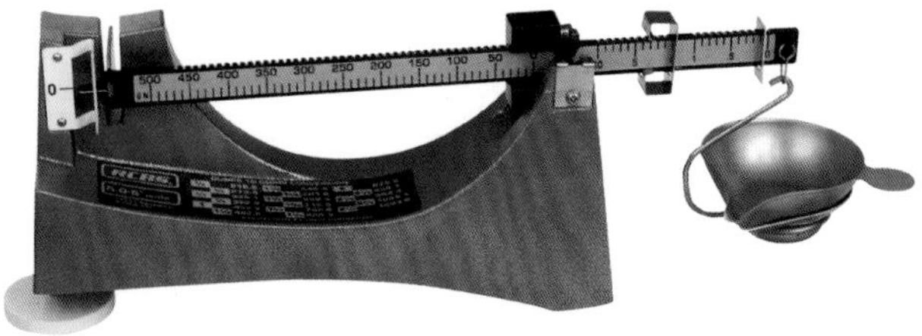

▲ Among the most popular powder scales, the RCBS 505 is all you need to make superior handloads.

Your bench is a most important item. I've fashioned several over the years, all with a few things in common. First, they're sturdy. A press handle exerts a great deal of leverage, and you must expect a few recalcitrant cases—sizing that takes muscle on the down-stroke. A thick case neck you forgot to lube can resist the expander ball mightily, requiring a weight-lifter's tug to free the hull. Ordinary tabletops won't hold up. Neither will single sheets of plywood or planking. On one bench, I used 2x6s with a sheet of three-quarter-inch plywood on top. Where I mounted tools, I installed an additional layer of 2x6s underneath. A press has big mounting holes for a reason:

▲ Powder measures come in many sizes. Adjustments and level of precision usually determine price.

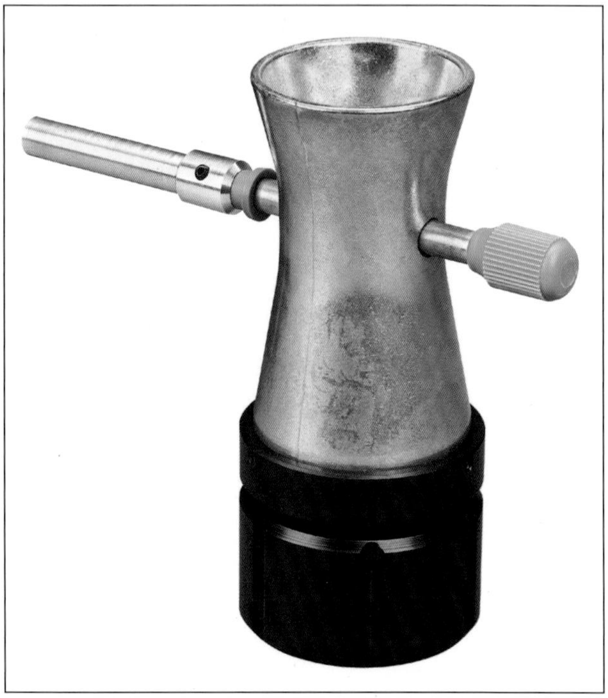

▲ The RCBS powder trickler is an inexpensive solution to getting those last grains on the scale neatly.

They accommodate heavy machine bolts. You're not to use wood screws or small lag screws. Snug the nuts on hefty flat washers from below. Better that you don't cinch the nuts down from the top, lest you stress the cast press base. For the same reason, you'll want to ensure first that the base is flat on the bench and evenly supported by it or washers; and you'll snug the nuts as you would an automobile wheel—incrementally, on opposing bolts.

I much prefer a concrete base for a bench. It needn't be as thick as that in a missile silo or under a hammer-forging machine. But it's a more solid foundation than wood flooring over stringers. If you've no shop or basement on concrete, you can reinforce flooring under a bench with heavy plywood.

Whatever it rests on, the bench must have sturdy legs. I use 4x4s or paired 2x4s. Angled bracing with screws keeps those supports rigid under load. On a bench I fashioned from a heavy butcher's table, horizontal ties at ankle level support a bench-length shelf for powder and other lightweight components. A kitchen-counter unit I salvaged from an old house made a fine bench, after I added a thick plywood top and 2x6s for tool mounting. The unit's 1950s-era construction included heavy, clear lumber that doesn't budge under a press stroke.

A smooth, splinter-free top without cracks allows you to easily sweep up spilled powder and keep your bench spotless. Handloading, you'll use precision-ground tools and measuring devices that go three decimal places past visible. You don't want to work on unfinished barn boards that gather dust and grit. I sand tops smooth and usually apply three generous coats of spar varnish. Substitute epoxy finishes if you prefer. Unlike a gunstock, you're not looking for a classic oil finish. Varnish and epoxy seal pores faster and are more durable.

▲ You'll want a full tray of shell-holders to accommodate every case you might load. They're cheap.

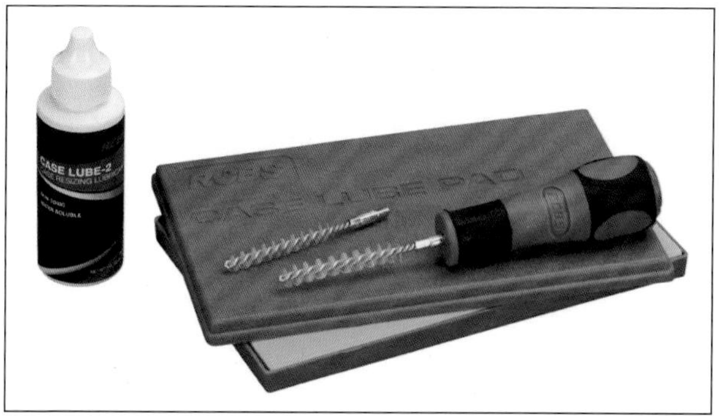

▲ The RCBS case lube kit includes a pad, brushes and lube to help cases move easily through the die.

▲ For handloading away from the shop, clamps will secure presses. No full-length sizing of .50 BMGs!

BABY THOSE TOOLS!

Tool steel is not rustproof. When steel is stripped dry for measurements, or when oil is removed by sizing or cutting, apply a thin coat of oil or grease before storing tools. A rag protects them from your sweaty hands. Except those permanently mounted on your bench, store tools and measuring devices in a cool, dry, dust-free place—in their original boxes when convenient. Before running brass through new dies, swab the dies with mild solvent (I use Hoppes No. 9), followed by a dry patch to remove packing grease and other foreign material. Make sure you clean every fired case thoroughly prior to lubing. Sand and other grit picked up from hulls ejected onto the bench or the ground can ruin tooling!

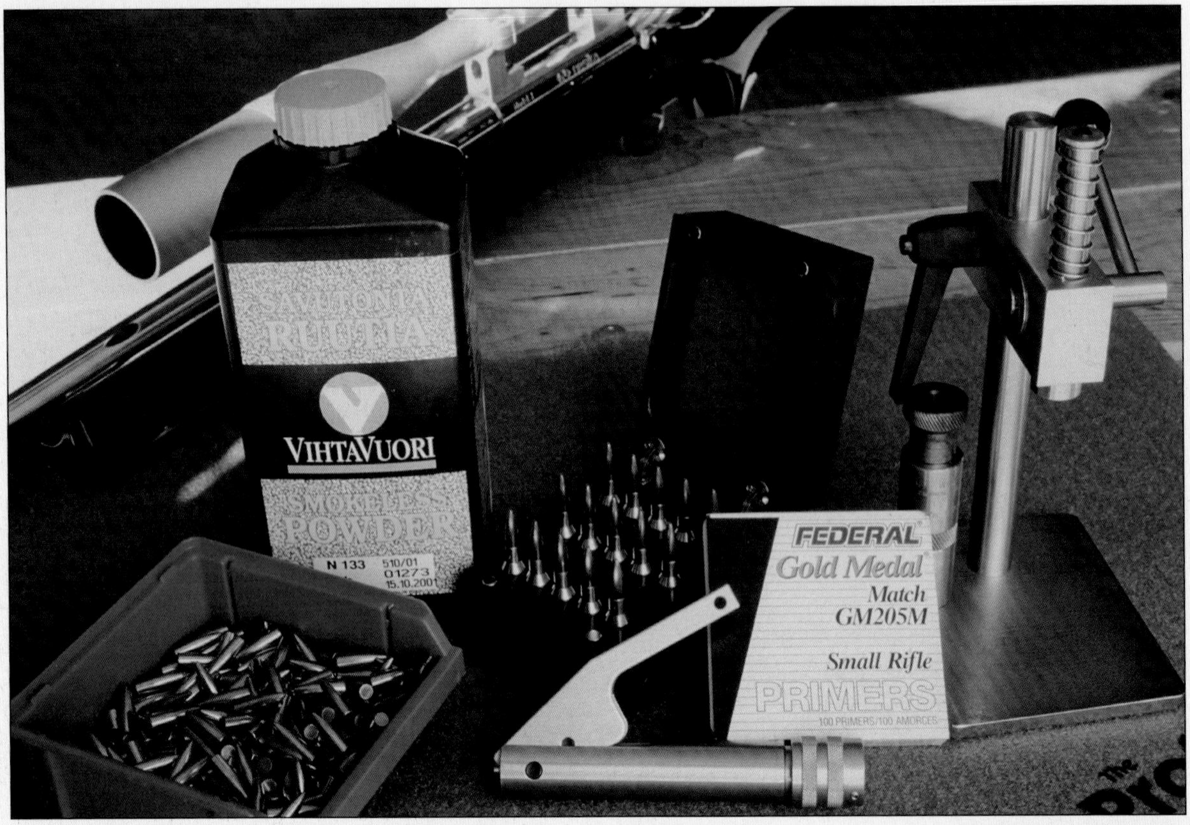

▲ With priming tool in front, arbor press right, this benchrest shooter is equipped for precision handloading.

Chapter 4: Headspace Is Not IQ

When you pull the trigger, several events follow fast. The striker's blow detonates the primer's shock-sensitive compound. Flame jets through the flash-hole in the primer pocket, igniting gunpowder in the case to produce high-pressure gas. As the brass case is ductile, it yields to that pressure, ironing itself to the chamber wall. Still expanding, the gas thrusts the bullet forward into the bore. At the same time, it pushes the case head back against the bolt face.

Peak gas pressure can exceed 30 tons per square inch. But the case doesn't respond uniformly to it. The case is thick at the web, a solid partition of brass around the flash-hole. At the mouth, that brass is much thinner. As the front of the hull presses tight to the chamber, the thick base remains near its original diameter. Now, if the case is supported by the bolt face, everything is OK. But it's hard to ensure that an unfired cartridge will fit tightly against the face, because it would be very difficult to chamber. A cartridge longer by a gnat's lash would not chamber without great effort. So chambers are cut to allow for variation in ammunition. But if there's too big a reach between the bolt face and the point in the chamber that stops the cartridge up front, you have a condition of excess headspace. That's trouble.

Headspace is not the size of a rifle's chamber. It is the distance from the face of the locked bolt to a datum line in the chamber that prevents the cartridge from moving forward.

The striker's blow pushes the cartridge forward until it contacts the datum point in the chamber. Case expansion sticks it there. Again, the case head isn't stuck because it is thick and doesn't expand as much, so it moves rearward to meet the bolt face. The case stretches as gas pressure, leveraged against the bullet and the case shoulder, moves the head to the rear. The case just forward of the web can stretch a bit without damage. But excess headspace can permit it to stretch too far. Repeated firings "work-harden" the case, reducing its elasticity. After several stretchings in a generous chamber, and subsequent sizings, this case can crack, or even separate, spilling gas. Faster than the bullet itself, the gas jets through orifices and along corridors in your rifle action. It can make its own paths, too, tearing the rifle asunder.

In the days of low-pressure black-powder cartridges, headspace was arguably less critical than it is now, when even mild hunting rounds generate 30,000 pounds per square inch. Ambitious loads register 65,000! This thrust doesn't last long; it doesn't

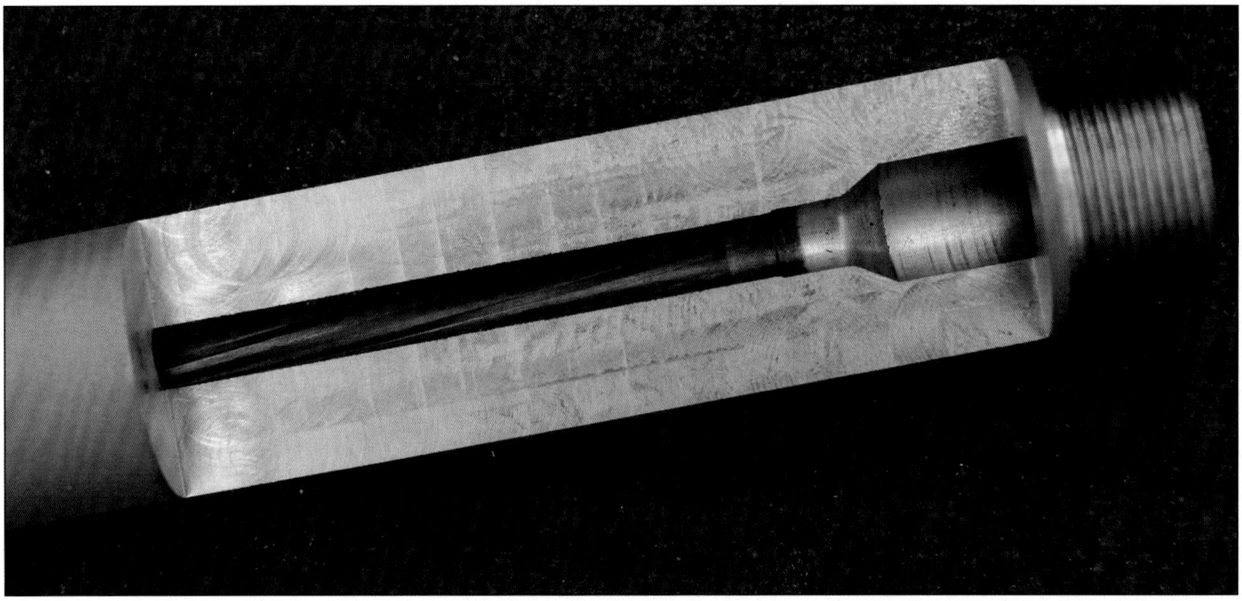

▲ Chamber dimensions affect headspace and case expansion. The throat affects breech pressures.

have to, to propel a bullet or wreck a rifle. On a graph, the pressure rises steeply after a short horizontal line reflecting delay between primer detonation and powder ignition. Pressure typically peaks within a millisecond (1/1,000 second). Its decline is relatively gradual as the bullet advances, increasing the volume behind it. The faster the powder, the steeper the curve, both sides of the peak. Two to three milliseconds after the striker hits the primer, pressure has dropped to zero.

The term "headspace" originated when all metallic cartridges had rims—the .30-30, for instance—so the first measurements were made from the bolt face to the leading edge of the rim. Now the forward or datum line varies with cartridge design. A straight, rimless case like the .45 ACP headspaces at the case mouth, because that's what stops the round in the chamber. On a belted magnum, the stop is the front of the belt. The datum line for rimless bottleneck rounds like the .30-06 and .270 lies on the shoulder. Ditto for rebated cases like the .284 Winchester. Semi-rimmed cartridges could headspace on the rim, but the measure for the .220 Swift is from the shoulder. The same goes for the .38 Super Automatic pistol round. Hornady designed the semi-rimmed .308 and .338 Marlin Express to headspace on the shoulder.

Gunsmiths measure headspace with steel "go" and "no go" gauges inserted in the chamber. The "go" gauge is typically .004 to .006 shorter than the "no go" gauge for rimless and belted cartridges. The bolt should close on a "go" gauge but not on a "no go" gauge. Theoretically, if the bolt closes on a "no go" gauge, the barrel should be set back a thread and rechambered to achieve proper headspace. However, many chambers that accept "no go" gauges are still safe to shoot. A "field" gauge has been used to check chambers (mostly military). Seldom seen now, it's roughly .002 longer than a "no go" gauge.

Minimum and maximum headspace measurements are not the same as corresponding minimum and maximum *case* dimensions. A .30-06 chamber should measure between 1.940 and 1.946, bolt face to shoulder datum line. A .30-06 case registers between 1.934 and 1.940, base to datum line. Case gauges machined to close tolerances perform the same check on cartridges that headspace gauges do in chambers. An obvious difference: case gauges are female and cannot accurately gauge headspace. A change in case

◀ The .45 ACP case headspaces on the mouth, so case length matters a great deal in 1911 pistols.

▲ The Short Magazine Lee Enfield's bolt has a separate head, which can be changed to tune headspace.

▲ Fine finish, precise dimensions of Redding dies ensure proper sizing, correct base-shoulder measure.

dimensions alters the relationship of the cartridge to the chamber. Reducing head-to-datum line measure of a case can result in a condition of excess headspace, even if the firearm checks out perfectly!

Once, preparing cases for the wildcat .240 Hawk, I set the die to full-length resize, so cartridges would easily fit the chamber. The die had been made to reduce the neck diameter of the parent (.30-06) case without changing the datum line. Alas, my first shot blew gas from every port of the Remington 700 action. The case showed a circumferential crack ahead of the belt. I compared sized cases with the fired hull. Sized .240s were shorter by .1 inch! So I backed off the sizing die, then advanced it incrementally as I tried sized cases in the rifle. When I was at last able to close the bolt on a case, the die was .1 inch above the shell-holder, the measure of the difference between fired and unfired hulls. The die was far too short for this rifle's chamber. When the striker fell, it moved the short-sized case forward in the chamber. The shoulder expanded into the chamber, while the rear of the case backed up .1 inch against the bolt, pulling the brass apart just ahead of the web.

As I've pointed out, neck sizing makes great sense if you're handloading for one rifle and it has a properly round chamber. There's no sense over-working the brass with full-length re-sizing. Belted cases, especially, benefit from limited sizing, because chambers for belted rounds are often cut generously in the shoulder area. The headspace dimension, after all, is the distance from bolt face to belt face (.220 to .224, "go" to "no go"). Full-length-sizing these magnums, you may reduce head-to-neck measure considerably each time, so the hull stretches a lot at each firing. Soon you'll see a white ring around the case just ahead of the belt. If you insert a straightened paper clip with a small "L" bend at the end and feel the inside of the case there, you may detect a slight indentation—a thinning of the case wall. Discard that case before it separates!

Chambers for Improved rifle cartridges (hulls "blown out" to reduce taper and increase shoulder angle, to boost capacity) should have the same headspace measure as the standard cartridge. That's why you can fire factory ammunition in an Improved chamber safely and wind up with Improved cases.

◀ Both these 7mms, the long .280 and short-action 7mm-08 are rimless and headspace on the shoulder.

The front-end elasticity of a new case lets it stretch to hug the Improved chamber wall. But, of course, you can't fit Improved cases in a standard chamber. Recently, a hunter who I knew to be packing a .280 Remington for a safari told me about picking up some costly .280 Improved ammo. "That won't chamber!" I blurted. Nothing ruins your day like a bolt that won't close when you're halfway around the world.

Headspace can change over time, as some compression of locking lugs and seats occurs with each firing. Many firings with heavy loads can drain the elasticity of the steel in lock-up and cause a permanent increase in headspace. Enterprising shooters with old rear-locking lever rifles have kept them in service by peening case rims carefully from the side to boost rim thickness. But the real fix for excess headspace is to trim and rechamber the barrel.

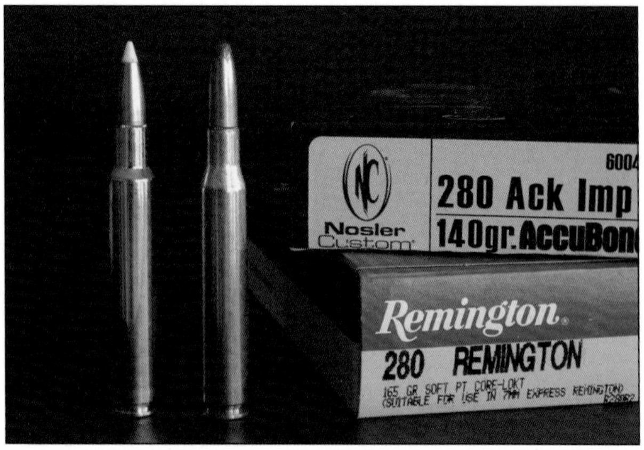

▲ The .280 (right) can be safely fired in .280 Improved chambers to form the sharper Ackley shoulder.

Chapter 5: Pressure

Copper units of pressure (CUP), the common measure, doesn't tell everything you should know about the gas driving your bullet, because the figure says nothing about the pressure *curve*. Dave Emary, Hornady's senior ballistician, has an extensive military background in ammunition. He has also designed and helped bring to production several sporting cartridges for Hornady, including the .17 HMR, .308 and .338 Marlin Express, and the Ruger Compact Magnums and 6.5 Creedmoor. "Pounds per square inch (PSI) fails, too," he emphasized. "Like CUP, any such measure is just a figure in time. But the *progression* of pressure matters. You can increase velocity by extending the peak of the pressure curve forward without jacking that curve higher." I knew he'd follow with a review. I'll paraphrase:

▲ Loaded to modest pressures at its 1892 introduction, the 7x57 could be throttled up in Ruger's No. 1.

When spark from the primer jets through the flash-hole and ignites the powder charge, gas forms to replace the consumed propellant. The gas quickly expands to occupy a much larger space, increasing pressure inside the case and, as heat rises, accelerating fuel consumption. Following the pressure peak—typically within a millisecond after the powder starts to burn, the pressure comes back down. This decline is relatively gradual as the bullet moves forward, increasing the volume of the bore behind it. The faster the powder, the steeper the curve, both sides of the peak. Area under the pressure/time curve translates to bullet velocity. Two to three milliseconds after the striker hits the primer, including the brief delay before powder combustion, the bullet is gone.

The .300 Weatherby Magnum thrusts a 180-grain bullet out the muzzle of a 26-inch barrel about 1.25 milliseconds after gas pressure overcomes neck tension to accelerate that bullet on its way. This data, showing pressures and velocities from case mouth to muzzle, were adapted from a pressure-time curve in the text *Any Shot You Want*, Art Alphin's A-Square loading manual.

Time (seconds)	Pressure (psi)	Velocity (fps)	Distance (inches)
0	0	0	0
0.0001	12,000	60	0.02
0.0003	36,000	500	0.60
0.0005	60,000	1,400	2.80
0.0007	42,000	2,350	7.40
0.0009	24,000	2,970	13.80
0.0011	6,000	3,250	21.30
0.0013	100	3,300	26.00

Notably, pressure peaks when the bullet has moved only about 3 inches, even with the slow fuels appropriate for the big hull and modest bore of this popular magnum. Pressure drops off fast, too, losing 90 percent of its zip in the next 18 inches of barrel. But the bullet continues to accelerate, even as pressure behind it diminishes. Between 7 and 21 inches, pressure loss totals 36,000 psi. But bullet speed increases 300 fps! With very little pressure remaining behind it at the muzzle, the bullet is still accelerating! The

▲ Pressure curves matter in short-barrel self-loaders. Duplicate factory loads to ensure proper function.

value of a long barrel is clear, even if nearly all of it is used to control the tail of the pressure/time curve.

Hornady's Dave Emary observed that, "we get higher speed from our Light and Heavy Magnum ammo (now Superformance) by pushing the pressure curve forward so the peak occurs when the bullet is 3 inches out. The powder in those cartridges has 4 percent more nitroglycerin than ordinary double-base propellants. Surface deterrents slow the intitial burn so the bullet doesn't outrun the burn so soon."

Pressure/distance curves and pressure/time curves differ in slope, but both are steeper at the start than at the finish. The area under a pressure/distance curve represents the energy imparted to the bullet. Of course, not all of that is available downrange. Much is lost to heat, case expansion, friction between bullet and barrel, even bullet rotation. Pressure/distance curves matter to designers of gas-operated rifles that must tap the gas at some point in the bullet's bore travel. Too little pressure, and the bolt won't move far enough or briskly enough to clear the fired case. Too much, and the violence can damage action parts.

Measuring gas pressure is no easy task. In fact, pressure figures stayed out of reach until the mid-1800s, when Alfred Nobel and an American named Rodman separately solved that nettlesome problem. Rodman's "crusher" solution is a factory procedure not easily performed in a home shop. A small piston is slid into a hole in the barrel of a test gun, and a copper or lead pellet is inserted snugly between the

▲ Rifle barrels at Black Hills Ammunition are used to measure pressures as well as check accuracy.

top of the piston and a stationary anvil. When the rifle is fired, the piston presses against the pellet or crusher, shortening it. The difference in lengths of the crusher before and after firing is converted mathematically to CUP or LUP (lead units of pressure). Copper crushers are either .146 in diameter and .400 long to start, or .225 in diameter and .500 long. The choice depends on application. Copper crushers work best for rifle and handgun loads that generate substantial pressures. Lead crushers (.325 x .500) typically register the low-pressure loads in rimfire rifles, early revolvers and shotguns (though small-diameter copper crushers can be used). After crushers are calibrated in a press, measurements from firearms yield "Tarage Tables" that enable technicians to calculate the pressure.

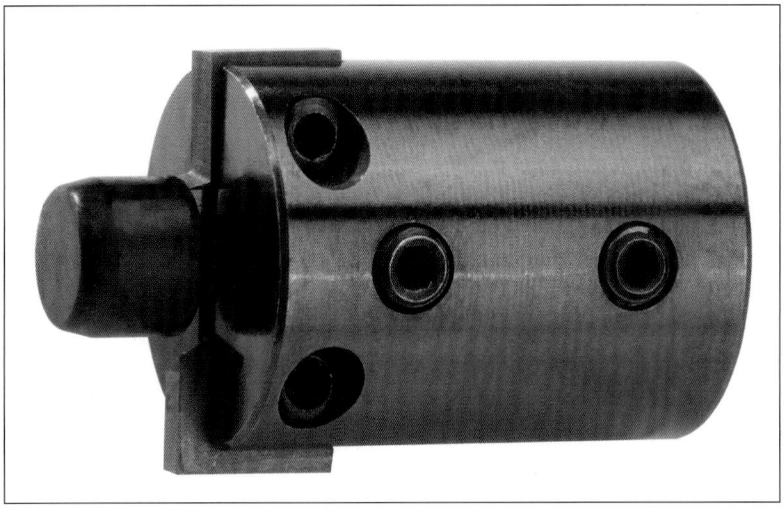

◀ Trimming cases keeps stretched necks from contacting the chamber mouth and crimping the bullet.

Crushers don't register *peak* pressure accurately because the flow of the copper is slower than the change of pressure in the chamber. When the moving piston comes to a halt, the reading is skewed in the opposite direction. There's no balancing out—just conflicting forces.

Copper units of pressure and lead units of pressure are not the same; nor can they be interchanged with measures in pounds per square inch. CUP value *may* coincide with psi value; for example, SAAMI lists 28,000 as maximum average pressure for the .45-70—in both CUP and psi units. The .243, however, has maximum average pressures of 52,000 CUP and 60,000 psi. There's no easy way to convert CUP to psi or vice versa.

Acceptable breech pressures for smokeless centerfire cartridges are determined by the Sporting Arms and Ammunition Manufacturers' Institute. They range from around 42,000 psi for the .30-30 to over 62,000 psi for frisky magnums. Some rifles safely digest proof or "blue pill" loads generating more than 100,000 psi. But some rifle actions, some steels and even some serial number ranges within models put a cap on safe pressures that's low by modern standards. Famously, US Springfield 1903 receivers to serial number 800,000 (1917 vintage) were of case-hardened, low-carbon steel, not as stout as the double-heat-treated receivers that followed. These acceded, in 1927, to even stronger nickel-steel receivers, at SN# 1,275,767.

▲ Early cartridge rifles, like this 1873 Springfield, fired low-pressure black-powder loads one at a time.

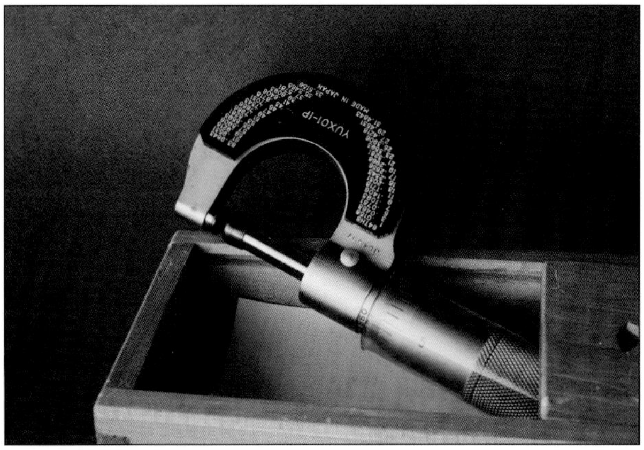

▲ Case head expansion—a measure of pressure—can be done with a micrometer. Note protective caps.

Without gauges, you can't target the cartridge-specific pressure values SAAMI designates as safe maximums. Still, a fired case can tell you something about pressures. It won't show how *much* pressure a load generates, or whether or not you were out of your gourd when you chose the powder; but it can tell you when pressures are running above or well below reasonable levels. Head expansion is the first thing to check if you think a load might be too hot. Measured with a micrometer, head expansion of more than .001 suggests you reduce the charge. But a .001 bulge at the web can become .005 a tad farther forward. Dave Emary, at Hornady, told me it's best to measure forward, because you get more reaction from the brass there. An extruded primer may or may not signal high pressures. A big striker (firing pin) channel in the bolt can also cause primers to extrude or crater. A flattened primer is a more reliable yellow light. If the shoulder of the primer blows out tight to the case head around the pocket, your load is almost certainly at the edge of sensible. If cases extract with difficulty or you find loose primer pockets, back off!

Emary notes that pressure high enough to affect the extraction or appearance of a fired case is already well above SAAMI spec. "You start to pierce primers at about 70,000 CUP, and get blown cups at 80,000."

Some savvy shooters have indulged their tech cravings with a piezoelectric gauge. It registers gas pressure via electric charge delivered through a transducer from a crushed crystal. Pressure applied to the crystal yields a transducer reading in pounds per square inch. Conformal transducers are installed in the barrel like crusher pistons. External barrel-mounted transducers can be removed for calibration checks.

▲ Smith & Wesson's .460 generates higher pressures than do other revolver rounds. The revolver is stout—handload with great care!

▲ Primer type can affect pressures. Wayne uses standard large rifle primers for charges to 65 grains.

The strain gauge is another pressure-testing option. Developed for the handloading market by Dr. Ken Oehler, it's essentially a sprig of wire you glue to the barrel's exterior at the chamber. When you fire, the chamber expands and the wire stretches. Wire length is then compared with a previous measure to get a stretch reading that translates into pressure. These readings do not equate with readings from a crusher or piezoelectric gauge. The strain gauge is most useful after you read pressures from factory loads and maximum recommended loads. Comparing values, you determine *relative* pressures of your handloads.

Dave Emary points out that a strain gauge attached to the barrel can't be calibrated to a standard, as can his Heise Gauge—a device, like the Doppler machine in his lab that handloaders with fewer than three Maseratis can ill-afford.

THE BIG PINCH

Anything that impedes easy release or fast travel of the bullet from the case can boost pressure to levels that make rifles cringe. Some years ago, working up loads for a .338-06, I got an unusually sharp jab of recoil. The bolt handle wouldn't budge. After letting the rifle cool, I managed to open the bolt with a length of 2x4. The primer had ironed itself flush with the case head, evidence of pressure well in excess of 70,000 psi. I checked my loads. Columns of the slow powders were lightly compressed, eliminating the possibility of over-charging. I confirmed powder types. What I *hadn't* checked until then was the length of the case relative to that of the wildcat chamber. A case mouth contacting the front of the chamber as the bolt turns into battery is pressed into the bullet. Upon firing, it holds the bullet against gas pressure. A crimp applied by a loading tool opens to release the bullet, but one imposed by the chamber gives the case mouth no room to relax. A similar condition can result from a tight chamber neck—albeit a snug neck makes chambering difficult because you must push the cartridge forward some distance with no help from cam surfaces. It's easy to keep cases trimmed to within SAAMI length. Pay special attention to chambers on wildcat rifles. If you suspect incipient contact, trim cases .03 short for safety.

◀ Its rotating bolt suits the Browning 81 to handloads with pressures too high for traditional lever guns.

Chapter 6: Giddy-Up!

Automobiles and airplanes move us around much faster than camels, bicycles, or feet. But compared to a bullet, an automobile at highway speed isn't much quicker than tree sap. That sedan rolling along at 60 mph covers 88 fps. Bullets from ordinary deer loads clock 2,500 fps. A jet airplane cruising at 600 mph is 10 times faster than the car, but still only a third as speedy as most bullets. Hot small-bore rifle loads reach velocities half again higher than 2,500 fps.

SPEED: THE INVISIBLE

Understanding bullet flight isn't necessary to measure bullet speed. But absent a grasp of exterior ballistics, speed is just a number. For decades, after clever people came up with ways to get approximate velocities, the bullet's arc remained an enigma.

A measure of speed tells you nothing directly about the shape of a bullet's trajectory. But speed and the physical characteristics of a bullet help you predict its arc and gauge its effectiveness.

Measuring the speed of missiles that couldn't be seen and tracing their paths proved difficult for shooters early on. But in his 1537 book on ballistics, a brilliant Italian named Trataglia postulated that bullets indeed traveled in arcs, a radical idea when many people assumed they flew straight until spent, then fell abruptly. Trataglia determined the barrel angle that would give a bullet its greatest reach was 45 degrees. That's much steeper than the angle at which a modern bullet would start on its longest travel. But Trataglia's conclusion was valid, because at the lead-ball speeds of long ago, gravity had a greater effect than air resistance on a projectile's path. Bullets from today's smokeless rounds, clocking two and three times the speed of sound, are influenced less by gravity than by drag.

▲ David Miller shot this fine Coues buck far away with a Sierra MatchKing in his .300 Weatherby.

In a seventeenth-century trajectory study for the Venice arsenal, Galileo dropped cannon balls from the Leaning Tower of Pisa. He affirmed Trataglia's finding of 45 degrees as the launch angle for maximum range and further concluded that because the pull of gravity was constant, bullet paths were parabolic. His experiments did not take drag into account because, again, at that time it didn't matter. Compared to the acceleration of gravity, drag on a cannonball dropped from a window was of no account at all!

Many decades passed before Englishman Benjamin Robins devised a ballistic pendulum. Firing a bullet of known weight into its heavy wooden bob, also of known weight, Robins calculated velocity by measuring the pendulum's swing. Colleagues in the 1740s could hardly believe that a musket ball could be driven 1,500 fps! As incredible were Robins' findings on drag. Low swing readings farther from the bob indicated that drag on the musket balls might approach 85 times the force of gravity! Measurements of drag would eventually bear out the results of these trials—after development of the chronograph.

Sir Isaac Newton had died only fifteen years before Robins began his pendulum experiments. In his universal law of gravitation, Newton declared that the force of gravity varies with altitude. Sir Isaac's fundamental laws of mechanics, and his development of calculus (In Germany, Leibnitz labored over calculus at the same time), would help describe bullet flight. Newton showed a relationship between drag and the *square* of the projectile's speed. He also concluded that drag increases with the density of air and the bullet's cross-sectional area. Given the limitations imposed by the pendulum, he could not know that bullets approaching the speed of sound (1,120 fps) set up terrific drag.

During the late 1800s, scientists conceived the idea of a "standard" bullet, of certain dimensions and weight and with specific flight characteristics. The best-known versions were by Krupp in Germany and the Gavre Commission in France. The Krupp standard bullet was a flat-based conical, 3 calibers long, with a 2-caliber ogive. Shortly after the Krupp data were published, a Russian colonel named Mayevski developed a mathematical model that showed the drag deceleration of this bullet. It became the basis for tables by U.S. Army Colonel James Ingalls. First published in 1893 and revised in 1917, the Ingalls tables featured a standard Krupp bullet, similar in form to modern hunting bullets. Deriving ballistic coefficient, or *C*, was the next step. While matching bullets by shape and weight yields serviceable *C* values, velocity plays a hand, too. As drag increases with velocity, you can't expect the same bullet launched at different speeds to produce the same *C*.

▲ Long ogives help bullets retain velocity. Standard seating allows these to easily clear the magazine.

Technicians at Sierra Bullets tell me: "It's common to observe differences of 10 percent between calculated *C*s and those determined by firing tests." Still, you can get a usable value with this formula: $C = w/id^2$, where *w* is bullet weight (pounds), *d* is bullet diameter (inches) and *i* is a variable called "form factor." *C* includes sectional density and the bullet's weight divided by the square of its diameter. Form factor has to do with the bullet's profile. Long, pointed bullets with tapered heels (boat-tails) have high sectional densities and high *C*s. Blunt bullets of the same weight have high sectional densities, but less aerodynamic form, so lower *C*s. Traditional hunting bullets have *C*s ranging roughly from .200 to .450.

VLD (Very Low Drag) bullets with long, gradual ogives are an attempt to increase *C* and flatten trajectories. Some medium-bore (.243-.338) VLD match and hunting bullets boast *C*s exceeding .600. Changes in *C* do not cause linear changes in drag, which most directly affects bullet drop. A bullet with a *C* of .600, started at 3,000 fps, falls about 58 inches at 500 yards. A bullet with a C of .400 sags 65 inches.

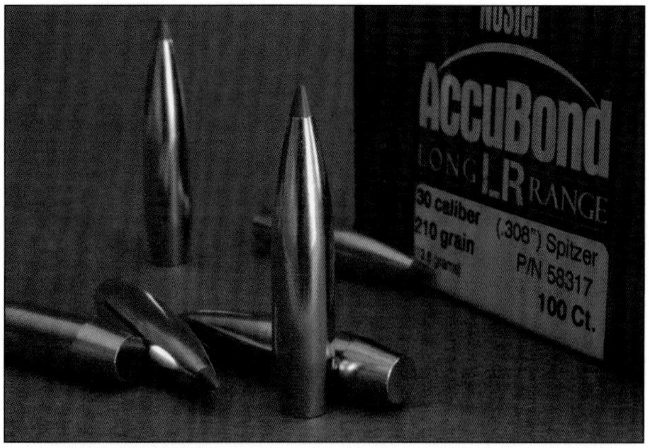

▲ High ballistic coefficient yields high speed downrange. These Noslers excel for long shots at game.

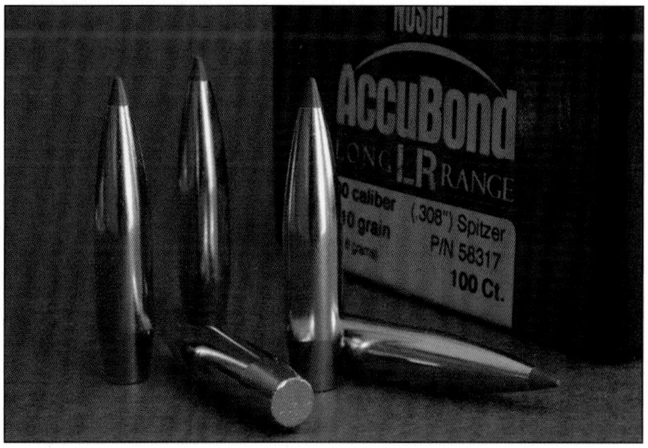

That's not much more, given the 33-percent change in *C*. But at distance, high *C* benefits you more than does a quick launch. The faster bullet has a higher deceleration rate and has shed its advantage at distance, where high *C* exerts proportionately more influence.

If you reduce the velocity of bullets with *C*s of .400 and .600 from 3,000 to 2,500 fps, both show substantially more drop over 500 yards. The ".600" bullet drops 85 inches—27 inches more than it did at a velocity of 3,000 fps. The ".400" bullet drops 96 inches—31 inches more than with the faster start.

A change in *C* has a larger effect on bullet flight downrange at high muzzle velocities than at low ones, because as bullets speed up, drag increases as a percentage of the forces impeding flight.

HEADLONG AFTER LAUNCH . . .

Every bullet decelerates as soon as it escapes the thrust of powder gas—that is, as soon as it exits the barrel. Air resistance and friction, plus turbulence set up in flight, cause deceleration. Kinetic energy measured in foot-pounds is a function of bullet weight and the square of bullet velocity, so as the bullet slows, it loses its authority. As velocity falls off, gravity is pulling the bullet to earth at the accelerating rate of 32 fps/s. The accelerating rate of drop and the decelerating rate of forward travel lead the bullet in a parabolic arc, steeper downrange than near the muzzle. The basic shape of all bullet arcs is the same, but the actual drop measure at any range, and the "flatness" of the arc over any portion of it depend on the physical properties of the bullet, its launch speed and atmospheric conditions.

Ballistic coefficients change markedly near the speed of sound.

Magazine length and practical seating depths can limit the use of VLD bullets in rifles designed around cartridges traditionally loaded with shorter bullets.

CLOCKING BULLETS

Chronographs are a century old, but it wasn't that long ago when Texan Dr. Ken Oehler designed and built the first chronographs meant for consumer use. Before Oehler's instruments, chronographs were found only in the laboratories and shooting tunnels of ammunition companies. They were fixed in place. They were very costly. Consequently, shooters could only take the catalog ballistics charts at face value, and hope their handloads were producing the pressures and bullet speeds listed in loading manuals. Now every serious shooter I know has a chronograph. Portable and easy to use, some are less expensive than an ordinary riflescope!

Portable chronographs have screens—electric eyes—set a short distance apart on a bar or directly on the electronic box whose innards compute and

▲ Fast-stepping bullets can land killing blows with light recoil. Kelsey's small bullet was well aimed.

◀ Chronographs (here an RCBS AmmoMaster) are now affordable, easy to use, a must for handloaders.

▲ Scott Harrold of Quarter Minute Magnums makes use of fast, precise handloads at great distances.

deliver velocities. The chronograph measures the time lapse (hence, "chrono") between the bullet's passage over the first screen and its passage over the second. Just as you can compute the number of miles per hour your car would travel at a given speed by clocking it for a mile, so you can learn bullet speed in feet per second by timing bullet flight over a short distance. Some chronographs allow you to adjust the gap between screens. The greater that span, the more accurate the read. The chronograph must be precisely calibrated for the screen-to-screen measure.

You get lots of information besides speed readings from a chronograph. It also delivers average velocities for strings of several shots. An average or mean value is the sum of recorded velocities divided by the number of shots fired. The instrument tells you the extreme spread (ES) as well—that is, the range of velocities, slowest to fastest. ES is useful because you want *uniform* speed from your loads. While it's unrealistic to expect all shots to stay within 5 fps of each other, I've often seen 100 fps variation between slowest and fastest readings. It's unlikely that with such swings in velocities you'll keep bullets in small groups. If a hunting load delivers good accuracy and adequate speed, and ES stays within 25 fps or so, the ammo shouldn't disappoint you. Some loads do better; some work hard to meet that standard.

Another number you get from modern chronographs is standard deviation. Credited to American statistician Karl Pearson, this term appeared in the late

▲ New powders (recently 4166) keep turning up at Hodgdon to serve fast-steppers like the .22-250.

▲ Leslie found a high-speed, light-bullet load in a 7mm Magnum just right for her first pronghorn.

1890s. Without wading into mathematics, which had me in a headlock from grammar school through my PhD studies, I can summarize standard deviation (SD) as the positive square root of the variance. What's variance? It's the sum of the squares of the deviations from the mean of the chronograph readings divided by a number that's one less than the number of shots fired. A high SD indicates plenty of spread in your data—a great deal of variability among your readings. A low SD means that most of your readings were clustered close to the mean.

There's more to milk from standard deviation. With it, you can construct a bell curve that shows how velocities group around the mean and, for any given speed range, the percentage of shots likely to fall within that range. Occasionally, you'll get a reading you don't believe. Perhaps the chronograph didn't register the bullet's passage properly. Or the load was somehow defective. One rule of thumb to keep SD useful: Throw out any reading more than 2.5 times the SD from the mean.

When setting up a chronograph, position the screens to block direct sunlight to the electric eyes. There's no bullet shadow without some background light. But in my experience harsh light can bring inconsistent readings. Translucent plastic on Oehler Sky Screens softens the light hitting the bullet and the eyes. Check the screens to be sure the distance between them exactly matches the setting on your instrument. You are measuring a very small segment of the bullet's path, over a fraction of a second. A .30-06 bullet that exits at 2,800 fps spends only one seven-hundreth of a

▲ Big country, here in southern Texas, begs speedy, flat-shooting handloads for sure long-range kills.

second between electric eyes spaced 4 feet apart. Any error you make in locating the screens or calibrating the chronograph will affect the reading.

I adjust my the screens and my shooting position on the bench so my bullets pass 4 to 5 inches over the electric eyes, and perpendicular to the screens. Bullets on angled paths, horizontally or vertically, induce error. If you switch rifles or scoot your rest on the bench to refine your position, check the angle of your barrel. Often you'll have moved enough to skew the bullet path relative to the Sky Screens. If the horizontal angle is severe, you may get no read, as the bullet's shadow misses an eye. That's a wasted shot. Testing small batches of handloads, you can ill-afford such blunders!

THE INFLUENCE OF BARREL LENGTH

Short barrels make for lighter rifles that point fast and handle with agility in thickets. The cost: an abbreviated pressure chamber. That is, the bore releases the bullet and the gas behind it before the gas has given its all. Velocity is higher with long barrels—at least, until they become so long that friction exceeds the push of the fuel. (Incidentally, bore dimensions and rifling type also affect pressures and bullet speed.)

How much bullet speed you lose with each inch you take from a barrel depends on the length you started with and on the cartridge, powder, and bullet. Ditto if you're chasing velocity gains with a longer barrel. The only sure way to determine the effects of

BRAKES ON THE BULLET

The retarding effect of air friction is like a big parachute. In a vacuum, a 150-grain .308 bullet fired at 2,700 fps at a 45-degree upward angle can fly 43 miles! The same bullet fired at the same speed and angle through earth's atmosphere hits the ground about two miles out, sapped by air resistance 56 times as strong as gravity! Drag comprises several factors. Their sum depends on bullet speed, weight and profile, as well as axial spin and atmospheric conditions. The higher the velocity, the stronger the drag. Jacket texture affects "skin friction." A sharp nose reduces "pressure drag," but so does supersonic speed. "Wave drag" results from the shock of a bullet traveling above the speed of sound. "Base drag" comes in the bullet's wake, a kind of suction.

▲ The .308, .30-06, .300 Win. Mag., .300 Ultramag—each .30 performs best with different powders.

changing barrel length is to chop a very long barrel shorter an inch at a time. But even these tests can leave you scratching your head. Trials conducted by A-Square with a .300 Winchester pressure barrel measured velocities at 1-inch increments from 28 down to 16 inches. Loads of 70.5 grains IMR 4350 with a 150-grain Nosler Ballistic Tip, and 78.0 grains RL-22 with a 180-grain Sierra Spitzer gave these results:

BARREL LENGTH	150-GRAIN VELOCITY, FPS	180-GRAIN VELOCITY, FPS	LOSS, FPS, 150/180
28 inches	3346	3134	
26 inches	3268	3089	78/45
24 inches	3211	3016	57/73
22 inches	3167	2966	44/50
20 inches	3108	2930	59/36
18 inches	3014	2874	94/56
16 inches	2903	2748	111/126

Velocity loss per inch of barrel length varies from a low of 22 fps to a high of 56 fps for the 150-grain bullet, 18 fps to 63 fps for the 180-grain bullet. Note that rate of velocity loss increases substantially as the barrel is cut shorter than 20 inches. Logic tells us we're cutting into the bell of the pressure curve.

Hornady's .300 and .338 RCM cartridges were designed to deliver high speeds in carbine-length barrels. Mitch Mittelstaedt, who headed the project, explained to me that with new proprietary powders, his team was able to "tighten" pressure curves so the .300 RCM behaves like ordinary .300 magnums in 24-inch barrels but doesn't lose as much enthusiasm in carbines. "Velocity of .300 WSM bullets falls 160 to 180 fps when barrels are chopped from 24 to 20 inches; RCMs lose 100." With chronograph guru Ken Oehler, I chronographed .300 RCM loads from the 20-inch barrel of a Ruger carbine. The Oehler 35 gave me readings of around 2,840 fps with 180-grain bullets.

▲ Early on, Winchester's .264 sales trailed the 7mm Remington's. Both are superb long-range rounds.

IT'S NOT JUST THE LOAD!

Bullet velocity varies not only with the powder type and charge, bullet weight and barrel length. It's influenced by chamber dimensions, throat shape and length and bore finish. A tight chamber reduces the amount of energy lost in case expansion. So does a tight throat. But a long throat that allows the bullet to move before engaging the rifling lands, and permits long seating of the bullet to increase powder space, enables a handloader to add fuel, boosting velocity. That long throat is generally thought to be less than desirable for accuracy; but on hunting rifles it's no liability. Roy Weatherby employed long throats and ambitious loadings to give his magnums lots of pep. John Burns, one of the principals in the early days of GreyBull Precision, insisted that long throats *cut to a minimum diameter* sacrifice no accuracy but afford more throttle than the short throats commonly associated with target rifles.

Small loads of fast powder dump all their energy quickly. You won't get much more speed from a rifle in 9mm or .45 ACP than you will from a pistol. Rimfire fuel burns like tinder; .22 Long Rifle bullets top out in just 16 inches of barrel. Hornady's Dave Emary tells me the .17 Mach 2 and .17 HMR get little or no lift after 17 inches.

▲ The .30-378 Weatherby Magnum, faster and more powerful than most hunters need, remains a top seller!

Chapter 7: Testing Handloads

Some things I can't explain: how bees fly and sockeyes find their way upstream, why Congress spends so much.

Handloading isn't so mysterious. But occasionally you get the inexplicable. I once charged .30-06 cases with mid-range loads of a proven powder—and got half a dozen hang-fires. I still don't know why.

Recently I assembled some loads for the .338 Norma, a short .338 Lapua. All 285-grain Barnes TSXs keyholed, tumbling into the target end over end. No indictment of these sleek bullets, these results seemed only to show my rifling pitch was too gradual for them—the twist too slow for such long missiles. The puzzle: 300-grain Sierra MatchKings flew straight and cut tight groups. While the lead-core Sierra is shorter for its weight, it and the lighter TSX are very nearly the same length! TSX bullets have produced excellent accuracy in other rifles.

▲ In far-away places, you'll want handloads that function flawlessly. Check each one before you leave!

Such conundrums keep me humble. Expectations dashed over many decades of handloading have confirmed the value of repeated testing. Once you've finished seating bullets in a batch of gleaming new cartridges, your handloading journey is only half completed. Its next leg is at the range.

NO-WIGGLE TESTING

Five minutes from my house there's a bench. I helped design it, but more talented people built it. The top is a trough of heavy iron, broad as a pool table. It holds 4 inches of concrete and rests on legs of well casings thick as cannon barrels, also filled with concrete. They're sunk so deep, heat from the earth's core may have cured the footings.

This bench doesn't creak when you lay a heavy rifle across sandbags. It doesn't quiver when you squirm to re-position a rest. You could hog-tie a steer on this bench and it wouldn't budge.

The only thing I don't like about this bench is that it's about as portable as the Pentagon.

Royal Stukey knows about steers. He cowboyed in another life, and "was happiest in the hills, on horseback." There, and as a hunting guide, he indulged his long affinity for rifles and shooting. Now 53, Royal is a decade into an enterprise that began with a blank check. "A client wanted a portable shooting bench that was really steady. I couldn't find one. So he told me to build one."

Mechanically inclined, Stukey complied. His first benches had flaws, but because cost wasn't an overriding concern, those benches quickly got better. "Our real breakthrough was the floating nut plate," said the entrepreneur. "Most of the wobble in portables come from the junction of legs and top. One day I got the idea of a self-centering plate." It's a clever arrangement. The legs grip the top with 5/8 bolts at

▲ In lightweight "woods rifles," accuracy like this is very good—and hard to beat with handloads.!

bench. The frame is of 1.5-by-2-inch heavy angle iron. Fourteen screws secure the 32-by-40-inch top, of three-quarter-inch birch plywood. It's triple-coated with marine varnish both sides—six coats on edges.

Royal Stukey's bench can be quickly assembled and taken apart without tools. The 30-pound top and 35-pound leg package are designed for easy carry, one in each hand. A Contico box, incorporating a seat, comes separately. It can hold a man's weight in shooting accessories. Set up, the bench itself has a 36x44-inch footprint and works well on uneven ground.

"We contract powder coating of the metal, and I have another fellow building tops to our specs," said Royal. "I do the welding and other metal-work here in our shop. Assembly, too." The shop, in Powell, Wyoming has grown since Brownells and Sinclair International have put Stukey's bench in their catalogs. "That's been a real blessing for Jeanie and me." Jeanie is Royal's wife, an active partner in the business.

"She handles orders, records and anything having to do with computers. Thanks to her and my customers,

▲ The best commercial ammo, like handloads, gets hand-inspected—here at Black Hills Ammunition.

we've put solid portable shooting benches all over the country. And in countries I've not yet visited!"

Stukey won't likely go on tour soon. Bench orders keep him busy. "We get a lot of business from riflemen who've tried other portable benches. They own custom and semi-custom rifles. They handload. They expect tight groups. They know if you can't be still, the most expensive rifle and scope is just a pile of wasted money. I can't afford to ship a bench that wiggles."

At this writing, Royal Stukey markets his cleverly designed benches at *shootingbenches.com.*

Another worthy support for handloaders wanting to scotch the wobble in ammo trials comes from South Dakota. With his own sophisticated shop, Wally Brownlee could live anywhere. Watertown makes sense because, Wally pointed out, "prairie dogs live a short drive away. *Lots* of prairie dogs."

In the nearly two decades since I've known him, Mr. Brownlee has turned out several types of beautifully machined rests. The Model 1000 is one of my all-time favorites: portable, adjustable, sturdy. His pedestal-style Model 2500 shooting bench is more expensive.

"But it's a bargain if you want convenience as well as accuracy," he insisted when walking me through the prototype. A bench unlike any other, the 2500 will spoil you. It's not a four-legged table. The piano-style seat with barstool and auxiliary footrest swings on a spindle stout as the propeller shaft on a battleship. A 38x42-inch table of laminated wood on a frame of angled alloy encompasses a 12x12-inch plate astride a 9-inch bearing at the table's center. This bench rotates 360 degrees! An adjustable brake lets you tune friction to your liking, so you can swing quickly or with more deliberate effort. Of course, you can lock it in place. There's no movement when you settle into the rifle. "You can adjust table height from 36 to 52 inches," said Wally. "There's a tilt adjustment

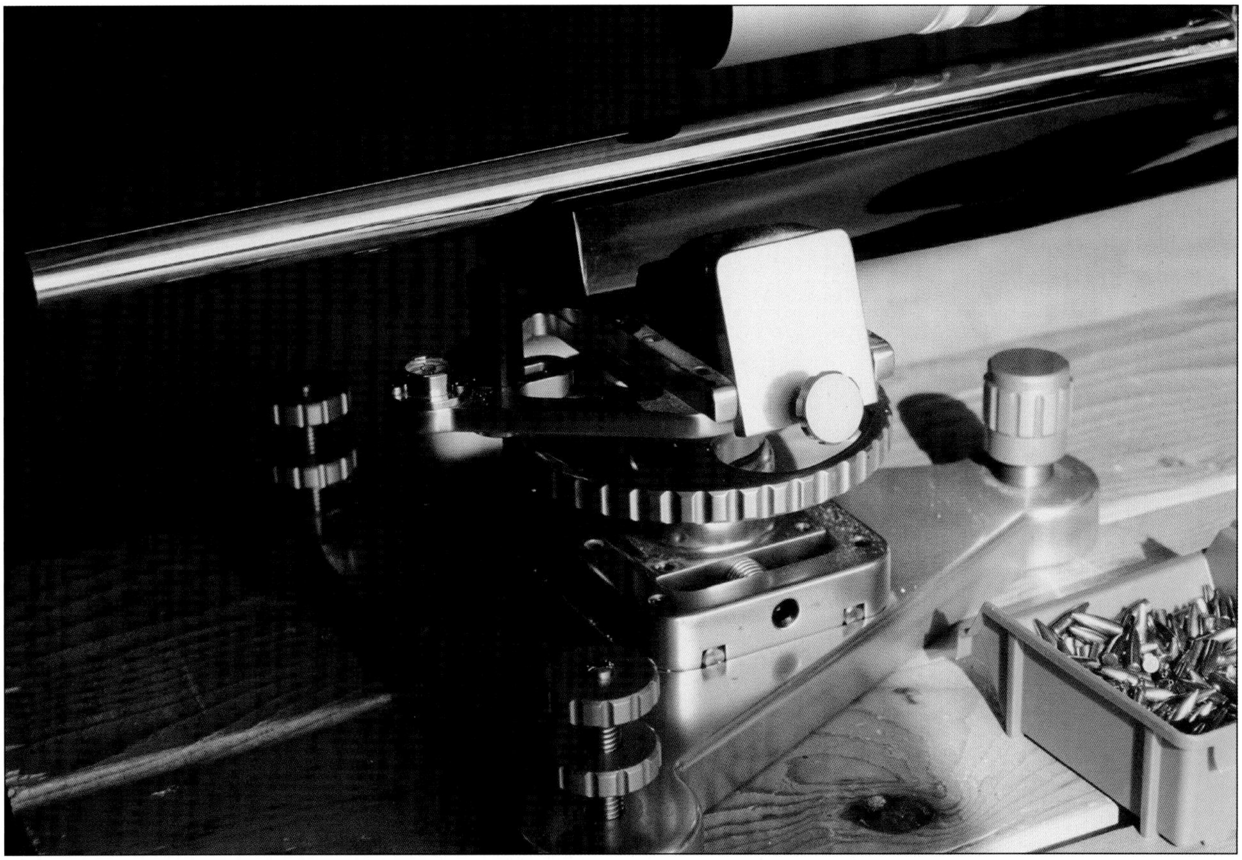

▲ This benchrest forend cradle is fully adjustable, to ensure stability and consistent rifle support.

for leveling on uneven ground." Thermal-wrap keeps the top cool, if you forget Brownlee's awning on a warm day. A tripod of 32-inch folding legs includes heavy-duty plastic feet don't mar floors or pickup beds. They resist movement on grass.

The quality of this bench is evident in both materials and machining. "All major metal parts are aluminum," Wally told me. "Hey, it's a portable!" That said, the generous dimensions of those parts, with their adjustments, give his product substantial heft. "It weighs 114 pounds complete," he admitted. "But it's made to hand-carry in three pieces." The center assembly (spindle, plate and legs tucked into a 24x33-inch package) weighs 70 pounds, the top with frame 34. Add 10 for the seat. Surely overbuilt for Friday night card games, Brownlee's shooting table excels for range work as well as sniping in poodle pastures. It's not just stone-steady; it's *comfortable*. It puts you higher than many benches, above tall grass. Your feet rest on a rail or hanger, not on the ground. Brownlee's 2500 bench is a tour-de-force in engineering and manufacture. "It's American made, too," he reminded me. "Right here in Watertown." This bench and Wally's other shooting supplies can be found at www.targetshooting.com.

Whatever its design, your bench is only part of the rifle's support. It's a foundation for your rest. Sandbags still suffice, but you're better served by a mechanical rest with close-tolerance adjustments that ensure consistent support and let you get a precise hold without imparting tension to the rifle. Such are standard equipment at Benchrest matches, where marksmen compete with rifles and handloads capable of one-hole groups.

If your budget isn't up to a benchrest-class rest, you still have options. Many hunters use polymer rests like those in Caldwell's line, which includes the recoil-absorbing Lead Sled. Available from Midway USA, these rests offer great value. Brownells and Sinclair catalog a host of others. Hunting suppliers like Cabela's do, too.

Whatever the rest, remember that any variation in rest-rifle contact, or hand pressure on the rifle, can affect point of impact. Your body position on the bench must also be consistent. One other tip: Make sure the rifle can move in recoil. That's not an issue when you're firing from the shoulder. But some rests provide a butt bracket with a stop behind the pad. If you load a Lead Sled too heavily, or otherwise brace your .475 DinoBlaster from behind so it can't retreat at the shot, you may find the rifle's receiver walks right out of the stock!

A QUICK, EFFICIENT ZERO

A zero is actually a distance—the second (and downward) crossing of the bullet's arc through the straight line of sight. The first crossing is near the rifle, commonly at about 35 yards for centerfires zeroed at 200 yards. A .22 rimfire zeroed at 75 brings sightline and bullet arc together first at 25.

Illustrations showing bullet trajectory relative to the sightline have given the impression that the bullet rises above the sightline. Not so. A bullet starts dropping as soon as it leave the muzzle, victim to the inexorable tug of gravity. It never rises above the line of bore. However, the sights (or scope) direct your eye in a line not parallel with the bore but at at angle to it. So the sightline cuts below the bullet's arc near the muzzle. Then, far off, at a zero range you determine by adjusting the sights, the bullet crosses the sightline a second time, falling below it.

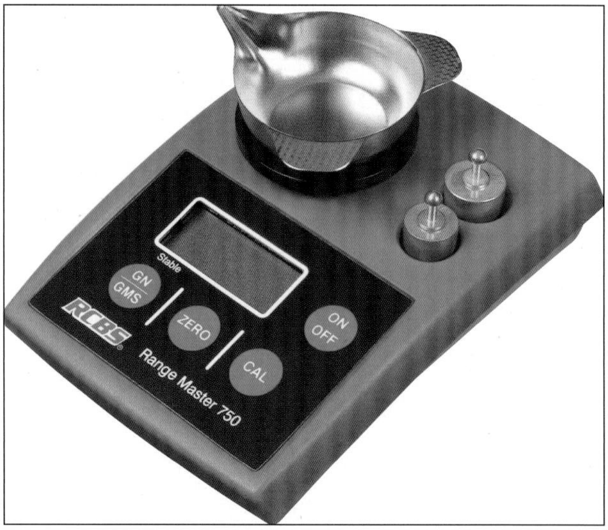

▲ Working up loads is faster with electronic scales like this, from RCBS. Takes little bench space too!

ACCURATE BY ANY STANDARD!

Marksmen have used various measures to gauge rifle and handgun accuracy. The most enduring is group size, measured center to center between the outside bullet holes. While bullseye shooting is still popular, and steel plates add interest to long-range matches, group size still determines the winner in the benchrest game. The first official Benchrest match occurred in 1947 in Johnstown, New York. Riflemen obsessed with accuracy soon swelled the ranks of benchrest competitors. The first world championships happened in France in 1989. Special rifles, handloads and optics have since enabled shooters to drill tiny groups. In the UK, a recent event produced a .135-inch five-shot knot at 100 yards, a 6.908 group at 1,000—in trying conditions. The tightest ever at a sanctioned 1,000-yard match spanned less than 2 inches!

While "minute of angle" is a common unit in gauging accuracy, it isn't so widely understood. An angular measure, actual measure varies with distance. At 100 yards, a minute is 1.047 inch; but rounding to 1 inch makes sense. At 200 yards, 1 MOA is 2 inches; at 300 it's 3 inches, and so on.

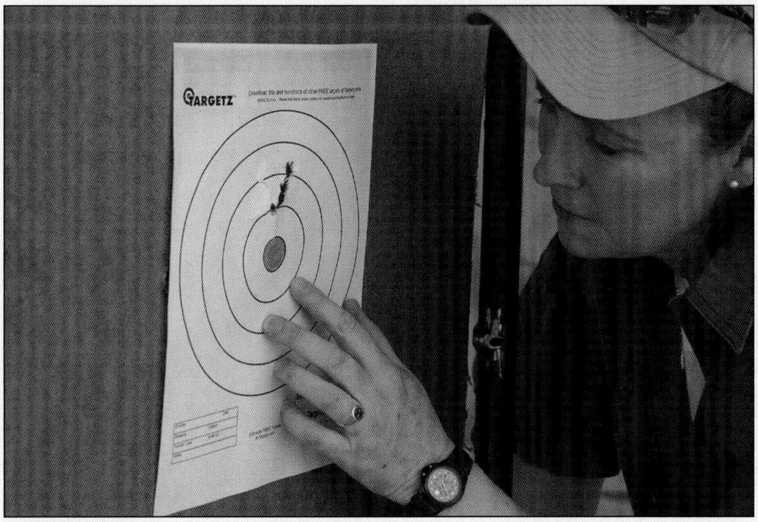

▲ For most big game loads, a 200-yard zero makes sense. At 100, bullets will strike 2 to 3 inches high.

▲ The author's 300-yard group with a Browning A-Bolt in the then-new .270 WSM miked under ½ MOA!

Zeroing, or sighting in, enables you to tap your ammunition's reach. And reach, after all, is one of the main reasons for the existence of rifles!

While these days long shooting brings to mind desert ranges and shots at game on the far side of yawning western canyons, riflemen first officially tested themselves at distance in the East—at Creed's farm on Long Island, then across the Appalachians. In Pennsylvania during my youth, riflemen squinting through Lyman Super Targetspots and 2-inch Unertls imperiled resident woodchucks as far as half a mile across quilts of rolling alfalfa. Those barrel-length scopes perched on rifles heavy as the stones anchoring the hedgerows. Varminters favored high-octane

.22s, from the Swift to the then-wildcat .22-250—and less enduring hotrods like the .220 Weatherby Rocket and the .219 Donaldson Wasp. The .22 Newton and .228 Ackley hurled hefty (70- and 90-grain) .228 bullets in flat arcs.

Long shooting at big game has become something of a trend now, though the ethics of shooting beyond sure-kill range are hotly debated. No matter what the game or the distance, hunters haven't the target-shooter's luxury of zeroing in advance for the exact yardage to their target. So they must settle for a zero that delivers quick, acceptably centered hits up close without excessive bullet drop at distance. For truly long shots, they rely on load data—drop and drift values determined first on a chart or a computer, then by firing.

▲ Chronographing is an essential part of testing handloads. Ensure the screens are precisely positioned!

Zeroing takes time and consumes ammunition. Here's how do do it most efficiently:

Attach your scope in rings as low as practical so you get full cheek support when aiming. Locate the scope tube well forward to get a full field of view when your face crowds the comb nose—as it will when you fire from prone or sitting, or even offhand when the shot is urgent. You'll lose valuable time if you must pull your head back to find the target or to avoid getting bumped on recoil! Cinch base screws very tight, and snug ring-screws alternately as you would lug nuts on a wheel to get firm, even pressure.

With the bolt removed or the breechblock on your single-shot dropped, lay your rifle on a rest or sandbags, and center a distant object in the bore. (My practice is to target a rock on a bank a quarter mile off.) Without moving the rifle, dial the scope reticle onto that object. This "bore-sighting" should put your first bullets near point of aim at 35 yards, where you'll have placed a box or frame with a generous paper target. Pump and lever rifles, and autoloaders, can be bore-sighted with a collimator. Just slide the spud into the muzzle and, with your scope adjustments, center the grid with your reticle.

Settle your rifle on sandbags or a commercial rest. If necessary after your first shot at 35 yards, adjust the sight, moving it the direction you want the bullet to go. Most hunting scopes have quarter-minute clicks, each graduation of the windage and elevation dials moving point of impact one-quarter inch at 100 yards. Don't bother refining point of impact up close; just get it within a couple of inches of center. Move the target to 100, then 200 yards, where, for all but short-range loads, you'll want a hunting bullet to hit point of aim. That's your zero range. While hunters expecting long shots zero at greater distances, they're setting themselves up to miss high at midrange, where many big game animals are killed. A 200-yard zero allows you point-blank aim to at least 250 with modern loads. That is, your bullet will strike no more than 3 vertical inches from point of aim to that yardage—close enough to stay well inside a deer's chest. Very flat-shooting loads pinch this variation to 2 inches. You can also nudge the zero for such cartridges out to 250, extending point-blank range to just over 300. A zero beyond

▲ Testing with iron sights, use a target big enough to see clearly. You'll get surprisingly small groups.

250 compels you to hold low where shots are more frequent and more often urgent.

Now fire three-shot groups from hunting positions at 200 yards. The paper will not only point up any change in point of impact, but also measure your marksmanship. If in the field you employ a sling or a bipod, use it when refining your zero. A tight sling enhances accuracy but can pull groups to 7 o'clock. "Loading" your bipod by pressing the rifle forward adds consistency, especially on hard surfaces but can also affect point of impact.

After zeroing, thoroughly clean your rifle and run a lightly oiled patch through the bore. Let the barrel get stone-cold, then fire again at 200 yards to check point of impact. Pay attention to the first and second shots. They're the shots that count when you're hunting. Save the cold-barrel target for more shots after your rifle is again clean and cold. A composite group from different days should form a small knot.

I once ran accuracy tests of 74 hunting loads, in chamberings from .243 to .338. A few shot tiny groups from my hunting rifles, but the average for *all* three-shot groups was 1.7 inches. The average for five-shot groups: 2.1 inches. By some standards, that's not very impressive, but it's representative of what you can expect from factory ammunition and preliminary handloads. Until proven otherwise, you needn't settle for average accuracy. A .270 Model 70 Winchester that delivered 1.3- and 1.7-inch groups with two types of ammo drilled .6-inch groups with

BENCHREST'S BAR FOR ACCURACY

Handloaders owe much to the benchrest game, with its impossibly high standards for precision. Benchrest shooters have also come up with many rifle and cartridge innovations now enjoyed by hunters.

On July 7, 2007 in IBS (Benchrest) competition at the Thunder Valley, Ohio range, Tom Sarver fired five shots into a 1,000-yard group that measured a scant 1.403 inch. That's .14 minute of angle! Almost as remarkable: the knot was centered, scoring 50-5x. It bested, in the Light Gun category, a 1.546-inch group shot by Rich DeSimone five years earlier—a performance then thought "untouchable." Sarver used a wildcat cartridge on a shortened .338 Lapua case. With 85 grains of H1000, his .300 Hulk kicked 240-grain MatchKings from a quintet of hulls reportedly on their 58th loading!

Not even a year after Sarver drilled his incredible target, Joel Russo used a 21-pound Bruce Baer rifle in .338 Big Baer (an Improved .33-408) with Lawton action and Krieger barrel to punch a .44-minute group *at 1,680 yards!* Four of those five bullets went into 3.806 inches—well under a quarter minute! He performed this feat at the fabled Williamsport range, home of Pennsylvania's 1,000-yard Benchrest Club since 1967.

two others. A Remington 700 in .338 Winchester Magnum that disappointed me with a 3.6-inch group also printed one that miked sub-MOA.

Realistic accuracy standards vary. A rifle that shoulders quickly for elk in cover lacks the mass to compete in a benchrest heavy-gun match. Its magazine robs rigidity from the receiver. A scope of modest power delivers the wide, bright field needed on a hunt, but not the precision required for one-hole groups on bullseye targets. Bullets that blast through elk, balling up in perfect mushrooms under the off-side hide with less than 10 percent weight loss, don't fly as uniformly as MatchKings at 600 yards.

▲ On hunts, handloads must function without a hitch. Cycle all loads you'll carry. Keep them clean.

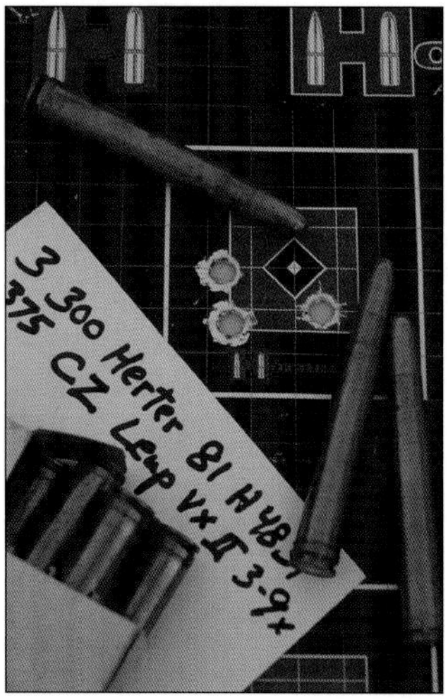

▲ Handloads stored well still perform. These were 30 years old when Wayne dug them out for a test.

THE IMPERATIVE OF FUNCTION

A load that doesn't take your head off or shred your rifle is but one step along the road to utility. It must be accurate, too, and, if for hunting, deliver the terminal performance you want. It must also cycle without hitch through your rifle. Long ago, on safari with .375 handloads, I got into a running battle with a Cape buffalo. To my chagrin, the cartridges I was frantically jamming into the Model 70 wouldn't enter the magazine below the top spot on the follower. While my ammunition didn't exceed maximum overall length on the charts, and I'd chambered every round to check feeding, I hadn't pushed each to the bottom of the box. I found in this moment of truth that the old square-shouldered Winchester solid bullets, while easily clearing the front of the magazine, contacted its radiused front corners below the top position. My four-shot rifle became a two-shot rifle. Lesson: Run all hunting loads from the belly of the magazine up to ensure function!

▲ At the range, test-cycle every hunting load from the bottom of the magazine up through the chamber.

▲ In hunting, the load matters very little unless you can shoot well in field conditions. Practice helps!

Chapter 8: Born in the Barracks

Notwithstanding a rich history of cartridges and characters from the annals of wildcatting, some of the most useful and enduring rifle and handgun cartridges have arrived in uniform. The .30-06, surely. Both the .308 and .223 also owe their geneses to military projects. So too the .45 ACP. Even the .45-70 and the .45 Long Colt benefited from their tenure in the U.S. Army. I'm probably one of few who mourns the early demise of the .30-40 Krag, a contemporary of the similar .303 British. The Brit lasted from 1888 through the Second World War, while the Krag enjoyed only a decade in service, beginning in 1892. Both were fine mid-capacity cartridges. Their rimmed, tapered hulls don't raise the pulse of shooters brought up with cell phones. Pity.

.308 TO .338

If there's not a .30-06 in your battery, you've probably had to tender an excuse before now. It's not that other deer rifles won't kill as effectively or that other cartridges aren't as versatile. You own an '06 to pay homage. The cartridge is older than female suffrage. It went to Alaska when miners were still plodding the Chilkoot trail. With the .30-06 we won two world wars. It was a charter chambering in the Winchester Model 70 and is still arguably the most versatile big game round ever. You can live without a .30-06, as you can without a towel rack in your bathroom. But why would you?

The .30-06 cartridge was conceived in 1900, when engineers at Springfield Armory began work on a battle rifle to replace the .30-40 Krag-Jorgensen. Their prototype emerged in 1901. Two years later, the Model 1903 Springfield appeared. Its .30-caliber rimless cartridge headspaced on the shoulder, like the 8x57 Mauser. A 220-grain bullet at 2,300 fps made the .30-03 a ballistic match for the 8x57 and a 236-grain bullet at 2,125.

A year after the .30-03's debut, Germany switched to a new 154-grain 8mm spitzer at 2,800 fps. The

▲ Arguably, more mule deer have fallen to the .30-06 than to any other cartridge.

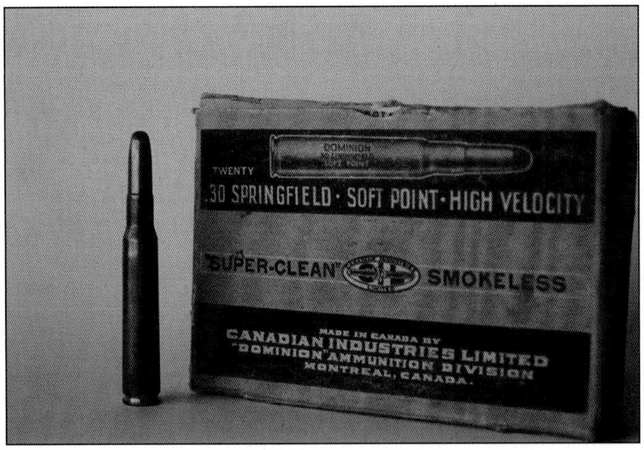

▲ First loaded for infantry arms, the .30-06 soon appeared in hunting ammo—here vintage Dominion.

Americans countered with the Ball Cartridge, Caliber .30, Model 1906. It spat a 150-grain bullet at 2,700 fps. Then someone decided to shorten the case .07, to .494. All .30-03 rifles were promptly recalled for rechambering.

World War I demonstrated that bullets of high ballistic coefficient increased effective range, so the Army replaced the 150-grain .30-06 bullet with a 173-grain spitzer at 2,646 fps. This M-1 cartridge pestered soldiers to 5,500 yards. It hiked recoil, too. In 1939, the Army adopted the M-2 load. With a 152-grain spitzer at 2,805 fps, it functioned better in the Garand than did heavy-bullet loads. US troops used it throughout World War II. At the same time, it established an enviable reputation on the target range.

When I was a lad, you could buy surplus military '06 ammo by the bucket. But savvy shooters kept it far from their *good* rifles. The reason: potassium chlorate primers deposited corrosive salts in the bore. Though Remington developed its non-corrosive Kleanbore priming in 1927 (and commercial rounds featured non-corrosive priming exclusively from about 1930), military cases were fitted with corrosive FA 70 primers as late as 1952! Corrosive priming, for all its faults, does not weaken the case. Mercuric priming, on the other hand, attacks brass but won't harm bores. Since the Korean War, the only domestic '06 ammo to avoid has been a run of Western Match cartridges with Western "8 ½ G" primers. These are corrosive and mercuric.

First in surplus infantry rifles, the .30-06 became a popular hunting round. In 1937 it appeared in the new Winchester Model 70. Over the next quarter-century, the 70 sold in 18 chamberings. More than a third of the rifles shipped (208,218) were .30-06s!

Well-credentialed in all the world's game fields, the .30-06 will handily take any North American animals and all but a few huge beasts abroad. It shoots flat too. Given 200-yard zeros, the .30-06 strikes within 2 vertical inches of the .300 Winchester at 300 yards. It's chambered in more rifles than any other cartridge, save, now, the .308. You can buy ought-six ammo in outposts from the Canadian North to sub-Saharan Africa. Such ubiquity endears it to any traveler who has lost luggage. Many august riflemen have loved and handloaded the .30-06, including:

- Jack O'conner, who favored 53 grains IMR 4320 behind 150-grain bullets,
- Townsend Whelen, who launched 165-grain boattails with 58 grains 4350,
- Warren Page, who claimed fine accuracy with 180-grain bullets, 55 grains 4350,
- Ken Waters, who capped 50 grains Norma 203 with 180-grain bullets.

A broad selection of .30-caliber bullets suits the .30-06 to bullseye shooting, as well as to game from coyotes to brown bears. Planning a hunt for Alaskan moose and Dall's sheep, I didn't have to look past a converted Springfield in .30-06, with iron sights. It downed both animals cleanly. The .30-06 is a superb elk cartridge. In my surveys of members of the Rocky Moutain Elk Foundation, it shared top spot in popularity with the 7mm Remington Magnum. It ranked among the first six picks of Washington elk hunters 20 years before the 7mm Magnum appeared!

A reader once castigated me for writing in another publication that the .30-06 was essentially the equal of the 7mm Remington Magnum. With 150-grain bullets out of the blocks, the 7mm wins. You'd expect it to; it has a bigger case. But comparing the 180-grain '06 bullet with a 175-grain bullet from the Magnum, you'll find the advantage diminishes. In fact, if you pick Hornady's Superformance or Federal's High Energy .30-06 180-grain loads, or handload to match

▲ One of the most versatile big game cartridges, the .30-06 is easily handloaded, still wildly popular.

them at 2,820 fps or better, you'll generate the 3,180 ft-lbs of energy standard for the heavy-bullet load in the 7mm Magnum.

To 300 yards, there's less than an inch difference in point of impact between 180- and 150-grain bullets in the .30-06, at 400 only 2 inches. But the heavier bullet has a 20 percent weight advantage that translates to deeper penetration. During my youth, some hunters preferred 220-grain .30-06 loads for the biggest game. But a 220-grain round-nose Core-Lokt starts at only 2,410 fps, and these days, few riflemen want to sacrifice that much speed. A 200-yard zero with a 220-grain '06 load requires a 3-inch lift at 100 yards. Beyond 200 yards, that bullet drops like a stone: 13 inches at 300 yards, 31 inches at 400. Better to zero these long, blunt bullets at 150 yards and limit shots to 250 or so.

It's hard to improve on the .30-06, and when you find something better, there's a good chance it derived from the .30-06! The .270 Winchester did, and of course the .25-06 (1969) and .280 Remington (1957). Then there's the .35 Whelen, another Remington adoption. Among contemporary wildcats, the .30-06 Improved and .338-06 are more popular than the .375 and .400 Whelen. The 6.5-06 has a modest following, as does the 8mm-06.

Pushing the '06 shoulder out to 40 degrees increases case capacity slightly, but you'll gain only 50 to 70 fps for your efforts. I own two .30-06 Improved rifles, both carved from 1903 Springfields. One of them

▲ A lightweight rifle, this Kimber shoots very well with .30-06 handloads: IMR 3031, 150-grain Hornadys.

took the biggest elk I've shot, a Wyoming bull that dropped to a 180-grain Nosler Partition.

The .308 Winchester began life in the early 1950s as the T-65, a military cartridge to supplant the .30-06. Shorter and lighter in weight, but nearly as potent, it still serves soldiers as the 7.62x51 NATO in machine guns and selective-fire shoulder arms like the M14 and FN-FAL. In 1952, Winchester added this round to its commercial line as the .308. Offered in Winchester's lever-action Model 88 and autoloading Model 100 rifles, as well as the Model 70 Featherweight, it soon jumped across brands and became a top-selling round in the likes of the Savage 99 and Remington's 760 pump and 742 self-loader. Shortly, the .308 ranked as one of the most popular choices in short-action hunting rifles of all stripes. Though clearly less capacious than the '06, the .308 launches bullets nearly as fast (within 100 fps). Given sleek profiles, .308 bullets in all hunting weights pass the 500-yard mark with 1,200 ft-lbs of energy.

To give snipers greater reach while tapping the potential of new rifle mechanisms and improved optics, Research Armament Company trotted out a powerful new round in 1983. The .338 Lapua, based on the .416 Rigby hull, was designed to launch a ballistically efficient 250-grain bullet at 3,000 fps. Bell Extrusion Labs, Ltd. produced new brass. Sweden's Norma and Finland's Lapua ammo firms eventually loaded the first commercial cartridges. After Research Armament built rifles under Navy contract, Dakota offered its Longbow rifle in .338 Lapua. Now this fire-breather has been chambered in several affordable "tactical" rifles for commercial sales, by such companies as Savage. It has become the darling of shooters who enjoy banging steel at extreme range. In Afghanistan, US snipers have used the round to make hits at ranges far beyond the reach of the .30-06 and .308.

▲ The .308, an American round, is chambered worldwide—here in the smooth, accurate Steyr SM 12.

◀ The .308 (7.62x51 NATO) is widely chambered. Here it serves a super-accurate McMillan rifle.

▲ AR rifles come in many configurations, two action sizes. This is a new lightweight Wilson in .308.

◀ Lightweight bullets keep ARs controllable; can nip very tight groups, especially with standard twist.

THE .223

Features that distinguish martial hardware change with time. Bayonets have been replaced by the selective-fire option. But the profiles of some military rifles differ little from those of popular sporting models. To soften the image of infantry arms, industry apologists have taken to calling any self-loader of AR-15 design "the modern sporting rifle." While even those of us enamored of hand-checkered French walnut admire the ingenuity in Eugene Stoner's space gun of the 1960s, this seems a spineless euphemism. It is also untrue. You'll see many, many more Remington 700s in deer camps than you will AR-15s. Only if you march the term "sporting" from its traditional place in the hunting field to the confined arena of the three-gun match does the AR qualify as *the* rifle.

Enough of that. Whatever the shape of your pet hunting rifles, handloading can blur, if not erase, the lines separating them from their military forebears. Ammunition from your bench can suit any rifle to any purpose worthy of the bullet's weight and speed.

The number of prairie dogs shot with the .223, or 5.56 NATO, is growing almost as fast as our national debt. This cartridge reigns in Moundville, because the ammunition is inexpensive and doesn't crack your molars when you set it off. The .223 has also generated a spate of super-accurate hollowpoint, softnose and poly-tip bullets, from 35 to 80 grains in weight, with dozens of flat-shooting factory loads. Its military forebear, the .30-06, produced a cornucopia of hunting loads too, but over many more years.

In 1957, the .223 appeared as an experimental round for Armalite's AR-15 combat rifle. Adopted in 1964 as the 5.56mm Ball cartridge M193, it owed much of its success to Bob Hutton, technical editor of *Guns & Ammo*. With Gene Stoner of Armalite, Hutton put a 55-grain bullet in a hull a tad longer than the .222's. With an exit speed of 3,250 fps, the M193 load met the requirement for supersonic speed at 500 yards and was issued to US forces in Vietnam. In 1980 it earned the blessing of NATO countries, which substituted the FN-designed 62-grain SS109 boat-tail bullet that penetrated mild steel. The SS109 left the muzzle at 3,100 fps and hit harder at distance than did the 55-grain boat-tail. Faster rifling twist (to 1-in-7) gave it superior accuracy as well. The US Army called this new load the M855.

The .223's small, high-velocity bullets were designed to shoot people, relatively fragile creatures. Fifty years ago, soldiers firing .30-caliber rifles in jungle environs were, it seemed, over-gunned. Most hits happened up close; the targets were child-size. In the thickets of Southeast Asia, rate of fire and magazine capacity counted for more than downrange energy. Ammunition weight mattered because a selective-fire M16 could chatter through a magazine while an infantryman of the old school cycled the bolt twice on a Mauser or Springfield. The .308 (7.62 NATO) in the M14 rifle reduced cartridge weight and length below those of the .30-06, but didn't appreciably lighten a soldier's pack. The .223's bullet weighed only a third as much as the .30-bore spitzers of mid-century. And it laid people low.

Whether you choose factory loads or roll your own, .223 hunting bullets fly flatter and, by some measures, hit harder than lever-gun loads once thought deadly on big game. The .44-40's 200-grain bullet in a Winchester factory load registers 630 ft-lbs of energy at exit, 450 at 100 yards. That's substantially more than the .38-40 (540 and 325), a great deal more than the .25-20 (410 and 275). But it falls short of the energy generated by Winchester 55-grain .223 Ballistic Silvertip: 1,280 and 1,005 ft-lbs. A 117-grain .25-35 bullet, widely considered adequate for whitetails at modest range, just matches the muzzle energy

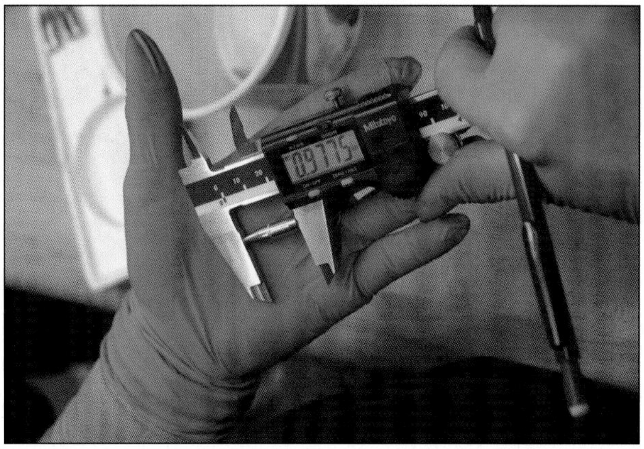

▲ AR actions put limits on bullet length. Long bullets also require sharp rifling twist for best accuracy.

of the most ambitious .223s. At 100 yards, it is 100 ft-lbs weaker. At 200, where 55- and 60-grain .223s retain 780 ft-lbs (and the Hornady 75 TAP tops 900), the 117 .25-35 yields only 620.

You could argue that .223 bullets weren't designed for big game, that the killing power of a 200-grain .44-caliber bullet is under-rated in energy tables. Still, Winchester's 64-grain Power Point, started at 3,020 fps, has about the same muscle as the 55-grain, and nearly 20 percent more mass. Hornady's 60-grain TAP FPD load boasts 9 percent more bullet weight than the standard 55-grain. It floors deer with shots through the forward ribs. So too the 62-grain Remington Core-Lokt Ultra Bonded, leaving at 3,100 fps with 1,325 ft-lbs. Federal's 64-grain softpoint at 3,050 fps carries equal authority. A Hornady 75-grain TAP FPD, clocking 2,790, lands a heavier blow at distance than do its brethren with faster starts.

This is no defense of the .223. The world is full of more effective deer cartridges. But recent .223 factory loads are much better suited to deer hunting than were the first. Handloaders can match them, and sometimes beat them. Bullet choices abound, and include truly innovative missiles, like the DRT missiles I've used on whitetails and tested in gelatin blocks. (CorBon, of Sturgis SD, loads .223 ammo with these lead-free bullets.)

Dynamic Research Technologies is based in Grant City, Missouri. The DRT bullet is powdered metal in a copper jacket. Upon striking flesh, the jacket ruptures and the core disintegrates. There's little left to recover. But the wound channel is broad, and deep enough to destroy both lungs. DRT literature makes much of hydraulic damage and the bullet's centrifugal force. Even gimlet-eyed skeptics have been convinced that bullets that turn to dust can flatten big deer. After a few days afield, I was. One whitetail facing me stood just long enough for a careful shot with my Smith & Wesson M&P15. The animal spun and sprinted, expiring at full throttle to pile up against a tree 65 steps from where it had been hit.

"We've found that DRT bullets needn't plow through the lungs, or even reach them," said Dustin Worrell as he sliced through the diaphragm during the autopsy of a doe hit by another hunter a little far back. "We've killed deer cleanly with .223s that didn't enter the chest cavity. As the bullet turns to tiny particles it releases all its energy in one quick burst. The shock to the liver and other vital organs is lethal, even if those organs show no bullet channel." Dustin, with his father John Worrell, have pioneered the manufacture and marketing of these bullets. Developed in a US government project for the .45 ACP, the DRT design is counterintuitive in this era of "controlled expansion" bullets—especially when you apply it to small-bore rounds like the .223.

The bullet that took my buck had been reduced to a few jacket shards inside. Two deer I'd killed with .223 DRTs on an earlier hunt had succumbed quickly, their lungs minced by high-speed dust. Like Harold Beal, who'd done definitive work with sintered .45 ACP bullets, John and Dustin have put various bullet shapes and materials to the test. During my visit, a gelatin trial showed the lethal behavior of a 79-grain tungsten-core .223. Heavier than lead, and more costly, tungsten DRTs deliver more thump within practical length limits.

Certainly, the impetus behind this bullet (and others for the .223) is the popularity of the AR-15 rifle. From factory and bench, there's been a steady proliferation of hotrod loads that dismember prairie dogs and send rockchucks into back-flips. Match bullets that print half-minute groups followed persistent efforts to make AR rifles half-minute capable. Because many states don't sanction .22s for big game, deer loads for the .223 got less traction at the drawing board. AR-15 manufacturers chose instead to chamber their rifles for new cartridges.

AR ALTERNATIVES

Remington's 6.8 SPC (Special Purpose Cartridge) owes much to the 1906 introduction of the .30 Remington, essentially a rimless .30-30 fashioned for the company's square-back Model 8 autoloading rifle, new that year. The .25, .30, .32 and .35 killed deer reliably at woods ranges in the Model 8 and the slide-action Model 14, trotted out in 1912. Scope sights and the evolution of bolt rifles would eventually nudge both off-stage. At .421, rim diameter of the .30 Remington is the same as that of the .25 and .32, but smaller than the .35 (.460). The .308 and .30-06 mike

.473 across the base. This dimension matters because in its quest for a twenty-first century infantry round, the Army focused on cases that would cycle in AR-15 and M16 actions. Opening the bolt face from .375 (standard for .223s) for larger hulls was permissible, given the requisites of more power up close and flat flight for easy torso hits to 500 meters. Changing bolt throw, magazine length or receiver dimensions were not options.

The 6.8 SPC emerged quietly, the US Army Marksmanship Unit and 5th Special Forces Group lopping the .30 Remington hull from 2.05 inches to 1.69, or .07 shy of a .223 case. They fashioned a 23-degree shoulder and reduced neck diameter from 7.62 to 6.8mm (.277 inside), same as Winchester's .270. The finished body measures 1.295 inch long, the neck .290. The hull has 17 percent more capacity than the .223. A 115-grain bullet was as long as could be practicably loaded for an OAL of 2.26. At 300 yards, that bullet packs 1,000 ft-lbs of energy, about the same as a 100-grain softpoint from a .243. Here's how the 6.8 SPC compares to similar cartridges.

	Muzzle	100 yds	200 yds	300 yds	400 yds
6.8mm SPC,115 OTM (Remington)					
velocity, fps	2800	2535	2285	2049	1828
energy, ft-lb	2002	1641	1333	1072	853
arc, inches	+2	0	-9	-26	
.257 Roberts, 117 SPBT (Hornady)					
velocity, fps	2780	2550	2331	2122	1925
energy, ft-lb	2007	1689	1411	1170	963
arc, inches	+2	0	-8	-24	
.250 Savage, 100 PSP (Remington)					
velocity, fps	2820	2504	2210	1936	1684
energy, ft-lb	1765	1392	1084	832	630
arc, inches	+2	0	-9	-28	
.243 Winchester, 100 PP (Winchester)					
velocity, fps	2960	2697	2449	2215	1993
energy, ft-lb	1945	1615	1332	1089	882
arc, inches	+2	0	-8	-23	

Remington engineers who joined the military design team in 2001 had no mandate to develop the 6.8 SPC as a hunting round. But that seemed a logical course. Bolt rifles followed. The first 6.8mm SPC rifle to come my way was a Remington 700. Zeroing at 600 yards, I settled into prone and peered through the Leupold 6.5-20x scope at paper the size of a small garage door. It looked small as a postage stamp.

Bang! The rifle barely hopped. The target didn't stay long in the pits. It arose with a white marker on the X. With no sight adjustment, I fired nine more shots. Only two leaked into the 9-ring. A rifle that hits at long range in gusty wind but pampers your shoulder and eardrums is easy to love! In the Southeast that deer season, I carried a Remington Model Seven in 6.8. When a big doe appeared, I steadied the crosswire of the Kahles and pressed the trigger. The deer dropped, kicked convulsively and lay still. A month later, I took a second deer with the 6.8 SPC in a T/C pistol. The doe was quartering to me when I unleased a 115-grain Core-Lokt. She dashed off into the Kentucky woods. A few minutes later, I was at the carcass. The bullet had angled to the off-flank, retaining just over half its weight.

In bolt rifles, the 6.8mm SPC won't threaten the .243, .260 or 7mm-08. Still (despite lukewarm promotion by Remington), the 6.8 remains one of the most versatile cartridges for the AR-15.

The .204 Ruger is more specialized, kicking lightweight bullets away at 4,000 fps with negligible recoil. It's a popular AR chambering now.

In 2009 Remington, first to list a commercial AR attired just for hunters, chambered its R-15 rifle for the new .30 Remington AR round. This .30 has the case head of the .308; but OVERALL LENGTH ? is that of the .223. A 125-grain AccuTip or Pointed Core-Lock from the .30 Remington runs neck-and-neck with 150s from the .308. Another fine .30 is Bill Wilson's (Wilson Combat) 7.62x40. It's a .223 hull trimmed and necked up. Wilson's own ARs cycle it silkily. With 110-grain TTSX bullets, I've shot tiny groups. The 7.62x40 is deadly far out of proportion to its size. Still-hunting hogs in cover, I downed a muscular boar with one bullet that raked forward from the center ribs, opening violently but driving to the off shoulder.

Big-bore enthusiasts welcomed the .450 Bushmaster, its case derived from the 6.5-284. Hornady loads with 250-grain FTX bullets clock 2,200 fps. In the Deep South, the Bushmaster is a favorite of hog hunters. Then there's the potent .458 SOCOM, brainchild of Marty ter Weeme. Allegedly he chatted up Tony Rumore at a Bar-B-Q, asking about AR uppers for the .440 Corbon and .50 Action Express. Using Starline brass, Marty rebated the rim of the .50 AE to .473. Manson Precision sent a reamer, CH Tool & Die a sizer. A 20-round .223 magazine holds just seven .458 SOCOMs, but each 300-grain bullet exiting at 1,900 fps carries 2,400 ft-lbs of punch! I've managed half-minute shooting with a Wilson rifle in .458 SOCOM. Bill Alexander has earned plaudits for the similar .50 Beowulf, a 325-grain Speer leaving a 16-inch, 1-in-9 barrel at 1,950 fps.

As well known as the Beowulf is the 6.5 Grendel, also from Alexander Arms. Essentially a 6mm PPC necked up and blown out, the Grendel case barely reaches mid-shoulder on a .223. But it holds more powder than even the 6.8 SPC. A 123-grain Scenar bullet leaves a 20-inch Lothar Walther barrel at 2,600 fps and stays supersonic beyond 1,000 yards. Ditto Les Baer's almost-identical .264 SBC.

Brian Scheutz, of Seattle-based Olympic Arms, chambers routinely for the 7.62x39 and the .300 Fireball, a necked-up .221. Nostalgic customers buy his .222s. Brian and his crew have adapted the AR-15 mechanism to handgun cartridges: 9mm, .40 S&W and .45 ACP—the 9 and .40 with Glock magazines! The company builds ARs for the WSSM line too: 223, .243 and .25. Uppers for these rounds have special bolts and carriers, but they fit standard lowers. The .300 Olympic is a hotrod on the .243 WSSM case.

▲ Powders for ARs include those chambered to pistol cartridges and the many other .223 alternatives.

The most talked-about AR-15 cartridges of late are the .300 Whisper and the .300 AAC Blackout, derived from the .221 Fireball and .223 Remington hulls. These two .30s are very nearly the same, but the Blackout has the blessing of the Sporting Arms and Ammunition Manufacturers' Institute. The Whisper should chamber in the slightly larger Blackout chamber. Dimensional differences are so slight, the reverse can also be true—though not universally so. Hornady loads Whisper ammunition with a 110-grain V-Max bullet at 2,375 fps and a 208-grain V-Max at 1,020. The latter, with a 220-grain spitzer at 1,010 fps from the .300 Blackout, is subsonic. The "tactical" value of subsonic bullets is clear enough; less apparent is any benefit to recreational shooters or hunters. More useful: the 125-grain softpoint load at 2,215. One of my pals, a seasoned ballistician at a company manufacturing subsonic ammo, tells me it does not always shoot accurately. The .300 Blackout case measures 1.368 inch. OAL: 2.26 inches. Bullets fly best from a 1-in-7 twist.

As cartridges for the AR-15 action have proliferated, so have rifles. A decade ago, when shooters anticipating the 2004 sunset of the assault weapons ban throttled back on AR purchases, Mark Malkowski drew from idle parts and machinery to build left-hand AR-15s. The southpaw entrepreneur kept pace as the market strengthened. So emerged the Stag rifle. A Stag 7 in 6.8 SPC impressed me with its features, function, fit and finish. Hogue over-molding on grips added control. That rifle delivered minute-of-angle five-shot groups with a variety of loads, including the Remington Core-Lokt Ultra and Hornady V-Max.

Ruger's SR-556 sports a hybrid chamber designed by the company's gifted engineer, the late Roy Melcher. It's proportioned to yield the fine accuracy of shorter-throated .223 barrels without increasing pressures, as some .223 barrels do when fed 5.56 NATO ammunition. SR-556 barrels are cold-hammer-forged. The 1-in-8 rifling of the VT version is steeper than the 1-in-9 twist of its siblings, to stabilize long match bullets. Ruger configures its AR rifles primarily for hunters.

The AR-15 mechanism scaled up for the 7.62x51 NATO (.308) round is significantly heavier but accommodates truly potent cartridges, including the .243, .260, 7mm-08, .338 Federal and .358. Add the .250 and .300 Savage, if you favor pre-Depression rounds, the 6.5 Creedmoor if you prefer high ballistic coefficients. Randy Luth, who founded DPMS, was quick to add such chamberings to its Panther series, insisting the rifles cycle every commercial load without hiccup. (DPMS and Bushmaster have since been absorbed by The Freedom Group of companies, which controls Remington.)

Rock River's LAR-8 Varmint A4, another .308-class rifle, carries the double-edged blade of mass that counters recoil and steadies your hold but also leaves you tired on the mountain at sunset. The LAR-8 .308 differs from the daintier AR-15s most noticeably in its bolt latch. The release is not a hinged tab on the left side, but a shoe forward of the winter (oversize) trigger-guard. The 26-inch heavy stainless barrel has a target crown (ditto the alternative 20-inch barrel). The button-rifled bore is cryogenically treated and air-gauged. Twist: 1-in-10. Rock River claims its rifle will shoot into a minute of angle, and my test rifle bore out that claim. The tightest group (.6 inch) came from Remington 150 Core-Lokts. Swift Sciroccos (Remington loads) shot into a minute of angle, as did Hornady's A-Max and Federal-loaded MatchKings.

Just a sampling of the Armalite's legion spawn, these flat-black assemblies of soul-less stampings might indeed induce boredom, were it not for the interesting cartridges we feed them—and the power and accuracy we once attributed only to bolt guns!

5.56 OR .223?

While they fire the same bullets, and the cases look the same and are both considered signature cartridges for the AR-15 rifle, the .223 Remington and 5.56 NATO are not identical. The rifle chambers aren't either. A barrel cut for the .223 Remington has a shorter throat and steeper lead, in front of a neck section that's a bit smaller in diameter than one for a 5.56. Because the .223's main perceived use was in varmint rifles, where accuracy mattered, this initial chamber design made sense. The 5.56, intended for military use where high rates of fire and dirty conditions could impede easy chambering, was accurate enough if it delivered 3-minute groups. Function mattered more; hence, generous 5.56 chambers. Their extended throats also better accommodated the long tracer bullets that could hike pressures in rifles bored to suit midweight varmint bullets. Some sporting-rifle chambers are cut to permit safe use of 5.56 ammo while retaining the precision needed for shooting prairie dogs. All .223 cartridges can be used in barrels marked for the 5.56 NATO. While you shouldn't encounter problems using 5.56 ammo in a .223 rifle, it's a better idea to feed it .223s.

▲ The .45 ACP also has military roots. Here an inspector used magnification on Black Hill .45 loads.

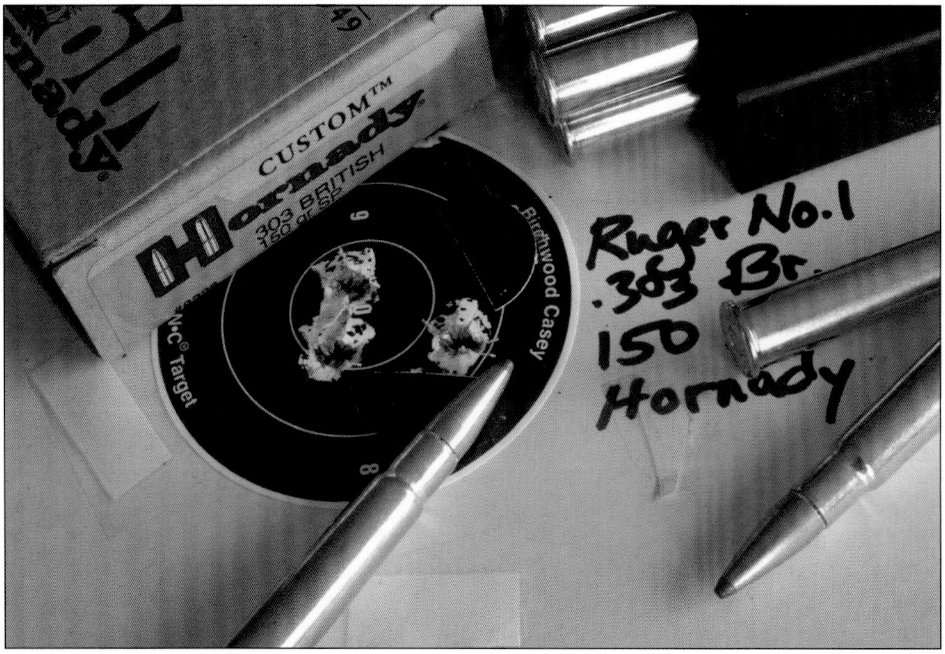

◀ Another military veteran, the .303 British, has been given new life with commercial Hornady loads.

▲ This 1873 Springfield was made only briefly in .50-70, one of the first metallic cartridges in uniform.

Chapter 9: Wildcats

Seventy years ago I visited Cooper's Landing, Alaska. Well, not actually. It was just a few weeks back as I write this, and not in the Far North, but at my loading bench. Seating bullets for a Winchester 71 in .450 Alaskan, I could only imagine those post-war wildcatting days when gunsmith Harold Johnson designed the round. Based on the .348 case, it is a potent cartridge that can hurl 400-grain bullets at 2,150 fps. The .450 Alaskan trumps the British .450-400 that in an even earlier time seemed a match for Bengal tigers and tough African game. The last of Winchester's big-bore lever rifles suited the hardy sourdoughs in woolens and shin-high boots, probing alder jungles for brown bears and willow thickets for moose.

▲ This husky wildcat was made by necking down the old .404 Jeffery (c. 1910) to take .358 bullets.

You had to work up the courage to drive a 500-grain bullet from a rear-locking lever rifle. Ackley matched the Alaskan with his jaw-jarring .450-348. The .450 Fuller joined these bruisers in the 71. Ralph Payne and John Howell also developed wildcats on the .348. Perhaps the most sensible change: a simple neck expansion to .358, to accommodate the generous and versatile suite of .35-caliber bullets.

Not that the parent .348 as factory loaded was a flyweight. Its 250-grain bullet left the muzzle at 2,350 fps and churned up 3,000 foot-pounds—as much as a .30-06 (the .348 holds 10 percent more fuel). But the blunt bullets required in the 71's tube magazine limited reach. The 71 didn't last long. Production began in 1935, ending in 1957 as hunters turned to scoped bolt rifles spewing pointed bullets at Mach 3.

"See what you can do with it." Steve Kerby had loaned me his 71 in .450 Alaskan, with a batch of .348 cases, months earlier, but other projects got in the way. At last I shut the door to the twenty-first century and pawed through my stash of powders. I picked Scot 3032, H322, H4895 and Winchester 748, to use with bullets from Northern Precision, Hornady and Speer, 325 to 400 grains.

Expanding a .348 case to .45 caliber is best done in two steps. RCBS forming dies with .30-to-.40 then .40-to-.45 expander balls yield a straight, tapered case. Next, firing a loaded round in a .450 Alaskan chamber puts a shoulder into the hull and reduces body taper. I hand-weighed powder charges and seated bullets without crimping. Had these been hunting loads, I'd have crimped the bullets in place, because the stiff recoil of the .450 Alaskan can jam bullets back in their hulls in the magazine. To form cases, I loaded the first-generation rounds in the chamber singly.

Boom! Even without elk down-range, shooting the 71 and home-brewed loads was great fun. All the cases emerged beautifully formed, with no pressure signs—though one charge drove 400-grain Speers at nearly 2,100 fps.

Alas, I had to return that fetching 71. But I learned that Steve also had a Browning (Miroku) 71 reproduction, whose chamber had been reamed to .348 Improved. "Have you developed loads for that?" I asked. Obligingly, he swapped it for the Alaskan.

▲ Ultrasonic case cleaners (here an RCBS) give wildcatters brilliant hulls to form into new cartridges.

▲ A compact .33-caliber wildcat cut this group with a 200-grain Speer and 43.5 grains Accurate 2015.

With a set of RCBS dies, I turned out a handful of loads that shot close to a minute of angle. With that rifle, I bellied to within 100 yards of a Wyoming pronghorn and with the bead on its shoulder triggered a 200-grain softnose. The animal tipped over without a twitch. It was a satisfying shot—much more so than had I used a scoped bolt rifle with factory ammo.

Not that I've a grudge against turnbolts. Jim Busha of Colorado Springs even adapted the .348 to that action by turning off case rims and cutting extractor grooves. He dubbed his wildcats line "Heavy Express." With 40-degree shoulders and reduced body taper, these rounds added nearly 20 percent to the .348's case capacity. Jim experimented with a variety of bullet diameters.

Stout and versatile, a bolt action is your best bet for wildcatting. Dozens of different cartridges fit the same magazine and bolt face. Just change the barrel or cut a new chamber, and you're ready to load for another cartridge. I've followed this routine to indulge my wildcat fantasies, mostly with Improved cartridges, which are easy to form and a cheap and practical way to boost a rifle's horsepower. A .30-06 Improved on a Springfield action downed one of the biggest elk I've shot. Like John Nosler and many other shooters, I'm sweet on the .280 Improved. I killed an elk with my .35 Whelen Improved. While I like that cartridge, the small difference in diameter between body and neck gives little shoulder to bump, so there's not much increase in case capacity over the standard .35 Whelen. With a 26-inch barrel, I get another 200 fps; but much of that, I suspect, comes from that additional 2 inches at the muzzle.

Some wildcats come from the benches of experimenters willing to submit them to SAAMI. They include rifle-makers with ideas for a proprietary cartridge line. Roy Weatherby developed his magnums in this fashion. So did Don Allen (Dakota) and John Lazzeroni. Kenny Jarrett of "beanfield rifle" fame has several wildcats with his label, from the .220 Jaybird to the .338 Kubla-Khan a .378 Weatherby necked to .33. Jarrett's .243 Catbird is a necked-down .270 Winchester, with the shoulder blown forward. His .300 Jarrett, on the 8mm Remington Magnum hull, is ballistically a .300 Weatherby.

Speed and power are compelling seductresses. Many wildcats carry more sizzle than utility. The .408 CheyTac (Cheyenne Tactical) was developed for

▲ The wildcat 6.5 Redding, a necked-down .308, appeared years before the similar .260 Remington.

military snipers by John Taylor and Bill Wordman. Its case, based on the .416 Rigby, holds enough slow powder to drive 419-grain bullets 3,000 fps. These missiles, hand-turned from a copper/nickel alloy, remain supersonic beyond 2,200 yards and deliver more energy than a .50 BMG past 700! A 305-grain .408 spitzer can be started at 3,400 fps, about what you can get from a 50-grain bullet in the .223. As the CheyTac can generate 7,700 ft-lbs of muzzle energy, it has more thump than hunters need. And more recoil than you'll want.

But wildcats run a broad gamut, from .17 to .50, tiny to gargantuan. Rimmed and rimless, straight and bottlenecked, they number in the hundreds. Actually, thousands. Last time I checked, Dave Kiff, who supplies the industry with many specialty dies under the shingle of Pacific Tool & Gauge, had drawings for 6,000 case designs!

Handloaders charging wildcat cases would be well served by math that could tell them, after first shots, how many grains to pile on starter loads to get top speeds safely. Alas, there's no such thing. Slight increases in velocity over a ladder of stiffer loads can lull you into thinking that for every, say, 2 grains, you'll get 50 fps, and pressures will climb as predictably. Not so. Pressures can spike suddenly as charges near case capacity, and each powder behaves differently as you approach safe limits. For example, here's a list of loads I've tried in the wildcat .35-404:

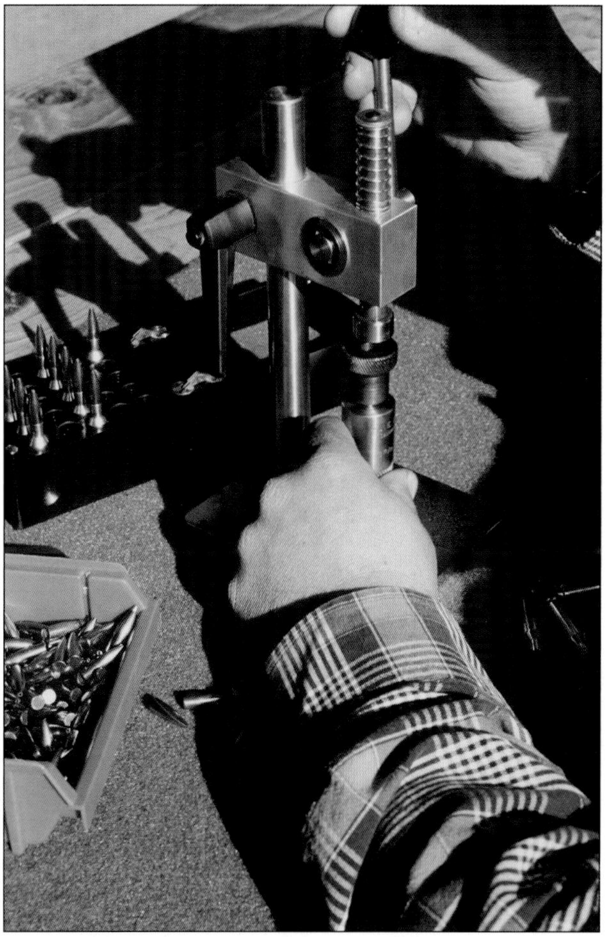

▲ Cartridges with a reputation for accuracy may just be more carefully loaded—here on an arbor press.

95 RL19 250 Speer	3141
97 RL19 250 Speer	3200
91 RL22 250 Speer	2930
100 RL22 250 Speer	3130
100 H1000 250 Hornady	2904
103 H1000 250 Speer	3123
92 H4831 250 Hornady	2935
95 H4831 250 Hornady	3019
95 3100 250 Speer	3043
97 3100 250 Speer	3126

Note that RL-19 adds about 30 fps per grain, RL-22 about 22 *at these levels in this case*. Adding 3 grains of H1000, however, bumps velocity 180 fps—60 per grain! I got a similar rate of increase from

Accurate 3100, while H4831 behaves more like RL-19. These results came from powders similar in burn rate, with same-weight bullets near practical (comfortable) velocity limits. Conclusion: you're smart to add powder cautiously. You can't assume that any of these powders will act the same in a .30 Mashburn hull as they do in the .35-404, or that they'll give the same increments of push at all charge weights.

Sometimes you'll nudge charges ever higher without seeing much more giddy-up in the bullets. In one of my .338-06 rifles, I got these chronograph readings:

76 H4831 210 Partition	2927
77 H4831 210 Partition	2907
78 H4831 210 Partition	2916

The temptation here is to bump the charges a little more, because nothing's happening. Actually, the variation you'll get chornographing some loads can hide the build-up of pressures and even velocities. While the analogy isn't perfect, you might liken such a dilemma to the task of starting a fire on a windy day. Dousing a pile of sticks with lighter fluid as matches flare out, you might conclude you need more and more lighter fluid because nothing's happening. Spare yourself and your rifle: hike charges gradually!

Wildcat cartridges that have crossed my bench include the .270 Redding, developed by Richard Beebe at Redding on the .308 hull decades before the .260 and 7mm-08. I prefer the Redding's 30-degree shoulder. An earlier short .270 arrived in the 1940s, when F.R. Krause of Albuquerque and Roy Triplett of Cimarron, New Mexico necked down the .300 Savage, set the shoulder back for a .270-length neck and steepened the shoulder angle to 28 degrees. Charles Evans and Bliss Titus put their brand on this round, now commonly ascribed to Mr. Titus. It's a good fit for Model 99 rifles originally barreled to .300 Savage (.308 magazines aren't the same and can handle a broader suite of cartridges). As rising production costs torpedoed the 99 in 1997, the .300 Savage and derivatives lost their shine. The .270 Titus can drive 130-grain bullets at over 2,700 fps.

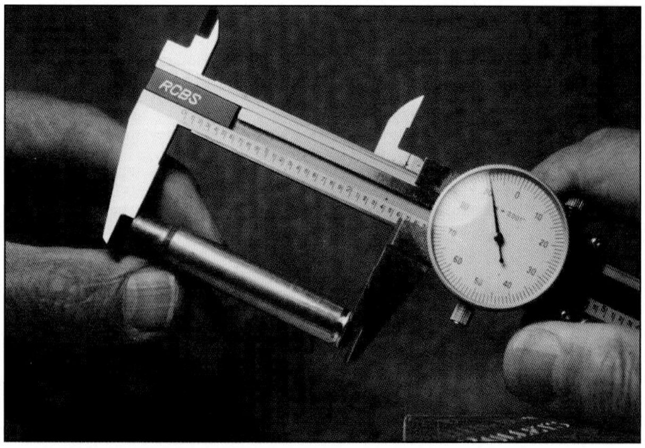

▲ A dial calipers is exceedingly useful. Handloading wildcats, case length can be a crucial measure.

More ambitious is P. O. Ackley's .270-257 Improved. The disparity between this cartridge and the 7x57 Improved is no greater than that between the .270 Winchester and .280 Remington. Each of these pairs is pretty much identical, launching same-weight bullets differing in diameter by .007. The .270-257 Improved has just about the same case capacity as the .270 Winchester. Neither matches the .270 Howell, wildcatted by veteran handloader and gun guru Ken Howell. That hull has the common .473 head but a longer body, to beat the .270 Winchester by 150 fps. Howell wildcats include several other useful rounds.

Hawk wildcats hew to the 2.50-inch case length of the '06 clan and short belted magnums. Fred Zeglin and Bob Fulton, both living near Casper, Wyoming during the mid-1990s, designed Hawks from .240 to .411. Fred built me a rifle in .411 Hawk, which I used to kill a caribou. No surprise to me or Fred, or, probably, the caribou.

Other wildcats have seduced me. Some, like fleeting romances, were quickly forgotten. The best earned a permanent place on the die shelf and rifle rack—but, in truth, offer little I can't get from factory-loaded alternatives. Any short list of favorites would surely include the .25 Souper.

In his *Handbook for Shooters and Reloaders*, P. O. Ackley wrote of the Souper: "This cartridge is quite similar to the Improved .250-3000 but came at a much later date and did not gain popularity to any degree. It is made by necking the .308 Winchester case to .25 with no other change. Coming after the

▲ One of Wayne's favorite wildcats is the .25 Souper, a .243 necked up. It trumps the .250 Improved.

introduction of such fine and popular cartridges as the Improved .257 and of course the very fine standard .257, it [has] little to recommend it over existing [.25s] similar in design. . . ."

Though the .25 Souper won't match the .257 Roberts Improved, it's a furlong ahead of the .250 Savage and trounces .257 Roberts factory loads. In short actions, it's a better fit than the Roberts, which derives from the 2.235-inch 7x57 hull, as does the 6mm Remington. Both are a tad long for rifle actions developed around the 2.015-inch .308 and offspring. You must seat bullets well into the powder space of the 7x57 and its progeny, negating somewhat the value of the longer hull. Better to use a cartridge that matches the magazine when a mid-weight bullet is seated with its base at or near the bottom of the neck.

Nit-picking, perhaps. But the field of hunting cartridges is so crowded now, handloaders are often reduced to conjuring significance from trivialities. If you're content with your .250 Savage, .257 Roberts or .25-06, a wildcat .25 probably has little appeal unless you can be satisfied and curious at the same time. I like those three cartridges, but I prefer the .25 Souper.

It was a love affair long denied. The late *Field & Stream* shooting editor Warren Page may have written the first text I read on this round. The hull seemed nicely proportioned. The useful range of bullet weights and styles appealed to me. So too the ease of forming cases. While you can neck down the .308, I prefer to neck *up* the .243. There's just .014 change in neck diameter, light work for an expander ball.

Oddly, decades passed before I got serious about a rifle in .25 Souper. Capable Texas gunmaker Charlie Sisk came up with a short Remington 700 action and a 24-inch Lilja barrel with 1-in-10 twist. He squared the bolt face, lapped in the lugs and trued up the receiver and barrel shank. Before assembling the metal, he installed one of his own recoil lugs.

"It looks like an ordinary Remington washer," he explains. "But it's not stamped out. Mine are machined from 416 stainless steel, then bored and surface-ground by CNC. The result is a lug that's true and flat. They fit the barrel perfectly. I make 'em .200, .300 and .500 thick." I chose a .300 lug.

Charlie favors Brownell's Acraglas for bedding, and he used it on this 700. "My father had an old Farmall tractor whose radiator sprung a leak. Rather than pulling it for repair, we mixed some Acraglas to dab on the hole. It's held for more than 20 years." Charlie concedes that if Acraglas had failed as bedding compound, he'd keep it around for tractors. But it helps his rifles shoot very well.

Charlie installed a Timney trigger and a Hi-Tech Specialties stock from Mark Bansner. One-piece Talley alloy mounts add little weight, with a look to complement the rifle's classic profile. They align the Swarovski 3-9x36 (one of my favorite hunting scopes) right in front of my eye.

Recoil, as you might expect, borders on the negligible. The rifle hops like a .243. But the Souper accommodates heavier bullets. It has significantly more capacity than the .250 Savage, a tad less than the .257 Roberts. You can beat the Souper with the Improved Roberts in long actions. But deer won't notice a difference. Here's how handloads in the .25 Souper compare to its factory-loaded competition (table on following page).

The Sisk .25 Souper printed seven three-shot groups at or under .75 inch. No signs of excessive pressure surfaced on the Winchester cases or primers. I got no sticky bolt lifts with any of these loads—though they are ambitious and, of course, should be approached cautiously. Ackley, by the way, lists 87-grain bullets at 3,400 fps, a 60-grain at 4,000, both with IMR 4320.

COMPARISONS OF .25 SOUPER WITH FACTORY-LOADED .24S AND .25S

Cartridge	Load	Muzzle velocity (fps)	Group size (in.)
.243 Winchester	Federal factory, 85 Sierra	3320	
	Federal factory, 100 Nosler Partition	2960	
6mm Remington	Remington factory, 100 PSPCL	3100	
.250 Savage	Remington factory, 100 PSP	2820	
.257 Roberts	Remington factory, 117 SPCL	2650	
.257 Roberts	Hornady factory, 117 SST	2780	
.257 Roberts	Federal +P factory, 120 Nosler Partition	2780	
.257 Roberts	Hornady Light Magnum factory, 117 SST	2940	
.25-06	Federal factory, 90 Sierra Varminter HP	3440	
.25-06	Remington factory, 100 PSPCL	3230	
.25-06	Remington factory, 120 PSPCL	2990	
.25-06	Hornady Light Magnum factory, 117 SST	3110	
.25 Souper	41 IMR 4064, 87 Hornady	3335	.75
	43 H380, 87 Hornady	3200	1.50
	44 H414, 100 Nosler Ballistic Tip	3170	.05 (best!)
	48 RL-19 100 Nosler Ballistic Tip	3325	.35
	46 H4350 100 Speer	3240	.85
	44 W760 100 Speer	3140	2.00
	40 Vihtavuori N-150 100 Sierra	3090	.85
	39 Varget 100 Sierra	3077*	1.15
	43 H4350 115 Nosler Ballistic Tip	3097*	1.00
	45 A3100 115 Nosler Ballistic Tip	2720*	1.00
	44 H4831 115 Nosler Partition	2917*	1.10
	46 RL-22 115 Nosler Ballistic Tip	3030	1.50
	44 WP Big Game 110 Berger VLD	3145*	.75
	44 Vihtavuori N-160 110 Berger VLD	3020	.35
	47 WMR 117 Sierra flatbase	2885	.25
	46 WP Big Boy 117 Sierra flatbase	2730	.75
	45 NMR 120 Hornady	2945	.35 (2 shots)

* Wider variations in chronograph readings than attributable to the loads may have been caused by bright sunlight on the chrony's screens. The gremlins left after I installed new shade.

Whatever the shape of your ideal cartridge, wildcatting is a graduate course in handloading—and, like graduate research, titillates your curiosity with the dual rewards of exploration and discovery.

▲ Before the .300 Winchester appeared in 1963, wildcatters got a potent .30 by necking down the .338.

A SHELF FULL OF MANUALS

Even when handloading a common cartridge, you'll do well to buy several manuals. While you can safely rely on one, you'll get data for more powders and a wider range of "maximum" loads as you add volumes. Wildcatting, you'll want as many references as you can muster, to check multiple loads for cartridges of similar dimensions and capacities. I usually spread three or four manuals on the desk when picking loads for a new cartridge. Working with the .270 Redding, for example, I sifted many .243 loads, dozens more for the .308. Soon I knew which powders should work best, and had a feel for starting loads. With "from-scratch" rounds, I load 5 to 10 percent below charges I think will prove useful. Commercial rounds in factory-chambered rifles permit a less conservative approach. Manuals are more conservative now than was the case before every other suit on the street was a class-action attorney.

THE MYTH OF ACCURATE CARTRIDGE

Are there cartridges with a bent to accuracy? It's hard to say any is *inherently* accurate, even if proven by able marksmen in rifles that shoot one-hole groups. Ace gunmaker D'Arcy Echols has his list of favorites. It includes the 7x57, .308, .30-06, .300 H&H, .300 Winchester, .375 H&H—even the wildcat .458 Lott (the .375 case necked up). He'll add the .300 Weatherby if he can cut the chamber with a short throat. He doesn't like the .280 Remington or Winchester's .338 quite as well. "Temperamental to handload." But just about any cartridge, given its best load in an accurate barrel, will print tight groups. The barrel matters a great deal, and it seems no two are identical. Echols once replaced a disappointing barrel with one of the same make, weight, twist, chamber—and groups shrank!

He warns against predicting long-range accuracy at short yardage. One of his .300 Weatherbys averaged .6 for three shots at 100 yards. But it would also average .6 at 200 and shoot into an inch at 300! That powerful round was hardly developed for punching one-hole knots in paper. But D'Arcy's do. With another of his .300s, I nipped a .115 group at 100 yards. Still, another averaged .360 *for 10 groups*. One tested at 300, 400 and 500 yards kept the mean spread to a half-minute of angle!

For years the .222 was the darling of the benchrest circuit, but PPCs and others have unseated it. Handloading can turn an ordinary cartridge into a winner. There's no magic in a number.

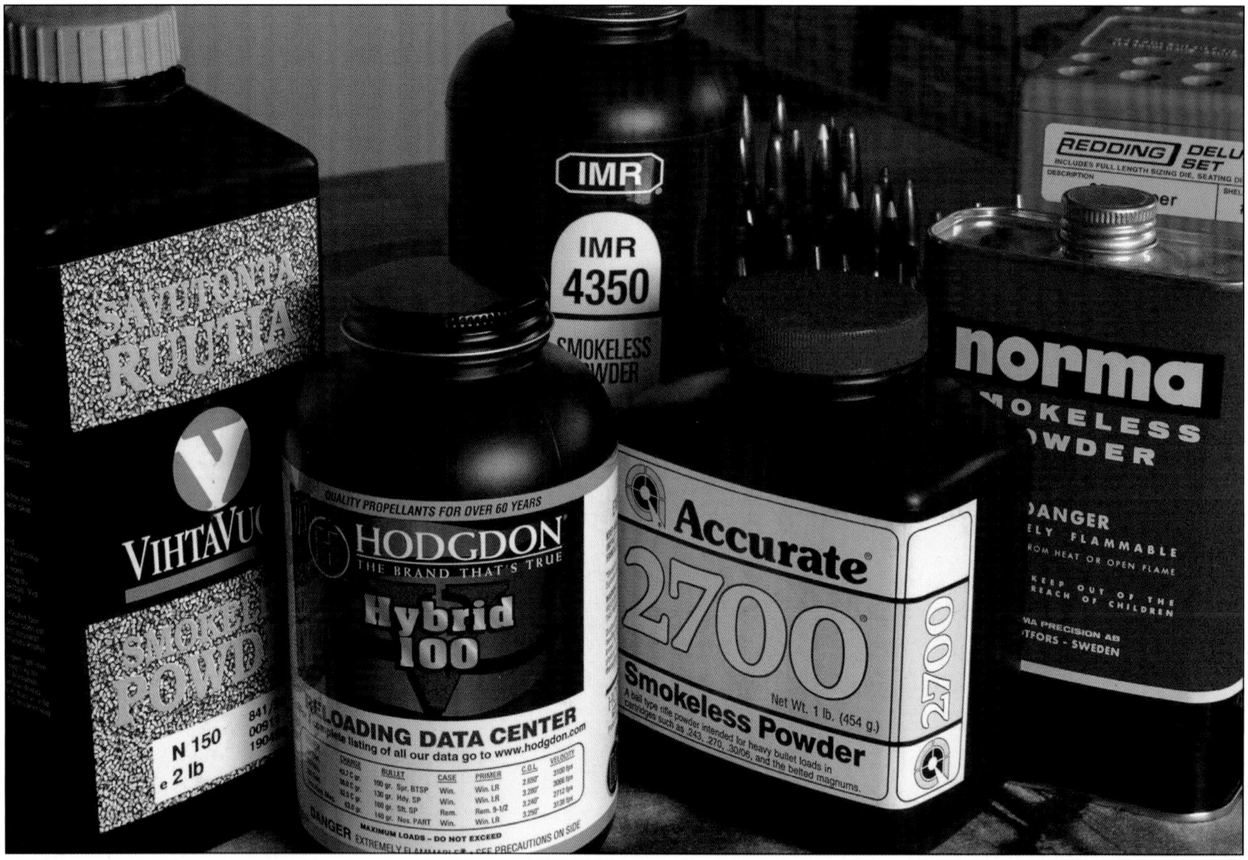

▲ Early wildcatters would have welcomed the wide selection of powders available to handloaders now.

A CHAMP BY ANY OTHER MEASURE

Several wildcat cartridges have become commercial successes—most famously, perhaps, the .22-250 and .25-06. The .338-06, an efficient, versatile hunting round, was long overdue for factory adoption when Art Alphin pushed this easily-fashioned wildcat through SAAMI hoops to establish its dimensions. Weatherby had the gumption to chamber it the trim, six-lug Mark V Ultra Lightweight. I thought both the rifle and Norma-loaded Weatherby ammo would wow shooters. I was wrong. In 2004, three years after it listed the round, Weatherby dropped the .338-06. "Shooters look to us for high-velocity rifles," shrugged a Weatherby source. The .338-06 remains, in my view, one of the best big game cartridges ever. Alas, to date it has had one of the shortest commercial tenures of any wildcat.

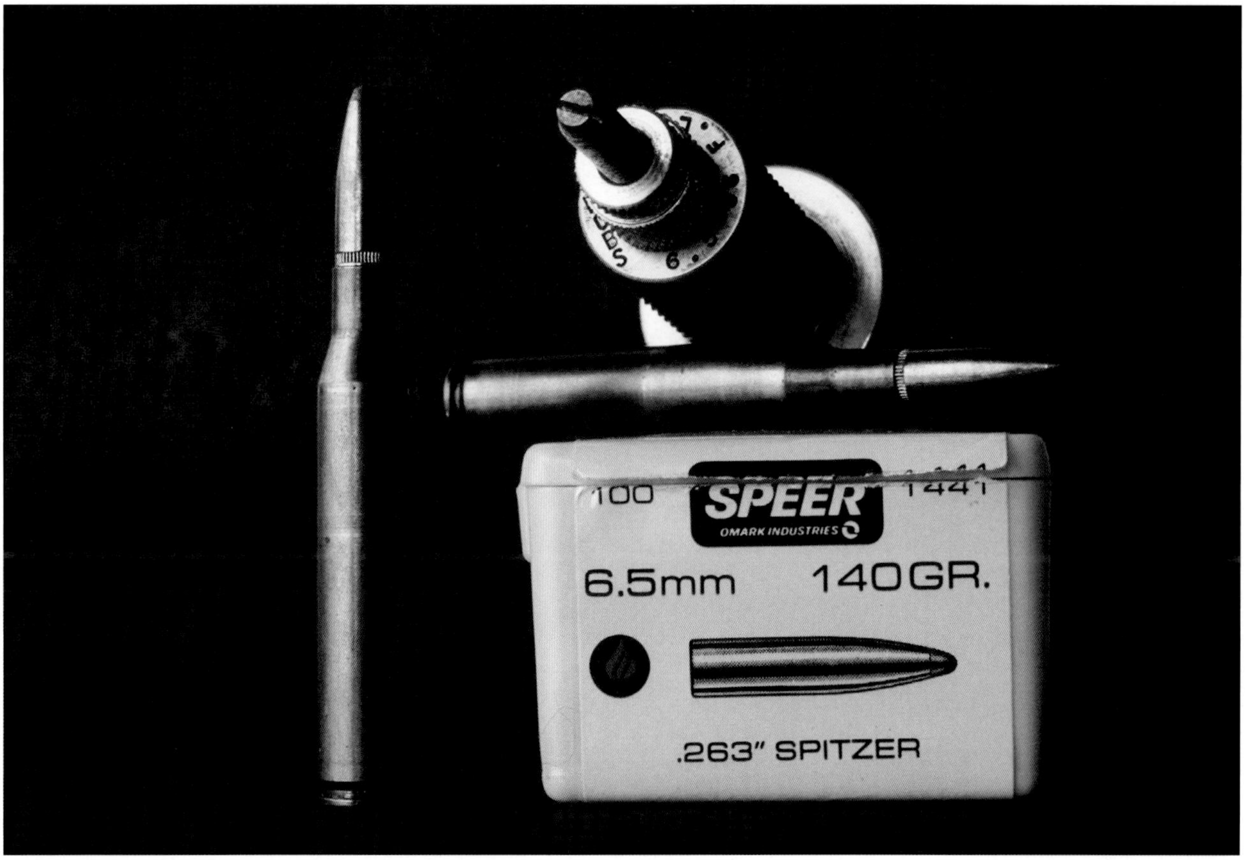

▲ The 6.5-06 (.30-06 necked to .264), is a useful wildcat that never caught on. Too similar to the .270?

Chapter 10: Fast-Steppers Gone Factory

The siren call of high velocity has long inspired handloaders to develop "Improved" cartridges and wildcats. Most of this work has focused on small-bore rounds because their applications most effectively make use of quick bullets. Also, recoil is less intimidating while hurrying little hollowpoints along than when throttling up missiles big enough to upend brown bears.

TINY, WITH STING

Your first gun may well have been a .17. A Red Ryder, perhaps. Or one of those potent Daisy M-25 pumps a pal used to put a welt on my brow before we decided BB-gun fights were the height of folly. Those smooth-bores, like Olympic-class air rifles that drill one-hole groups at 10 meters, have .177 bores.

Centerfire .17s for coyote country, 'chuck pastures and prairie dog towns are actually .172s.

Of course, there are other differences. Speed, for instance.

The .17 Remington, introduced in 1971 in the Model 700 rifle, starts 20-grain AccuTips at 4,250 fps, 25-grain hollowpoints at 4,040, by factory charts. Surely P. O. Ackley had such figures in mind when experimenting with .17s on the .218 Bee Improved case at the end of World War II. Later wildcats on the .222 and other hulls led, in 1965, to the .17/223, fashioned by Dave Wolfe. The .17 Remington was also based on the .223, though Remington set back the 23-degree shoulder to lengthen the neck.

The .17 Remington was hailed by Midwest fox hunters, as its frangible bullets vaporized inside, leaving pelts undamaged. Complaints had to do with bore cleaning. You needed a skinny rod and special brush. Untended .17 bores fouled badly. Few hunters would fire enough rounds to see throats erode, but many expected damage. Bullets clocking Mach 4 weren't kind to steel, the gas pushing them even less so.

Decades earlier, shooters had said the same about the .220 Swift.

In the 1950s I was young, music came from phonographs and you could buy a new Chevrolet for $1,500. That decade brought wildcatting to a fever pitch. New cartridges proliferated on loading benches as riflemen ratcheted up bullet speeds. Varmint shooters fashioning .17s drew laughs at first. But tiny 25-grain bullets clocking over 3,300 fps flew flat and hit surprisingly hard, with little noise and almost no muzzle jump, from cases as small as the .22 Hornet Improved. P. O. Ackley had found the .218 Bee and .222 Remington hulls as big as any .17 bullet could justify. Clocking 3,800 fps, the hot .17 Mach IV was essentially a necked-down .223 chopped from 1.75 to 1.40 inches. It was offered by the O'Brien Rifle Company of Las Vegas.

Interest in .17 bores subsided in the 1960s. Riflemen hailed Remington's adoption of the .22-250 in 1965. Then, in 1970, the .17 Remington appeared. With a 25-grain bullet exceeding 4,000 fps, it promised to inflict the bore-fouling headache that had plagued .17 wildcatters decades earlier. But clean propellants and moly-coated bullets mitigated this problem.

The .17 Remington Fireball, introduced in 2007, is a necked-down .221 Fireball (developed for Remington's bolt-action XP-100 handgun in 1963). A shortened .222 Remington, the original Fireball earned a small but faithful following. The .17 Fireball mimics the .17 Mach IV, with a 1.41-inch case and a 30-degree shoulder. It launches a 20-grain AccuTip V bullet at 4,000 fps. The .17 Fireball has replaced the .17 Remington in the 700 rifle. But the older cartridge still appears on Remington's ammo roster.

Milder than the Fireball is Hornady's recent .17 Hornet. Though .17s on this diminutive case date

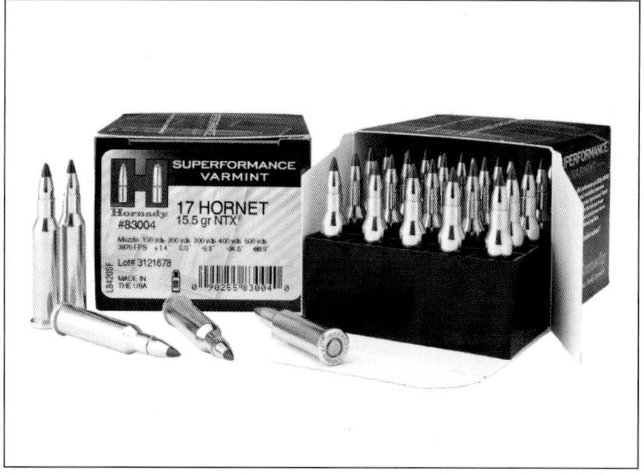

▲ With its tiny, super-accurate bullets, Hornady began loading the .17 Hornet—to nearly 3,900 fps!

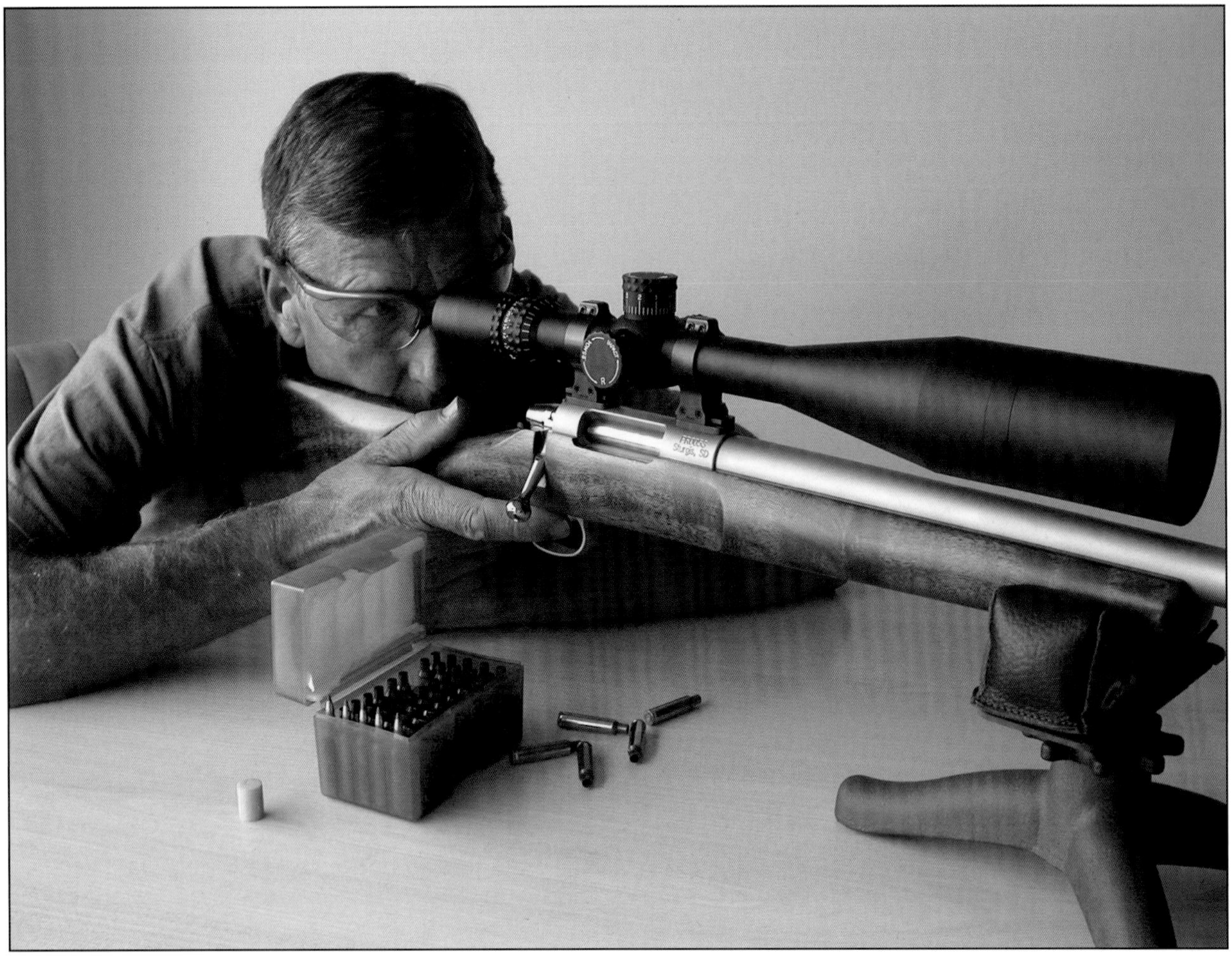

▲ Wayne fires a Nesika rifle in .20 Tactical. This super-accurate rifle has little recoil, shoots very flat.

to the halcyon wildcatting days after the war, this is the first cataloged. It's a frisky pup indeed, 15-grain NTX bullets clocking 3,860 fps, a 20-grain V-Max at 3,650! Few rifles are so chambered; the dimensions of this dainty round suit it neither to rimfire receivers nor short-action centerfires. Ruger does offer it on a modified 77/17 rimfire mechanism.

WILD CHILD

Now, in 2015, the .22-250 is either 50 years old or 80. Its 1965 debut in the Remington cartridge line-up came with SAAMI blessing. But by then it had logged more field time than the .270 or .300 H&H Magnum. It had won bucket-loads of benchrest medals and almost certainly accounted for more 'chucks, foxes and coyotes than any other centerfire .22.

The .22-250's parent is the .250 Savage, developed by Charles Newton. Schooled in law, Newton soon left legal practice to design rifles and cartridges. In 1905 he necked the .28-30 Stevens down to .22. Between 1909 and 1912 he fashioned the .25 Special on the .30-06 case, and a similar 7mm (think .25-06 and .280). His .256 Newton, a 6.5mm round on a slightly shortened '06 hull, proved less popular than its successor, the .250-3000. Introduced in 1913 on a 1.912-inch case for short-action rifles, this quarter-bore cartridge was so named for the velocity of its 87-grain load, which Savage chose over the 100-grain bullet recommended by Newton. The lightning speed

▲ Handloading the .250 Savage can yield ammo to trump factory loads, limited and long unchanged.

of 3,000 fps was good ad material. The .250-3000 became, later, the .250 Savage.

Roy Chapman Andrews, an explorer who led expeditions for the American Museum of Natural History, called the .250-3000 "the most wonderful cartridge ever developed." But smallbore enthusiasts also hailed Newton's .22 High Power, which he'd developed in 1911 on the .25-35 case. Hunters fired the High Power's .227 bullets (achieving 2,800 fps) not just at rodents, but also at game as big as deer, even tigers! Meanwhile, accuracy buffs had turned from dropping-block and lever-action rifles to bolt-actions. By the 1930s, wildcatters J.E. Gebby, J.B. Smith, Harvey Donaldson, Grosvenor Wotkyns and John Sweaney had come up with a .22 on the .250 case. A version by Gebby and Smith, circa 1937, became the "Varminter"—a name copyrighted by Jerry Gebby.

It is astonishing that the .22-250 trundled along for 30 years as a wildcat while, in 1936, the Swift made the charter list of chamberings in the Model 70 Winchester. Even as Swift shooters lamented short case and throat life, the .22-250 stayed in its shadow. The Swift's capacious hull allowed 4,110 fps with 48-grain bullets. But the Varminter nipped at its hocks. Afield, these two hotrods are equals.

Now the Swift has faded, while the .22-250 enjoys international acclaim. It's chambered in every varmint-class rifle I can think of, domestic and foreign. It even made Remington's list of ill-fated EtronX cartridges developed for electronic ignition.

With 50-grain bullets at 3,800 fps, the .22-250 carries more than 500 ft-lbs of energy to 400 yards —a knockout blow to any 'chuck, fox or coyote. That bullet starts as fast as a 40-grain spitzer from a .223, but it bucks wind better and, at 400 yards, outpaces the .223's by 270 fps. For deer the 6mms excel, though 55- and 60-grain bullets in the .22-250 have taken boxcar-loads of whitetails. A 60-grain .22-250 bullet at 3,600 fps beats a 75-grain .243 bullet off the blocks by 200 fps and is still faster at 400, where it delivers 600 ft-lbs. Loaded to 3,500 fps, 64-grain spitzers from the .22-250 send more energy to 100 yards than do 170-grain softpoints from the .32 Special!

Handloading the .22-250 is easy. Pick from myriad bullets of 40 to 70 grains and from a generous array of powders midrange in burning rate—AA2520, H335, IMR 3031 and 4320, Winchester 748, BL-C(2), RL-15, Vihtavuori 140, TAC and Varget, for example. Faster fuels like RL-7 and IMR 4198 work as well. Hodgdon's new IMR 4166 Enduron propellant reduces the copper fouling resulting from the .22-250's high bullet velocities. You'll find plenty of accurate, quick-stepping factory loads for this cartridge from Black Hills and Federal, Hornady, Remington and Winchester. These offerings represent the range of bullet weights and types available for the .22-250, and velocities you can expect from handloads.

.22-250 LOADS

43-grain TNT (Speer, Federal)

	Muzzle	100 yds.	200 yds.	300 yds.	400 yds.
Velocity, fps	4000	3250	2620	2070	1590
Energy, ft-lbs	1530	1010	655	405	240
Arc, inches	-1.5	+0.9	0	-6.1	-20.8

50-grain AccuTip (Remington)

	Muzzle	100 yds.	200 yds.	300 yds.	400 yds.
Velocity, fps	3800	3339	2925	2546	2198
Energy, ft-lbs	1603	1238	949	720	536
Arc, inches	-1.5	+0.8	0	-4.9	-15.9

60-grain SP (Hornady)

	Muzzle	100 yds.	200 yds.	300 yds.	400 yds.
Velocity, fps	3530	3131	2768	2433	2122
Energy, ft-lbs	1660	1306	1021	789	600
Arc, inches	-1.5	+1.0	0	-5.6	-17.1

Standard rifling twist for the .22-250 is 1-in-14, which suffices for most common varmint bullets. But the advent of extra-heavy .22 spitzers, and lead-free poly-tips long for their weight, has sent shooters to 1-in-12 rifling. In general, if you stick with lead-core bullets no heavier than 55 grains, the 14-inch spin should work fine. For 60- to 70-grain jacketed spitzers, and the 53-grain Barnes TSX, 1-in-12 excels.

SIXES IN TRACK SHOES

When the '06 was still less than a decade old, Charles Newton developed his .256, which drove a 129-grain .264 bullet at 2,760 fps. Case head and rim diameters matched those of the .30-06; but the case was .04 shorter. The .256 had barely cleared the starting blocks before its prolific designer came up with a .250 on a more compact case. Newton handloaded 100-grain bullets to 2,800 fps. But Savage, for whom he developed the round, chose instead to load 87-grain missiles at 3,000 fps. The .250-3000 was a hit in 1899, then in Model 99 lever-actions; but later competition from the .257 Roberts and .243 throttled its sales in bolt rifles. Winchester and Remington catalog a single 100-grain .250 load apiece. In an accurate Cooper Model 54, the best I can manage from either of these loads are groups the size of pool balls. But handloads of 34 grains IMR 4895 pushing 87-grain Sierras at 3,065 fps deliver .6-inch knots!

I can't say why Newton skipped the 6mm bore. He could easily have hot-rodded a 6mm. The first of these—at least, to achieve commercial standing Stateside—had arrived in the 1895 Lee straight-pull bolt rifle. Also called the .236 Navy, the 6mm Lee Navy was chambered in 15,000 infantry rifles. Its 112-grain round-nose bullet left the muzzle at an uninspiring 2,560 fps. That long missile mandated a sharp rifling twist: 1-in-7½. The .220 Swift on the Lee Navy's semi-rimmed case followed in 1935, the last year commercial .236 ammo was produced.

Not until the 1955 would US companies again tool up for 6mm cartridges. But the early 1920s brought them to life in the British Isles, where Holland & Holland introduced the .240 Flanged Nitro Express and the .240 Belted Nitro Express, or .240 Apex. Both fired 100-grain .245-diameter bullets, the belted version at 3,000 fps, the flanged (for double guns) at 2,900. Purdey's .246 Flanged, with 100-grain .253 bullets at 2,950 fps, came two years before the 1923 debut of the .242 Vickers Rimless Nitro Express with .249 bullets at 2,800. Meanwhile, in Germany, Halbe and Gerlich made rimmed and rimless versions of the .244 Halger, essentially a necked-down 6.5x57 that allegedly kicked an 87-grain .243 bullet out the muzzle at 3,700 fps! The popularity of these rounds was limited by their circulation and their distinctive diameters (.243 to .253). The Depression of the 1930s and another world war sealed their fate.

Wildcatters kept sixes alive during the early post-war years. The 6mm International on the .250 Savage case, and Fred Huntington's .243 Rockchucker on .257 Roberts brass are best-known. In the 1950s Warren Page and Remington's Mike Walker came up with the .243 Page Pooper, a forerunner of the .243 Winchester. Walker developed the 6x47 from the .222 Remington Magnum. Other 6mms were necked-down versions of the .30-30, .303 British, .30-40 Krag, .30-06. The 6mm Arch derived from 6.5x55 brass.

The other day I came across a copy of a letter written by Warren Page, then shooting editor at *Field & Stream*, to Ralph Davis, of the M. G. S. Bullet Company. It's a window into the times. The query on 6mm bullets surely reflected a need in the handloading community and may well have put one more flagstone on the path to the .243 and .244. I'll excerpt:

Dear Ralph,

Nice to hear from you again, and I hope that things are booming in the bullet business—certainly seem to be generally in the field of handloading equipment.

Right now I am messing around with the 6mms. On the rack awaiting a chance to get up to Remington for some chronograph shooting of the .243 Rock Chucker built by Homer Brown. He is also working up for me a lightweight deer rifle, on that same case, built around a 722 Remington action. I think there's a good deal of possibility in the 6mms and wouldn't fall over dead if sometime there were a commercial cartridge using that bullet diameter. Also, I am in the works of getting together a 6mm bench rest rifle—am awaiting word now from Hal Mallett of H & M Tool Company regarding reamers for a necked-down version of the .308 WCF case, a "design" more or less my own—accomplished simply by fiddling around until Brown and I can get a die that would squeeze the .308 down to 6mm and leave a fairly sharp shoulder on it! No calculations, just guesswork, but it looks as good as some of those that the boys sweat over! Have my barrel ready for it. Hence it would appear that I could use some 6mm bullets if you've got some that you figure are really hot.

Then I'll have to run some more accuracy tests and some more chronograph dope on my 7mm Washburn Short Magnum which I used up in the Yakutat last spring, and in Wyoming last fall—Art Washburn and I have done a few more shenanigans with it and I'll probably have to rework all my charges. I have chronograph dope on the original barrel with 160- and 195-grain bullets—want also to rerun that and to incorporate data on 180- and 200-grain slugs. In the meantime, I got curious about .33's and am having a .333 OKH made up on short Magnum brass by Charlie O'Neil. Do you make any .33 caliber bullets? Fred Barnes does and I have a few that I got from England, but I am not sure whether you swage any in that diameter or not. . . .

Sure wish I knew how many bullets were sold to handloaders each year. Al Freeland told me the other day that he sold 7,800,000 in a year, and his shop is not primarily a handloaders' shop. Do you have any idea as to what the total might possibly be? Nobody but nobody has any conception of exactly how many reloaders there are in this country. I get more damned mail on that than almost anything else except shotgun muzzle attachments!

Incidentally, in 6mm I have some spire-point bullets which are of the 2D type, and I suspect were made by you . . . They shot quite well in my .243 Rock Chucker and look to be a very slick job of bullet making—I am inclined to believe that I can use considerably stiffer charges with this type of bullet. . . .

Most sincerely yours,
Warren Page
Shooting Editor

In 1955 Holland & Holland squeezed the .300 H&H neck to 6mm and announced the .244 H&H Belted Rimless Magnum. Its 100-grain .244 bullets rocketed away at 3,500 fps. Stateside that year, more practical, efficient designs appeared. Factory loads for

Winchester's .243 (on the .308 case, with original 20-degree shoulder) fired 80- and 100-grain bullets. Remington's .244 (on the .257 Roberts hull, but with steeper 26-degree shoulder) came out with 75- and 90-grain bullets. That slight disparity proved decisive at market. Barrels in .243 had 1-in-10 rifling, those in .244, 1-in-12. Rumor spread that .244s would not stabilize 95- to 105-grain bullets. Sales tipped in favor of the .243, as many riflemen wanted a 6mm that would kill deer as well as coyotes and rodents. Now, while long bullets do like faster twist, a Remington 722 in .244 shot very well for me with bullets to 100 grains.

Sometimes perception trumps fact. Remington responded in 1963 with a "new" 6mm. In truth, it was identical to the .244; but Remington barrels marked 6mm were (and are) rifled 1-in-9. Loaded with with 80-, 90- and 100-grain spizers, this round has taken root but still lags the .243 in sales. Ballistically, the two are close, the edge going to the 6mm with its greater case capacity. But short actions require deep seating of long bullets in the 6mm hull. Early on, claim gnomes in some ballistics labs, .243 factory loads were tested in 22-inch barrels, 6mm ammo in 26-inch bores. And .243 cartridges were commonly held to 47,900 psi, versus 51,000 for 6mms. So velocity differences were exaggerated. When both cartridges are handloaded to 50,000 psi with IMR-4350, both clock about 3,100 fps with 100-grain bullets.

While it has been widely chambered and ranks among the most popular of centerfire rounds, the .243 is arguably under-appreciated. Many .243 rifles go to youngsters, women and beginning hunters, the implication being only square-jawed marksmen can brook the recoil of "real" big game cartridges. Verily, almost everyone shoots better with rifles that don't kick hard. Repeat whacks to the gums can quickly put a flinch in your shooting routine. A .243 with

▲ The short powder column of the 6mm BR delivers surprising velocity and, more important, precision.

100-grain bullets pops you only half as hard as a .280 with 160-grain loads. A .300 Winchester with 180s is three times as violent!

An 85-grain Federal Trophy Copper bullet from a .243 exits at 3,200 fps, about what you'll get from a 55-grain missile leaving a .223. At 400 yards drift in a 10-mph crosswind is 21 inches for the .243, about 33 for the .223. The .243 reaches 400 steps with nearly 1,000 ft-lbs of energy; the .223 retains less than 500. The .243 is unquestionably a better cartridge for game bigger than coyotes. After the .243 had been afield a season, an industry survey recorded its harvest of 83 animals, mostly deer. Of those, 60 were instant one-shot kills. Thirteen other died within 200 yards. Only half a dozen had to be trailed.

At this writing, you'll find about 40 factory loads for the .243. There's a sampling at the bottom of the page.

Last month, at this writing, I carried a Savage bolt rifle in .243 on three deer hunts. Its Federal-loaded 95-grain Ballistic Tip bullets downed three bucks, each with one shot through the front ribs, at 90, 200 and 240 yards. There were no exit holes, no blood trails, but in each case the lungs were pulped. The deer all ran a short distance (30 to 40 yards), dying in stride.

Rifles in .243 and 6mm shoot flat, hit surprisingly hard and are delightfully pleasant to fire. If you present one of these sixes to a youngster or to your sweetheart, release it only on condition that you can borrow it back, "to develop better handloads for you, Honey."

A .243 ON STEROIDS

Since 1955, the only other hot 6mm to achieve commercial success has been the .240 Weatherby Magnum. It arrived in 1968, hurling 90-grain bullets at an advertised 3,500 fps and 100-grainers at nearly 3,400. The .240 derives from no other cartridge. Its 2.5-inch belted case with signature radiused shoulder has a head diameter of .473 (not .532, as on magnums fashioned from the .375 H&H). So it fits the same bolt faces as the .243. But the .240 Weatherby is a long-action cartridge—in dimension and performance a 6mm-06. Introduced in the Weatherby Mark V rifle, the .240 has made the leap to the company's more affordable Vanguard line. Twist rate: 1-in-10.

FROM QUARTER-BORE TO 6.5

When the .30-30 courted deer hunters in 1895, it had little competition. The first sporting round loaded with smokeless powder, it hurled a 160-grain bullet at nearly 2,000 fps—scorching speed for the day. Thirty-bore cartridges got another boost when the .30-06 Springfield became the US service round. The .270 broke the .30-bore mold in 1925. Flat-shooting, with the power to kill elk-size game, the .270 also drew praise for its mild recoil. Not until 1962, when Remington announced its 7mm Magnum, would a big

.243 LOADS

			Range, yards		
Manufacturer; bullet weight, type	Muzzle	100	200	300	400
Hornady 58 V-Max					
velocity, fps:	3925	3465	3052	2676	2330
energy, ft-lb:	1984	1546	1200	922	699
arc, inches:	+0.7	0	-4.4	-13.8	
Rem. 75 AccuTip BT					
velocity, fps:	3375	3065	2775	2504	2248
energy, ft-lb:	1897	1564	1282	1044	842
arc, inches:	+2.0	0	-5.2	-15.0	
Win. 95 Ballistic Silvertip					
velocity, fps:	3100	2854	2626	2410	2203
energy, ft-lb:	2021	1719	1455	1225	1024
arc, inches:	+1.4	0	-6.4	-18.9	

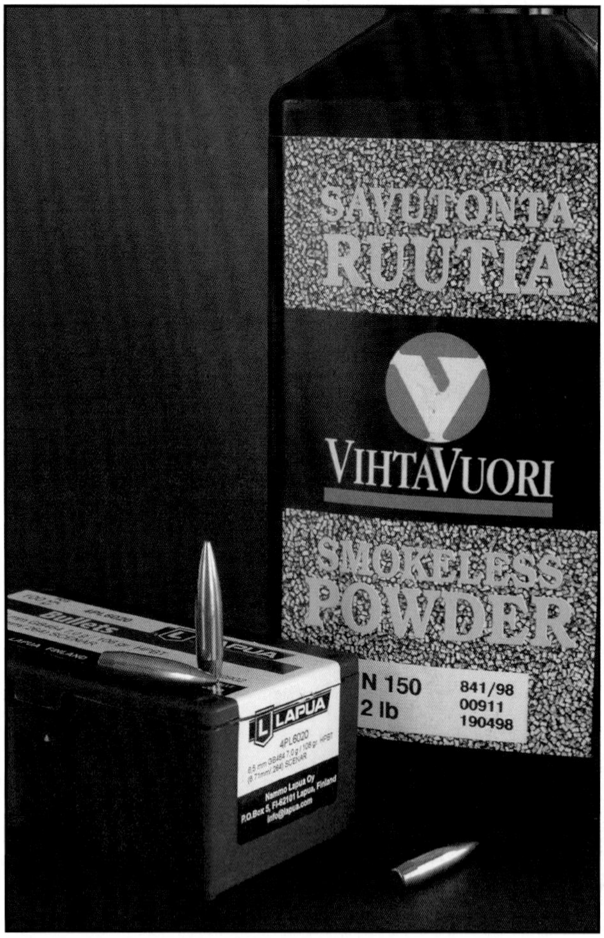

▲ The Finns have fine products for handloaders, and, with other Scandinavians, adore the 6.5 bore.

game round bring such a tide of kudos. A year after that, Remington adopted a popular wildcat, the .25-06. An ideal cartridge for deer-size game at distance, the .25-06 has since appeared in a great number of bolt-action rifles. It remains popular, if not wildly so.

Bracketed ballistically by 6mms and short-action .25s on one side and the .270 and belted 7mms on the other, the .25-06 had to shoulder its way into the growing roster of US hunting cartridges. At the same time, 6.5mm (.264) cartridges fell flat. The 6.5x55 Swedish Mauser, introduced in 1894, deserved better. It is a versatile cartridge, and adored in its home country. Though traditional 156-grain round-nose bullets loaf downrange at about 2,550 fps, Swedish hunters think that's fast enough. The 6.5x55 has killed more Scandinavian moose than any other cartridge. Explorer Frederick Courtney Selous and celebrated hunter W. D. M. Bell used the similar 6.5x54 Mannlicher-Schoenauer on beasts as imposing as elephants. Its long blunt solids penetrated pachyderm skulls. Charles Sheldon found the 6.5x54 adequate for Alaskan brown bears, sheep and moose. Trim Mannlicher-Schoenauer carbines did much to endear it to riflemen.

I've used the 6.5x55 successfully on elk, with 140-grain bullets at 2,650. Intelligent case design means smooth feeding and efficient powder burn in short barrels. I once carried a Swedish 1896 carbine for Wyoming pronghorns. The Williams aperture and 18 ½-inch barrel made the little Mauser a delight in hand. A single Norma-loaded 120-grain Ballistic Tip dropped a fine buck—instantly—in a rain-storm. Loaded with match bullets, the 6.5x55 has performed well in international 300-meter competition.

Still, post-Depression hunters in the US gave even steeply discounted 1894, 1896 and Model 38 Swedish Mausers a tepid reception. The 6.5x55 couldn't match the reach of US Springfields. Wildcatters working with .30-06 brass favored .25-caliber bullets to .264s, perhaps because the .270 was so much like the 6.5-06 and commercially available.

High-octane 6.5s date back to Charles Newton's .256, in 1913. It was a ballistic whiz, pushing its 129-grain .264 bullet at 2,760 fps. With modern powders, you can easily add 150 fps. The .256 case was similar and size and profile to the .270's.

Europe didn't long limit hunters to the ordinary, if efficient 6.5x55. In 1938 the Germans came up with the 6.5x68 Schuler, on the 8x68 hull. In Spain I once had to borrow a rifle to hunt ibex. "Shoot from here," said my guide, when we spied a ram just a little closer than Morocco. He insisted his 6.5x68S shot so flat I wouldn't have to hold high. I politely demurred. After we'd hiked a bit closer, he again urged me to fire. The ibex still appeared no bigger than a gnat. I held firm, sneaking alone inside 200 yards, where a 120-grain softnose laid the ram low.

When in 1959 Winchester announced its .264 Magnum, the 6.5's star might have risen. Based on the company's belted .458 Magnum introduced three years earlier, the .264 Winchester Magnum is nearly identical to the 7mm Remington Magnum. Bullet

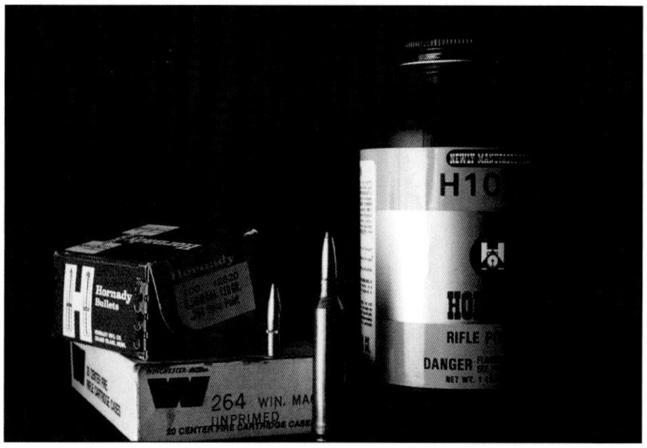

▲ Winchester's .264 appeared in 1959. It requires very slow powder, drives 6.5mm bullets very fast!

diameter differs by a mere .020. In those innocent days, after concluding my $30 Short Magazine Lee Enfield didn't reach far enough to kill every deer I wanted to bag in a hunting career yet young, I got hungry for a .264. Months of milking cows left enough coin in my jeans to snare a Mark X Mauser action and a Claro blank from Royal Arms. A winter later, I thumbed three gleaming cartridges into the rifle's belly. But I'd neglected to bed the lug tighter than the tang. The figured Claro splintered at my first shot. My tearful road back finally yielded a whitetail buck.

Like me, Winchester's hot 6.5 stumbled at the start. Announced as a long-range marvel in 1959, it spat 140-grain bullets at 3,200 fps, 100s at a blazing 3,700. But instead of promoting its new round as a flat-shooting cartridge for deer and elk, Winchester billed the .264 Magnum as a hotrod pick for deer and rockchucks. Full-page magazine ads showed the .264's maw, with the caption, "It makes a helluva noise and packs a helluva wallop!" But blast and recoil were unsettling for a deer and 'chuck round. Remington sealed the .264's fate with the 1962 debut of its 7mm Magnum, with 150-grain and 175-grain bullets for the West's biggest game. Winchester dealt another blow to the .264 with its scandalous 1963 overhaul of the Model 70 rifle, just as Remington's fetching 700 hit the stage.

While the .264 Winchester can't comfortably handle the 160-grain bullets that distinguish 7mm magnums in elk country, the ballistic coefficients and downrange energy retention of sleek 140-grain 6.5 bullets give them real authority at distance. Alas, only a few such bullets were available then. Winchester put another nail in the .264's coffin when it reduced starting velocities in its ballistics tables from 3,200 fps to 3,030 for the 140-grain Power Point. "Why, you might as well shoot a .270!" exclaimed shooters. To be fair, the .264 Winchester handloaded to its poten-

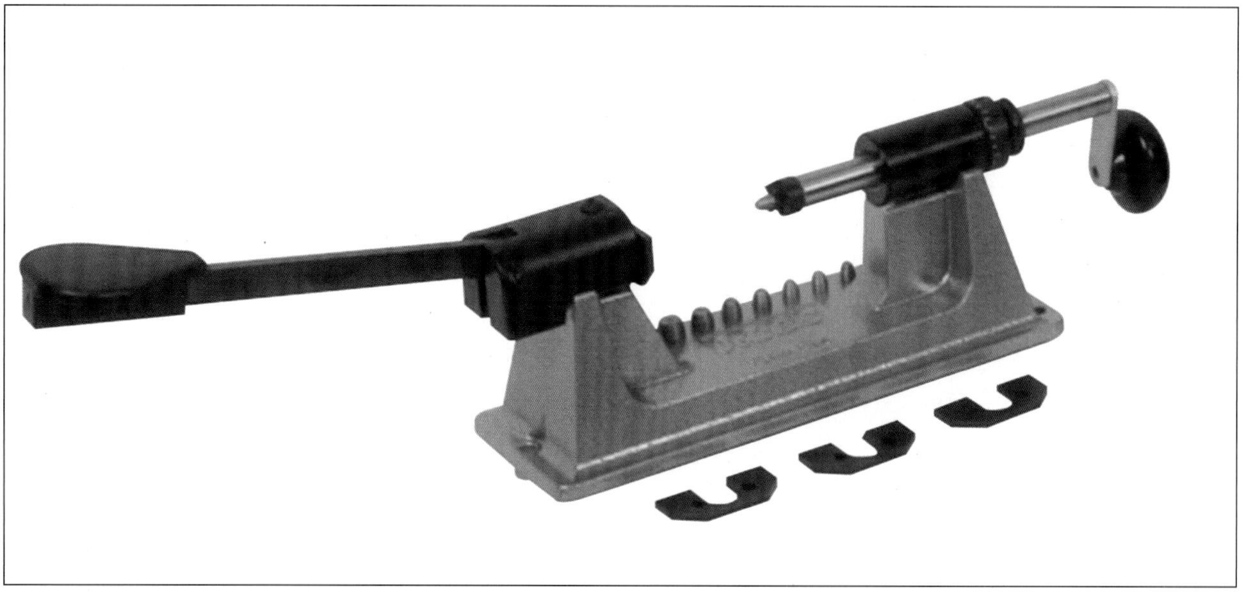

▲ Trimming cases, standard procedure for handloaders, is especially important with hot loads.

tial and fired in a Winchester M70's 26-inch barrel can push 140s faster that even the original factory claims. With slow powders like IMR 7828 and RL-25, I've clocked Sierra spitzers at over 3,300. No signs of excessive pressure.

Remington entered 6.5 territory in 1966, with the 6.5 Remington Magnum, a belted round that, with its sibling .350, appeared in the Models 600 and 660 carbines, manufactured 1965 to 1971. These rounds employed the belted hull that began life in 1912 with the .375 H&H, and was cut to 2.5 inches in the 1950s to produce the first short belted magnums. The .308-length actions of the 600 and 660 required even shorter cartridges; the 6.5 and .350 Magnums have 2.15-inch cases. Ballistically, the 6.5 Remington Magnum matches the 6.5-284. Muzzle blast from both the 6.5 Remington and .264 Winchester is grim in short barrels. The Model 660 wore a 20-inch tube, Winchester's .264 M70 Featherweight a 22-inch.

Shorter but friskier than Sweden's 6.5x55, the .260 Remington appeared in 2002. The .308 hull necked to .264, it trails the versatile 7mm-08 at market, largely because the 7mm got there first. I've seen .260s take a variety of big game once thought best hunted with .30-06-class rounds. On the last day of a Colorado hunt, I spied elk on distant slope, then sneaked to an opposite ridge and bellied the last yards in deep snow. Prone, I leveled the Kimber 84M and settled the Leupold's crosswire. A fat cow spun at my shot, dashed downhill, then tumbled to a stop in a flurry of snow, laid low by the 120 Nosler Ballistic Tip.

A growing number of shooters are taking to the 6.5-.284. This necked-down 7mm started out as a wildcat in long-range competition, with bullets of high ballistic coefficient. While now such bullets are available in all popular diameters, the .264 bore claims some of the most accurate. VLD bullets in 6.5mm keep the 6.5-284 in 1,000-yard competition. This rebated cartridge also excels for game as heavy as elk. I killed a bull at 300 yards with a 140-grain Nosler Partition from an E.R. Shaw rifle in 6.5-284. The animal collapsed instantly. Like other mid-length rounds, this 6.5 excels in 3-inch bolt actions like those by New Ultra Light Arm. Norma loads the cartridge. So does Black Hills. Lapua lists 6.5-284 brass.

The current popularity of AR-15 rifles made a new, smaller 6.5 round all but inevitable. The 6.5 Grendel's 1.52-inch case is shorter than the .223's; loaded length is the same. Lou Palmisano had set the stage as early as 1984 with his 6.5 PPC. The Grendel came in 2002, courtesy Bill Alexander

◀ The 6 PPC, here with Wilson die, proved itself (and the merits of short cases) in benchrest events.

(Alexander Arms) and Arne Brennan, who'd chambered a prototype in an AR rifle in 1998. The latest rendition, Les Baer's .264 LBC AR cartridge, has a case essentially the same as the 6.5 Grendel's. Chamber dimensions differ slightly. Both 6.5mms are quite accurate. Arne Brennan fired a 600-meter group with the Grendel that miked less than 1.2 inches! Velocities range from 2,900 fps for 90-grain bullets to 2,500 for 129s.

The most celebrated 6.5 of late has been the 6.5 Creedmoor, announced by Hornady in 2009 and named for the famous New York shooting range (originally Creed's Farm) that hosted early long-distance rifle competitions. The 6.5 Creedmoor, developed for target shooters *and* hunters, has a shorter case than the .260 Remington, but the same .473 head diameter. Truncating the hull and keeping the shoulder well to the rear, "you can seat long bullets without exceeding permissible OAL in short-action magazines," said Hornady's Dave Emary, who developed the round. Powders from the firm's LEVERevolution project were tweaked to deliver .260 Remington velocities from the Creedmoor's smaller case.

An obvious choice for deer hunting, the 6.5 Creedmoor might, I reasoned, serve for bigger game. Then I got a fine Magnum Research rifle, one of its carbon-fiber barrels threaded to a short Remington 700 action. GreyBull Precision supplied a 4.5-14x Leupold VX-3 with GreyBull's long-range reticle. Its 1/3-minute elevation stem sported a dial calibrated for Hornady's 129 SST in the 6.5 Creedmoor. Putting the dial to work on steel targets at long range, I rang the metal with uncanny regularity.

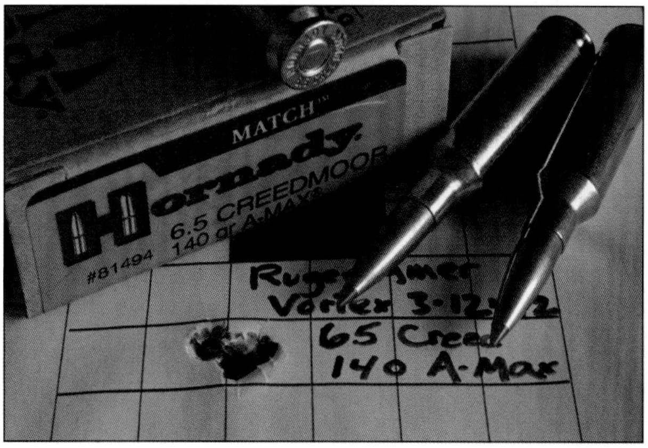

▲ Recent, from Hornady, the 6.5 Creedmoor is deadly on deer. Factory loads shoot flat, accurately.

In the field, of course, closer is always better. Alas, when Ray Milligan and I spotted a bull, there was no way to approach. Dead-still air, front-lit ribs and a steady prone position coaxed me. "Remember how you and that rifle performed at the range," whispered Ray. I crushed the trigger. Dust erupted beyond the five-point. He sprinted, wheeled and crashed into the sagebrush. The SST had drilled both lungs. That 600-yard shot was twice as long as any I had attempted at elk in 35 years of hunting.

Subsequent shooting with Ruger rifles in 6.5 Creedmoor, both on deer hunts and a South African safari, bolstered my confidence in the cartridge. So did a long-range match in Utah that stretched shots to 1,200 yards. But this delightful round, like every other, has a practical limit.

"It's too small," said Andrew. The Professional Hunter steered me through a grassy basin below an amphitheater of towering rock. When we spied a bedded eland bull far off, I bellied forward alone. At 150 yards, bereft of further cover, I slinged up, steadied the reticle—and declined a quartering shot as the bull stood and turned in one motion. Then another bull appeared, pausing in a slot in the thorn. I fired.

Andrew and I looked in vain for blood. Half an hour later, our Bushman tracker whistled. Hopes sank when we saw the tiny drop. For the next hour we tracked the bull uphill. Suddenly, the thick spiral horns winked above a bush 90 yards ahead. We dashed forward, up, up. The great splayed prints showed the bull had turned toward a brushy canyon. We stopped, my lungs heaving. Then a rock rolled. The eland lunged up the far side, 200 yards off. Jamming the rifle onto Andrew's sticks, I triggered a shot offhand as the bull quartered away. Behind! I flicked the bolt, fired again as the bull offered one final chance.

We found him dying. I stood to the side, relieved but half regretting my first shot. That GMX had landed well, centering the near lung, ranging to the off-shoulder. My final bullet had driven forward from between the hams, slicing the dorsal aorta near the spine. A lucky hit.

"An eland takes some killing," said Andrew quietly.

▲ The Nosler .26 is best paired with very slow powders, and long, sleek bullets that retain velocity.

More horsepower in a 6.5 came at the 2014 SHOT Show, with the introduction of the .26 Nosler. Brass became available a few weeks later—as did the chambering in Nosler's Model 48 Heritage rifle. At this writing, factory-loaded ammo is still in the "promised" stage.

Like many modern rimless (not belted) magnums, the .26 Nosler derives from the .404 Jeffery, a British number released in 1910. Don Allen used the .404 hull early on for his Dakota line (through .375). The rims on these and their brethren fit bolt faces sized for the .532 rims of most belted rounds. But ahead of the extractor groove, belt-free case design yields larger body diameter, which means greater capacity.

With a loaded length of 3.34 inch, Nosler's .26 fits a .30-06-length action. The hull is 2.59 inches long, between that of 2.50-inch short belted magnums and the .300 Winchester Magnum's 2.62-inch case. The Nosler's 35-degree shoulder is set well forward, almost as far as the short-necked .300 Winchester's. Nosler brass is beautifully finished. Readying my first .26 handloads, I did find the pockets snug for my CCI Magnum Rifle primers. Bullets seated without a snag, case necks gripping them firmly. I seated them first out to magazine length, checking by chambering to ensure there was no land contact.

Nosler fashioned the .26 to push its 129-grain AccuBond Long Range bullets at 3,400 fps, and to hurl 140-grain Partitions at 3,300. With 3,385 ft-lbs of energy at the muzzle and an even ton at 400 yards, the 140s carry a haymaker punch. On the charts, it outclasses original .264 Magnum loads by 100 fps—and Winchester's current anemic .264 listing by 270 fps.

As I had no Nosler factory ammunition, I handloaded Nosler brass with what seemed appropriate powders. The company's 120-grain Ballistic Tips joined the 129s and 140s on my bench. Mason Payer at Nosler suggested 82 grains Retumbo, 93 grains US 869 as maximum for the 129. He listed 86 grains US 869 as tops for 140s. I didn't have that powder on hand. With other super-slow fuels, my Oehler recorded these average speeds (Caution: These are not recommended loads! Reduce charges by 5 percent to start!)

.26 NOSLER LOADS

120 Ballistic Tip, 79 Vihtavuori N165	Vel: 3456 fps	
120 Ballistic Tip, 82 IMR 7828	Vel: 3703 fps	(maximum!)
129 AccuBond LR, 83 Magnum	Vel: 3449 fps	
129 AccuBond LR, 81 H1000	Vel: 3403 fps	
129 AccuBond LR, 80 RL-25	Vel: 3474 fps	
140 Partition, 78 Retumbo	Vel: 3318 fps	
140 Partition, 85 Accurate 8700	Vel: 3339 fps	
140 Partition, 81 Magnum	Vel: 3431 fps	(maximum!)

I'd hoped to nip cherry-size groups while firing through Skyscreens with a Sightron SIII 6-24x scope. Alas, strong, gusty winds spread shots horizontally. And I ruined a half-minute group by nudging the last bullet with my clavicle. Though a couple of

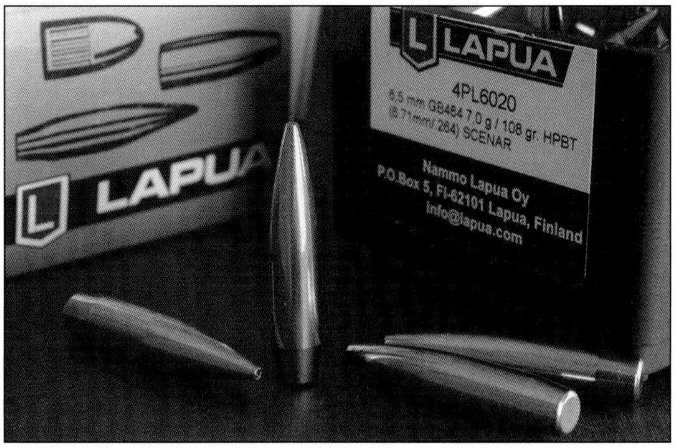

▲ Lapua's 6.5mm match bullets have a reputation for accuracy. At 108 grains, these are lightweights.

loads were disappointing, all the others promised to fulfill the Nosler pledge of 1-MOA accuracy for its M48. The 129 AccuBond LR powered by 81 grains H1000 came in at almost exactly the target speed of 3,400 fps and drilled a .8-inch group with my first trio of bullets. I figure 3,700 is about as fast as a 120-grain bullet should go, and 3,400 fast enough for a 140. While these ambitious loads left primers a tad flat, neither they nor any other load gave me sticky bolt lift. The rifle fed, extracted and ejected without fault.

Of course, Nosler's new plum has the liabilities attributed to the Winchester round 55 years ago: It burns lots of fuel behind a skinny bullet. You'll want a long barrel to accelerate it. And the throat will show erosion sooner than that, say, of a .308's. Efficient the .26 is not! Still, efficiency is hardly a universal measure of value. It doesn't raise the pulse or push horizons. Hunters who crave bullets that rocket past 400 yards in a blink and shoot as flat as the curve of the earth may find the .26 Nosler just plain sensible!

▲ Fastest 6.5 yet! Nosler's .26 trumps even the .264 Winchester Magnum, uses same-length action.

ROCKET LAUNCHER!

Nosler came up with its own rifle to chamber the fast-stepping .26. The Model 48 Heritge boasts a traditional push-feed, twin-lug bolt action, a two-position thumb safety that does not lock the bolt. The side-mounted extractor and plunger ejector operate in an enclosed bolt face. The adjustable, single-stage trigger is nicely positioned to the rear of the guard. A Model 70-style button secures a hinged floorplate. All bottom metal is alloy. The stainless, hand-lapped 26-inch barrel has a slender but not whippy profile, with 1-in-8 rifling. Steel parts are Cerakoted satin black. Nosler fitted well-figured, conservatively shaped walnut to the Heritage, checkered in generous 20-lpi point patterns. A shadow-line cheekpiece and slight palm swell accentuate the butt-stock, capped by a 1-inch Decelerator pad with the Nosler insignia.

Nosler offers the 48 in 17 chamberings. Synthetic-stocked versions have pillar- and glass-bedded actions, with an alloy bedding rail in the hand-laid aramid. The 48 Outfitter features a 22-inch barrel with open sights. Remington 700 bases fit all M48s.

BULLETS TO STRETCH YOUR REACH

The 60 years following John Nosler's development of the Partition bullet in 1947 brought many other bullets from the Bend, Oregon firm—Zipedo, Solid Base, Ballistic Tip, AccuBond, E-Tip, Nosler Solid, Ballistic Tip Lead-Free, to name a few. In 2012, John Nosler died at 97. Bob Nosler and his son, John, have continued to grow the product line, with Safari and Vamageddon bullets and with centerfire ammunition featuring the panoply of Nosler missiles. Long Range bullets appeared recently, first a 210-grain for .30 magnums, with six others to follow, in .264, .284 and .308. Ballistic coefficients start at .561! Thank the sleek ogives, long tapered heels. Gray polymer noses distinguish Nosler's LR bullets at a glance. To 300 yards, ordinary boat-tail bullets behave about the same as LRs. Farther on, high ballistic coefficients rule. At 500 steps, you'll see 2½ inches less drop with LR bullets, from 150 to 200 ft-lbs more punch.

◀ Fast sixes to handload: from left, .243, 6mm, .240 Weatherby, with the .30-06 for comparison.

Chapter 11: The Shift to Short

While "short magnum" has a contemporary ring, hurling bullets at high speed from stubby cases dates to the early days of smokeless powder. Charles Newton's snappy .250-3000, developed before the First World War, had a bit less case capacity and a tad more body taper than current short magnums, but it is certainly of the same cloth. The .300 Savage (1920) and the .308 Winchester and its offspring (1950s) packed tough-game punch into short rifle actions.

As has happened throughout the history of metallic cartridges, competitive shooters birthed and tested the short-coupled case designs that have blossomed into popular hunting rounds. On the benchrest circuit in 1974, Lou Palmisano and Ferris Pindell reshaped the .220 Russian (a necked-down 7.62x39) to form what would become the .22 PPC. A 6mm PPC followed. From base to 30-degree shoulder, these hulls measured barely over an inch, though rim diameter approached that of the .30-06. Palmisano figured that the short powder column would yield better accuracy. Proving the PPC's superiority over the .222 and 6x47 in a game already dominated by one-hole groups might have taken years. But in surprisingly short order, the two accomplished riflemen convinced colleagues to try their new rounds. Two of the top 20 rifles in the Sporter class at the 1975 NBRSA championship matches were chambered for PPCs. By 1980, 15 of the top 20 shooters used a PPC. In 1989 all of the highest Sporter scores were shot with PPCs, plus *every one* of the top 20 Unlimiteds and 18 of the 20 best in the Light and Heavy Varmint classes!

"Short" belted magnum hunting cartridges had appeared with Winchester and Remington labels during the 1950s and 1960s, after Roy Weatherby had wildcatted his .257, .270 and 7mm Magnums in the early 1940s. Hardly short by current standards, they

▲ Short (rimless) magnums impress hunters who must hit tough game hard with lightweight rifles.

brought the performance of leggy Holland & Holland rounds to rifle actions scaled for the .30-06 and kin. Of much more benefit than a slightly abbreviated bolt throw was the affordability and availability of military actions and mid-century sporting rifles in .30-06. These became home to the 7mm Remington, and the .300 and .338 Winchester Magnums. Weatherby's sub-.30 magnums also fit these mechanisms, though Roy was loath, at the time, to release his cartridges to the great unwashed. He focused his considerable marketing skills on hunters of means.

In 1992 short *rimless* magnum rounds appeared in Don Allen's Dakota line. The 7mm, .300, .330 and .375 Dakota cases, based on the .404 Jeffery's, measure 2.50 to 2.57 inches, but hold more fuel than contemporary short belted magnums. At 97 grains (water), the .300's case capacity is just 3 grains shy of the 2.85-inch .300 Weatherby's.

John Lazzeroni ventured into cartridge design in the mid 1990s, coming up with a stable of gigantic rimless rounds. Then John turned his attention to shorter cases. The case heads on his .243 and .264 short cartridges mike .532—standard dimension for an ordinary belted magnum and the head on Lazzeroni's long .257 Scramjet. His 7mm, .300, .338 and .416 have .580 case heads like their full-length counterparts. John named his cartridges with metric measures:

- 6.17 (.243) Spitfire: 85-grain bullet at 3,618 fps
- 6.71 (.264) Phantom: 120-grain bullet at 3,312 fps
- 7.21 (.284) Tomahawk: 140-grain bullet at 3,379 fps
- 7.82 (.308) Patriot: 180-grain bullet at 3,184 fps
- 8.59 (.338) Galaxy: 225-grain bullet at 2,968 fps
- 10.57 (.416) Maverick: 400-grain bullet at 2,454 fps.

The 8.59 (.338) Galaxy, introduced in 1997, ranks among my favorites. With it I killed a Montana whitetail at long range and a bull elk up close in timber. Though the Galaxy case is just 2.05 inches long, it has more capacity than the .338 Winchester Magnum's! John mated his cartridges to rifles of his own design. They're of high quality and very accurate.

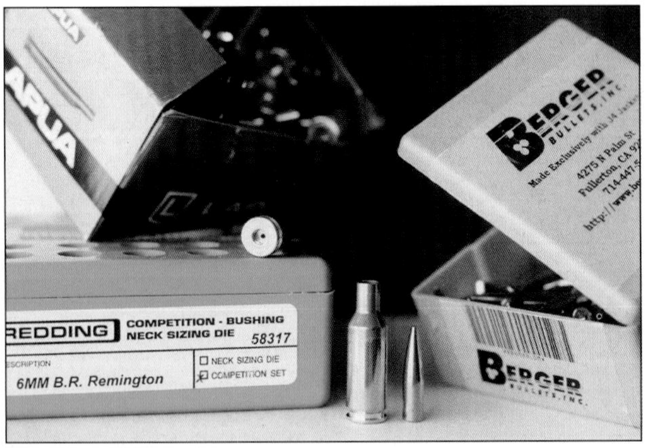

▲ Benchrest shooters explored the advantages of short cases early, with the PPC and others like this.

My L2000SA Mountain Rifle has a Jewell trigger and 24-inch Schneider barrel and weighs just 7 pounds.

Dick Davis, a lifetime competitive shooter, used a rifle in Lazzeroni's 7.82 (.308) Patriot to set a world record for 1,000-yard benchrest score in 2003. He put 11 of 15 Berger bullets into a 7-inch 10-ring! "I like this short .30 partly because my loads are so consistent," he told me. "A 10-fps difference in exit speed causes 2 inches of vertical dispersion at 1,000 yards. Uniformity matters out yonder!"

Just before the start of the twenty-first century, Winchester announced its .300 WSM. Slightly longer and, with a .532 base, not quite as broad as the Lazzeroni Patriot, the .300 Winchester Short Magnum performs like the belted .300 Winchester Magnum (1963). At 2.76 inches, the .300 WSM *cartridge* is little longer than the earlier .300's 2.62-inch *case*!

Browning apparently approached Winchester with the idea for the WSM early in 1999. Browning and U.S. Repeating Arms Company redesigned their bolt-action rifles for the .300 WSM, initially loaded with 180-grain Fail Safe bullets at 2,970 fps and 150-grain Ballistic Silvertips at 3,300. Though it had the jump on Remington with its first short magnum, Winchester did not then register a 7mm. Remington soon unveiled .300 and 7mm Short Action Ultra Mags, the .300 a ballistic twin to the .300 WSM. Just enough shorter to fit a Model Seven action, the Remington rounds hold slightly less powder. Winchester steamed ahead with a .270 WSM and a 7mm WSM, then a series of Super Short Magnums. The .223, .243 and .25 WSSMs are

▲ Janice has warmed to the .300 WSM for most of her hunting, but took this buck with a belted .30.

▲ The .270 WSM trumps the longer .270 Win. by 200 fps. Wayne took the first elk with this round.

▲ The efficient short-action .270 Redding wildcat comes close to the .270 Winchester ballistically.

based on the .300 WSM trimmed from 2.10 to 1.67. Next to the .22 WSSM, a .22-250 looks tall. But there's more capacity in the WSSM case, and the round has a 200-fps velocity edge.

Hornady arrived late to the short-cartridge party but with two superb rounds. The .300 and .338 Ruger Compact Magnums use new powders formulated to excel in short rifle barrels. Mitch Mittelstaedt, who headed the RCM project at Hornady, explained that these propellants enabled his team to compress pressure curves so the .300 RCM behaves like ordinary .30 magnums in 24-inch barrels but doesn't lose as much enthusiasm in carbines. Inspired by the 2.58-inch .375 Ruger hull, the .300 and .338 RCM share its .532 head and base. Capacities average 72 and 68 grains of water. (Remington .30-06 cases hold 67 grains, Winchester .300 WSM cases 79 grains). Ruger Compact Magnums are loaded to the same 2.84-inch overall length as WSMs and cycle through WSM magazines; however, you can slip four RCMs into most three-shot WSM boxes.

I used a delightfully nimble Ruger 77 in .300 RCM on a British Columbia moose hunt soon after the round appeared. The moose I found the last afternoon fell as though struck by the hammer of Thor.

Handloading short magnums, you can often employ incrementally faster powders. The claim that you get less recoil than with belted magnums is technically true: A smaller charge of faster powder means less ejecta. But felt recoil depends on several factors, some of which have greater effect.

◀ The .300 Ruger Compact Magnum was engineered by Hornady for high velocities in short barrels.

▲ This moose fell to one shot from Wayne's Ruger in .300 RCM, a short, very efficient magnum.

Short Magnum comparisons

Cartridge	Bullet Weight	Muzzle Velocity	Cartridge	Bullet Weight	Muzzle Velocity
.223 Rem.	55	3240	7mm Rem. Mag.	140	3150
.22-250	55	3680	7mm SAUM	140	3175
.220 Swift	55	3800	7mm WSM	140	3225
.223 WSSM	55	3850	7mm Ultra Mag	140	3425
.243 Win.	100	2960	.30-06	150	2910
6mm Rem.	100	3100	.300 SAUM	150	3200
.243 WSSM	100	3110	.300 WSM	150	3200
.240 Weatherby	100	3400	.300 Win. Mag.	150	3250
.257 Roberts	117	2780	.325 WSM	200	2950
.25-06	115	2990	.338 Federal	200	2630
.25 WSSM	115	3060	.338 Win. Mag.	200	2950
.257 Weatherby	115	3150	.340 Weatherby	225	3065
.270 Win.	130	3060			
.270 AHR	130	3150			
.270 Weatherby	130	3200			
.270 WSM	130	3275			

"You can't declare without exception that short hulls favor faster powders than do longer belted cases," cautioned Chris Hodgdon. "Ideal burn rate depends on capacity, neck reduction, bullet weight—even, in some cases, bore and rifling." We've found very slow powders like Retumbo excel in the .270 WSM, but that in the .300 WSM H4350 works a bit better than H4831." While these powders are also proven champs in belted magnums, "short cases give you more power per grain. In the .300 WSM you need only 64 grains H4350 to get 2,950 fps from a 180-grain AccuBond. In the .300 Winchester Magnum the recommended maximum charge of 67 grains yields 2,920 fps." Chris added that some of the spherical powders Hodgdon sells are even better picks for short hulls. In my experience, Winchester 760 and H380 work well for light and midweight bullets in compact .30s, and in the .325 WSM.

Short magnum fans were blessed recently with Hodgdon canister powders from LEVERevolution and Superformance projects at Hornady. "Our Superformance powder is truly versatile," Chris Hodgdon enthused. "In a burn-rate chart, it lies between H4831 and H4350. But it trumps both in

▲ Short magnums from the United States have become popular, and are commercially loaded worldwide.

short barrels and delivers top speeds from compact cases like the WSMs, RCMs, SAUMs and the short Lazzeronis."

To my knowledge, I shot the first elk ever killed with a .270 WSM and a .300 SAUM, probably the first killed with an 8.59 Lazzeroni Galaxy. The .223 WSSM has taken deer for me. Elk and Africa's biggest antelopes have fallen to a .300 WSM and a .325 WSM, Australian buffalo to a 7mm WSM. I've seen short magnums in the hands of other hunters take many more animals. Most rimless short magnums are a bit more efficient than their belted counterparts, but that alone doesn't mean they're better. Short magnums require steeper stacking in the magazine or more belly in the rifle to achieve the same capacity. They don't feed as smoothly as slimmer rounds that enter the chamber at a gentler angle.

We may not be making cartridges *too* short yet, but we're mighty close!

◀ From left: .22 Hornet, .223, .22-250, .220 Swift—and the stubby .223 WSSM, as fast as the Swift.

◀ With their longer flame duration, magnum primers suit "new short magnums" as well as belted.

Chapter 12: Handloading the Old-Fashioned Way

Misfires. You'll rarely get one with centerfire ammunition, but they're irritatingly common with muzzle-loaders. "The key to reliability is to keep the rifle clean," says Chris Hodgdon. "Breech plug and nipple especially. Between firings, swab the bore with a damp patch, followed by a dry one. When you put the rifle away, clean it with water, dry it thoroughly, and apply a light film of oil. Overnight, on a hunt, remove the cap and leave the rifle where it won't warm up. Bringing it into a heated cabin on a chilly fall evening can cause condensation on the metal. All black powder is hygroscopic and will absorb moisture condensed in the bore. Wet powder may not ignite!"

On a Utah hill once, after a snow, I tracked a buck through thick cover that all but cancelled any chance for a shot with my muzzleloader. About to despair, I spotted the deer crossing a small opening 90 yards ahead. Quickly I knelt, thumbed the hammer and squeezed off a shot. Click! The buck paused a step short of oblivion. I could do nothing but re-cock and try again. *Ka-Boom!* The explosion almost surprised me. The Barnes bullet struck the deer audibly. It lunged away, then collapsed in a flurry of sunlit snow. I still can't say why the first hammer strike failed to detonate the primer. I was pleased the second did.

▲ Wayne took this fine Utah mule deer with Pyrodex pellets at 90 yards. Iron sights of course.

Another time, in the Arctic, I borrowed a pal's muzzleloader to hunt caribou. Eventually I spied one where dips in the tundra allowed me to belly close. Prone, I cocked the side-hammer T/C Hawken and, as the bull ambled to within 30 yards, crushed the trigger. The plume of white smoke was expected. But I felt hardly any recoil. The caribou trotted off. I re-charged the rifle, then picked up the trail. Heart-shot, the animal hadn't gone far. But the patched ball hadn't exited. At camp, I asked my friend about the load. "Oh, that. It started out as 90 grains," he mumbled. When pressed, he explained that the local Inuits were lining up to fire his rifle the day before I arrived, "so we halved the charges to double the shooting."

Though most sportsmen know it as the traditional propellant for muzzle-loading rifles, and as the choice of purists in cartridge guns for Cowboy Action shooting, black powder still has military uses. It's in the detonating charges for high-energy propellants in artillery shells, and propels ejection seats clear of aircraft. As in the nineteenth century, it comprises sulfur, charcoal and saltpeter. They're ground fine and mixed at 3 percent moisture. Pressed into cakes, the powder meal is then fed into a granulating machine. Screens segregate particles by size; they're polished in revolving wooden barrels. Most black powder is labeled A-1, Fg, Ffg, FFFg, FFFFg and FFFFFg, in decreasing order of granule size. Bigger grains generally burn slowest and work best pushing heavy balls or bullets. Very fine black powder is suitable only for priming charges and pyrotechnics.

In 1976, his smokeless powder business well established, Bruce Hodgdon agreed to distribute a new product called Pyrodex. This black-powder substitute had its start in the Seattle-area laboratory of a young but talented shooter named Dan Pawlak. Dan's goal during the early 1970s was to develop a fuel that would match black powder in appearance

▲ Pyrodex serves hunters in remote places. This bull fell to a Maxi-Ball, a Thompson/Center caplock.

and density, produced similar smoke and smell, and yield comparable velocities—at pressures any black powder gun could bottle. The compound would be stable and easy to ship, releasing shippers and shooters from the onerous regulations governing black powder. Specifically, Pawlak wanted his propellant to dodge the Class A, High Explosive label applied to black powder, and to pass Flammable Solids tests, so it could be handled like smokeless.

Experienced propellant engineer Mike Levenson joined Pawlak in the venture. Within two years the pair developed a steel-gray fuel that met some of Dan's criteria. They dubbed the product Pyrodex, an abbreviation for pyrotechnic deflagrating explosive.

Pawlak's work caught the eye of Warren Center, at the gun firm of Thompson/Center. He phoned R. E. Hodgdon, urging him to consider a joint financial venture to back the young man. In January 1975 Hodgdon traveled to Seattle and found the strapping 6'4" entrepreneur in his Issaquah mobile home, next to a private airstrip and a well-equipped ballistics laboratory. The transducer pressure guns, oscilloscopes and test data convinced R. E. that Pawlak was serious, talented—and onto something.

By this time Mike Levenson had left the project. Linn Emrich helped underwrite Pawlak's work. Refining Pyrodex, Dan increased its potency and reduced its range of pressure variation. He made it burn cleaner but smell like black powder. He even changed the color to black. For Pyrodex production, Pawlak began remodeling Excoa, a former explosives facility on Taylor Mountain north of Issaquah.

Before submitting Pyrodex to government tests, Pawlak arranged his own. Detonator trials were most severe: An igniter was placed in one canister of ten 1-pound canisters in a case. To pass this test, the

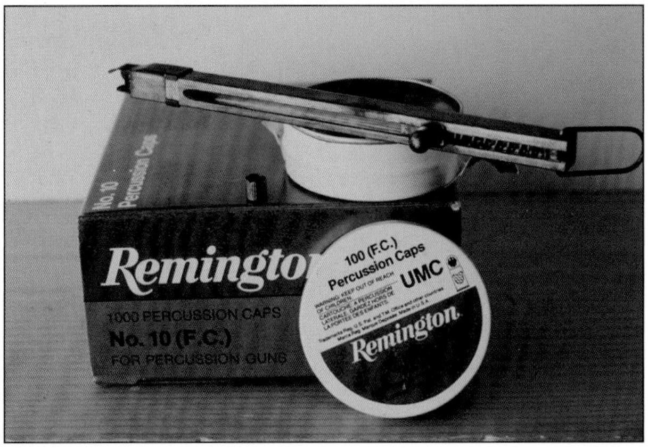

▲ Percussion caps employ the muzzleloader's nipple as an anvil. The brass sleeve speeds capping.

▲ Black powder accoutrements (from left) powder measure, bullet starter, caps, capper, MaxiBalls.

ignited canister could not cause detonation in the others. While even smokeless powders occasionally failed this exercise, Pyrodex passed repeatedly. In fact, the subsequent Department of Transportation lab report stated: "Pyrodex is probably a little safer than conventional smokeless powder because [Pyrodex] ignition temperature is considerably higher."

The first shipment from Pyrodex Corporation was slated for May 1976. Hodgdon agreed to act as sole distributor, and to market Pyrodex as "the replica black powder." The propellant gained credibility when it was approved by the National Muzzle Loading Rifle Association for use in its matches. Then, on January 27, 1977, tragedy struck at Pawlak's Issaquah plant. Three tons of Pyrodex flashed off, killing the entrepreneur and three technicians.

In the aftermath, Pyrodex underwent further testing. Again, it was deemed less hazardous than smokeless propellants. Directors of Pyrodex Corporation and the board of Hodgdon Powder Company met to discuss the product's future. Cathy Pawlak, Linn Emrich, Dave Wolfe, Neil Knox and R. E. and J. B. Hodgdon concluded that Dan would have wanted his project to continue. They agreed to build a new Pyrodex mill on an abandoned B-29 base near Herington, Kansas, 130 miles from Hodgdon's distribution center. In May 1979, after three years and numerous delays, the $1.5-million plant began turning out canisters of Pyrodex. They reached retail stores in early 1980.

Pyrodex soon became available in three grades: RS, the equivalent to FFg black powder, works best as the main charge in most muzzle-loading rifles. P, which mimics FFFg in burning characteristics, is for small-bore rifles and pistols. Pyrodex "Select" appeared in 1991 as a specialty powder for sabot and heavy conical bullets. Six years later, Hodgdon announced Pyrodex pellets, each a 50-grain (equivalent) pill easy to pop into the muzzle. No measuring required. But each pellet had an "ignition pad" on one end, which was easier to ignite than the main part of the pill. "It's really a couple of grains of black powder," explained Chris Hodgdon. "So you orient the first pellet with the pad toward the cap."

Pyrodex was followed by Triple Seven, "essentially Pyrodex without the sulfur," said Chris. "It's a cleaner fuel, with a bit more energy than Pyrodex." Triple Seven Magnum pellets each carry 60 grains of propellant, ten more than the standard pellet. Triple Seven residue can be washed away with water only —no need for the traditional hot soapy wash. White Hots, even more recent, have earned a reputation for consistency. "It's the most versatile muzzleloader fuel we've found," Chris told me. "We get excellent accuracy with a range of bullet types. Velocities match those from Triple Seven." He added that these black powder substitutes were developed with hot ignition in mind. Best performance comes with 209 primers. A standard 209 suffices for White Hots, but Winchester Triple Seven 209 primers excel. Reason: ordinary

▲ Hunting with caplocks like this replica Hawken brings riflemen back to handloading's roots.

209s sometimes push Triple Seven pellets down the bore at ignition, before the pellets are fully engulfed, leaving a ring in the bore. Winchester reduced gas output in its Triple Seven 209, so pellets are less apt to move prematurely.

Are pellets better than granular powder? They're certainly more convenient. Either form loads easily from the plastic charging tubes I prefer—if your hands are steady. When they're shaking with cold or because you just missed a records-class buck, powder can spill all over your boots. A pellet charge also burns more completely in the bore, according to Chris Hodgdon, who uses them in his own T/C and CVA rifles. He told me of shooting a fine whitetail at 105 yards with a 250-grain Hornady SST in front of two White Hot pellets and a standard 209 primer. Earlier he killed a mule deer buck at 180 steps, with a 300-grain Power Belt driven by three White Hots.

For elk hunting, you'll want a stiff propellant charge behind a bullet with enough weight to drive deep. I start with 90 grains of granular powder; Chris works loads up from 70. We both stop adding thrust at about 130 grains. Unlike smokeless powder, black powder and its substitutes don't take guns apart at some redline charge. But you get incrementally less benefit from additional fuel the higher you go. For instance, 70 grains of FFg pushes a .490 round ball with a .020 patch at about 1,750 fps. At 80 grains, you get 1,840, at 90 grains 1,925, at 100 grains 1,990. Meanwhile, recoil ratchets up. Expect the same law of diminishing returns from Pyrodex black powder substitutes.

The Pyrodex project has made shooting muzzleloaders more convenient, and the brand will no doubt

BLACK POWDER FROM THE BREECH

Comparing rifles, handloads and marksmanship is old entertainment in Europe, where German- and Swiss-style *Schuetzenfests* included plenty of beer and sauerbraten. The first *Schuetzenfest* on record in the US occurred in New York at the close of the Civil War. In the European tradition, most firing was done offhand at 200 yards.

A decade later, Remington's Lewis L. Hepburn modified the Rolling Block rifle in efforts to beat Irish sharpshooters who'd triumphed at Wimbledon in 1873. The Irish had challenged any American team to another match. Six men would fire three "rounds" of 15 shots, one round each at 800, 900 and 1,000 yards. Targets measured 12 feet high and 6 feet wide, with a 3-foot-square bullseye. An Amateur Rifle Club conducted tryouts for the American team. The fledgling National Rifle Association and the cities of New York and Brooklyn put up $5,000 each to build a range on Long Island's Creed's Farm. Deeded to the NRA for $26,250 in 1872, it would be called Creedmoor.

In September, Americans with breechloaders upset the Irish with their muzzleloaders, 934 to 931.

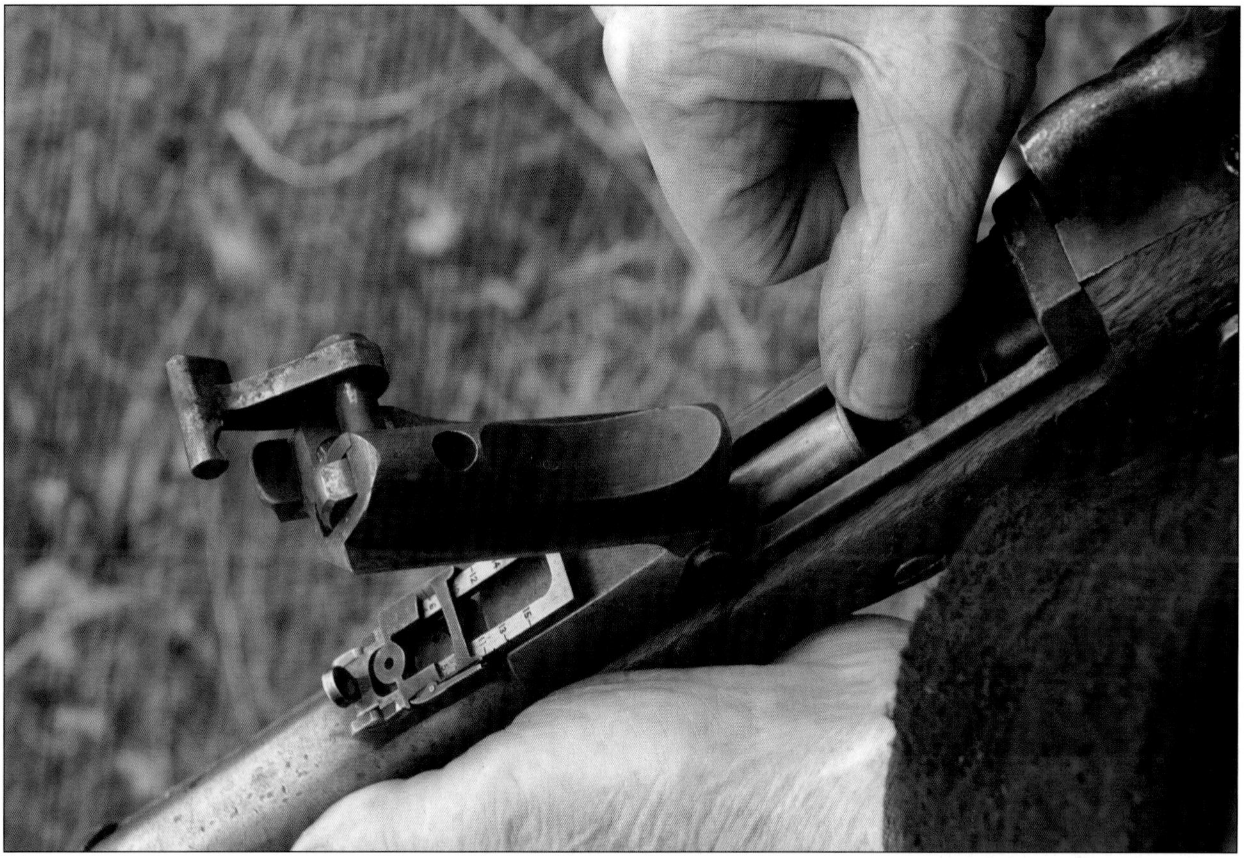

▲ Among the first metallic-cartridge military rifles was the "trapdoor" Springfield of 1873.

LONG AND LONGER

The most celebrated long-range rifle of the black-powder era was undoubtedly the 1874 Sharps. A double-set trigger boosted its 1878 price to $44. More recently, this Sharps appeared with Tom Selleck in *Quigley Down Under*. The film included Selleck's long shot at a bucket, which inspired the 1,000-yard Quigley match near Forsyth, Montana. The bucket-shaped target is 44 inches wide at the top. Many shooters nail it routinely with iron-sighted black-powder rifles lobbing bullets at 1,300 fps!

Long shooting was redefined in late June 1874, in the Texas panhandle village of Adobe Walls. Billy Dixon and 27 other frontiersmen were roused at dawn by 700 Comanches thundering in from the east. Led by Chief Quanah Parker, the Indians killed three whites before retreating under heavy rifle fire. But two days later, on the 28th, some warriors still lurked nearby. As legend has it, 15 appeared on a bluff almost a mile off. Dixon, a renowned buffalo hunter, was urged to take a poke with the saloon owner's 50-caliber Sharps. To the astonishment of all, as the echoes of the shot died, one of the Indians came off his horse. The distance, surveyed: 1,538 yards.

Was a hit at that range possible? Surely. Probable? Hardly. Whether or not you believe that Billy Dixon downed a Comanche at over 1,500 yards with a black-powder Sharps, you have lots of company!

continue to grow as it adds specialty propellants. The current generation of black powder shooters may not remember news of the 1977 Issaquah disaster. But they certainly know about Pyrodex. Legions would say it's the best propellant ever for a front-stuffer. Dan Pawlak would have liked to hear that.

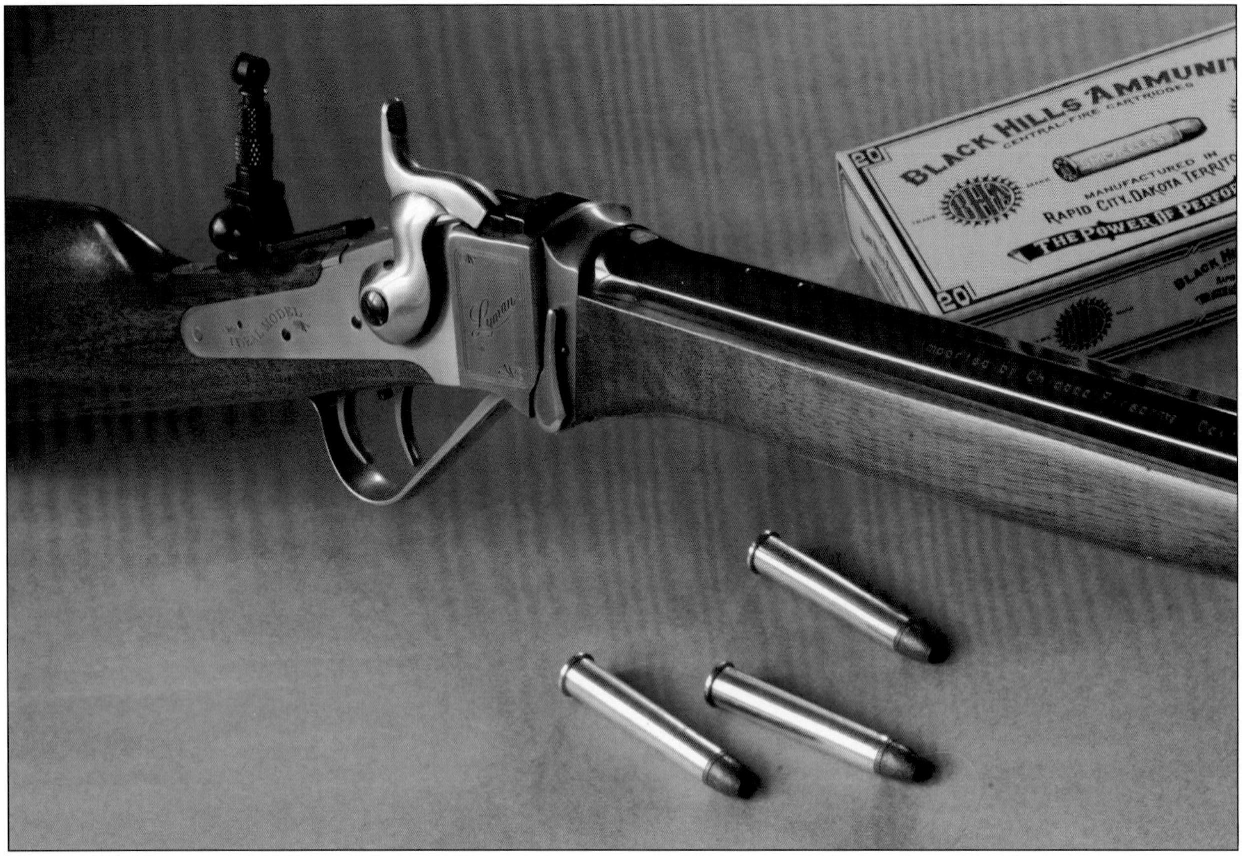

▲ Lyman, of Ideal fame, makes loading tools, but also imports fine replicas of early American rifles.

Chapter 13: Colonial Loads

The development of rifles and ammunition in Great Britain and continental Europe during the seventeenth and eighteenth centuries differed from that in North America. In the heyday of the British Empire, much of the *big* game hunting occurred in far-flung frontiers. The great animals of southern and eastern Africa heavily influenced rifle design. Black-powder loads and, later, metallic cartridges were fashioned not to kill large numbers of game at distance (as were, arguably, rifles and loads for the American plains), but to bring huge beasts to earth with one shot.

BEFORE SAFARIS WERE FUN

The Dutch settled the Cape of Good Hope beginning in 1648. The first hunters there relied on heavy bullets from big bores to down Africa's heavy game. Samuel Baker carried a 4-bore rifle firing a 4-ounce (1,750-grain) silk-patched lead bullet in front of 16 drams (437 grains) of black powder. In 1840, at age 19, he commissioned this 21-pound smokepole from George Gibbs. It had 2-groove rifling in a 36-inch barrel. In 1869 Baker ordered a 3-bore from Holland & Holland. It fired a 5-ounce (2,187-grain) bullet. Sir Baker died in 1893, at age 72. His fame helped Harris Holland and Holland's nephew, Henry, establish their iconic London firearms business, which Harris, a tobacconist, started in 1837.

Explorers like Baker predated even the popular use of percussion ignition. Of course, so did the first of Great Britain's storied rifle-makers. By the time German immigrants to the United States were building Kentucky rifles in Pennsylvania, the Irish firm of Rigby was turning out fine dueling pistols in Dublin. Rigby's genesis in 1735 makes it the oldest of British firms still selling rifles. It developed the .450 Nitro Express 3 1/4-inch cartridge in 1898 when it began representing Mauser in England. Thirteen years later it introduced the rimless .416 Rigby, a versatile and still popular bolt-action round for Africa's big game. After a tortuous history marked by intrigue, impending bankruptcies, and changes in ownership, Rigby's name has recently resurfaced on beautifully sculpted rifles. Per originals, they're built on Mauser actions.

▲ Tobacconist Harris Holland, with nephew, Henry, started the great London firm Holland & Holland.

In 1856, after French firearms designer Lefaucheux unveiled a hinged-breech gun at the London Exposition, James Purdey introduced a series of Black Powder Express rifles and cartridges. Lightweight .450- and .500-bore bullets left at a sizzling 1,700 fps! BPE rounds yielded in the 1890s to cartridges that achieved 2,100 fps with cordite powder and heavier bullets. Nitro Express rounds proliferated around the turn of the century. The .500 NE hurled 570-grain bullets at 2,150 fps, the .577 NE 750-grain missiles at 2,000, the .600 NE 900-grain slugs at 1,950. All were of flanged or rimmed design, for dropping-block or hinged-breech rifles.

Around 1907, Great Britain barred import of .450 rifles to India and Sudan, where colonial rule was challenged, and the country's resources highly val-

▲ Early hunters in Africa's colonies relied on black powder, huge lead bullets. At right, the .30-06.

ued. India was a lucrative market for gunmakers, who shipped them to maharajahs as well as to high-level British officers sporting for tigers. The industry responded to the ban with new cartridges. Holland & Holland necked the .500-450 to .465, Eley the .450 No. 2 to get a .475 No. 2. Joseph Lang used the .500 3 ¼-inch as raw material for the .470. In a rare fit of charity (or brilliance), Lang released it to the trade. Result: the .470 NE became one of the most popular double-gun rounds of all time!

Here are some well-known British big-bores, from the transition of black to smokeless powder:

- 1880s—.450-400 BPE, 270-grain bullet at 1,650 fps
- 1896—.450-400 NE 3-in. (Jeffery), 400-grain bullet at 2,100 fps (Jim Corbett)
- 1896—.500-450 NE 3 ¼-in. 480-grain bullet at 2,175 fps (5,050 ft-lbs)
- 1896—.500 NE 3-in. (.510 bullets), 570-grain bullet at 2,150 fps
- 1896—.577 NE 3-in. (.585 bullets) 750-grain bullet at 2,050 fps
- 1898—.450 Rigby 480-grain bullet at 2,150 fps
- 1901—.600 NE (Jeffery w/ .622 bullets), 900-grain bullet at 1,950 fps
- 1903—.450 No. 2 NE 3 ½-in. 480-grain bullet at 2,175 fps (5,050 ft-lbs)

Modern smokeless powder did not suddenly appear to displace black. Semi-smokeless propellants in

▲ A Zimbabwean game ranger holds an ancient Martini, possibly rebarreled from .577-450 (c. 1871).

the United States had a counterpart in Great Britain called cordite. So named for its spaghetti-like form, cordite was easily inserted in straight cases, and suited long bottleneck rounds with gentle shoulders. Pressures from cordite loads accommodated double rifles of that era.

The dizzying array of proprietary big-bore cartridges for British double rifles at the onset of the twentieth century did not generate multiples of bullet weights and designs, for three main reasons. First, options in bullet construction were then limited; hunters had to lean on bullet diameter and mass to land a lethal punch. Secondly, in that day gun bearers commonly accompanied hunters, so packing additional rifles on safari made as much sense as changing loads in one. Finally, double rifles require regulation. That is, the barrels must be joined to shoot as close as possible to the same point of aim at a specified distance. This is a painstaking operation. A rifle was regulated for only one load; only by wild chance would other loads converge on the target.

As bolt actions proved their merit on battlefields, hunters noted that they were also less costly than the hinged-breech and dropping-block mechanisms hand-fitted in London. Bolt mechanisms were sturdy and accurate too. Soon cartridges appeared to give them real muscle.

William Jackman Jeffery established his gun business with a partner, Davies, in 1889. He died in 1909, a year before the rimless .404 Jeffery appeared. His brother Charles and, later, a nephew, Pierce, kept the business in the black until mid-century. Holland & Holland rescued it in 1960. Jeffery was later sold again.

The rimless .416 Rigby and the .425 Westley Richards with rebated rim (smaller than case head diameter) arrived between 1909 and 1911. The .500 Jeffery and .505 Gibbs followed. They were loaded to higher pressures than was permissible in double rifles. Most rounds that gained traction in magazine rifles, however, were of smaller bore, and easier on the shoulder.

Some notable hunters relied on big-bore double-rifle cartridges even as they made the switch to magazine rifles. The famous tiger hunter Jim Corbett used a .450-400 3-inch with a 400-grain bullet at 2,100 fps. Fielded by Jeffery in 1896, it was among a flurry of cartridges with very similar—sometimes the same—numbers that must have confused rifle buyers of the time. Most were proprietary, made for their orignator's own rifles but not chambered in others. The conventional wisdom concerning appropriate bullet weights and velocities for tough game, dictated in part by available steels and propellants, was widely shared. Almost all gunmakers in Great Britain fashioned their double-rifle rounds to kick bullets out the muzzles at between 2,000 and 2,200 fps.

Big-bore cartridges that took advantage of the strength of the Mauser bolt action delivered plenty of punch. But loads didn't push velocity envelopes. The British had found that heavy bullets at 2,200 fps killed the toughest game, and because such animals were commonly shot at very close range, flat bullet arcs mattered not. These five loads all acquitted themselves well in the years leading up to, and following, the Great War:

- 1910—.404 Jeffery, 400-grain bullet at 2,125 fps (also called the 10.75x68 Mauser)
- 1911—.416 Rigby, 410-grain bullet at 2,370 fps
- 1909—.425 Westley Richards, 410-grain bullet at 2,350 fps
- 1911—.505 Gibbs, 525-grain bullet at 2,300 fps
- 1920 or so—.500 Jeffery, 535-grain bullet at 2,400 fps (also introduced as the 12.7x70 Schuler)

Long after these potent rounds became popular, some hunters shunned their recoil. W. D. M. Bell killed elephants with the 7x57, the .303 British, the .318 Westley Richards. Introduced in 1910, the .318 is a ballistic match to the .338-06. The .333 Jeffery that arrived in 1911 may have inspired the .333 OKH (O'Neil, Keith, Hopkins) Smokeless powder that drove long, blunt bullets of great sectional density. It also yielded results that surprised hunters weaned on ponderous black-powder rifles. Careful study of elephant skulls showed Bell just where to aim from all angles. His full-jacketed small-bore bullets had no trouble lancing the skull and brain.

NUMBERS FROM THE BUSH

Don Heath, a professional hunter with whom I've shared the trail, has had several close calls with elephants. The last bull he shot as I write this fell so close that the animal's trunk broke Don's arm. "In Zimbabwe," he tells me, "80 percent of injuries inflicted on hunters by animals are caused by leopards. But 80 percent of fatalities are due to elephants. If an elephant wants to kill you, and you don't shoot it dead before it reaches you, your chances of surviving that scrape are very, very slim." In round numbers, elephants that reach you with lethal intent are 100 percent successful.

TWIN TUBES TO TURN-BOLTS

As the effectiveness of small-bore rifles in the hands of skilled marksmen became apparent, more hunters on safari chose lightweight bolt-actions over ponderous, costly doubles. At the turn of the century the array of loads popular in magazine-fed rifles included infantry rounds of the day (the 7x57, 8x57 and .303 British), but also some fast-stepping commercial numbers.

- 1906—.280 Rimless Ross with 140-grain bullets at 2,900 fps
- 1912—.275 Belted Rimless NE (H&H) with 140-grain bullets at 3,100 fps
- 1915—.280 Rimless Jeffery with 140-grain bullets at 2,800 fps

In the 1920s a couple of 6mms appeared: the .246 Purdey (a .253, flanged) with 100-grain bullets at 2,950 fps, and the .240 Belted Rimless NE with 100-grain bullets at 3,000 (a.k.a. the .240 Apex).

One of my favorite cartridges from this era, the .303 British, arrived in 1888 with 215-grain .311 bullets over compressed charges of black powder. A capable infantry round, it went smokeless in 1892, velocity reaching nearly 2,200 fps. Later sporting powders accelerated 180-grain softpoints to over 2,500. Various forms of the .303, in the Short Magazine Lee Enfield, served British and Canadian forces into the 1950s. That SMLE mechanism is smooth, and the only turn-bolt I've found that will cycle a full magazine of empties without a hiccup.

Our first short belted magnum cartridges from Winchester and Remington in the 1950s and 1960s owe their genesis to the .375 H&H, introduced in 1912 as the .375 Belted Rimless Nitro Express. It neatly bridged the gap between the slow, heavy bullets of double rifles for dangerous game, and the lightweights ideal for Africa's antelopes. With 300-grain softpoints and solids at over 2,500 fps, the .375 shot flat and hit hard. It killed farther than hunters needed to reach with iron sights, and floored big, angry beasts up close with assuring certainty. Steeply tapered, with a shoulder angle of less than 13 degrees, .375 rounds also chambered eagerly, for fast follow-up shots.

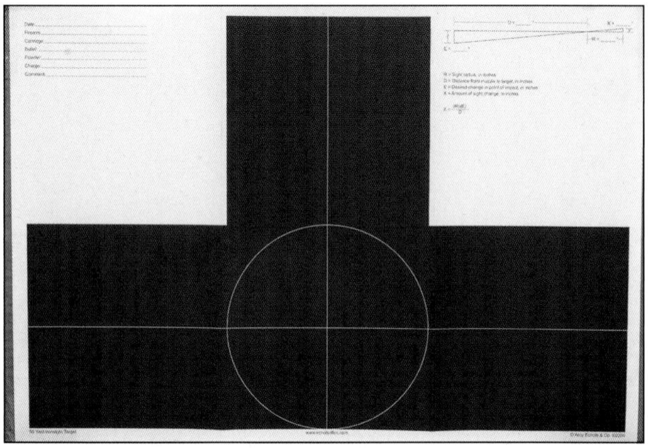

▲ Gunmaker D'Arcy Echols designed this target to help with zeroing, accuracy test with iron sights.

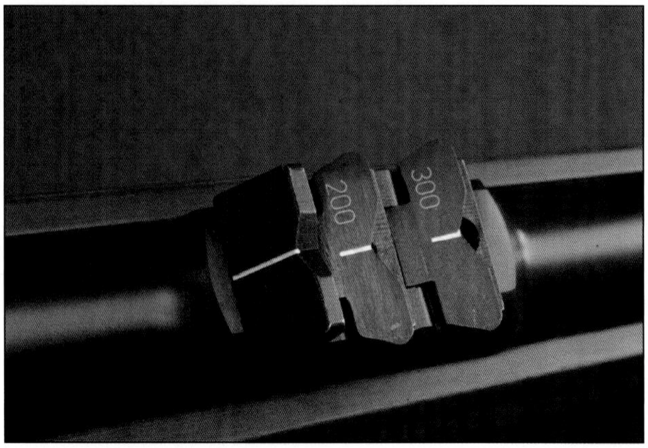

▲ Wayne avoids folding leaves. No matter the load, one sturdy, foolproof leaf suffices to 100 yards.

In his book, *African Rifles and Cartridges,* John Taylor praised the .375 H&H: "I've had five of these rifles . . . and have fired more than 5,000 rounds of .375 Magnum ammunition at game. . . . One [rifle] accounted for more than 100 elephant and some 411 buffalo, besides rhino, lions. . . . Though my formula gives [the .375] a Knock-Out value of 40 points . . . that does not really do full justice to it."

Taylor recalled a buffalo he hammered with a 300-grain solid from his .375 double. "The bull dropped to the shot but in an instant was up again. . . . I gave him the left barrel fairly in the center of his great chest. . . . He crashed on his nose [and] keeled over—stone dead."

Taylor rightly noted that bullet construction has much to do with killing big game. He once shot a waterbuck at 40 yards with a 235-grain .375 bullet at 2,850 fps. The animal ran and had to be shot again because the copper-pointed bullet "literally disintegrated against the spine . . . making [only] an appalling surface wound. . . ." Taylor liked the .375 with 300-grain solids, which gave "deeper penetration than any other bullet I have ever used." He warned against solids not hard enough to maintain their form.

The first Cape buffalo I shot ran off, and I clobbered it quartering away with a German 300-grain solid from my .375. A couple of hits later, the bull expired. Autopsy showed the second bullet had entered at the last rib, but instead of driving to the far shoulder had "gone banana," bending then carving a hooked path that ended just under the hide behind the *near* shoulder. Its arc kept it clear of the vitals. Not good.

Despite early bullet failures, the .375 H&H Magnum has earned its immortality; it's no closer to obsolescence now than the automobile. The original light-bullet load, a 235-grain softnose at 2,800 fps, is dead. The 270-grain softnose remains popular. Nosler's 260-grain AccuBond hits harder at 200 yards than a 180-grain .30-06 bullet at the muzzle, and flies as flat. For game the size of buffalo, 300-grain Swift A-Frame and Trophy Bonded bullets by Federal are my pick of softpoints. In full-throttle loads, they bring two tons of energy to 50 yards. Several firms market superb 300-grain solids. At 350 grains, Woodleigh's long solids pack more weight (and sectional density). I used one to shoot an elephant between the eyes at slingshot range. The animal collapsed, dead while it was still falling, the bullet lodging in its flank.

The .375 has wide appeal partly because it can be chambered in bolt rifles as lively as a .30-06. Most hunters can point such a rifle more deftly than they can a heavier, if shorter, double. And they can fire it without fear of turning their cheek or shoulder the color of old cheese. Whatever the mechanism, rifles for the .375 H&H don't require the steel of those built to hurl 410- to 570-grain bullets half an inch in diameter. A .375 can be built trim and lithe. Quick handling makes first hits faster, and can help send more bullets into crippled animals than might be possible with a ponderous big-bore.

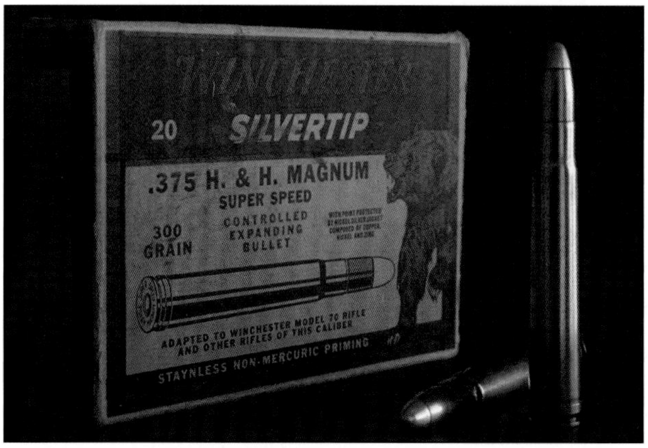

▲ Introduced in 1912, London's .375 H&H soon made its way Stateside. Here, an early factory load.

▲ The taper of the .375 H&H makes for smooth feeding. Crimping helps guard against bullet creep.

▲ A nimble .375 by Montana Rifles helped Wayne kill this leopard with a quick shot at 11 steps.

Agility is too seldom given its due in sporting rifles—especially those used on dangerous game. A few years ago in Namibia, I dashed around a bush to the cry of a tracker who'd come suddenly upon the leopard we'd been trailing. My .375, a svelte arm by Montana Rifles, leapt to my cheek like a shotgun and all but fired itself. The cat rocketed into the air with broken shoulders. It died as it hit the ground, 11 yards away. A heavy rifle would have been slower in hand, slower to point, perhaps a split second too late to the party.

Magazine capacity for .375s exceeds that of rifles storing larger rounds in a box of roughly the same size. With one in the chamber, some rifles (CZ 550s, for example) give you six shots before you must dig in your pockets. Such capacity served a friend well when a Cape buffalo charged, absorbing his first several bullets, plus two from his PH's .505 Gibbs. Close enough to touch with a fly rod, and with blood in its eye, the tank-tough buff fell to the last .375 bullet in my pal's rifle.

A rimmed form of the .375, for double rifles, also appeared in 1912: the .375 Flanged Magnum Nitro Express. But the more powerful belted round works just fine in hinged-breech mechanisms, and the flanged version is pretty much dead.

One of the great all-purpose cartridges still, the .375 H&H begat the .300 H&H Magnum.

Also called the Super .30, the .300 H&H appeared Stateside in the Western Cartridge Company's 1925 catalog. Like its parent, it was too long to pair comfortably with 1898 military Mauser actions or the US Springfield. Magnum Mausers kept both these 3.60-inch cordite-era cartridges alive until the 1937 debut of Winchester's Model 70.

The .300 H&H is more versatile than the .375 in North America, and a delightful .30 in hand. It is commonly said to have surprisingly mild recoil. It was upstaged in shorter actions by the .300 Winchester and .308 Norma Magnums (based on the H&H case), then the .300 WSM and other powerful .30s on beltless hulls. But now the Super .30 is enjoying a bit of a revival. More .300 H&H rifles and factory loads are available than in my youth. With frisky handloads, it matches the .300 Winchester ballistically. Between the world wars, it was also a popular pick for long-range target matches.

If the .375 H&H has a Continental counterpart, it is the 9.3x62 Mauser. Developed in 1905 by Otto Bock in Germany, the "nine-three" gave farmers in Africa's German colonies a cartridge adequate for the toughest game. It soon became popular in Europe on hunts for red deer and wild boar. The 9.3x62 fires a .366-diameter bullet—286 grains in factory loads that drive that beefy missile at around 2,360 fps. Handloaders can duplicate (and trump) that speed with mid-range powders like IMR 3031, 4895, 4320, and 4064. Other fine choices: RL15, Accurate 2015, Vihtavuori N135, and Varget. The 9.3x62 has very nearly the same base and rim diameters as the .30-06, and is about the same length. Closer, physically, to the .35 Whelen than to the .375 H&H, it carries significantly more up-close muscle than the Whelen. It has proven so effective in Africa as to warrant exemption, in some places, from the ".375 minimum" rule for dangerous animals. A friend has used it for almost all of the dozens of elephants and Cape buffaloes he's shot, and has stopped charges with long, lethal Woodleigh solids in his nine-three.

For years the only .366 bullets commonly available Stateside were from Speer. But recently the 9.3x62 has gained a higher profile, with bullets from other makers and loaded ammo from Hornady and Federal as well from Norma, which offers excellent Oryx and Woodleigh loads. I used a CZ 550 in this chambering

▲ Dating to 1905, the 9.3x62 found great favor as a bolt-rifle round for big game in southern Africa.

POWDER AND BRASS

The British Eley Brothers made paper cartridges as early as 1840. Metallic cases permitted stiffer loads, but gunmakers and Eley opened the throttle with care. When cordite first became available, it was held to low (black-powder) pressures because 1) metal cases of the day were thin and prone to stick in hot chambers, 2) big-bore rifles routinely wound up in the tropics, where the sun baked barrels and ammunition, and 3) cordite is temperature-sensitive—even ambient heat can cause pressure spikes.

In 1902, Eley introduced the .450 No. 2. It and "No. 2" cartridges that followed have heavier brass than their parents. Subsequent consolidation of Eley and Kynoch under the shingle of Imperial Chemical Industries, Ltd. gave hunters the celebrated Kynoch ammunition, in yellow and red boxes. From 1925 on, Kynoch hulls were made stout for nitrocellulose powders. During the early 1960s, Berdan priming gave way to reloadable Boxer cases in the Kynoch line. But in 1963 the firm dropped its sporting ammunition. A new company, Kynamco, has taken up the manufacture of classic British big game rounds in a modern, if rural, facility north of London.

on a moose and mountain goat hunt. The moose fell to one shot at 40 yards. The goat took my softpoint quartering away at about 200. A second hit anchored the tough animal. With proper bullets, the 9.3x62 is adequate for any North American game. It's not a flat-shooting round by modern standards, but 250-yard shots make perfect sense.

The best bullets for the 9.3x62 weigh from 250 to 286 grains. A 250 can easily be driven at over 2,600 fps. Federal lists a Barnes TSX load that carries a ton of energy past 300 yards. Loaded stiff, this bullet, and the 250-grain Swift A-Frame and 285-grain Oryx, merit a 200-yard zero. Figure a foot of drop at 300. Zeroing at 150 is more practical for blunt 9.3 bullets, including the old bantamweight: a 232-grain softpoint with modest sectional density.

BIG-BORE NOTES FROM DOWN UNDER

Handloading manuals abound. But Woodleigh's is unique. Now pending publication, it describes loads for the big-bore cartridges—many obscure, many fabled—for which Geoff McDonald developed and manufactures Woodleigh Bullets.

Nearly 40 years ago, Geoff traveled from his family farm ("Woodleigh") in southern Australia to the Northern Territories. The hunt yielded his first buffalo, and campfires with Dave Lindner, a bear of a man with the bush-savvy of Aboriginals. Linder shot animals "on control" for the government. A firearms enthusiast with sophisticated tastes, he mourned the dearth of bullets for early British double rifles.

Back home, Geoff set about making those bullets. It was a daunting task, as the originals were not of common diameter. The proprietary cartridges that dominated big game fields during the transition from black to smokeless powder were rules unto themselves, dimensions determined seemingly at whim. Also, bullets from the black-powder loads struck at lower velocities than those developed on the eve of World War I. Both softpoints and solids had to be engineered either for specific loads or to perform across a wide range of impact speeds.

While Woodleigh bullets sifted the market as handloading components, and appeared in Norma's factory-loaded ammunition, fellow Australian Graeme Wright earned kudos for his fine book, *Shooting the British Double Rifle*. It featured Woodleigh bullets. I decided to visit McDonald's operation.

I came by the back door, traveling through northern Australia, where Wright graciously loaned me a W. C. Scott double in .500 Nitro Express for a try at buffalo. My bolt-rifle upbringing glared as I muffed easy shots. But a couple of bulls obligingly collapsed. Soon that double, plain but vault-tight and beautifully balanced, was pointing as naturally as my arm. "That's why they're favored for dangerous game," smiled Graeme. Dave Lindner concurred, pulling from the shadows at camp a couple of lovely British doubles likewise fueled by Woodleigh.

Geoff McDonald and I made our way south, into bucolic countryside. The ancient tooling in his farmstead shop didn't impress me. But the bullets did. I marveled at the tolerances and Geoff's attention to jacket design and uniformity. A family enterprise with few employees, Woodleigh lavishes great care on its products as if each missile were a custom creation. Result: Bullets from this corner of Australia have emerged as a measure of superiority—the best available for vintage sporting rifles. They've also become the top pick for safari-bound hunters with high-octane cartridges like the .458 Lott. Woodleigh bullets appear in dangerous-game cartridges by Norma and Federal.

When Geoff and Graeme committed to a handloading manual, I knew it would be comprehensive, and painstakingly accurate. The draft includes more than data for odd-size British bullets. For example, Geoff has told the tale of John Marozzi's Hydrostatic design, which he adopted at Woodleigh. This hard-hitting, square-nose solid now has a polymer cap for slick feeding. Dave Lindner has been tapped to share his bush experiences with this and other bullets. I can't think of another book that depends as heavily on field results as this one. Ballistic gelatin is a great aid in proofing bullets, but it doesn't match the massive bones and muscles of buffalo! And McDonald has tested his loads in an eye-popping assortment of bolt-action and double rifles.

As to data, the Woodleigh manual will comprise two main sections. "American and European Cartridges" covers more than 80 hunting rounds, from the 6.5 Mannlicher-Schoenauer to Geoff's own behemoth .530s. "British and Double Rifle Cartridges" details both obscure and historically important rounds, and other big-bores, like the .470, popular after a century. It lists "loads within expected velocity range" so you can duplicate pressures as well as velocities of original factory ammo.

Geoff McDonald and Graeme Wright have conspired to produce an exhaustive, entertaining, and informative book with data and descriptions you'll find nowhere else. This tome belongs in your library, even if there's no Holland Royal sidelock in your gun case!

BEFORE YOU TOOL UP . . .

I enjoy handloading fat bullets for shoulder-crushing cartridges. Their size and heft better suit my big fingers than do the slippery little spear-shaped missiles suitable for prairie dogs. But if you choose a .22 over your .505 to chase gophers from the garden, or if you wish to test a costly "stopping" rifle before you buy it, tooling up and ordering handloading components for that big-bore doesn't make sense. Enter factory loads for safari-class rounds. Federal and Hornady pioneered in this market. "We don't sell many boxes of .470s," confided a pal at Federal. "But we do very, very well with those we do."

▲ Biggest big-bore sporting round? The .700 Nitro Express dwarfs all, here with the more versatile .243.

Eleven cartridges .40-bore and up define Nosler's Safari stable. The .404 Jeffery has a 400-grain Solid, the .500-416 a 400-grain Partition. The .416 Rigby and .416 Remington Magnum come with 400-grain Partitions and Solids. The .458 Winchester and .458 Lott launch 500-grain bullets (properly driven 2,100 fps in the Winchester case). You get 500-grain Partitions in the .450 Rigby and 500-grain Solids in the .470 NE. The .500 Jeffery and .500 NE carry 570-grain Solids, the .505 Gibbs Solids of 525 grains.

Norma's African PH stable boasts Woodleigh softs and solids, .375 H&H to .505 Gibbs. The 12 cartridges include four rimmed numbers for doubles, including the .375 Flanged. For many Norma loads, you can get the company's own brass-alloy solid bullets—also listed for the 9.3x62 and the .416 Taylor (the .338 Winchester Magnum necked up).

▲ The .458, Winchester's first commercial short, belted magnum, had the muscle of much larger rounds.

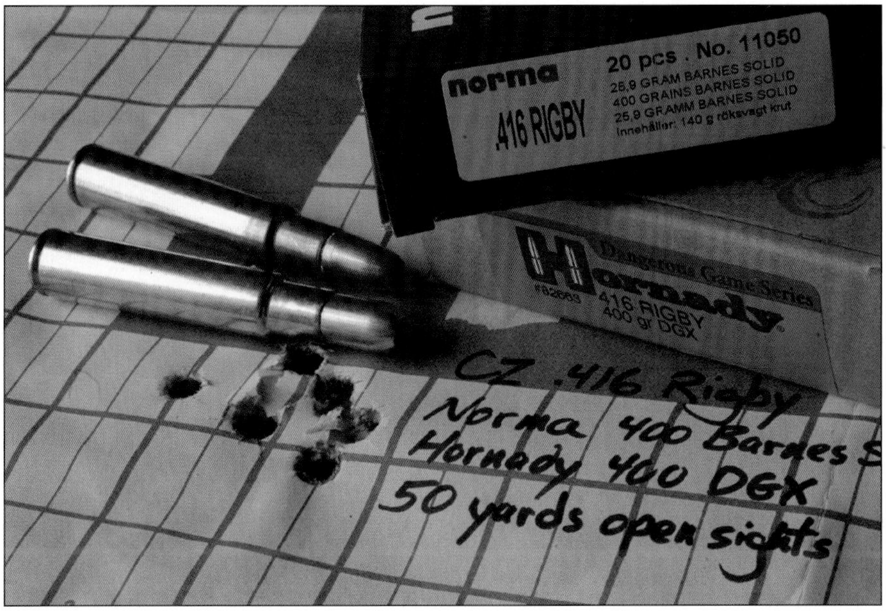

◀ New big-bore bullets, handloaded and in factory ammo, deliver fine accuracy, same impact point.

◀ Booming interest in "safari" rifles and early cartridges has put new tooling and dies on the market.

Chapter 14: More on Bullets

Lead bullets that fit the bores of muzzleloaders are fairly easy to make. Frontiersmen cast their own. You can too, with a pot and a mold.

CASTING YOUR OWN

When I was just a year old, the *Ideal Hand Book*, published by the Lyman Gun Sight Corp., told do-it-yourself riflemen and handgunners how to make bullets. It urged them to buy "an IDEAL Bullet Mould, an IDEAL Dipper, a melting pot that will hold between five and ten pounds of metal, such as the IDEAL Melting Pot, some bullet metal and . . . beeswax, tallow or sal ammoniac for fluxing the metal."

It allowed that with one of the new electric furnaces on the market "which are very convenient for home use," the dipper is unnecessary.

Casting bullets is still a good way to save money and get an extra measure of satisfaction from your loads. While times have changed, the basics of bullet casting have not. Briefly, here's the process, and some ancillary items to scrounge before starting:

You'll need a heavy wooden stick to strike the mold's sprue cutter, and a container, preferably of metal, that will accept the dross skimmed from the pot.

Fold an old blanket or towel to form a cushion on which to drop hot bullets. Fresh from the mold, bullets should never be dropped on a hard surface or against each other. Nicks and dents affect accuracy.

With all materials at hand, heat the lead until it melts completely. Then add the tin (it will melt at once). Now add an acorn-size hunk of beeswax or tallow and stir the metal well. The smoke from either of these fluxing greases can be ignited with a match, if it doesn't ignite itself. Fluxing mixes the metals in the alloy and causes any impurities to rise to the surface, where they can be skimmed off. Bright, clean metal remains. Always flux before skimming!

▲ Big game bullets must fly flat and accurately, expand at distance but remain intact here, up close! (Gene Brehm photo.)

Now, with the ladle about half full of metal and the hole in the bullet mold horizontal, place the spout against the hole and turn mold and ladle together to a vertical position, allowing the cavity to fill. Remove the ladle, leaving some metal in the sprue hole. With your wood striker, slice off the sprue with a sharp blow to the sprue cutter. Open the mold and let the bullet fall on the folded blanket or other pad. If the bullet doesn't drop, tap the mold with your stick. Never use a metal tool to strike the mold!

The first bullets from a mold may be wrinkled on the surface, indicating traces of oil in the cavity, or a failure to get the mold hot. Bright, shiny bullets that don't fill out in the corners may also indicate a cool mold. If the lead has a frosted appearance, the mold and metal are probably too hot—though these bullets are as serviceable (excepting, perhaps in some small-bore loads) as those with a brilliant finish.

While the bullets cool, keep them separated on a soft surface.

The number of molds available for rifle and handgun bullets approaches the count of stars in the summer sky. Credit many shooters tweaking bullet design over decades. While cast-bullet enthusiasts are relatively few in this age of jacketed missiles, some shooting matches still permit only cast bullets. A pal routinely places well in competition with his .30-06, a rifle that probably can't remember when the last cupronickel jacket skated down its bore.

Bullet molds usually cast bullets slightly larger than their finished size so that they can be forced through a die of final diameter to true them up and remove imperfections. But before sizing, lead bullets must be lubed—their grooves filled with grease. For this, Ideal built its Kake Kutter, with instructions: "Stand a number of bullets on their bases in a pan or shallow box. . . . Pour melted lubricant around the bullets so that it is deep enough to cover all the grooves. Allow the grease to cool [in the lubricant]. The Kake Kutter is used to cut the bullets out of the grease, each bullet pushing the preceding one up through the Kake Kutter. If you have a cartridge case of suitable inside diameter you can make your own Kake Kutter by boring out the head of the case."

A quicker, arguably easier method is to melt the lubricant in a container of such depth that bullets can conveniently be immersed, one at a time, with your fingers. After dipping a bullet to fill its grooves, stand

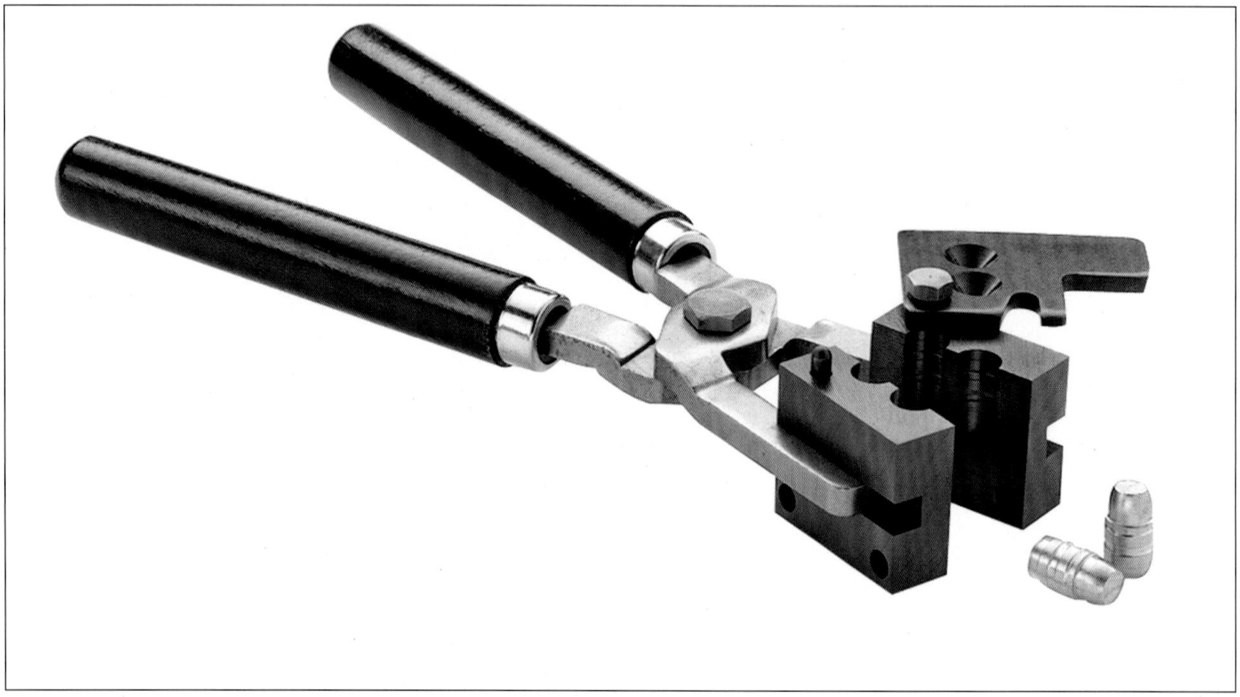

▲ Bullet molds (here from RCBS) are available for handloaders who cast their own. It's an art unto itself!

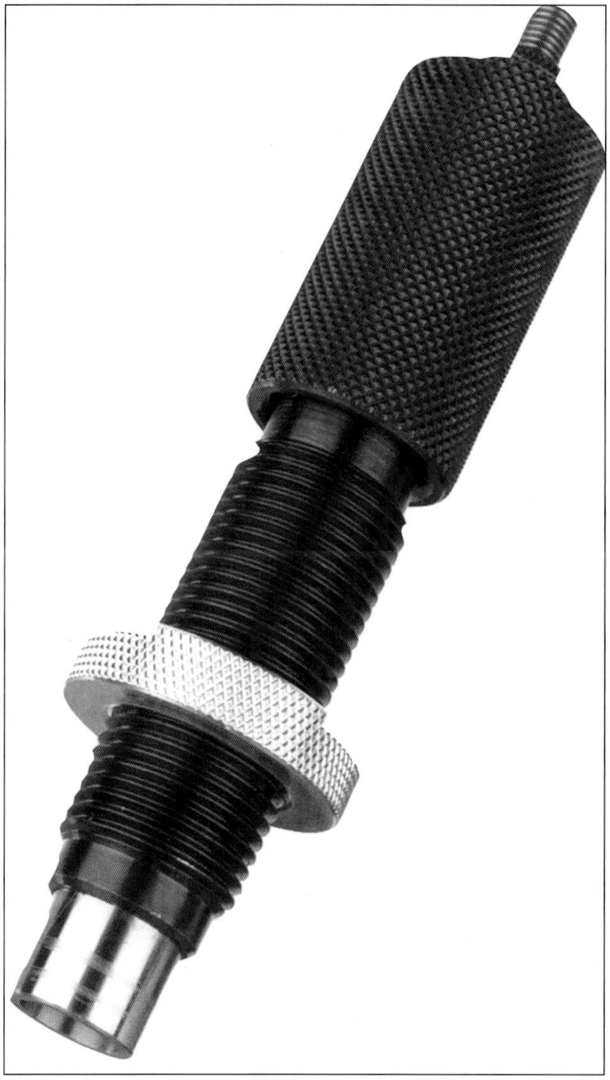

▲ Forster's seating dies with inner sleeves align bullets precisely, so they enter hulls without tipping.

it on its base on a board or sheet of paper. The lube will coagulate around the cold bullet. When set, the excess lubricant can be trimmed with the Kake Kutter or a similar sleeve. If the bullets are held in the hot lubricant long enough to warm them, excess lubricant will shed itself. If they're allowed to get *too* warm, lube will run out of the grooves.

Sizing now produces a finished bullet. Ideal's Bullet Sizing Chamber of the 1950s comprised a die and a punch to fit the standard bullet for each diameter. This punch drove the bullet through the die base first. A point-first orientation, though intuitive, leaves the base vulnerable to deformation, which typically affects bullet flight more than does minor damage to the nose. Tooling for this operation hasn't changed much since jacketed bullets became widely available. As the die gives a cast bullet its finished dimensions, it also packs grease into the grooves.

Incidentally, bullets with bands of different diameters are intended to be used as cast.

Even for low-velocity loads, pure lead isn't suitable for bullets in cartridge firearms. Too soft to resist skidding and deformation during its thrust into the rifling, lead strips from the bullet's shank and adheres to the rifling. Each bullet, its accuracy impaired by its torn surface, leaves more lead in the bore, the build-up further reducing the barrel's ability to deliver bullets to the same place. Of course, pure lead is also easily damaged in handling. Alloying lead with tin makes the bullet harder. These metals mix well when heated to liquid states (easily done on a kitchen stove). When they solidify the lead will contain up to 11 percent tin in a true alloy. A tin component exceeding 11 percent will crystallize.

The *Ideal Hand Book* advised beginners: "A mixture of 1 part tin to 30 parts lead will be hard enough for revolver bullets and bullets for use in rifles with charges of black powder. A mixture of 1 part tin, 15 parts lead will make a suitable mixture for all-around use." For bullets equipped with gas checks (metal caps over the heel to prevent the powder gas from melting the bullet at higher velocities), "the best mixture is an alloy of 1 part tin to 10 parts lead."

▲ Lead bullets, here in Black Hills loads, remain a great match for lever guns like this 53 Winchester.

Lyman supplied "several alloys of different degrees of hardness." It recommended a gas or electric source of heat, but acknowledged that "millions of excellent bullets have been cast over coal fires and the kitchen coal range. . . ."

The *Hand Book* recommended these alloys for various applications. While much in the shooting industry has changed since I was a tyke, the numbers still make sense!

Revolvers—Not softer than 1 part tin to 40 parts lead. Alloys as hard as 1 part tin to 10 parts lead or 1 part tin, 1part antimony to 20 parts lead may be used with entire satisfaction.
Automatic Pistols—1 part tin to 10 parts lead or 1 part tin, 1 part antimony to 20 parts lead. Alloys as soft as 1 part tin to 20 parts lead can be used, but soft bullets are more liable to damage.
Rifles, Black Powder—1 part tin to 16 parts lead if bullets are undersized. With bullets of groove diameter or larger, use 1 part tin to 10 parts lead or 1 part tin, 1 part antimony to 20 parts lead.
Rifles, Plain Base Bullets—1 part tin to 15 parts lead with light loads. For normal loads use 1 part tin to 10 parts lead or a 90-5-5 mixture of lead, tin, and antimony.
Rifles, Gas-Check Bullets—1 part tin to 10 parts lead or a 90-5-5 mixture of lead, tin, and antimony.

Cast-bullet enthusiasts know antimony also hardens lead, but they avoid using antimony alone, as it can crystallize out when the alloy solidifies or freezes. While a home-cast lead-antimony bullet will feel harder than a lead bullet, the lead actually embraces antimony crystals in a soft matrix. Bullet scarring and bore leading may still result. A lead-tin mixture better binds antimony crystals. Alloys of lead and tin also melt better, cast better, and size better than lead with antimony only (which expands when it cools, so the alloyed bullets "cast large").

For all the hurdles imposed by antimony, it is an invaluable component of rifle bullets, jacketed as well as cast. It raises the melting point of the bullet alloy while boosting its hardness. Antimony is used commercially in the manufacture of bullets built for Mach 4 flight from centerfire rifles.

Alloying bullet metal, bear in mind that each component has its own melting point. Antimony's is too high to reach on a kitchen stove. Veteran bulletcasters weigh out the appropriate dose and break it up by pounding it fine with a hammer. They melt the lead and bring it to a red heat, then add the antimony and cover the molten surface with powdered charcoal to keep the lead from oxidizing. They stir the mix and flux with bees' wax or sal ammoniac. The antimony melts.

Antimony, however, is lighter than lead and will float on the surface of molten alloy. A layer of antimony is your cue to increase the heat and again flux the metal. Never skim the metal without fluxing, as you'll selectively remove the lighter material and change the character of the alloy. Keep alloys well mixed to avoid

▲ A variety of bullets for targets, hunting, and defense are available for handguns. Here: cast and JHP.

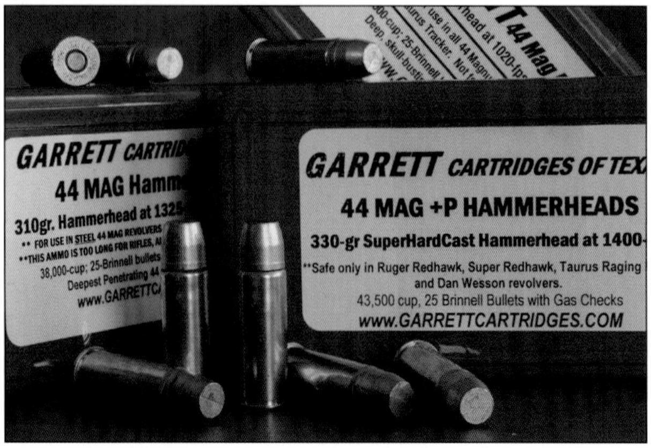

▲ Hard-cast bullets are the foundation of frisky Garrett loads for big-bore handguns and rifles.

a batch of bullets too high in tin or antimony—and soft bullets from the bottom of the pot.

Metal crystal formation is affected by the time of cooling. Expect large crystals if the metal cools slowly, small ones if cooling is rapid. When the mold and metal are so hot that it takes several seconds for the sprue to solidify, bullets may appear frosted, courtesy of the large crystals formed by extended cooling.

In black-powder days, bullets were usually made several thousandths of an inch smaller than the groove diameter of the barrel. Black powder burns (and builds pressure) so fast that it delivers a blow to the bullet base. While the peak pressure didn't match that of progressive smokeless powders that arrived beginning in the 1890s, that slap was sharp enough to upset a lead bullet base. "Bumped up" at launch, the bullet would better fill rifling grooves. Still, work by Lyman and shooters casting lead bullets proved that harder bullets sized to groove diameter yielded accuracy equal to that of soft bullets. When several shots had to be fired without cleaning, the harder alloys were superior, as they produced less leading in the bore and less deformation in the bullet shank and base. (Bullets for some revolvers may be sized as much as .003 larger than groove diameter).

Velocities at which plain-base lead alloy bullets can be driven are limited by the temperature and pressure of the powder gas—and the duration of thrust. Bullets melted by the gas pushing them are hardly useful! Gas-cutting occurs when gas melts the side of the bullet and surges ahead of it, spraying molten bullet metal into the bore, where it adheres to the rifling. Once lead becomes attached to the steel, it picks up more lead from subsequent bullets. Gas-cutting can cause leading regardless of the bullet alloy.

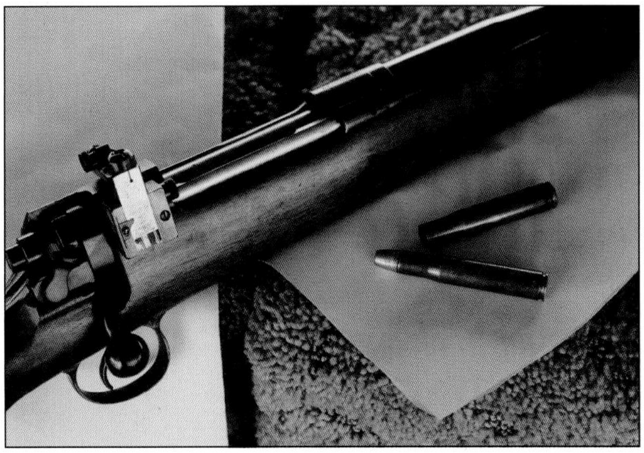

▲ Cast bullets suit bolt rifles too. This 1917 Enfield '06 is fun to fire with mild, accurate, cast loads.

SLUGGING A BORE

To get the best performance from any rifle or handgun, the bullet must fit the bore. Barrels drilled and rifled on modern machinery are wonderfully uniform. Bores of rifles and handguns built more than a century ago—and even custom black-powder arms to this day—can vary in dimension. Slugging a barrel to get exact land and groove measures makes sense, especially when you're casting your own bullets.

First, clean the bore, finishing with an oiled swab. Get a lead slug just over groove diameter—or use a bullet of that caliber, "bumping it up" slightly in a vise or with a hammer. With light blows from the hammer to a short brass rod, tap the slug into the bore from the muzzle. A ring of lead should shear off, indicating the slug is big enough to contact the bellies of the grooves. With longer rods, continue tapping or pushing the slug through the bore. Catch it on a soft cloth to prevent deformation. Measure across the opposite ridges (grooves in reverse) with a micrometer caliper. You'll get groove diameter, the measure that counts when you're tooling up to cast and size bullets.

To reach higher velocities with homemade bullets, John Barlow, who developed Ideal's original tooling for handloaders, devised the gas-check. (No doubt other shooters had this idea too.) A gas-check is a shallow gilding metal cup attached to the base of a cast bullet. It endures the heat and pressure there better than does a lead bullet base. Gas-check bullets can be driven 200 to 300 fps faster than lead bullets without leading, and they better resist damage in handling.

Gas-checks fit on bullets made especially for them. They can be gently tapped onto bullet bases before lubricating. A bullet sizing chamber then seats the gas-checks firmly. Ideal's old No. 45 Lubricator and

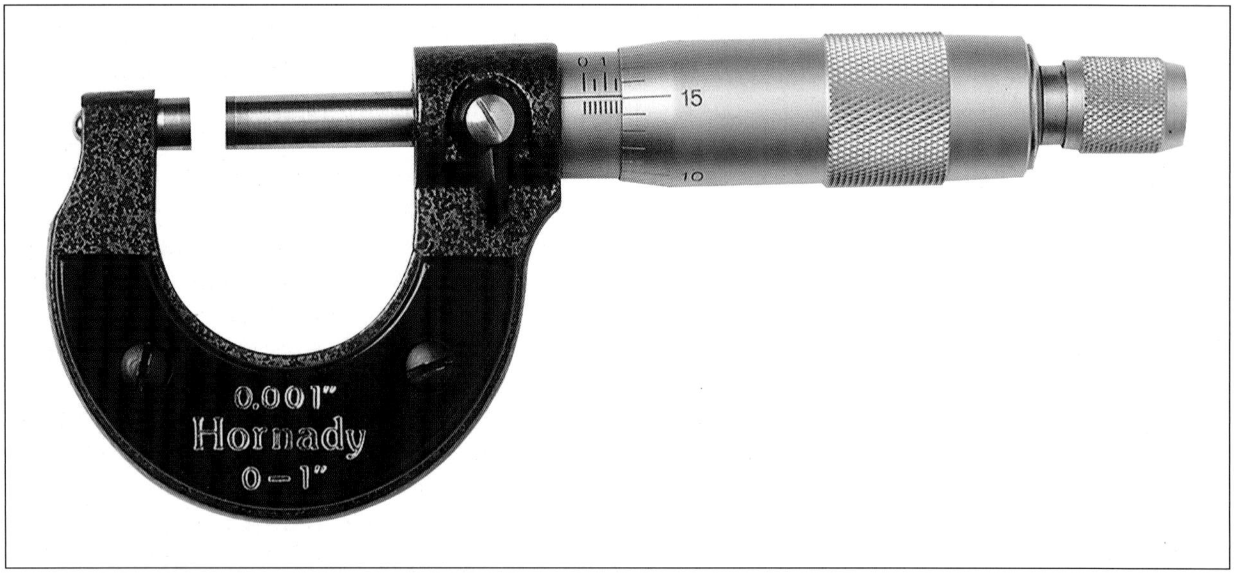

▲ Custom bullet-makers should hew to industry standards re: diameter. Use a micrometer to check.

BRASS TO MATCH CAST BULLETS

Casting bullets from wheel-weight lead, once a popular hobby, still entertains shooters who get special satisfaction from "made-from-scratch" ammo. It also makes sense for "high-volume" handgunners and for enthusiasts with vintage firearms or those using hard-to-find cartridges. Brass cases for old-time and obscure military rounds can be tough to locate too. But Starline, in Sedalia, Missouri, specializes in these hulls. Its current list includes 75 mostly uncommon numbers like the .38 Short Colt and .38 Super Comp, the .45 S&W, .475 Wildey, and .500 Linebaugh. Rifle cases include those for the .38-55, .40-65, .45-100, .50-90, .56-50 Spencer. . . .

Sizer, used with an inside punch having a concave surface, installs gas-checks in a jiffy. The cavity fits the gas-checks and prevents lubricant from being forced under the bullets. Flat-faced punches should be used with plain-base bullets.

FROM GREASE GROOVE TO JACKET

The high velocities achievable with smokeless powder generate lead-melting heat, pressure, and bore friction in the bore. In the 1890s, bullet jackets showed up to prevent leading and ensure accuracy. These were paired with harder cores that better retained their shape under the terrific stresses imposed by smokeless propellants.

Early .30-06 bullets were jacketed with an alloy of 85 percent copper and 15 percent nickel. It did not hold up at .30-06 velocities, and fouling rendered rifles inaccurate. Tin plating reduced fouling, but over time, tin "cold-soldered" to case mouths and could cause pressure spikes. Some necks even exited with the bullets, squeezing with protest through

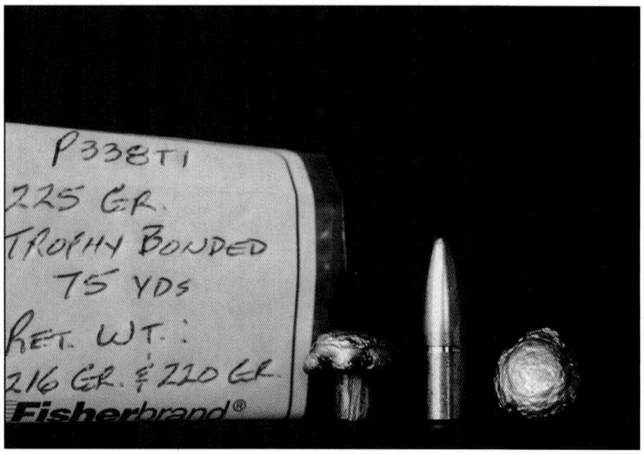

▲ Upset like this, with high weight retention, makes the Trophy Bonded a top choice for tough game.

Springfield bores! An alloy of zinc and copper, 5-95 or 10-90, solved this problem. It became known as gilding metal.

The cores of rifle and handgun bullets have evolved to accomplish specific tasks. Almost all have a dash of antimony to make them harder. The usual ratio for rifles: 97.5 percent lead, 2.5 antimony. Sierra uses three alloys for rifle bullets, with antimony proportions of 1.5, 3, and 6 percent. I don't know of any commercial bullets with more than 6 percent antimony, and some big game bullets have unalloyed lead cores to yield cohesive mushrooms as they upset in game. Thick copper or copper alloy jackets on these rifle and handgun bullets keep their soft cores from fragmenting.

▲ Big bullets from the .577 Nitro Express, right, then the .505 Gibbs are now matched in effect by the short .458.

Core blanks for most modern jacketed bullets are lopped from lead wire extruded from bar stock, then annealed to prevent expansion during forming. Even "pure" bullet lead has traces of copper, zinc, nickel, arsenic, aluminum; but only by design are these metals permitted in significant amounts. As little as .1 percent copper can cause hard spots.

Bullet jackets are formed by impact extrusion or a "cup-and-draw" process. Drawn jackets begin as wafers punched from sheet metal. Formed over a series of dies, they become progressively deeper cups that are eventually trimmed to length. After insertion of the lead core, the bullet is shaped and finished off at the nose. Jackets given the impact extrusion treatment arrive at the punch press as sections of annealed rods. The press slams them into cups with 60 tons of force. Bullets like the Nosler Partition have cavities fore and aft so must be punched twice. (Original Partitions had machine-turned jackets.)

Hornady gets its lead in ingots, which are melted and formed into cylindrical blocks the size of a roll of freezer paper—albeit much heavier! A massive press squirts these cylinders, cold, through dies to form the wire that's then cut into bullet lengths. Antimony content is specified at purchase, from 0 to 6 percent. Most Hornady bullet cores have 3 percent antimony. Jacket cups punched from sheets are held to tight tolerances because concentricity is vital to accuracy. Hornady holds it to just .003 "runout."

Bullet shape influences accuracy and arc. Though it would reduce drag in the barrel, lengthening the nose to shorten the shank gives the nose greater leverage if it swings off the bullet's axis in flight. A long nose also mandates a more gradual curvature forward of the shank—which increases the chance for misalignment in the throat, and subsequent yaw. "A short transition is best, so the bullet is forced quickly into full contact with the rifling," says Hornady's Dave Emary, who prefers to keep the ratio of bearing surface to diameter 1.5 or higher. "Nose type and other variables affect that ratio." He points out that the "secant ogive" profile of Hornady Spire Points reduces nose weight. "Tangent ogives yield more rounded form. We've used the secant ogive for years to minimize air friction. It doesn't necessarily mean a sharper junction between the conical and cylindrical sections of the bullet; but it can appear that way." (Secant and tangent refer to the point from which an arc, its radius measured in calibers, scribes the outline of the bullet nose. As it has been explained to me, tangent ogives start perpendicular to the bullet axis at the cylinder-cone juncture. Secant ogives begin behind that point.)

To accommodate crimping, some bullets are given cannelures. Once common, and still advisable in safari rifles and powerful lever-actions with tube magazines, cannelured bullets aren't needed for the most popular loads in bolt rifles. They've been retained on bullets used in heavy-recoiling rounds for both rifles and pistols to guard against bullet creep and to smooth some cartridge profiles for better feeding in autoloading mechanisms. Many factory loads are still crimped. Except where specifically required, the process is commonly viewed among handloaders as the unnecessary addition of another variable. Most cannelures are rolled on; Nosler cuts the crimp in its 210-grain .338 bullet.

▲ A hunting partner admires one of Wayne's bucks. The .35 Whelen bullet penetrated lengthwise.

The smallest variations in bullet dimensions and weight can influence point of impact. Jacket and core must be held to close tolerances. Rich Maccholz of Sierra Bullets insists jacket concentricity is the key to accuracy. "Sierra MatchKings nip tiny groups because we take extra care with jackets. We allow .0003-thickness variation at the bullet base, .0010 at the nose. Jacket tolerances for Pro-Hunter (flat-base) and GameKing (boat-tail) bullets are almost as tight: .0005 at the base, .0015 at the nose. Weight limits for match and hunting bullets are the same: .3 grains maximum variation on finished bullets. Maximum runout is the same too: .0001 at the nose." Sierra makes its own jackets, using two to five draws to bring the cupronickel from strip to cup. Test lots of 168-grain 30-caliber match bullets that don't shoot into *¼ inch* at 100 yards can send the entire batch back to the production line!

Hornady's Dave Emary agrees that jacket concentricity is important. "Another thing to mind is the distance between center of gravity and center of pressure. It's hard to measure because it's only there when the bullet is moving. For a bullet that flies point-on, CP doesn't matter. But if there's lift or yaw, a CP that's far from CG affects stability." A tapered heel or boat-tail moves center of gravity back, away from the center of pressure. "That's one reason flat-base bullets commonly shoot as well as or better than boat-tails. Another is that flat-base bullets are easier to keep uniform; there's one less angle on the heel. Also, when the shank of a flat-base bullet clears the muzzle, there's no tail for powder gas to wag." On average, Dave tells me, flat-base bullets go to sleep sooner in flight.

Hornady's Spire Point softpoints have been a mainstay of deer hunters for decades. Now the firm also makes A-Max (Advanced Match Accuracy) spitzers for competitive shooting. The V-Max, introduced in 1995, shares the A-Max's plastic nose insert. A very thin jacket gives the V-Max explosive effect on small animals. The SST (Super Shock Tip) plastic-nose bullet for big game

▲ Fast, flat-shooting, lightly constructed bullets excel for pronghorns. Tamar's Kimber is a .270.

◀ Short softpoint bullets, throttled down, tame potent rounds like the .458 Winchester for light game.

followed. "We got the SST designation from a 1950s Hornady bullet board," recalls Emary, "It's now our premier deer bullet." The Hornady InterBond is essentially a bonded version of the SST, to floor tough game.

"Most bullets that expand readily and reliably in deer can be made to shoot very accurately," says Rich Maccholz. "Thin gilding metal jackets and lead cores allow ballisticians plenty of freedom in nose design. We're not so constrained by length limits as we would be with solid-copper bullets or even thick jackets. The more lightweight material you have in a bullet, the longer it will be for its weight. At some point you must reduce weight to get the design you want, or put up with a bullet too long to stabilize in standard rifling—or a bullet that requires deep seating into powder space." He adds that heavy bullets can be very accurate. But the heaviest bullets have round noses and fly in steep arcs.

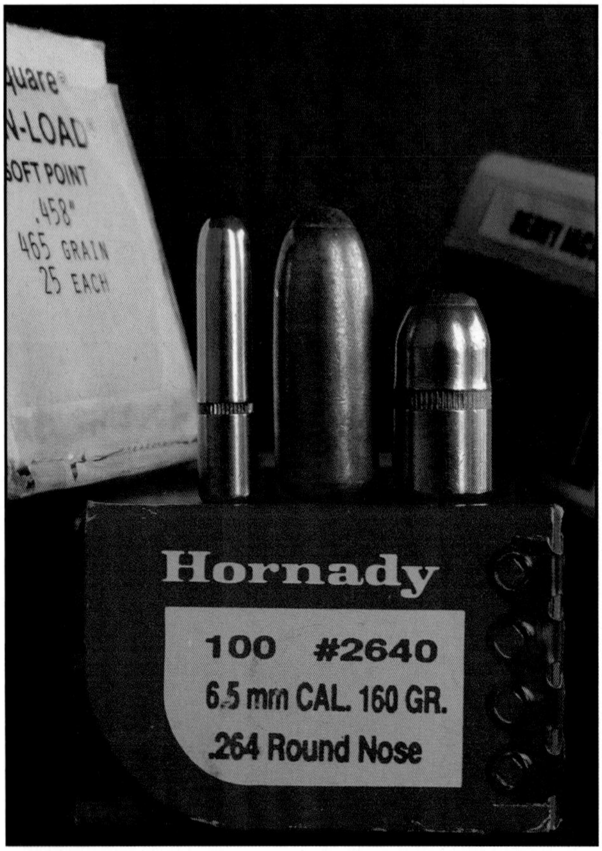

▲ Long, slender bullets (left) have high sectional density; they drive deeper than short, thick bullets.

The bullet's tip has less to do with accuracy than does a uniform base. And it has very little effect on trajectory. "If the meplat, or bullet tip, is less than 15 percent of the bullet's diameter, you won't get any flatter flight with a sharp bullet," declared Alan Corzine, then a ballistician for ATK (Federal). "The ogive or curve of the bullet from about .1 back from tip to shank matters more. A perfectly formed heel doesn't affect the arc, but it's essential for fine accuracy." He agreed with Dave Emary that round-nose bullets often fly more accurately than spitzers.

To test the effect of nose shape on accuracy, I once cut the noses off several .338 bullets halfway down the ogive. Bullet shanks were crushed in the jaws of my tool. Though now of different weights, and leading with ragged mouths, the bullets still shot into 3 inches at 100 yards!

Blunt bullets sometimes penetrate straighter than pointed bullets. Deformation that results in an unevenly weighted (not concentric) front or a lopsided ogive will cause the bullet to stray. Blunt bullets may drive more consistently through brush, but that's difficult to prove because it's nearly impossible to hit branches exactly the same each time in trials. I've found that both pointed and blunt bullets deflect on thumb-size limbs so badly that targets just 12 feet behind them show keyhole hits well off the mark.

A round-nose bullet has a weight advantage over pointed bullets of the same length, so it yields higher sectional density. But at long range drag eats momentum, which is why spitzers are more popular. Round-nose bullets can't battle drag as well, so they decelerate faster. A bullet losing speed is also losing energy. Because round-nose bullets move more slowly, they drop farther per unit of distance. For example, a 180-grain Nosler Ballistic Tip kicked from a .30-06 at 2,700 fps reaches 500 yards still clocking 1,887. The steep ogive of Swift's A-Frame, a partitioned softnose that yields picture-book upset, throttles that bullet from 2,700 at the muzzle to 1,648 fps at 500 yards. Result: the Ballistic Tip brings almost as much energy to 500 yards as the A-Frame does to 400! And it drops less from line of sight.

Now, polymer-tipped bullets do not always fly flatter than softnose bullets. The 150-grain Sierra GameKing loaded by Federal to 3,110 fps in the

▲ Iron sights and blunt bullets in his .303 Savage compelled Wayne to creep close. Memorable hunt!

7mm Remington Magnum reaches 500 yards traveling 50 fps faster than a Nosler Ballistic Tip of the same weight, launched at the same speed. Nor are polymer-tip bullets necessarily your most accurate choice. During a visit to Hornady's plant, I noticed a stack of targets with one-hole groups. They were shot with regular softnose bullets.

▲ The bullet ogive has a greater effect on trajectory than the tip. The base most affects accuracy.

▲ Polymer-tip bullets are no longer just for light game. Some have bonded or solid-copper shanks.

WHAT'S WRONG WITH THESE BULLETS?

Many moons ago, I found in the shooting tunnel of Hornady's Grand Island, Nebraska, factory a rack of gleaming Hart and Schneider barrels screwed into M70 and M700 receivers. This test battery did its work on a three-point, free-recoiling machine rest.

"What happens when a customer insists he got bad bullets?" I asked the attendant.

He smiled. "One of those fellows phoned the other day, said our bullets wouldn't cut a three-minute group. Because he was local, I asked him to bring his rifle to the factory, expecting I'd have to diagnose a problem. When he came in, the first thing I did was load up some of his bullets and bench the rifle. It shot into ¾ inch. To his credit, he took it gracefully. Not all customers do. Shooting can be an ego thing."

Some rifles are fussy about loads, and some bullets are fussy about twist rate. When bullets stray all over the target, the likely culprit is still the quivering mass of capricious protoplasm behind the trigger.

▲ Small-shop bullet-makers turn out fine specialty bullets like these softpoints for stiff .45-70 loads.

ENERGY OR KILLING POWER?

Measuring bullet energy in ft-lbs, you trump weight with speed, because this calculation includes velocity squared. Elmer Keith and other big-bullet proponents have urged measures emphasizing weight instead. Hornady has come up with a formula that strikes me as the best available for assessing a bullet's relative effect on game. Called H.I.T.S (for Hornady Index of Terminal Standards), it incorporates bullet weight and sectional density, ballistic coefficient and impact speed. Resulting three-digit values are easy to compare with those of other loads. Explaining the formula takes longer than pulling up *hornady.com* on your computer. Enter bullet weight and diameter and terminal speed—a H.I.T.S. number will appear.

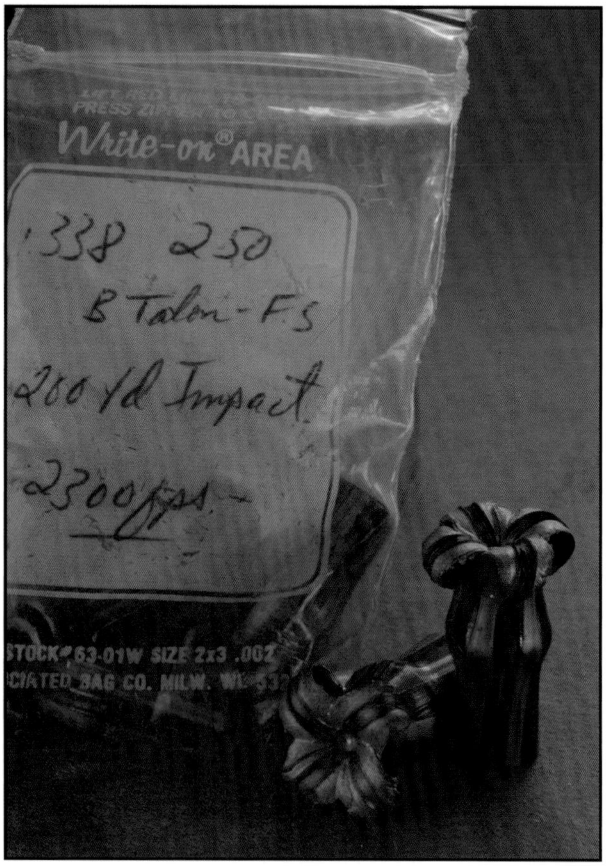

▲ Winchester's Fail Safe, a costly but effective bullet for tough game, is, alas, no longer available.

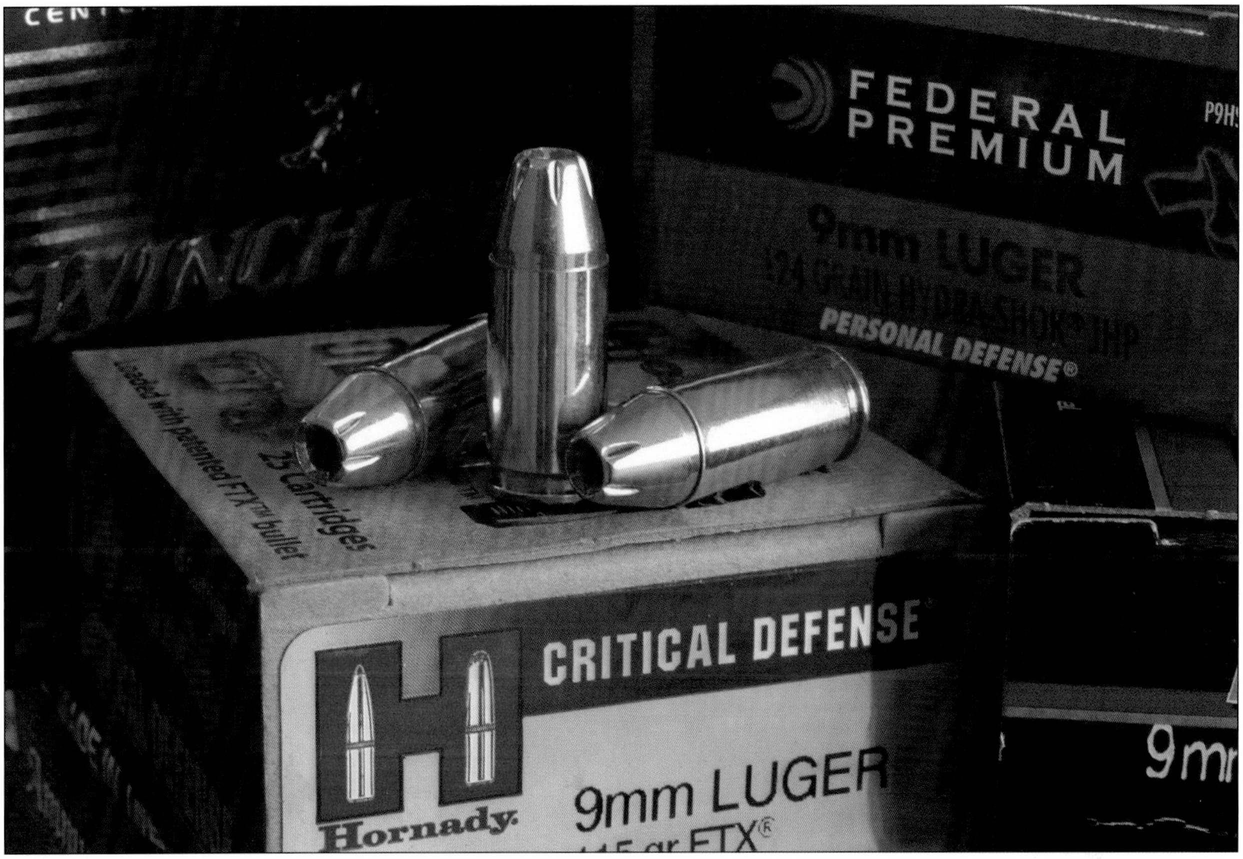

▲ Handloaders once pursued hunting ammo. Now many focus on handgun loads and bullets for defense.

Chapter 15: Bullets for Big Game

In hunting bullets, terminal performance can matter more than accuracy. Expanding bullets dump energy as they decelerate. A ruptured bullet nose hikes resistance, boosting deceleration rate and energy release as it carves a big, pear-shaped cavity. Its rotating nose petals tear tissue. Hydraulic pressure opens the channel still wider. A wound caused by a bullet upsetting to double original diameter is much, much bigger in volume and cross-sectional area than one from a bullet that doesn't open. The violence of upset increases with impact velocity.

In the early days of smokeless propellants, getting predictable but cohesive upset with adequate but not excessive penetration was a problem for bullet makers. Some .270 bullets shattered on contact with game, courtesy their 3,000-fps launch. Winchester tried to mollify whining meat hunters with a 150-grain load throttled to 2,675 fps. Market response was what you'd get for a sports car without high gear.

Subsequent bullet designs and materials have teamed up with high velocity to better deliver a lethal dose of bullet energy to tough targets. So-called "controlled expansion" bullets resist fragmentation on impact but expand to tear broad, deep wound channels.

THE CASE FOR BULLET INTEGRITY

"It's hard to make an all-purpose hunting bullet," observed one engineer—who chose to remain anonymous, lest such defeatism cost him his job. "An ordinary softnose comes close. Polymer tips look sporty but are a pain to make. For deep penetration, the jacket must be thick to slow setback of the tip on impact. Thick jackets are harder to keep concentric.

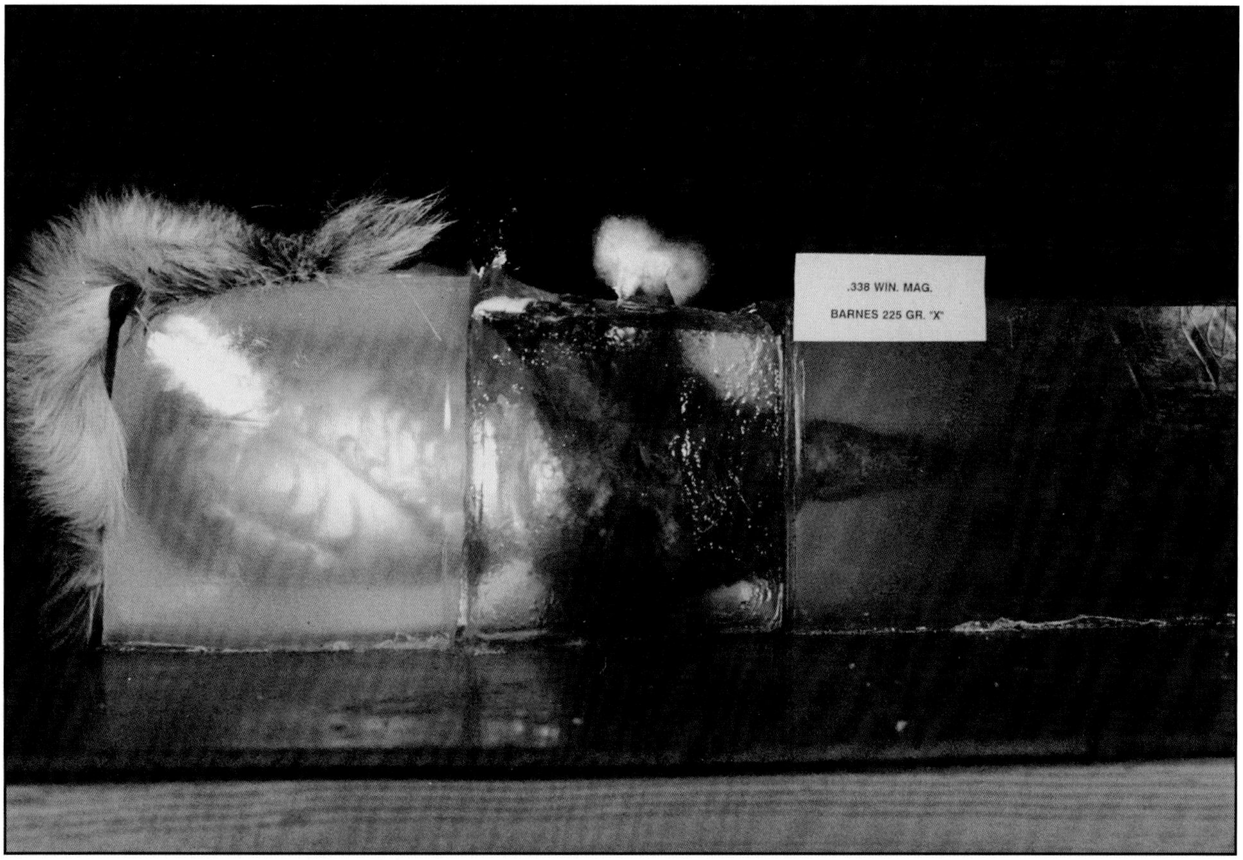

▲ Gelatin, here with deer hide, tests bullet upset. Note torque and violence in convulsing "wound" channel.

▲ No bullet can ensure against deflection. Julie's first shot struck a limb; a second killed this kudu.

Ditto, complex bullets. And remember: hunters expect the missile that flies flat, drills one-hole groups, and plows reliably through tough game after hitting it at Mach 3 to open on a pronghorn so far off that bullet speed has dropped to 1,600 fps."

Bullet nose design has a lot to do with how expansion proceeds. Small cavities and thick jackets keep hollowpoint bullets from fragmenting, but make upset less dependable. Among early hollowpoints, the Western Tool and Copper Works bullet with a tiny nose cavity delighted many American hunters. In Europe, DWM's "strong-jacket" missile had a long, narrow cavity lined with copper tubing and capped.

Westley-Richards of London fielded a bullet with a dimple covered by a metal lid that controlled upset.

The Remington Bronze Point was a hollowpoint with a peg in the hole. The peg's front half was a bronze cone forming the bullet tip. Impact drove the peg back to make the bullet blossom. Remington's current best seller, the Core-Lokt, proved less violent and more reliable. Winchester's early Precision Point had a cone of jacket material over the bullet tip and locked into the jacket proper. Three "windows" at the juncture of cone and jacket initiated upset. Subsequently, Peters developed the Protected Point. A cone capped its flat-topped lead core, whose front third was enveloped by a "driving band" under the jacket. The band controlled expansion. Each Protected Point bullet required 51 operations and three hours to make. Winchester followed with a less costly alternative, minus the driving band. It became the Silvertip.

High-speed impact stresses the marriage of jacket and core. The first jacketed softpoints were of round-nose profile, with lots of lead exposed so they'd open readily at exit speeds of 1,900 to 2,400 fps. But they came apart when pushed at over 2,700. Efforts to

▲ High-energy double-base powders give reach to sleek, controlled-upset bullets like this AccuBond.

keep bullets intact yielded the Peters Inner Belted and its spawn, Remington's Core-Lokt. The Speer Hot-Core process guaranteed adhesion by virtue of warm lead imprinting on the jacket. John Nosler devised a mechanical solution in 1947, after several softpoints from his .300 Magnum disintegrated on a moose. The Nosler Partition has a cupronickel wall dividing the core. However fragmented the nose, the heel drives on, a solid cylinder. Incidentally, Nosler wasn't the first with such an idea. The European H-Mantle is very similar. Before World War I, Charles Newton designed a wire-core bullet. In 1914 he wrote: "A copper wire is embedded in the center of the bullet point [to protect] the point against every deformation except upsetting." Newton's bullet had paper insulation between jacket and core so barrel friction wouldn't melt the core. He'd found evidence of lead seeping from bullets by drilling holes in the jackets, then firing into cardboard and observing lead smears.

Incidentally, the polymer tips now so popular have little to do with a bullet's terminal behavior, though they play a part, commonly as a wedge, to initiate upset. Internal design of the bullet behind the tip determines how a bullet will expand, and to what degree.

Many big game bullets developed in recent decades are touted for their "controlled expansion." But truly, all expanding bullets are designed and manufactured to yield specific results on target. Some are fashioned to unload their energy quickly—to burst violently upon impact. Animals as big as deer and pronghorns fold as if struck by bolts from Zeus. For moose and other heavy creatures, you'll want deep penetration to reach vitals, especially on quartering shots. All bullets begin to expand at about the same time: when they strike the target. Designers can't *delay* upset, because a bullet built to retain its shape on impact won't open after it has slowed inside the animal. What *can* be controlled are the rate and degree of bullet expansion and the bullet's integrity under stress.

The mid-section dam of the H-Mantle and later Nosler Partition is one way to ensure penetration after upset. The current Swift A-Frame combines that design with nose bonding. I like the A-Frame very much. A 140-grain .270 bullet that downed an elk

▲ The Swift A-Frame bullet makes the 7mm Magnum a match for any North American game.

▲ Swift's A-Frame bullets excel not only in centerfire rifle ammo, but handguns and muzzleloaders.

for me bulged the offside skin with 94 percent of its original weight in a double-diameter mushroom.

A modified Partition, the Partition Gold, was marketed by Winchester under the CT (Combined Technology) banner that marked collaboration between Winchester and Nosler. Partition Gold dams were positioned forward to limit weight loss if the nose came apart. A steel cup protected the heel. Winchester had pioneered such cups in its now-defunct Fail Safe bullet, behind a hollow, four-petal nose of copper alloy. The cup prevented the rear lead core from ballooning at the midsection and escaping through seams opened by the curling petal tips.

Chemical bonds have hiked retained weight above the 90-percent mark for many hunting bullets. Jack Carter's Trophy Bonded Bear Claw, now produced by Federal Cartridge, is the modern form of the Bitterroot Bonded Core bullet. The original Trophy Bonded and a new version with polymer tip compete with the likes of the Swift A-Frame and Scirocco, Winchester Power Max Bonded, and Remington Core-Lokt Ultra Bonded.

The Norma Oryx, from the Swedish ammo firm, features a tapered, gilding metal jacket scored at the

▲ Moose this big absorb hard hits. Bullet integrity ensures lethal penetration. This hunter used a .338.

nose for easy upset. The jacket is thicker at the shank, and "soldered" to the lead. A heavy heel section helps prevent deformation at the base. A test Norma has applied follows a longitudinal sectioning of the front end so only the central third remains attached to the heel. The nose slab is twisted 90 degrees. "Core and jacket don't separate," said Torb Lindskog, then Norma's CEO. While Oryx's flat meplat (squared-off nose) makes it look sluggish, the long ogive helps it slide through air. In .30-06 Norma ammo, Oryx bullets drilled a two-inch group for me—at *300* yards.

Woodleigh Weldcore softpoints appeared in 1984. "Two years after we started up," said Geoff McDonald, who operates Woodleigh in southern Australia. "The name is from our farm." Not long ago, he showed me that sheep station. Now in grain, its fertile fingers probe the crook of a shaded, serpentine river in New South Wales, 30 clicks north of Kerang. "My grandfather bought it in 1925," Geoff told me. The modest bullet facility occupies a small riparian plot nearby. There he and his family and neighbors build bullets for discriminating hunters. "I started with softpoints for the .450-400—thought I could better the commercial .458 softs I'd used on my first buffalo."

Geoff makes his bullet cores of commercial lead, "99.7 percent pure." Jacket material is gilding metal, 90 percent copper, 10 percent zinc. Since 1988 the jackets (heavy at the shank) have been bonded to the cores. Norma "African PH" softnose loads feature only Woodleigh Weldcore bullets. Weights and diameters span a range of uses, from small-bore cartridges to the biggest Nitro Express rounds. Weldcores give hunters heavy missiles they can't get elsewhere—350-grain bullets in .375 H&H, for example. These clock only 2,205 from a Sako Kodiak, but they hit like pile drivers. Sectional density is a whopping .356! For Australian buffalo, I carried 570-grain Weldcores in a century-old boxlock double rifle by Webley & Scott, a .500 Nitro Express. But even .375 and .308 Weldcores upended buffalo on that hunt.

Cataloged in 38 diameters, .264 to .700, the Weldcore is a blessing to owners of traditional rifles. Try finding .468 bullets for the .465 Nitro elsewhere! Or .330s and .333s for the .318 Westley-Richards and .333 Jeffery. Woodleigh also makes a Protected Point bullet, with a more streamlined ogive. You can load the 160-grain Protected Points in your 6.5x55, 180s in your .270. A 220-grain Weldcore adds close-range muscle to the .30-06 and .30 magnums. Need a dark-timber load for your .338? Try the 300-grain Weldcore. For handloaders who, like me, favor the .35 Whelen and .358 Norma, Woodleigh offers a 275-grain Protected Point and a 310-grain Weldcore. You can get both bullet types for the 9.3x62, in weights to 320 grains. Federal has loaded Woodleigh bullets since 1988.

▲ The .338 Ultra Mag (left) and .338-378 Weatherby hit hard and test bullet integrity in heavy game.

Heavy bullets of all stripes trade high velocity for momentum. But at normal hunting ranges, that is a better trade than many sportsmen think. With 71 grains RL-22 and a 200-grain Trophy Bonded bullet at 2,870 fps, my .308 Norma will down the toughest North American game. So will a 250-grain Swift A-Frame shoved by 61 grains RL-19 to 2,460 fps in my .338-06. The arc of such long, deep-driving missiles beyond 300 yards doesn't matter to me. I seldom fire at game that far off—especially not animals with the mass of a Harley cruiser and the constitution of a Peterbilt.

THE COPPER OPTION

Another way to reduce bullet weight loss and improve penetration in tough animals is to replace jacketed lead cores with solid copper alloy. First, a clarification: "Solid copper" bullets are not solid in the sense non-expanding bullets are solids. They're made to mushroom. A hollow cavity ruptures the nose,

▲ Bullet companies are now offering loads. You can still get the superb Barnes TSX as a component.

enabling pre-scored petals to peel back, increasing diameter and destruction. Here "solid" refers to the bullet's composition: either "pure" copper or gilding metal (copper/zinc alloy). The Barnes X and TSX are perhaps the best known of these bullets. Winchester has its Super X Power Core, Nosler the E-Tip, Federal its Trophy Copper, Remington its Premier Copper Solid, and Hornady the MonoFlex and GMX.

"Give up lead, and you give up speed in certain cartridges," said Hornady's Dave Emary. "Cases designed for full-capacity charges behind heavy lead bullets don't do as well with copper or gilding metal bullets, because to make weight, so to speak, these must be longer than lead-core bullets. You must put that extra length somewhere." Seating a bullet deeper reduces case capacity. Seating it to greater overall length can jam it in the magazine or throat. Any copper bullet with the dimensions of a lead-core bullet will be lighter. It won't retain its velocity as well or carry quite as much energy. Yes, you can start light bullets faster. But more speed at the muzzle won't offset a higher ballistic coefficient downrange. Also, because copper is harder than lead, and gilding metal harder still, you can't accelerate a non-lead bullet as fast as a traditional softpoint without hiking pressure. There's too much friction from that harder shank.

Another concern attending copper and gilding metal bullets is throat life. Most hunters needn't worry, though. While harder material accelerates barrel wear, few riflemen shoot enough to ruin a throat with these bullets. And competitive shooters have so far stayed true to lead-core designs.

Dave Emary told me solid copper hunting bullets include compromises in the nose. "You want an aerodynamic ogive, a pointed profile. But the small nose cavity in bullets of this shape won't start upset at low impact speeds. We can enlarge the cavity, but only at the expense of ballistic coefficient. More open noses also tend to shatter when driven fast into tough media. Copper bullets expand well in a relatively narrow velocity window. We can make lead-core bullets that drive deep when striking an elk at 3,000 fps but still open reliably in deer at speeds as low as 1,600. It's hard to make a copper bullet expand at under 2,000 fps unless the nose cavity is so big the front end disintegrates at 3,000." Bullets smaller than 6.5mm pose a challenge in nose design because there's so little material forward of the shank.

As for penetration, most copper game bullets drive deep, retaining more of their original weight than lead bullets and delivering a more symmetrical blossom, which tends to drive straighter. On average, petals on copper rifle bullets don't gape quite as widely as jackets on lead bullets, assisted by the smashed core. But while double-diameter upset of a lead bullet blasts a huge wound, damage from a copper bullet 1 ½ times its unfired diameter can be stunning, and its penetration deeper. Not long ago I shot a couple of Australian buffalo with Barnes TSX bullets. Both drove to the off-shoulder, tearing tissue well outside their channels. One hit the knuckle of the off-shoulder so

▲ Wayne broke the off-shoulder of this bull at 27 steps with a Barnes TSX from a .338. A fine bullet.

hard it shattered the wrist-thick bone at mid-section, several inches from point of impact.

Randy Brooks told me he was hunting when it occurred to him that most bullet failures involved lead loss. Not one to let a good idea lie, Randy built an all-copper bullet with a small nose cavity. He took that handmade bullet to Alaska and killed a brown bear. "I called it the X-Bullet because the nose peeled into four petals to form an X." In 1989 Randy and wife, Coni, bet their company on the X-Bullet. On safari in 1992, Coni used 225-grain X-Bullets in her .338 Magnum to kill 61 animals with one shot each.

Because the unalloyed copper X-Bullet fouled bores faster than the gilding metal (copper/zinc) of jacketed lead bullets, Randy machined three grooves into the shank to reduce friction and give the lands "somewhere to push that copper." Result: lower pressure and less fouling. In 2003 this new bullet became the TSX or Triple Shock. It delivered the deep penetration and near-100-percent weight retention of the X-Bullet; but it was more accurate. The Tipped TSX followed, then the MRX Bullet with tungsten-based Silvex core. The Triple Shock has since appeared in more than 60 configurations and has replaced the X-Bullet as the flagship product at Barnes (now a Freedom Group company with Remington). It is loaded by Federal, Norma, and Corbon. Meanwhile, the X-Bullet design has been adapted to Barnes handgun and muzzleloader bullets. Randy emphasizes that he pursued lead-free bullets to give hunters better mis-

▲ Corbon's flat-nose .475 bullets drive deep. Bullet shape and diameter ensure a big, lethal channel.

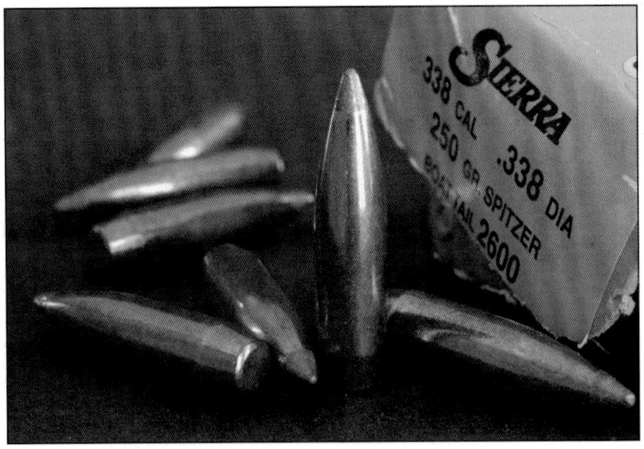

▲ Sierra's close tolerances and sleek bullet profiles appeal to hunters expecting long shots at big game.

siles, "not to avoid lead." In the 1980s bullet toxicity hadn't yet popped up as an environmental issue.

Over the last decade, however, lead in spent bullets has drawn public attention. A July 2008 ban on lead bullets in parts of California followed a lawsuit brought by the Center for Biological Diversity, the Natural Resources Defense Council, Wishtoyo Foundation, and Physicians for Social Responsibility, with representatives from other groups. They claimed spent lead bullets posed a hazard to condors feeding on hunter-killed game. Rather than fight the litigant's controversial cry that failure to ban lead bullets put the State at odds with the Endangered Species Act, California's Fish and Game Commission caved.

Since then, copper and copper-alloy bullets have propagated like ragweed. Another form of lead-free bullet is sintered (compressed) metal with a jacket.

Remington's Premier Copper Solid line of ammunition features polymer-tipped spitzers with two shank grooves. "They're designed to expand reliably over a wide range of impact velocities," said one of the Remington staff promoting the new missiles at the

▲ Wayne shot this buck with a 95-grain .243 Ballistic Tip. It did great internal damage and did not exit.

SHOT Show. "Our goal: double-diameter upset, with 98-percent weight retention in tough game."

Nosler's Combined Technology bullets, loaded by Winchester, include the lead-free E-Tip, which arrived in 2007. Nosler lists E-Tips as handloading components. Glen Weeks, centerfire guru at Olin's plant in East Alton, Illinois, claimed the E-Tip alloy of 95/5 (copper/zinc) "is as malleable as copper, but the Lubalox coating further reduces fouling." The design best suits bullets of at least .25 caliber. Weeks credits the E-Tip's accuracy partly to its one-piece construction. "More materials mean more variables." Also, the E-Tip's nose cavity extends below the ogive, so acceleration slugs the bullet into the rifling.

A sleek profile makes up for the relatively low sectional density of E-Tips. A 180-grain .30-06 E-Tip exiting at 2,750 fps passes the 400-yard mark at 2,099 fps—a touch faster than 180-grain Accubonds from Nosler. In game, E-Tips behave much like the TSX, driving deep with double-diameter upset. Glen said E-Tips need higher impact speed than most lead-core bullets to upset perfectly. "Still, at long range, E-Tips open as readily as traditional bullets." In 2011, Winchester followed its E-Tip with the Power Core 95/5. This gilding-metal hollowpoint lacks the E-Tip's polymer nose and Lubalox finish.

Nosler's Zach Waterman told me handloaders using E-Tips should start "about 2 grains shy of the charge recommendation for lead-core bullets. We've found best accuracy when bullets are seated .05 to .1 inch shy of the lands."

Hornady's lead-free GMX bullet appeared in 2009. The GMX (for "gilding metal expanding") is 95 percent copper, 5 percent zinc, same as Hornady's bullet jackets. These bullets expand reliably at impact velocities from 2,000 fps to 3,400 fps. "Typically, we get 99 percent weight retention in ballistic gelatin," said Jeremy Millard, who headed the GMX project. "We

▲ Be ready to fire again! Repeat hits with stout bullets from a 7mm-08 killed this outstanding warthog.

lose the plastic tip." The GMX looks and flies like an SST, though its nose cavity differs. Parallel-sided up front, it tapers to a point even with the base of the ogive, where expansion stops.

I first used a GMX on a moose quartering toward me at 95 yards. Shooting prone through thick forest, I sent the 150-grain bullet 105 yards to the near shoulder. The moose toppled over backward and didn't twitch. The bullet from my Ruger 77 in .300 RCM had shattered the scapula, minced the lungs, and lodged in mid-spine. Later, I took 6.5 Creedmoor ammunition with GMX bullets to South Africa and shot a variety of game with it, from dainty vaal rhebok to truck-tough eland. Exits were the rule on all but the eland—which, honestly, is best shot with bigger bullets than 120-grain 6.5s, no matter their design.

Accuracy with the GMX proved on par with that of jacketed bullets. Like the Barnes TSX, it has circumferential grooves. Hornady's team settled on two of standard cannelure width: .045. "Tests showed two grooves were better than one; three offered no perceptible advantage," explained Jeremy Millard. The grooves reduced full-diameter shank surface by 20 percent and allowed the shank material room to move under land pressure. Hornady chose gilding metal (5 percent zinc) over pure copper because it is less apt to foul bores. It's also more brittle. "A lot of work goes into petals to prevent breakage," said Millard.

The GMX shank was quickly paired with the soft polymer tip of FTX bullets in LEVERevolution ammunition. Hornady gnomes told me it was an arranged marriage to give lever-gun shooters a lead-free alternative. Announced in 2011, the MonoFlex or MFX resembles an FTX but features the GMX's cut cannelures. The 30-caliber MFX for the .308 Marlin Express weighs 140 grains, 20 grains less than its lead-core FTX counterpart. The nose cavity differs too. "Lead grips soft polymer stems firmly," explained one of the engineers. "But copper allows soft tips to slip. The longer MFX stem bottoms in a deep cavity, assisting upset."

Because the MFX intrudes farther into the case than does a lead-core bullet of the same weight, it can't be accelerated as quickly. So 140-grain MFX bullets exit about as fast as 160-grain FTXs.

▲ Wayne used a .30-30 on this Montana bull. For elk, bullet design is crucial when power is marginal.

The MonoFlex costs more than the FTX, partly because, like Hornady's GMX, it's made of more expensive material. But also, the MFX requires more handling and burnishing at the end to remove tiny scratches. I've shot two elk with MFX bullets in .308 Marlin Express loads. They performed like the FTX bullets that debuted in this cartridge. Perfectly.

Deep penetration, with high weight retention, can matter a great deal when you take on resilient game. But when handloading, you're smart to remember that the bullet is expendable, and must perform only once—also that it's effective only as it transfers its energy in the animal. One October I handloaded an ordinary softpoint instead of a less accurate "tough" bullet for an elk hunt. Days into this trip, as we descended a steep trail horseback, a bull elk popped up across a draw and ran. I piled off Paint and yanked the Model 70 from its scabbard. The bull was quartering away, just shy of timber, when my shot

▲ Wayne recovered these 165-grain Hornady GMX .30s from elk, one far, one close. Perfect upset!

▲ Bullets for the 7mm Weatherby were made for long-range hits. But Wayne shot this bull at 14 steps.

reached him. Trees swallowed him up. Wishing for an instant that I'd picked a stouter bullet, I hurried to the track, rifle ready. The elk had traveled just a few yards. The Power-Point, an ordinary deer bullet, had struck in mid-rib and angled forward across the top of the heart. It was balled up in shoulder muscle on the far side.

I was reminded, as we field-dressed that elk, of the hunter in turn-of-the-century British Columbia who'd bought a box of .303 Savage softpoints for his new lever rifle and proceeded to kill 18 big animals, including two grizzlies, with those 20 cartridges. A great testimonial for the softnose! Thousands of other hunters have similar stories. A Colorado game warden, whose job included shooting unwanted elk, used a .270 with ordinary 130-grain bullets. Jack O'Connor found that a winning combination on a wide variety of game. His wife Eleanor's 7x57 was deadly with handloaded 160-grain softpoints at 2,650 fps.

A bullet keeping 100 percent of its weight while penetrating game is no guarantee of quick kills. Mostly, death results from tissue destruction. Bullets so stout they lose *no* mass are unlikely to open wide enough or violently enough to dump all or nearly all their energy in the vitals. Missiles exiting a slender wound channel, with little deceleration, take much of their destructive energy with them. Even when the resulting wound is fatal, you may have to trail the animal to recover it.

I once watched a hunter shoot a bull elk at 250 yards with a .30-06. The elk took the bullet too far back, but the angle brought it to the off lung. A post-mortem showed that 180 Hornady was well minced.

"Not much left," mumbled the hunter, inspecting it.

"No," I said. "But that tattered bullet just gave you a whopping big elk. Be kind." There's nothing left of a grenade after it detonates, but grenades that stay in one piece do little damage.

I've seen dozens of elk shot dead with ordinary softpoints. A big bull tipped over backward and died right away after one shot through the lungs with a 130-grain .270 Hornady. Another mature six-point collapsed from a hit with a 145-grain Speer, courtesy of a .280 Remington. One fellow I know has killed a truckload of elk with a .250 Savage and Remington

▲ The Swift Scirocco combines high ballistic coefficient with a bonded core to ensure penetration.

Core-Lokts. Another uses 100-grain Hornady Spire Points in a .25-06. The .303 British has toppled many thousands of Canada moose with round-nose lead-core bullets.

When you want flat flight and deep penetration in tough game, copper and copper-alloy bullets offer an alternative to controlled-expansion jacketed bullets like the Nosler Partition, Federal's Trophy Bonded, and the Swift A-Frame. For deer hunting, I've not found lead-free bullets worth their high costs. Even with quartering shots, you can kill as cleanly—and sometimes more quickly—with an inexpensive softnose.

▲ David Miller uses match bullets on hunts. From his .300, they fly flat and kill pronghorns pronto!

WHAT'S IT MADE OF?

A century ago, bullets were just getting used to high speed. After the Great War, cupronickel, of 60 percent copper and 40 percent nickel, became the jacket of choice. Gilding metal (90 copper, 10 zinc) was first thought too soft for the friction generated by 150-grain bullets in .30-06 service ammunition; but Western Cartridge Company's Lubaloy jacket of 90 percent copper, 8 percent zinc, and 2 percent tin worked well. In 1922 Western provided Palma Match ammunition with 180-grain Lubaloy-coated bullets. When experiments at Frankfort Arsenal showed gilding metal endured high velocities, it became standard jacket material for rifle bullets. While Nosler used a 90-10 alloy for Partitions turned on screw machines before 1970, most bullet-makers now favor jackets of 95 copper, 5 zinc. Softer, almost pure-copper jackets up to .060 thick appeared on Bitterroot Bonded Core bullets. The high ductility of the unalloyed copper resisted shattering in tough going. These thick jackets made Bitterroots long for their weight and heavy for their diameter. Copper fouling mandated frequent bore cleaning. Barnes "Original" bullets, .22 to .600, wear jackets of pure copper, .032 and .049 thick. Barnes, a company dating to 1939, has focused of late on its all-copper Triple Shock bullets. Originals remain for big-bore and obsolete rounds like the .50-110 and .348 Winchester.

SINTERED, FOR EXPLOSIVE EFFECT

The cores of several new small-bore varmint bullets are of sintered metal—particles fused under pressure. Winchester's Ballistic Silvertip Lead Free comprises a gilding metal jacket and a compressed-copper core that disintegrates on impact. A polymer tip has a stepped peg securing it to the jacket. Space around the peg below the jacket mouth delivers the effect of a hollow nose. Lead-free varmint missiles have practical advantages over lead-core bullets. A 35-grain spitzer leaving in an eyeblink doesn't bounce the rifle hard. So you see target reaction. In rocky places, there's a reduced chance of ricochets.

The 35-grain Ballistic Silvertip Lead Free bullet is easy to handload in .223s to chart velocities of around 3,800 fps. You'll get 4,350 from it in the .22-250. Nosler's Ballistic Tip Lead Free is essentially the same, with the firm's signature color-coded tips for diameter ID. Barnes MPG (Multi-Purpose Green) and Varmint Grenade bullets employ cores of powdered copper and tin. The MPG is available in weights to 140 grains (.308) for deer. A 26-grain Varmint Grenade driven 4,200 fps from a .204 Ruger vaporizes in a strawberry. Hornady .204 and .224 NTXs are tipped hollowpoints with sintered cores. Remington's .223 and .22-250 Disintegrator ammo feature 45-grain sintered-iron bullets at 3,550 and 4,000 fps.

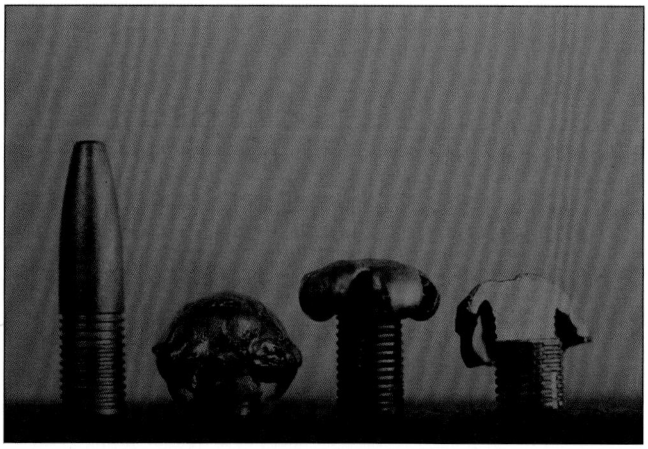

◀ This experimental big game bullet has a lead nose that expands and a copper shank that drives deep.

SHOOTING SECTION

Chapter 16: How to Hear When You're Old

Some things you can buy, some you can't. Ammunition and some handloading components are in short supply as I write this, but they're still in production. So are loading-bench hardware and firearms. Even rifles you can't afford have a price—one you might someday find cheap. As a lad I spent junior high lunch-hours at a local hardware store, ogling a Winchester 67 in the rack under a musty moose head. That single-shot .22 listed for $16.50. Such extravagance was then beyond my grasp.

But fortunes change.

Your health can change too. Lord willing, you get better after you get sick. You get stronger and faster with exercise. But Father Time will eventually put you in a slow wagon down a long ramp. Speed and strength leave you. Iron sights once in sharp focus get wooly edges.

And you can't hear . . . I said, YOU CAN'T HEAR!

If you're a handloader, you probably subject your ears to much more rifle fire than does the deer hunter who pulls Old Betsy from the closet once a year. Unless you shield them, you'll go deaf sooner.

In the old days, when otherwise intelligent shooters triggered all manner of firearms without ear protection, hearing loss was broadly considered a curse of old age. But we're all living longer—well, not *all* of us, but on average we cheat the Reaper out of years that would have been his when Winchester 67s sold for $16.50. Credit good dentistry and medical procedures that cost more than most of us are worth. My first shooting coach, who still remembers clearly his time in New Guinea during the build-up toward D-Day, recently drove the length of the United States and visited for a couple of days. At 92, he strides like a man half his age and still visits the local gym.

I digress. Earl still hears well too, thanks partly to the excellent hearing aids in his veteran's package. He

▲ Unwieldy? You soon get used to a suppressor, which is lightweight and reduces both noise and recoil.

▲ Protect your ears! Loading a rifle, you light a fuse to a bomb that will detonate near your face.

deserves them. But not even the most sophisticated hearing devices can match the marvelous audio gear that came to you at birth. Alas, it is easily damaged; and permanent hearing loss is just that.

Our inner ears can be physically wounded, of course—smashed or pierced. But by far the greatest threat to them is what they were designed to receive: sound. Measured in decibels, sound reaches you in a light-like spectrum or range. Instead of varying wave lengths that produce color, sound arrives in low and high frequencies. You don't have to be a musician to recognize changes in pitch. Sound also varies in its duration. Our ears can become deaf—literally!—to the constant rumble of machinery. I remember, after a long day plowing at full throttle, my young ears rang—though the noise didn't seem unpleasant as I sank the shiny steel in the Michigan earth and throttled up the Allis-Chalmers.

Of more concern to shooters is the sound of a shot. It's jarring because it's sudden. On a graph, it shows as a spike on the shallow surface of background noise. A blast over a murmur.

"We never wore hearing protection, even on the range," said Earl of his Army days. Unmuffled, the report of a .30-06 from a Springfield or a Garand can definitely impair hearing. Like a steady diet of donuts, frequent shooting without protection is worse than the occasional lapse.

According to audiologists, exposure to sounds exceeding 140 decibels can cause permanent ear damage. Now, 140 dB is not what you'll get standing next to a howitzer, a braked .50, or even that .30-06. The fine receptors in your inner ear get a 140-dB dose *from the muzzle of a .22 rimfire*. Centerfire rifles and handguns can deliver over 175 dB. Add a muzzle brake, or fire Bertha under a metal roof at the local range, and you boost the blast. Irreversible damage can follow even one loud report.

Of course, the shooting industry is sensitive to the threat of ear damage on the line. Most industry live-fire events include—and require—soft plugs for participants. But they're not always enough. On the range during annual SHOT (Shooting, Hunting and Outdoor Trade) Shows, I've been jarred by sharp and thunderous claps from short AR-15s and braked .338 Lapuas as manufacturers demonstrated these rifles under tin without preamble. In such conditions you need muffs *and* plugs.

I keep soft plugs in nearly every pocket, even if my plans call for no range time. I wear 'em when mowing the lawn, for occasional pokes with a .22. I take them hunting and put them in when time allows for shots at big game. For prolonged shooting from a bench, I wear muffs, often over plugs.

Muffs vary in price and protection. The best-known companies—Peltor, Pro-Ears, Leight—sell a range of passive models, with sound reduction ratings from 18 dB. I insist on a rating of least 28. Electronic muffs are more costly and increasingly popular. A switch lets you hear normal conversation, but the muffs arrest harmful sound before it bangs your ears. Slim models

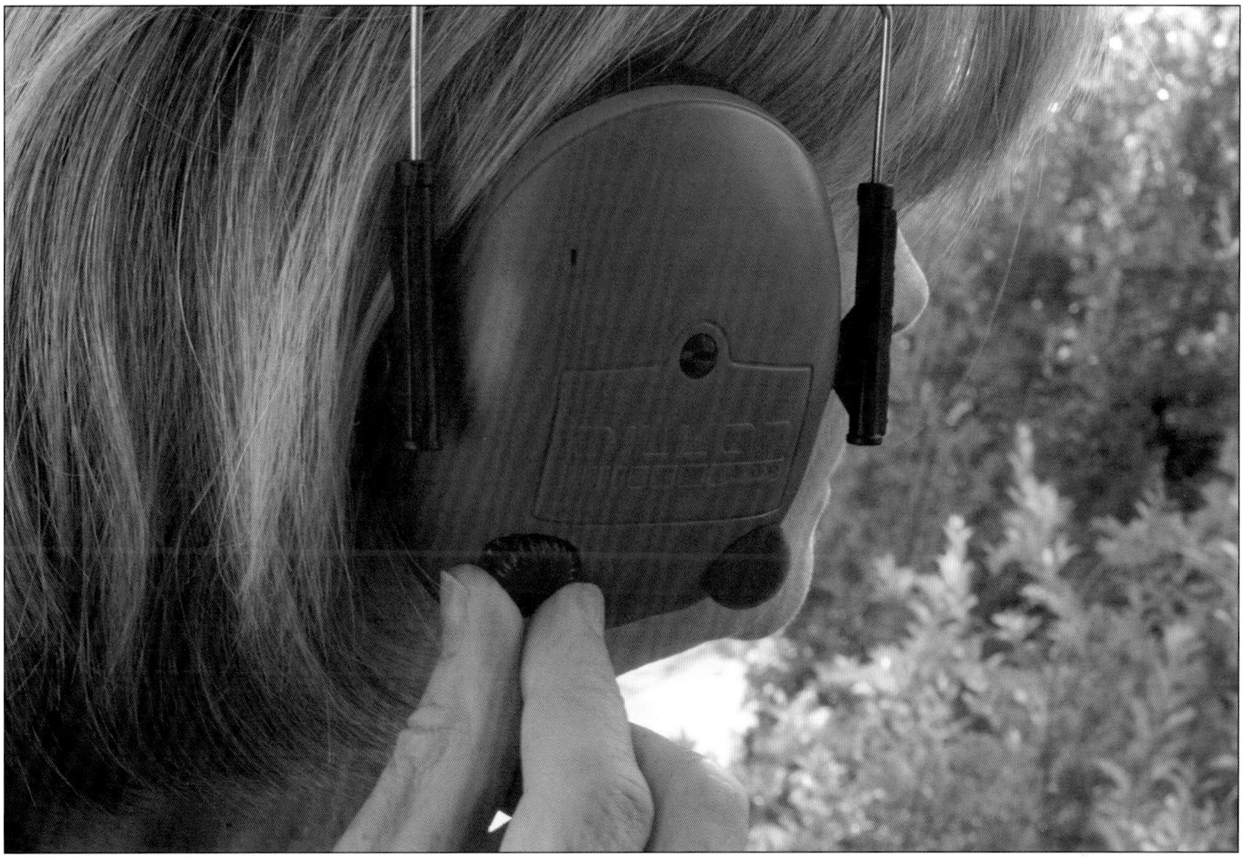

▲ Muffs are now available with switches so you can block only the sudden blast, not conversation.

let you hug the comb unhampered by the bulge that once made shooting with any muffs uncomfortable. Electronic earplugs and behind-the-ear devices are available too. Walker's Game Ear is hailed for its effectiveness, also for its utility afield.

A few companies offer custom-molded inside-the-ear protection. SportEar makes modestly priced plugs plus custom-fitted devices. The unobtrusive, battery-powered custom models not only shield your ears from harmful noise; they enhance your hearing! Before fitting mine, the SportEar people performed a hearing test across the spectrum of frequencies. My right ear passed muster. My left (nearer the muzzle because I'm right-handed) showed slight hearing loss. SportEAR crafted a set of ear-pieces from soft molds so they fit my ears exactly. They're color-coded, left and right. Each unit has a switch affording access to four programs. The first provides standard protection; the second enhances certain frequencies. The third and fourth also help you hear better over background noise. Of course, there's a volume control. SportEAR custom plugs are the Cadillacs of the industry.

Even with protection, some rifles deliver disturbing blasts. Brakes attenuate recoil by venting gas before bullet exit. The increase in noise can be substantial. If your rifle kicks hard enough to warrant a brake, consider a barrel-diameter model designed to minimize that additional sound. Texas rifle-maker Lex Webernick (Rifles, Inc.) used sophisticated equipment to measure sound levels from various brakes. He now manufactures his own. "While your distance from the muzzle affects the intensity of sound you receive," Lex told me, "your *location* doesn't seem to matter much." He added that brake design—size, number, position, and angle of vents—matters a great deal. "Of course, so do the load and barrel length."

▲ Walker's Game Ear protects your hearing while enhancing it, transmitting those little woods noises.

◀ SportEAR makes form-fitted earplugs with adjustments so you can tune hearing while protecting it.

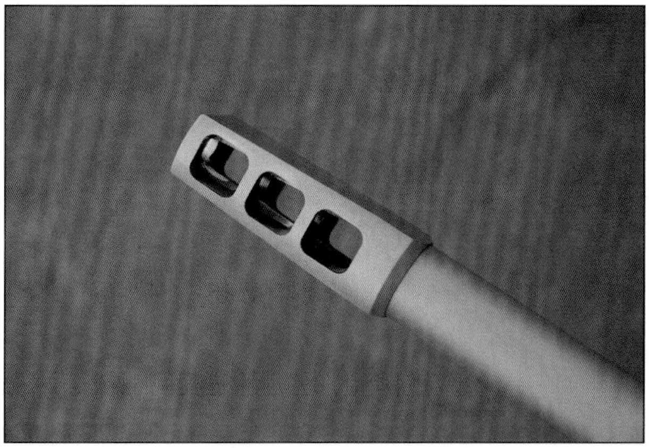

▲ Aggressive muzzle brakes tame recoil of violent cartridges, but the decibels can damage your ears.

Most hunting guides abhor brakes. At the elbow of a client firing at game, the hapless guide must endure that horrendous blast while spotting the effects of the shots.

Oddly enough, barrel-mounted suppressors, which reduce both recoil and noise, are heavily taxed in the United States and require a federal permit!

"Nothing can silence a shot," Darren Jones told me as he showed me the latest suppressors from SilencerCo, the Utah-based company that at this writing owns more than half the US market in these devices. "The 9-inch alloy Harvester models weigh only 11 ounces but reduce noise by as much as 34 decibels." Stainless steel baffles, he added, endure the heat and violence of .300 Magnum loads. Integral brakes cut recoil—as I found checking zero. The Remington 700 I'd chosen for a hunt with Darren, a .308 with a 1-6x24 Vortex scope, bumped me as gently as a .243.

SilencerCo offers several types of suppressors, and different sizes within type to match different bores. (Each suppressor will work on rifles with smaller bores, just not quite as efficiently.) The Harvester

▲ Tamar used a suppressed Sako in .270 on this Namibian impala. No hearing protection necessary!

comes in .30 and .33 and the heavier Saker in .22 and .30, with Stellite baffles "to endure the heat of extended rapid fire," said Darren. So does the Specwar, with its quick-detach mount. A Glock pistol equipped with an Osprey recoiled with all the violence of a .22.

This wasn't the first time I'd used suppressors. In Namibia and South Africa, as well as in central Europe, suppressors are common. Even England, with its draconian gun laws, encourages their use afield. I've carried suppressed rifles through African bush, over British heath, and in the forests of Germany and Austria. Women on my High Country Adventures safaris don't flinch with suppressed rifles.

Suppressors date at least to 1908, when MIT graduate Hiram P. Maxim (son of Hiram S. Maxim, of machine gun fame) formed the Maxim Silencer Company. His device, to mollify neighbors who might object to un-muffled target shooting, sold for as little as $3.25. But soon thereafter US Attorney General Homer Cummings proposed restrictions on some firearms to limit their use in crime. In 1934 the National Firearms Act passed in Congress. It imposed a then-exorbitant tax of $200 on suppressors. The NFA also restricted ownership of short-barreled rifles and shotguns and machine guns.

Increasing use of suppressors by military and law enforcement agencies, and their popularity with hunters abroad, have fueled improvements. Suppressors built by SilencerCo are lighter, more durable, and much more effective than their predecessors. In most places, these devices are legal. Currently, a handful of states in the upper Midwest and Northeast, plus California, are holdouts. But 38 states (more if you're in the law enforcement community or meet other standards) let you own a suppressor. Not all these states permit hunting with suppressors; some that do limit them to specified game and/or places. Recently, more states have shown a willingness to relax restrictions on suppressors. And why not? Ear damage from law enforcement and military firefights climbs 18 percent each year, resulting in disability payments exceeding a billion dollars annually! Makers of hunting rifles—Savage, Remington, Ruger, and others—now offer barrels threaded for suppressors. Civilian shooters snapped up 80,000 suppressors in 2013.

Buying a suppressor is an exercise in patience, but it's not difficult. Locate a Class III dealer, and indicate the product of your choice. You'll most likely buy from the manufacturer; the dealer acts as the conduit. With the dealer, you complete BATF Form 4 (5320.4). Then get a signature from your local law officer (as you would for a concealed-carry permit), and have yourself fingerprinted on two copies of FBI cards. Complete BATF Form 5330. Send two copies of Form 4, both fingerprint cards, and the Form 5330 to the BATF, with a check for $200 (a less onerous fee now than in the Depression, if no more palatable).

The agency will, in due time, approve you for a suppressor and notify the dealer, who'll order the product and let you know when to pick it up.

You can also form a trust or corporation to own that suppressor. Many shooters do. For details on this process, and for more information on rules regarding suppressors, go to *silencersarelegal.com*.

Suppressors no longer cost $3.25. Figure $300 to $900 to equip your deer rifle. Suppressors for sustained fire from battle rifles and for high-octane rounds like the .338 Lapua and .50 BMG cost more.

Not long ago, I carried a suppressed rifle on an aoudad hunt in Texas. In no time, I was threading that barrel extension through brush as if the rifle were a carbine. Some days later, I bellied atop a bench where a scattering of aoudad fed among razor-wire tangles of brush. A mature ram stood at just over 200 yards, but a screen of Texas spines blocked my muzzle. Unable to advance or to even sit lest one of the sharp-eyed animals spot me, I struggled into a perilously high prone position and fired. The stricken ram sprinted in a wide arc. My second TSX bullet met a branch and deflected. A third centered his lungs. He stumbled off a ledge and nosed into a steep slope.

The suppressor must have worked. I don't remember hearing a thing!

When as an adolescent I ogled single-shot .22s, hearing protection didn't enter my mind. Decades after many shots have pounded my naked ears, I'd like to spin back the clock and don muffs or use rifles with suppressors. Can't. But those options remain available to every shooter, to the end of that long ramp.

Chapter 17: Softer Shooting Isn't for Sissies

The reticle bounces about like a fly on a hot window. You're out of breath. The trigger's about to break . . . Oh no! It's gonna git me again! Now! NOW!

Recoil affects your shooting routine because it frightens you into doing things you know will not contribute to accuracy. Reduce recoil, and you'll get less pain and more center hits. Shooting will again be fun, as it was when you fired your first .22.

Accelerating a bullet from dead-still to gone in an eye-blink, you get recoil in return. Newton's "equal and opposite reaction" clearly applies to a bullet's launch. Recoil's kinetic energy is calculated this way: KE = MV2 / GC, where M is the rifle's mass, V its velocity. GC is a gravitational constant for earth: 64.32. Now, the derivation of V can put you to sleep, so I'll skip that. For a 180-grain bullet fired at 3,000 fps from an 8 ½-pound rifle in .300 WSM, rifle speed comes to roughly 15.2 fps. Plugging that into the formula (KE = MV2 / GC), you get this: 8.5 (15.2)2 / 64.32 = 30.5 foot-pounds of recoil—nearly twice as much as you'll get from mild loads in a same-weight .30-06.

Recoil that arrives as kick depends not only on the rifle's mass, but also a great deal on stock shape and your body position. Also, while bullet speed figures into energy calculation, its contribution to rifle "slap" does not. A bullet that exits fast dumps its energy fast. A rifle hurling a 405-grain .45-70 bullet at 1,800 fps delivers about the same recoil as a same-weight .338 Magnum launching a 225-grain spitzer 1,000 fps faster. But the .338's kick may well seem sharper. On a scale of gun-shy to gorilla, I'm on the wimpish end, acutely aware that when the trigger trips, a measured load of explosives will suddenly and viciously pound an unyielding stick of brass, steel and hardwood into my cheek and clavicle. Hugging a rifle has much in common with sitting on a stump over dynamite.

▲ Tough game requires a deep-driving bullet, but you must place it well. A flinch won't let you.

▲ Wayne's suppressed Remington in .308 helped him take this last-day aoudad—a challenging hunt!

You can reduce felt recoil by tying bricks to your rifle. A big-bore black-powder gun sold in 1875 by renowned elephant hunter William Finaughty proved uncomfortable for three successive owners. In a fit of practicality, the fourth tied a three-pound lead weight to keep the muzzle down in recoil. More popular methods these days include inletted lead (least expensive) and a mercury recoil reducer (most effective). For truly brutal rifles—those on the order of .378 and .460 Weatherby Magnums, and the .500 Jeffery—the mercury device has much to recommend it.

Stock shape matters too. A comb with lots of drop from comb to heel jumps up to hammer your chops. A sharp comb on a short stock adds pain. Straight combs with little drop and a rounded top are gentler. The forward-sloping comb on Weatherby's Mark V, like those of Scheutzen rifles with Tyrolean stocks, treats you well, recoil pushing the rifle away from your face. My agile, iron-sighted Mauser in .458, on the other hand, kicks like lightning with mule shoes. After three shots my head throbs, and I'm probing my jaw for fractures. If this diabolical lightweight didn't point like a 28-gauge Rizzini and stick 500-grain solids into cherry-size groups, I'd sell it.

Short stocks accentuate recoil when they jam your thumb into your nose. Crescent brass or steel buttplates put the pain on your clavicle. (Incidentally, frontiersmen fired those Kentucky rifles and early lever guns with crescent butts from the upper arm, not the shoulder; recoil from most black powder loads of that day was mild). A soft butt-pad can keep your thumb at bay by adding length to the butt-stock as it absorbs shock. The stock's wrist and forend can also help mitigate recoil, with dimensions that give your hands easy purchase. Checkering or slip-resistant synthetic texturing enhances control, especially when the stock is wet with rain or snow. Svelte stocks that respond nimbly offer less for your hands to grasp (and a smaller footprint on your shoulder, which intensifies kick). But a stock too thick for a wrap of your hand will jump free on recoil.

When you're prone and at a bench, your torso can't rock with recoil. Absorbing all the recoil a rifle delivers, without moving, is painful. Shooting uphill prone, you'll be closer to your scope than when firing from the sit, kneeling, or offhand. Recoil has often planted the ocular ring in my brow. Remember that when affixing a scope. Keep it as far from your eye as you can without compromising speed of aim.

Many powerful rifles now wear muzzle brakes, which send exiting gas through vents instead of letting it explode forward. Angled vents direct gas to reduce rearward thrust. Brakes needn't be unsightly. Some, like those from Rifles, Inc., are barrel-diameter, seamlessly fitted and relatively quiet. Still, brakes are not benign. Eruptions of dust or snow can obscure the target when you fire prone. Even brakes with small ports are noisy, and the most aggressive hit you with a deafening blast. Barrels chambered for the most potent hunting rounds are routinely equipped with brakes.

Remember when considering and using a brake that the people near you won't feel your rifle's recoil, stiff or gentle. But they will certainly notice the blast from

▲ A suppressor adds length but little weight. It reduces noise and kick, but shouldn't affect accuracy.

a brake! Hunting guides, close by their clients at the moment of truth, come to hate brakes. Competitors firing—and spotting—during long-range matches endure brain-rattling concussions from hot .33s and .50s.

Braked big game rifles demand that shooters make an uncomfortable choice afield: compromise their hearing of woods sounds by wearing ear protection, or damage their hearing at the shot without it. One solution: electronic muffs that allow you to hear unimpaired but that instantly block the sharp report of the rifle before it reaches your ears. Another option is to use a brake in practice, then replace it with an unvented sleeve of the same weight for the hunt.

If you replace a brake with a sleeve, check to see that point of impact doesn't change. Even same-weight tubes at the muzzle can have different effects on barrel harmonics and accuracy. Some rifle-makers now offer brakes that can be turned on and off by rotating a sleeve over the ports. Clever! A Savage Long Range Hunter I've used in steel-target matches at distance has such a brake. I keep it closed, because the 6.5 Creedmoor chambering doesn't require a brake. But with friskier rounds, such a device makes sense. Incidentally, you'll have to keep an adjustable brake clean to rotate it with your fingers.

▲ Recoil-shy shooters aren't all slightly built. Kelsey is, but uses a gentle load and places her bullets well.

▲ First safari, first wildebeest! Thea aimed carefully with a .30-06, the load adequate, not brutal.

Chapter 18: Shooting Well in Wind

The coyote came across a broad flat, orange in the early New Mexico sun. It loped easily, head swiveling, its near-white coat rippling in a brisk wind. The wind cut noiselessly across the muzzle of my 6.5 Creedmoor from 10 o'clock. "Come closer," I whispered. But at just over 200 yards the coyote pulled up, suspicious, facing me. Slinged up in a sit, it's all I can do to keep bullets in softball-size targets at 200. This breeze would move my shot to the edge of that zone. Tugging the sling high to add tension, I nudged the quivering crosswire to shoulder's edge and fired. The coyote collapsed.

Bullets never travel straight. In still air, gravity takes them in long parabolic arcs. When that air moves, it pushes the bullet sideways. Alas, unlike gravity, wind force and direction are not constant. In competition, I've fired through wind that straightened target flags one way while swinging wind vanes on the line in the opposite direction. A bullet sent through that gauntlet would, literally, fly a ziz-zag course. While wind at the muzzle has more effect on impact point than does an equivalent shift downrange, the bullet is more easily moved the farther it gets from the muzzle because downrange there's more time *per unit of distance traveled* for the wind to work its mayhem.

▲ Wayne accurately doped wind with LEVERevolution ammo in this Marlin with GreyBull scope to hit the gong from prone with six consecutive bullets—one each at 100, 200, 300, 400, 500, and 600 yards.

Wind speed and angle both matter. "Full-value" wind from 3 or 9 o'clock has the greatest effect because, like gravity acting on a bullet fired horizontally, it is pushing at right angles to the bullet's path. Wind from 12 or 6 o'clock has essentially no effect unless it is very stiff, and then the result may not be what you think. A bullet fired at a distant target across level ground is actually launched slightly nose-up and remains nose-up. Surface exposure due to the bullet's attitude affects its path—though insignificantly at hunting ranges. Unlike an arrow, a bullet is not heavy at the front and does not "porpoise." So you can ignore most headwinds and tailwinds. Remember that a bullet moving 3,000 fps bucks terrific resistance even in still air. It is, in fact, generating its own 2,000-mph headwind! What influence do you think a 20-mph headwind or tailwind will have on this bullet's flight?

Vulnerability to wind also depends on a bullet's speed and its ballistic coefficient, or C. Bullets of similar C, driven at the same speed, yield about the same drift. Consider a quartet of pointed bullets with Cs of .390 to .410: a 100-grain .243, a 130-grain .270, a 140-grain 7mm, and a 165-grain .308. Pushed at 3,000 fps, all drift about six inches at 200 yards in 20-mph crosswind. Drop C from .390 to .290, with, say, a 150-grain .308 protected-point bullet, and drift goes up 50 percent, to nine inches! Throttle the bullets, and drift increases as velocity drops.

My introduction to wind came in smallbore prone matches. When I moved outside from indoor three-position shooting, I felt as though I'd been plucked from a hotel pool and dropped into the North Atlantic. Savvy shooters learned prevailing winds on specific ranges, and the net effects of contradict-

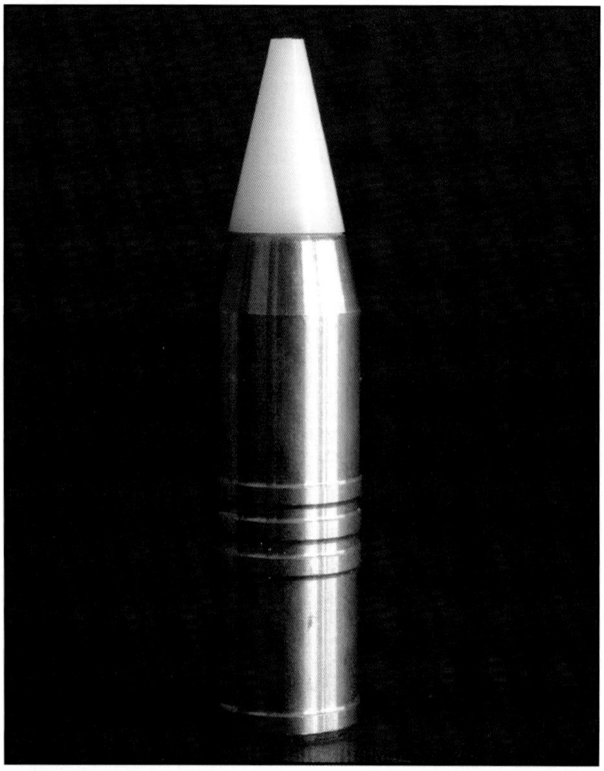

▲ This polymer-tipped brass bullet is experimental, for use in the potent .408 CheyTac sniper round.

ing flags. The Spokane rifle range, where I often competed, is on a riverbank. Wind typically angled across the firing line from 7 or 8 o'clock, bounced off the bank, and hit the targets from 4 o'clock. If you minded only wind at the line, you'd make a mistake. But if you waited for still conditions, you'd run out of time!

Hunting, you're not using a 12-pound .22 to nip dime-size X-rings. Bullets from most centerfire rifles can buck moderate breeze without significant deflection inside 150 yards. But at long range, even sluggish air can make you miss. A few rules of thumb can help, provided you can read wind accurately.

Remember that effective wind speed incorporates angle. A 10-mph right-angle push becomes a smaller problem as the wind shifts to 10 or 11 o'clock.

Double the wind speed, and you double the drift. Halve the wind speed, and you halve the drift.

Reduce the wind's angle from 90 degrees, and you reduce drift proportionately. Change the shot distance, however, and the drift may surprise you. For example, a 130-grain .270 bullet launched at 3,000 fps drifts less than an inch at 100 yards in a 10-mph wind. At 200 yards, it is three inches off course—four times as far as at 100! At 300 yards it drifts seven inches; at 400, thirteen. There's negligible drift at 100 yards, partly because the bullet arrives in just 1/10 second. There's not much *drop* at 100 either. Adding distance dramatically increases both. Drift for that .270 bullet at 500 yards is roughly 60 percent greater than at 400. For many popular centerfire rifle loads, a handy rule of thumb is to assume an inch of drift at 100 yards, then double that at 200. Triple the 200 drift at 300 and double the 300 drift at 400. For example:

Drift of an 85-grain .243 (Federal) Trophy Copper bullet driven at 3,200 fps in 10-mph right-angle wind

	Actual drift (inches)	Rule of thumb drift (inches)
100 yards	0.7	1
200 yards	2.9	2
300 yards	6.8	6
400 yards	12.5	12

In this case each estimate is within an inch of actual drift. Nobody I know can hold within an inch at 400 yards under hunting conditions, and darn few rifles will shoot even half that tightly. If you're firing a blunt 45-grain softpoint from a .22 Hornet, the rule of thumb fails beyond 100 yards, mainly because this is a relatively slow bullet decelerating at a high rate. By the way, lightweight bullets driven fast can show significant drift at distance because their low sectional density keeps C values low. A small-caliber bullet *heavy for its diameter* can thus buck wind as well as or better than heavier bullets from a bigger bore. For example:

Range (yards)	0	100	200	300	400	500
.30-06, 110-grain						
velocity (fps)	3330					1240
drift (inches)		1	6	15	30	52
.223 Rem., 55-grain						
velocity (fps)	3240					1270
drift (inches)		1	6	15	29	50

Sharp polymer bullet tips are all the rage now, but it's easy to lean too heavily on a sleek nose to win battles with wind. The ogive, or leading curve of the bullet between tip and shank, matters more.

Boat-tail bullets become an asset only at very long ranges or in gale-force winds. A 30-mph wind that shoves a flat-base 7mm bullet 17 inches at 350 yards moves a boat-tail bullet 15 ½ inches. Reduced drift afforded by a tapered heel at higher wind speeds is academic, given how hard it is to estimate drift in strong wind, or hold within two minutes of angle when your hat is leaving you at speed. Also, *percentage* difference in wind deflection between flat-base and tapered-heel bullets is about the same for a 10-mph wind and a 30-mph wind.

▲ On the peaks, wind can steal a shot. Learn to read it, dope it. Practice in wind with your handloads.

Another thing that affects bullet paths is the Coriolis effect. The earth's rotation causes a bullet to drift slightly right in the northern hemisphere, slightly left in the southern hemisphere. Get on a merry-go-round moving clockwise and toss a ball to someone else on the merry-go-round. The ball seems to curve left. Actually, it doesn't; only your frame of reference imposes that illusion. Coriolis acceleration for any bullet can be described by the equation: Y=2wVsin(latitude), where w is the earth's rotation rate (.0000729 degrees per second) and V is average bullet speed in feet per second. For a bullet moving 2,800 fps at a latitude of 45 degrees north, Coriolis acceleration is .30 fps/second, or about 1 percent of the acceleration of gravity. At 350 yards, you'll get a half inch of displacement. That's not enough to notice. At long range, Coriolis can be significant. Figure one-inch Coriolis correction for each second of bullet flight. F-16 fighter cannons aren't wired for Coriolis correction, a pilot told me. "But on-board computers are programmed for six-inch correction at 5,000 yards with Mark 82 or Mark 84 dive bombs."

A rotating bullet generates other forces that bend its arc. One of these is gyroscopic effect, which amounts to twice the Coriolis drift, and is thus negligible in most hunting situations. Spun by a right-twist bore, a bullet moves slightly right. Left-twist rifling pushes bullets left. Reason: torque within the bullet nudges its nose slightly in the direction of spin. There's a vertical gyroscopic component too, but you'll need a very accurate rifle to see it. The right-hand twist in my Remington 37 match rifle sends bullets to 4 o'clock in wind from the left and to 10 o'clock in wind from the right.

Wind doping is an acquired skill. Early in my competitive shooting career, fellow rifleman Dick Nelson (who helped Boeing engineer its moon vehicle) took me aside. "Learn to read the wind," he said, "and your bullets will hop through the X-ring like trained pigs."

Mirage is a visual distortion caused by heat waves rising from the earth's surface. If you don't see it, it's not there. Mirage doesn't move bullets; its dance shows you wind that does. Mirage can also show you a ghost target by floating the target image in the direction air is moving. You won't see mirage at all

▲ Strong wind can affect your hold as well as the bullet. A solid position trumps good wind doping!

distances at once. You'll see the strongest mirage, or the mirage at the distance for which your scope is focused. To get the most information about wind that most affects their bullets, match shooters typically focus their spotting scopes to read mirage just shy of the targets.

Mirage that's bumpy and moving slowly indicates light breeze. Flat, fast mirage clues you to stiff wind. When mirage suddenly vanishes with no change in light conditions, it's often because the wind has picked up. Mirage that boils vertically reflects a still condition—but beware, as a boil commonly precedes a reversal! Savvy competitive marksmen zero for light prevailing wind, then hold their fire during boils and reversals, shading and shooting during gentle pick-ups and let-offs.

On summer's prairie, mirage can help you hit. Fall hunting seasons bring cold weather, which all but cancels mirage. To read wind then, you must tap other indicators: nodding trees and grass, leaves and snow and mist that yield to wind.

In sum, moving air affects every shot. Like a spouse, wind brings you grief when you ignore it!

▲ With bullets of 650 to 750 grains, the .50 BMG dwarfs the .30-06 and doubles its reach in sniper rifles.

▲ The .50 BMG can require special tooling. Here: an RCBS priming tool just for the big .50.

WIND, GRAVITY, AND THE .50 BMG

Timing your shots to take advantage of favorable conditions can ratchet you quickly to the top of any scoreboard. During a short 48 seconds in a .50-caliber match, marksman Lynn McMurdo broke two 1,000-yard Light Gun world records. His five shots, sent lickety-split during a brief lull on New Mexico's Whittington Center range, all landed inside the X-ring: the first perfect score on that target ever! Center-to-center, McMurdo's outside bullet holes were only 2.97 inches apart. At 1,000 yards!

At extreme range, the .50 BMG has a distinct advantage. A ballistic coefficient of .500 is high for a .308 match bullet. But Hornady's 50-caliber A-Max has a C of 1.050. Launched at 2,750 fps, the big A-Max drops only 19 inches at 400 yards, 235 inches at 1,000—where a 178-grain match bullet at 3,000 fps from a .30 magnum falls *an additional 30 inches*! Drift disparities are equally stunning. A 10-mph breeze drifts a 750-grain .50-caliber bullet 26 inches at 1,000 yards—same as it pushes a .30-caliber 180 at 600!

MAKING SMALL GROUPS EASY

When testing handloads, pick a still day, or at least steady conditions. Switches in wind direction, with pick-ups and let-offs, spread your groups. But don't let wind steal your focus from fundamentals. Stay at the bench as much as you can, to avoid raising your pulse with unnecessary walking. Shoot with most of the sky's light behind you so the target comes clear easily. Take your time, making sure the bags or rest supports the rifle at the same places and with the same pressures for each shot, and that your hands grasp the rifle and rear bag the same. Consistency in all you do is crucial! At the target, there's no way you can distinguish the results of inconsistent handloads from those of inconsistent shooting.

▲ Shooting with a partner calling wind and the strikes can teach you more than solo practice.

Appendix 1: Handloads from Wayne's Bench

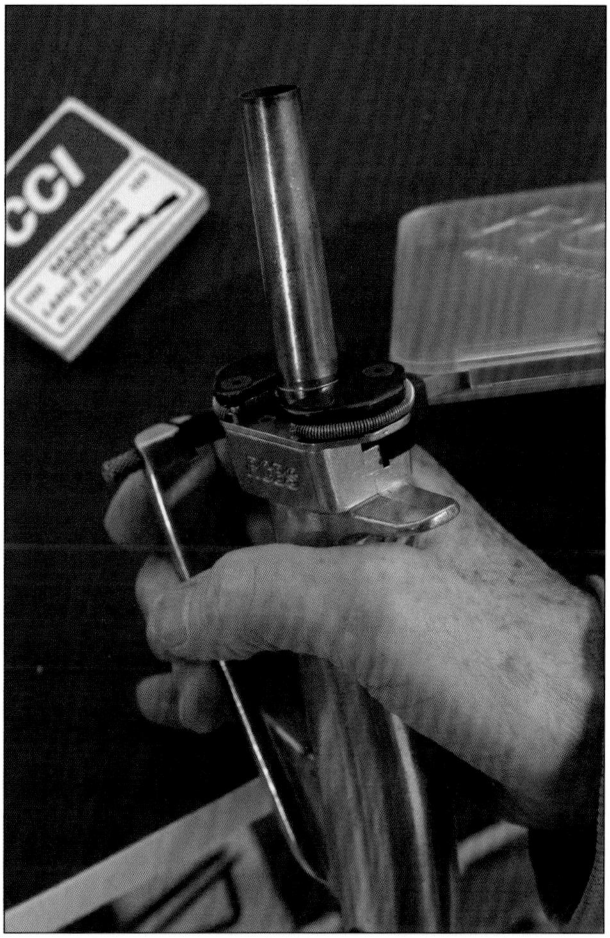

▲ Hand priming lets you feel seating resistance and depth.

After more than four decades of handloading, I've a long list of recipes that didn't work very well—starters that proved too modest to be useful, mid-level loads that showed wide velocity spreads or didn't shoot accurately, even some ammo so frisky it stuck bolts. I've purged such blunders from this section, a short list of handloads that worked well. Space constraints prevent a complete accounting. Of course, the usual caveats apply. To duplicate, start 5 percent off the listed charge. Be aware that in some cases, bullets may have been seated farther out than your rifle's throat or magazine permits. I've included factory loads that have performed exceptionally well. Asterisks (*) indicate loads that shot into .75 MOA—three-shot groups inside ¾ inch at 100 yards with the designated rifle.

Load	Velocity, fps
.204 Ruger, T/C Venture, 24 in.	
Fed 32 BTip	3860
Hor 32 VMax	3985
Win 34 JHP	3711*
Fed 39 BlitzKing	3467*
Hor 40 VMax	3630
.223 Rem, CZ 527, 22 in.	
Blk Hills 50 VMax	3189*
Win 53 HP	3224
Hor 53 HP Match	3135*
Fed 55 Bal Tip	3016*
Rem 62 HP Match	2767*
.223 Rem., Surgeon Scalpel, 18 in.	
Blk Hills 62 TSX	3026
Fed 55 BTip	3018
Fed 77 MK	2583*
Hor 40 VMax	3468
Hor 55 TAP	3049*
Hor 75 BTHP Match	2706
Lapua 69 HPBT	2907*
Win. 50 BSTip	3204
.223 Rem., Savage M25, 24 in.	
27 H335 40 Hor VMx	3580
27 H335 50 Spr TNT	3457
13 Blue Dot 45 VMax	3032
28 748 50 Speer Blitz	3452

6mm BR, Rem. 700 (Sisk), 22 in.

Rem 100 CL	2810
32 Benchmk 75 Hor	3265
30 H322 75 Hor	
28 RL-7 75 Hor	3240
32 RL-12 80 Rem PL	3020
31 2230 80 Rem PL	3115
32 BL-C2 85 Sie	3020
31 RL-12 85 Sie	3000
31 W748 85 Sie	2955
31 RL-15 88 Ber	3015
30 2460 88 Ber	3050
30 4064 88 Ber	3030
29 2230 90 Spr	2900
32 BL-C2 90 Spr	2915

.243 Win, Savage 14 Ltwt Hunter, 20 in.

Hor LM 85 IntBd	2963*
Nos 85 Part	3143
Rem 90 Scir	3014

.243 Win., Savage Edge, 22 in. 4/10

Win Suprm 55 BSTip	3711
Hor Vmt Exp 58 VMx 3680	
Fed Prem 60 HP Vmt	3507
Hor LM 85 IntBd	3062
Rem Premr 90 Scir	3069
Rem Prem 95 AccuTip	3128
Win Supr 95 BSTip	3066
Win Supr 100 BTSP	2949
Rem ExtRg 105 BTSP	2831

.243 Win., Savage 14, 22 in.

Win 55 BSTip	3613
Hor 58 VMax	3616*
Fed 60 HP	3398*
Fed 95 BTip	3025*

.243 Win., Win. 70, 22 in.

40 H335 70 Sie	3491
38 H335 80 Hor FMJ	3251*
42 H414 90 Rem	3107
Hor 95 SST	2910
Fed 100 Part	2808
Fed 100 Spr	2818
Rem 100 CL	2841
41 4350 105 Spr	2942

.243 Win., Mauser 98, 22 in. (Ackley Improved chamber)

47 4831 75 Sie	3123
48 H4831 85 Sie	3222
48 H4831 90 Spr	3196
45 H4831 100 Hor	2975

.240 Hawk, Rem. 700, 28 in.

50 4064 60 Sie	3550
52 4350 60 Sie	3550
48 Varget 70 Sie	3635
49 4064 75 Spr	3652
49 RL15 75 Spr	3583
54 Win760 80 Rem HP	3591
54 H414 80 Hor FMJ	3635
56 RL-19 85 Sie	3451
53 H4831 85 Sie	3270
54 H4831 85 Sie	3300
55 H4831 85 Sie	3325
54 3100 87 Hor	3366
53 H4350 89 Gardiner	3186
54 N160 90 Rem PSP	3223
55 H4831 100 Sie	3222
58 RL25 105 Spr	3260

.240 Hawk, Rem. 700, 28 in. (stiff loads)

51 Win 748 75 Hor	3954
50 Varget 75 Hor	3990*
52 4895 80 Rem	4037*
53 RL15 80 Rem	4055
58 4350 85 Sie	4040
54 Big Game 90 Rem	3474
58 RL22 100 Part	3420
58 H4831 100 Part	3480
58 WMR 105 Spr	3358

.250 Sav., Rem. 700, 22 in.

Win 100 STip	2695

.250 Sav., Savage 99, 20 in.

34 4895 87 Hor	2935
Rem 100 SP	2727
32 4895 100 Spr	2714

37 H4831 100 Sie	2370
37 W760 100 Spr	2683
37 H414 100 Spr	2756

.250 Sav., Cooper 54, 23 in.

37 H4831 117 PwrPt	2482
34 4895 87 Sie	3071
Rem 100 Spr	2784
Win 100 STip	2800

.257 Roberts, Dakota 76, 24 in.

Win 117 PwrPt	2773

.257 Roberts, Win. 70, 24 in.

41 4895 87 Sie	3155*
39 H335 100 Sie	3091
38.5 H335 100 Sie	3052
Win 100 Stip	2950
Fed 117 SP	2829
Win 117 Stip	2890
Win 117 PwrPt	2800
49 H4831 117 Part	2955*

.25 Souper, Rem. 700 (Sisk), 24 in.

41 4064 87 ho	3335
43 H380 87 ho	3200
44 H414 100 nobt	3170*
48 RL-19 100 nobt	3325*
46 H4350 100 sp	3240
44 Big Game 110 berg	3145
43 H4350 115 nobt	3097
46 RL-22 115 nobt	3030
45 NMR 120 ho	2945

.25-06 Rem, Wby Mk V, 24 in.

Fed 115 TB	3098

.25-06 Rem., Win. 70, 24 in.

52 H4831 115 BTip	2805
49 H4831 120 CL	2860
49 H4831 129 Hor	2727

.257 Wby., Wby. Vanguard, 24 in.

Wby 100 TSX	3464
Wby 110 AccuBd	3398
Wby 115 BTip	3312
Wby 120 Hor	3377

.256 Newton, custom Mauser, Buzz Fletcher, 24 in.

46 4895 129 Hor	2982
49 4350 140 Part	2888

6.5x55 Swedish, Mauser 96, 18 ½ in.

Lapua 108 Scenar	2722
Fed 120 MK	2539
Norma 120 BTip	2681
Hor LM 129 SP	2443
Fed 140 SP	2284
Rem 140 PSP	2337
Lapua 155 SP	2450

6.5x55 Swedish, Howa, 22 in.

Hanson 139 SPBT	2430
Fed 140 TB	2360
PMC 140 BTHP	2465

6.5x55 Swedish, Win. 70 (Webernick) 24 in.

Lapua 108 Match	3105
Fed 120 MK	2830
PMC 140 HPBT	2660
PMC 140 SPBT	2625
Lapua 155 SP	2690

.260 Rem., Kifaru, 18 ½ in.

Rem 140 CL	2400

.260 Rem., Sako, 22"

Fed 120 BTip	2934
Nosler 125 Part	2871
Fed 140 GK	2623
Rem 140 CL	2522

.260 Rem., Win. 70 (Webernick), 24 in.

44 4064 85 Sie	3426
42 4320 100 Sie	3129*
40 2230 100 Sie	3191*
41 W748 100 Sie	3112
46 W760 100 Sie	3211
38 H335 120 Part	2955
41 4064 120 BTip	3027

40 RL15 120 BTip	2959
46 H4831 129 Hor	2910
43 H414 129 Hor	2991*
46 RL19 129 Hor	2994
44 4350 130 SP	2822
45 H4831 140 Spr	2742
44 RL19 140 Spr	2802
43 4350 140 Spr	2908

6.5/08 Redding, Rem. 78, 25 in.

44 H335 85 Sie	3448
47 4895 85 Sie	3665*
44 4895 100 Hor	3309
42 H335 100 Hor	3225
43 W748 100 Hor	3117
43 4064 100 Sie	3028
44 4064 100 Hor	3072
43 RL15 100 Sie	3000
42.5 4895 100 Hor	3071
43.5 4895 100 Hor	3159
50 IMR4350 100 Hor	3168
40.5 2520 120 Spr	2860
41 W748 120 Sie	2874
40 H335 120 Sie	2936*
40 H335 120 Spr	3000
40.5 H335 120 Sie	2947
42 4895 120 Spr	2991*
48 RL19 120 Spr	2874
41.5 RL15 120 Spr	2842
42.5 RL15 120 Spr	2937
45 H380 120 Sie	2943*
44.5 W760 120 Sie	2861
44 H414 120 Spr	2800
45.5 H414 120 Sie	2838
46 IMR4350 120 Spr	2853
48 H4831 120 Spr	2809
49 RL19 120 Spr	2956
9.5 H4831 120 Spr	2991
47.5 RL19 125 Part	2852*
48 RL19 125 Part	2884
48 RL19 125 Part	2920
46 IMR4350 129 Acme	2916
48 H4831 129 Acme	2886
46.5 RL19 140 Hor	2735
47.5 4831 140 Sie	2760

6.5 Creedmoor, Ruger #1A, 22 in.

Hornady 129 SST,	2910
Hornady 140 AMax	2603

6.5 Creedmoor, T/C Icon, 24 in.

Hornady 129 SST	2939
Hornady 140 AMax	2647

.256 Newton, 98 Mauser (custom by Buzz Fletcher), 24 in.

50 RL15 85 Sie	3525
48 RL15 100 Sie	3300
54 RL19 100 Sie	3200
49 VV 140 100 Sie	3355
47.5 BigGame 129 Hor	3000
48 2700 129 Hor	2920
51 RL-19 129 Hor	2970
46 H380 129 Hor	2925
45.5 4895 129 Hor	2955
46 4895 129 Hor	2980
49 4350 129 Hor	2895
49.5 IMR4350 129 Hor	2910
50 RL19 140 Spr	2920
51.5 RL19 140 Part	2980
49 4350 140 Part	2890

6.5/284, Ultra Light Arms, 24 in.

56 H4350 85 Sie	3420
54 W760 85 Sie	3350
50 BL-C2 85 Sie	3400
49 4064 85 Sie	3430
49 N140 85 Sie	3350
54 H4350 100 Sie	3290
52 Big Game 100 Sie	3385
54 4351 100 Sie	3370
57 WMR 125 Part	3110

.264 Win., Win. 70, 26 in.

Rem 140 CL	3136
67 450450 120 sp	3382
68 7828 120 SP	3314
66 4831 125 Part	3420
66 7828 129 Hor	3288*
67 7828 129 Hor	3280
69 7828 129 Hor	3414
65 H4831 129 Hor	3324

67 H4831 129 Hor	3423
64 H450 140 Sie	3186*
64 H450 140 Spr	3170
66 H450 140 Sie	3249
64 H4831 140 Sie	3184
71 H570 140 Hor	3231
73 H570 140 Hor	3346
59 H4831 160 Hor	2815*
68 H570 160 Hor	2810
68 H570 160 Acme	2960

.26 Nosler, Nosler 48 Heritage, 26 in.

82 7828 120 BTp	3703
83 Magn 129 AB LR	3449
81 H1000 129 AB LR	3403
78 Retumbo 140 Part	3318*
85 AA 8700 140 Part	3339

.270/308 Rem. 78 (Redding chamber), 25 in.

47 H335 100 Hor	3470
46 2520 100 Hor	3264
45 2520 110 Hor	3134*
48 4064 110 Hor	3259
51 H380 110 Hor	3203
47 4320 110 Hor	3185
46 4895 110 Hor	3283
43 RL15 120 X	3022
41 H335 130 Sie	2922
42 H335 130 Sie	2958
43 2520 130 Spr	2938
44 4064 130 Sie	2954
45 4064 130 Sie	3007
45 4064 130 Spr	2954
46 4064 130 Spr	3037
48 H380 130 Spr	2949
43 4895 130 Spr	2927
43.5 4895 130 Spr	2967
44 4895 130 Spr	2984
45 4320 130 Spr	2932
49 H414 130 Spr	2917
50.5 H414 130 Spr	2977
45.5 W748 130 Spr	2938
44 RL15 130 Spr	2972
51.5 RL19 130 Spr	2932
48.5 W760 130 Part	2842
50 W760 130 Spr	2921
51 W760 130 Spr	3047
44 W748 140 Hor	2923
45 4064 140 TB	2880

.270 Redding, Rem. 700, 22 in. (data from Richard Beebe)

45.5 4895 110 Hor	3174*
46 4895 110 Hor	3207*
46 4064 110 Hor	3146
46.5 4064 110 Hor	3170
46 4320 110 Hor	3168
47 4320 110 Hor	3250
43 4895 130 Sie	2980*
43 4320 130 Sie	2932
43.5 4320 130 Sie	2980
43 4064 130 Sie	2900
44 4064 130 Sie	2963*
44.5 4064 130 Sie	2979*
45.5 4064 130 Sie	3078
45 4064 130 Sie	3132
50 W760 130 Part	3033
50.8 W760 130 Part	3100
51 W760 130 Part	3125

.270 Win., T/C Venture, 24 in.

Rem 100 CL	3432
53 4064 100 Hor	3465
57 4351 125 HP	3274
Fed 130 TSX	3156
RWS 130 HM	3002
Win 130 PwrPt	3004
61 RL22 130 SP	3202
60 3100 130 Hor	3252
60 H450 130 sp	3158
Hor 140 IntLk	3005
Norma 150 Oryx	2895

.270 Win., Win. 70, 24 in.

51 2520 100 Hor	3408
52 4895 100 Hor	3427
52 4064 110 Hor	3277
58 4350 110 Hor	3288
Fed 130 TSX	3098*
Rem 130 AccTip	2926*
Rem 130 CL	3006

59 H4831 130 Spr	2936
59 H4831 130 GS	2948
60 H4831 130 Spr	3101
59 3100 130 Spr	3048
60 3100 130 Spr	3099
60 H450 130 Spr	3050
53.5 W760 130 Hor	2976
54 H414 130 Spr	3020
58 RL19 130 Hor	2960
60 RL22 130 Spr	3075
59.5 W780 130 Part	3034
Fed HE 140 TB	3154
58 H4831 140 Hor	2984
59 H4831 140 Hor	3023
59 H4831 140 TB	3083
54 4350 140 BTip	2948
55 4350 140 BTip	3013
58 3100 140 TB	3010*
52 W760 140 BTip	2942
52 H414 140 BTip	2889
56 RL19 140 BTip	2972
59 RL22 140 Hor	2996
58.5 W780 140 BTip	3060
58 3100 150 Sie	2994
58 H4831 150 Sie	2980
58 H450 150 Hor	2876
53 4350 150 Sie	2885
55 RL19 150 Hor	2818
57.5 W780 150 Hor	2807

.270 Win., Win. 70, 24 in. (high reads)

59 H4831 130 SST	3146
58 Viht N160 130 SST	3118
57 H4350 130 SST	3199
59 3100 130 SST	3104
59 RL 19 130 SST	3167
55 W 760 130 SST	3173

.270 Howell, American Hunting Rifles, 25 in.

56 H380 100 Hor	3352
64 WMR 130 Spr	3256
64 H4831 130 Hor	3422
55 IMR4064 130 Part	3198
61 H414 130 Part	3272
63 A3100 130 Part	3104
62 RL-19 130 Part	3138
61 H4350 140 Armfld	3297
62 VV N160 140 FS	3361
63 H450 140 Sierra	3322
62 WMR 150 Spe	3119
62 H4831 150 Part	3216
62 RL-22 150 Part	3000

.270 WSM, Browning A-Bolt, 24 in.

Win 130 BST	3290
Win 140 FS	3115

.270 WSM, Winchester 70, 24 in.

Fed 130 X	3293
Win 130 BST	3369
Fed 150 Part	3261

.270 Weatherby Magnum, Mauser, 25 in.

Wby 100 Hor	3690
Wby 130 Part	3435
Wby 130 Hor	3455
Wby 140 Barnes X	3245
Wby 150 Part	3250
Wby 150 Hor	3145

7x57, Ruger No. 1, 22 in.

46 2230 100 ho	3102
46.5 H335 100 Hor	3115
45.5 RL15 120 Hor	2814
51.5 H380 120 Hor	2857
42.5 4895 140 Sie	2657
47 H414 145 Spr	2678
50 WW760 154 Hor	2680
49.5 H4831 162 Hor	2451

7mm/08, Savage 11, 22 in.

Rem 120 HP	3007
Hor LM 139	2924
Rem 140 CL	2785
Rem 140 SP	2804
Win 140 BSTip	2730
Win 140 FS	2777
Rem ExtRg 154 Hor	2575

7mm-08, Mossberg ATR 100, 22 in.

Hor LM 139 SST	2892*
Fed 140 TSX	2731
Fed 140 AccBd	2787
Rem 140 PSP	2756
Rem 140 AccTip	2805
Win 140 BST	2784*

7mm/08, Weatherby Mk V, 24 in.

Fed 140 BTip	2825

.280 Rem, Dakota 10, 24 in.

Hor LM 139 SST	3069
Fed 140 BTip	2891
Rem 150 CL	2771

.280 Rem., Win. 70, 22 in.

Rem 150 CL	2740

.280 Ackley Imp., Rem. 78, 26 in.

62 4350 100 Hor	3543
64 3100 100 Sie	3371*
60.5 4351 120 BTip	3401
58.5 H414 120 BTip	3313
63 4831 120 Hor	3261*
58 W760 120 Hor	3245*
57.5 W760 139 Hor	3076
60 4350 140 Sie	3197
62 H4831 140 BTip	
61 H450 140 Sie	3075*
60.5 RL19 140 Sie	3080
61.5 3100 140 BTip	3133*
55 H414 140 Sie	2992*
59.5 4351 145 Spr	3162
62.5 RL22 145 Spr	3149*
62 H4831 145 Spr	3104 Max
59 h450 145 Spr	2987*
59 RL19 150 Part	3004*
53.5 W760 150 Sie	2915*
54 H414 154 Hor	2861*
56.5 H4350 154 Hor	2898*
63 H1000 154 ho	2857
55 H4831 160 Hor	2870
57.5 H450 160 Sie	2864*
58 RL19 160 Spr	2884*
58.5 3100 162 SBase	2921
60 H4831 162 SBase	2972 Max
62 7828 160 Part	2960
62 7828 162 Hor	2971*
58 H4831 168 Sie	2841*
56.5 H450 175 Spr	2769
61.5 H1000 175 Hor	2707*

7mm Rem. Mag., Rem. 700, 24 in.

63 4064	100 Sie
73 3100 120 Hor	3515
71 7828	139 Hor
65 4350 140 SBase	3157
Rem 150 CL	3123
63 4351 150 Sie	3013
55 4320 150 Sie	2934
67 RL19 154 Jen	3074
66 H450 154 Jen	3040
67 RL-22 160 Part	2917
67 H4831 168 Sie	2930
68 W780 168 Sie	2881*
72 H1000 175 Spr	2947
78 8700 175 Spr	2912
77 H870 175 Hert	2870

7mm Rem. Mag. Tikka T2 Lite, 24 in.

BHA 140 BTip	3014*
Rem 140 CL Ultra	3086
Win 140 AccuBd	3064*
Win 150 PwrPt Plus	3104*
Hor 154 AMax	2996*
Fed 165 GK	2899

7mm Rem Mag, Remington 700, 24 in.

Jarrett 160 AccBnd	3047

7mm Rem. Mag., Win. 70, 24 in.

Win 150 PwrPt	2960
Rem 150 CL	2975
66 H4831 154 Jen	3080
65 H4831 160 Part	3005
64 H450 160 Spr	2886
79 H870 160 Spr	2946
Rem 165 SP	2838
Rem ExtRg 165 HP	2845

Rem 175 CL	2829
Speer Nitrex 175 GS	2838
77 H870 175 gs	2825

7mm Rem. Mag., Win. 70 custom, 26 in.

69 IMR 4831 140 BT	3220
71 RL22 150 Nos	3164
73.5 RL22 150 Nos	3288
71 RL22 160 Nos	3203

7mm Dakota, Dakota 76, 26 in.

Dakota 140 BTip	3220

7mm Wby. Mag., Wby. Mark V, 26 in.

Wby 150 X	3015
Wby 150 BTip	3290
Wby 175 Hor	3015

.30-30 Win., Marlin 336, 20 in.

Speer Nitrex 150 GS	2369

.300 Sav., Savage 99, 22 in.

Fed 150	2672
Hor 150 SST	2633
Rem 150 cl	2615
Win 150 st	2564
Rem 180 CL	2324
Win 180 ST	2310
Win 180 PwrPt	2320

.300 Savage, Savage 99, 24 in.

Rem 150 cl (24 in.)	2636

.30 Rem AR, R-15, 22 in.

Rem 123 FMJ	2812
Rem 125 AccuTip	2736
Rem 125 C-L	2742

.308 Win., Kifaru, 18 ½ in.

Rem 150 CL	2790
Rem 180 CL	2515

.308 Win., Rem. Seven, 20 in.

Rem 150 CL	2860
Hor 150 SST	2980

.308 Win., Sav 10, 20 in.

Rem MR 125 SP	2714
Hor LM 150 SST	3009
Win 150 ETip	2751
Fed 155 Match	2776*
44 Varget 165 IntBd	2681
BHA 168 Si MK	2600
Hor TAP 168 BTHP	2659
Fed LR 170 SP	2092*
Fed 175 MK	2461
Win 180 PwrPt	2590
Lapua 185 SP	2620

.308 Win., Sako, 21 in.

Musgrave180 SP	2753
Win 180 STip	2565

.308 Win., Rem. 78, 22 in.

Win 150 STip	2838
42.5 H335 150 SP	2745
42.5 H335 165 sp	2643
Hor 168 AMax TAP	2576
42 H335 168 no	2597
Military 172 Match	2738
Military Ball 173	2699
Rem 180 Part	2557
42.5 H335 180 SP	2595

.308 Win., RRA, 22 in.

Rem MR 125 SP	2645
Fiocchi 150 SST	2961
Hor LM 150 SST	3115
Rem 150 CL	2879*
Win 150 E-Tip	2863
Fed HE 165 TB	2857
Rem 165 Scir	2686
44 Varget 165 IntBd	2720
Hor 168 TAP AMax	2739*
Fed 175 MK	2685*
BHA 175 BTHP	2669
Lapua 185 SP	

.30-06, Rem. 78, 22 in.

Fed 150 SP	2907
52 RL15 150 SP	2879

59 W760 150 SST	2877
51 4895 150 SP	2818
56 H380 150 SST	2894
51 2520 150 SST	2881
53 4064 150 SP	2902
50 H335 150 BTip	2875
53 4895 150 SST	3020
59.5 RL19 165 Spr	2723
55 W760 165 Spr	2735
57 4350 165 TB	2732
56 H414 165 TB	2744
55 H414 165 BTip	2744
55 H414 168 Ho	2700
Speer Nitrex 180 SP	2772
58.5 RL19 180 Spr	2622
56 4350 180 HMtl	2606*
54.5 H414 180 BTHP	2640
54 W760 180 PwrPt	2614*
58 RL19 180 Hor	2759
58 RL19 190 Spr	2674
60 H4831 180 Spr	2683
60 H4831 180 Hor	2732
61 7828 190 Hor	2581

.30-06, Savage 116, 22 in.

Fed HE 165 GK	2949
Fed 165 TSX	2839*
Fed 165 BTip	2869*
Hor LM 165 BTSP	2865
Black Hills 168 BTHP	2746*
Blaser 180 HMtl	2835
Norma 180 Oryx	2649
PMC 180 X	2713
Rem 180 Scir	2722
Rem 180 CL Ultra	2750
60 H4831 180 Spr	2683
60 H4831 180 Hor	2732
58 RL19 180 Hor	2759
58 RL19 190 BTHP	2674

.30-06, CZ 550, 24 in.

Rem 125 MR	2625
Blk Hills 150 BTip	2960
Fed 165 GK	2961*
Hor 165 SST	2803
Jarrett 165 BTip	2806
Hor LM 180 BTSP	2895
Jarrett 180 Scir	2723
Win 180 BSTip	2759*

.30-06, Dakota 97 Outfitter, 24 in.

Fed 165 CoppTip	2890
Hor 165 BTSP	2760
Rem 165 CL	2835
51 4064 165 TB	2815
BHA 168 BTHP	2785
Fed 180 TBTip	2695
Fed 180 TBHE	2965
Norma 180 AccuBd	2685*
Norma 180 Oryx	2630
56 H414 180 A-Fr	2810

.30-06, Win. 70, 24 in.

Rem MR 125 SP	2500
Win 125 SP	2980
Fed 150 SP	2963
Hansen 150 SP	2894
Win 150 PwrPt +	3032
50 H335 150 BTip	3009
Fed 165 SP	2850
Hor 165 SP	2778
Rem ExtRg 165 SP	2765
Win 165 STip	2756
55 H414 168 Hor	2849
Fed 180 Part	2685
Norma 180 Oryx	2641
PMC 180 HP	2676
Rem 180 A-Fr	2738
Win 180 FS	2663
Win 180 STip	2620
58.5 H483l 180 PwrPt	2610
Rem 220 SP	2410
Win 220 STip	2375

.30-06 Ackley Imp., Springfield, 22 in.

60 4350 165 Spr	2837
61.5 4350 165 Spr	2810
62 H4350 165 TB	2915
61 H4350 165 SP	2853
61 H4350 180 PwrPt	2872

61 H4350 180 Hmtl	2844)
62 4831 180 PwrPt	2748
63 4831 180 PwrPt	2767
63.5 4831 180 cl	2724

.300 Heavy Express (.348 case), Rem 700, 24 in.

67 2700 140 X	3135
70 4350 150 Part	3240
66 4350 150 Cone	2951
60 4064 150 Hor	3225
61 Vit N140 150 Part	3180
60 IMR 4064 150 Hor	3225
65 H414 160 NorPr	3015
72 RL19 160 NorPr	3145
65 H414 160 NorPr	3015
67 3100 165 Spr	2860
62 W760 165 X	2886
67 Big Game 165 Sie	3080
70 Vit N160 165 Sie	3090
67 3100 165 Spr	2860
62 W760 165 X	2886
70 3100 180 Spr	3055
73 WMR 180 A-Fr	3050
67 RL19 180 A-Fr	2930
69 H450 180 Jen	3075 Max
67 RL-19 180 A-Fr	2890
70 VitN165 185 Ber	2896
73 H1000 200 Hawk	2860
72 RL25 200 X	2885
69 RL22 220 Part	2765

.300 H&H, Ruger #1S (Cabela's), 26 in.

Nos 150 AccuBd	3175
Fed 180 TSX	2993
Hor 180 IntBd DG	2939
69 H4831 200 Part	2823

.300 H&H, Win. 70, 26 in.

Win 150 STip	3130
73 H4831 150 BTip	3179
69 H4350 165 CL	3112
66 H380 165 Spr	3112
67.5 H380 165 Spr	3181 Max
72 H4831 180 CL	2997
67 4350 180 PwrPt	2961
69 4831 180 PrwPt	2917
71 4831 180 Spr	2944
71 H450 180 Spr	2919
70 3100 180 CL	2901
72 H4831 180 CL	2990
70 H4831 200 Part	2910
68 H450 200 Part	2855
69 w780 200 TB	2822
67 w780 220 Hert	2700

.300 WSM, Browning A-Bolt, 24 in.

69 H414 150 X	3301
68 W760 150 Hor	3159
63 Varget 150 Sie	3257
61 4064 150 Scir	3269
65 Big Game 165 SST	3131
66 H4350 168 X	3087
67 N204 168 BTHP	3144
Win 180 PP	2991
Win 180 FS	2944
71.5 N560 180 XLC	2947
68 RL19 180 Hor	3034
71 H4831 180 Oryx	3033
70 N160 180 BTip	3086
68 H450 180 FS	2896
70 RL22 185 Ber	2956*
70 WMR 200 Part	2804
66 AA 3100 200 Spr	2804
74 Big Boy 220 Sie	2763*

.300 WSM, Weatherby Vanguard, 24 in.

Fed 180 AccBd	3069
Win 180 AccBd	2990
Win 180 FS	2988

.300 Rem. SAUM, Rem. Seven, 22 in.

Rem 180 Partition	2941
Rem 180 C-L Ultra	2910

.30-338, Win. 70 (Freudenberg custom), 26 in. Lilja

72 H4350 165 Sie	3267
74 RL-19 165 TB	3345 Max
75 H4831 165 TB	3254
73 H4831 180 CL	3117
72 RL-19 180 TUG	3187

68 Win 760 180 A-Fr	3205
74 RL-22 190 Hor	3184
72 H450 190 Hor	3002*
73 Win 780 190 Hor	3048*
71 H4831 200 Hawk	2989
70 AA3100 200 Hawk	2992
73 7828 200 Hawk	2967

.308 Norma, Rem. 78, 27 in.

68 H380 150 Hor	3010
73 H4350 150 Part	3185
74 RL19 150 Hor	3095
69 Win760 150 Part	3050
67 2700 160 NorPr	2955
63 4064 160 NorPr	3020
80 Big Boy165 Spe	2990
68 H414 168 BTHP	2945
73 A3100 165 Spe	2970
70 Vit 160 165 X	2975
72 RL19 165 Hor	3000
75 H4831 185 Ber	2980
78 Big Boy 180 PwrPt	2900
69 H4350 180 Scir	3020
Nor 180 SP	3020
71 H4831 200 Part	2923
72 H4831 190 Hor	2944
73 H4831 180 CL	3025
68 H450 220 Her	2725
70 H450 200 TB	2889
71 H450 180 PwrPt	2984*
73 H450 180 Spr	3089*
71 3100 180 Spr	3054*
73 3100 180 PwrPt	3124*
74 RL22 180 TB	3135
68 RL19 180 PwrPt	2931
70 RL19 180 PwrPt	2967
68 4350 180 Spr	3023
70 4350 180 PwrPt	3060
66 w760 180 PwrPt	2967
68 w760 180 HMtl	3017
68 w760 180 Spr	3084*
70 w780 190 Sie	2833
72 w780 190 Hor	2869
72 RL22 190 Sie	3000*
70.5 RL22 200 TB	2944
71 RL22 200 Part	2955
71 RL22 200 TB	2885
70 3100 200 Part	2885*
70.5 3100 200 Spr	2940*
72 w780 200 Part	2892
76 1000 200 TB	2942*
67 RL19 200 Part	2821
76 1000 200 Part	2960
74 7828 200 TB	2958
74 7828 200 Spr	3020*
79 8700 220 Hert	2689
71 7828 220 Hert	2749
70 w780 220 Hert	2721
73 1000 220 Hert	2721
69 RL22 220 Her	2758
69 H4831 220 Hert	2779

.308 Norma, Cooper M56, 26 in.

Safari Arms 180 TSXa	2976
Safari Arms 180 TSXb	2888
Safari Arms 180 TSXc	3001*
Safari Arms 180 TSXd	2951
Norma 180 Oryx	3058
71 RL22 200 TB	2870

.300 Win. Mag., Win. 70, 24 in.

Herter 155 SP	3206
Rem ExtRg 178 BTHP	3035
Fed HE 180 TB	3034
Win 180 PwrPt	2945
73 H4831 180 Spr	2956
75 H4831 180 Spr	2998
75 H4831 180 Part	2977
Fed 190 BTHP	2895
Rem ExtRg 190 BTHP	2835
73 4831 200 Part	2813
69 4350 200 Part	2861

.300 Win, Ruger 77, 24 in.

Hor 165 IntBd	3053*
Jarrett 165 Sie HPBT	3195*
Jarrett 180 X	3089

.300 Win, Winchester 70 (Cabela's), 26 in.

Hor 165 IntBd	3076

Win 180 AccBd	3022
Fed 190 MK	2983
Win 190 STipBT	2883
Norma 200 Oryx	2676

.300 Win. Mag., Ruger No. 1, 26 in.

Rem ExtRg 178	3183
Fed 180 SP	2959
Rem 180 CL	2990
Win 180 FS	2940
75 H4831 180 Part	3040
76 H4831 180 FS	3095
Fed 200 TB	2916

.300 Dakota, Dakota 76, 24 in.

Dakota 180 Scir	2928

.300 Wby. Mag., Sako 75, 26 in.

Fed 180 TB	3202
Hor 180 IntLk	3061

.300 Ultra Mag, Rem. 700, 26 in.

92 RL19 150 Cone	3524
Rem 180 Part	3266
89 H450 165 Spr	3411
85 H4350 165X	3400
94 RL22 165 Hor	3551*
93 RL25 180 A-Fr	3271*
88 7828 180 Sie	3191
90 7828 180 Sie	3301*
89 3100 185 Berg	3264*
85 H4831sc 200 Part	3006
101 8700 220 Hert	3022
102 H870 220 Hert	3111*

.30-378 Wby. Mag., Wby Accumark, 28 in.

107 H4831 140 X	3733
105 RL22 150 BTip	3544
102 3100 165 TB	3536
108 H1000 165 Sie	3297
119 H870 180 Spr	3352
100 RL22 180 A-Fr	3265
120 H50BMG 180 Part	3234
114 8700 200 X	3264
116 H50BMG 200 Part	3126
102 RL25 200 Hawk	3184
107 RL25 200 Hawk	3241

.303 Savage, 1899 Savage, 20 in.

Win 190 ST	1790

.303 British, Ruger #1 RSI, 20 in.

Hor 150 IL SP	2644
PMC 174 MK	2332
Fed 180 SP	2370
Rem 180 CL	2382

.32 Win. Spl., Win. 94, 26 in.

Fed 170 SP	2209

8mm Rem. Mag., Rem 700, 24 in.

Rem 185 CL	
Rem 220 CL	2642

.338-08, Win. 88, 22 in.

46 2015 185 X	2730

.338-08, Win. 70, 24 in.

46 2015 185 X	2810

.338-08, Rem 700, 23 in.

42 RL7 180 BTip	2745
44 RL7 180 BTip	2870 Max
48 3031 180 BTip	2840*
49 4895 180 BTip	2805
42 4198 180 BTip	2750
51 BL-C2 180 BTip	2735
47 2230 180 BTip	2725
50 Varget 180 BTip	2755*
46 A2460 180 BTip	2740
49 4320 180 BTip	2700
50 2520 180 BTip	2730
46 H322 180 BTip	2775
45 Vit133 180 BTip	2760
48 Bnchmk 180 BTip	2815 Max
44 Xtermin 180 BTip	2640
47 Xtermin 180 BTip	2750
48 RL12 200 Hor	2555
46 2460 200 BTip	2660
48 Vit140 200 Hor	2565

49 Scot 4065 200 Hor	2585
47 2520 200 Hor	2555
48 2520 200 BTp	2575
50 BL-C2 200 Hor	2585
48 4064 200 Hor	2645
49 W748 200 Hor	2535
51 W748 200 BTip	2665
46 4895 200 BTip	2615
44 H322 200 BTip	2610
47 Varget 200 Hor	2505
49 RamTAC 200 Hor	2620
49 4320 200 BTip	2665*
49 2520 210 Part	2615
46 3031 210 Part	2650
49 H380 225 Armfield	2350
49 W760 225 Hor	2340
50 2700 225 Spr	2350

.338 Federal, Nosler 48, 24 in.

Fed 180 AccBd	2832
Fed 185 TSX	2797
Fed 210 Part	2665
48 2520 200 SP	2637

.338 Marlin Express, Marlin 1895, 24 in.

Hor 200 FTX	2570*

.338-06, Weatherby Mark V, 24 in.

Superior 210 Part	2765

.338-06, Husqvarna, 22 in.

57.5 4320 200 Hor	2677
58 4065 200 Hor	2708*
60.5 H380 210 Part	2663
61.5 W760 210 Part	2624
54 2520 210 Part	2658
54.5 4320 225 Part	2550
61 H414 225 Part	2610
56 4350 250 STip	2353
59 H4350 250 STip	2388
61 3100 250 STip	2376
61.5 H4831 250 STip	2374
57 H450 250 STip	2289*
60.5 H450 250 STip	2343*
54 W760 265 Hert	2244*
55 RL19 265 Hert	2225
57 re19 265 Hert	2270
56 H4831 265 Hert	2211
59 H4831 265 Hert	2284
54 4351 265 Hert	2289
56.5 4351 265 Hert	2332
53 H380 265 Hert	2305
58 H4831 275 Spr	2218
53 4350 275 Spr	2213
54 H450 275 Spr	2134*
56 H450 275 Spr	2186
54.5 3100 300 Barnes	2115

.338-06, Mauser, 25 in.

54 4320 200 Jen	2906
54 IMR 4064 200 Bltp	2830
54 RL15 200 Jens	2810
55 Scot 4065 200 Hor	2844*
56 4320 200 BTip	2781*
62 W760 200 Nos	2731*
62 H414 210 Part	2780
52 RL15 225 Nos	2608
60 H414 225 Nos	2698*
53 4065 230 Hawk	2627
62 H4350 230 Hawk	2720*
63 RL-19 230 Hawk	2695*
51 IMR 4320 250 Elkh	2542*
59 H414 250 SilvTp	2517*
59 4351 250 Elkhn	2636*
60 H4350 250 Elkh	2600
59 H4350 265 Hert	2387
61 H4831 265 Hert	2412
56 4351 275 Spr	2422
60 3100 275 Spr	2380

.338-300 WSM, Win. 70, 24 in.

65 RL15 180 BTip	3045
68 Big Game 180 BTip	2910
64 4064 180 BTip	3050
67 H414 200 Hor	2785
66 H380 200 BTip	2780
67 2700 200 BTip	2825
70 RL19 210 Part	2765
69 H4350 210 Part	2805
67 W760 210 Part	2785

68 H4831 225 Spr	2565
67 N160 225 Spr	2625
68 H450 225 Spr	2625
67 H4350 225 Spr	2665
69 WMR 230 Hawk	2500

.338 Win. Mag., Mauser (Echols w/ KDF brake), 23 in.

Win 200 PwrPt	2869
77 H4831 210 Part	2960*
73 3100 265 Hert	2639
75 7828 265 Hert	2645
72 4831 265 Hert	2596
72 3100 275 Spr	2582
74 7828 275 Spr	2573
72 4831 275 Spr	2546

.338 Win. Mag., Mauser (Meridian ID) 24 in.

76 H4831 200 Spr	2783
Fed 210 Part	2788
76 H4831 210 Part	2907
77 H4831 210 Part	2911
Fed 225 SP	2700
Rem 225 SP	2715
Win 225 SP	2759
Fed 250 Part	2615
Rem 250 SP	2612
72 H4831 275 Spr	2543

.338 Win. Mag., Rem. 700, 24 in.

Win 200 PwrPt	2815
71 4350 210 Part	2813
78 H4831 210 no	3002
75 RL19 230 Hawk	2856
72 4351 230 Hawk	2880
69 4351 250 STip	2680
69 4350 250 Sie	2752
67 4351 265 Hert	2619
72 4831 265 Hert	2590
71 H450 265 Hert	2558
75 7828 265 Hert	2617
73 3100 265 Hert	2663
67 4351 275 Spr	2592
67 4350 275 Spr	2600
68 4350 275 Spr	2621
72 H4831 275 Spr	2654
72 H4831 275 Spr	2622
72 3100 275 Spr	2568
74 7828 275 Spr	2563

.338 Win. Mag., Win. 70, 25 in.

Win 200 pp	2862
Win 250 sy	2598
Win 300 rn	2421
73 4831 250 Sie	2703
73 4831 250 Spr	2683
76 4831 210 Part	2927
77 4831 210 Part	2907
78 4831 210 Part	2916

.340 Wby. Mag., Wby. Mark V, 26 in.

Wby 200 SP	3193
Wby 210 Part	3172
Wby 250 Part	2966*

.340 Wby. Mag., Rem. 78, 27 in.

Wby 200 SP	3270
Wby 250 Part	2971
84 H4831 250 STip	2898
83 H450 250 STip	2870
83 3100 250 STip	2908
84 RL22 250 STip	2872
81 H450 265 Hert	2756
82 RL22 265 Hert	2771
81 3100 265 Hert	2795
83 H4831 265 Hert	2821
82 H450 265 Hert	2778
80 RL19 265 Hert	2790
81 H4831 275 Spr	2701
80 H450 275 Spr	2678
80 3100 275 Spr	2714
82 RL22 275 Spr	2739
78 RL19 275 Spr	2677
84 H1000 275 Spr	2620
78 W780 275 Spr	2620

.338 Norma, Remington/Montana custom, 26 in.

86 H4831 250 MK	2820
79 H4350 250 MK	2810*
85 3100 250 A-Fr	2814
87 RL22 250 A-Fr	2839

92 Big Boy 250 Sce	2736*
87 VV N165 250 Sce	2778
94 Mag 250 Pt Gold	2766
82 RL22 300 MK	2618
90 Magnum 300 MK	2625*
90 VV N570 300 MK	2761*

.338 Lapua, Sako, 26 in.

91 3100 200 Jen	3090
94 RL19 210 Part	3069
92 H4831 225 Hor	3058
91 RL19 225 Part	3023
90 H450 250 Sie	3061
91 RL22 250 Lapua	2947
98 H1000 250 Sie	2971
90 H4831 250 Elkh	2896
98 IMR 7828 250 A-Fr	3110 Max
86 H450 275 Spr	2684
85 AA 3100 275 Spr	2700
87 RL22 275 Spr	2721

.338-378 Wby. Mag., Wby. Mark V, 26 in.

Wby 250 Part	3005

.348 Win., Win. 71, 24 in.

Rem 200 CL	2415 (Improved chamber)
Win 200 STip	2442 (Improved chamber)

.348 Ackley Imp., Browning 71, 24 in.

58 N150 180 Speer	2750
54 H322 180 Speer	2734
59 4064 180 Hawk	2670
58 RamTAC 180 Hawk	2680
56 RL15 200 Hor	2464
57 RL15 200 Hor	2500*
57 Varget 200 Hor	2520
57 2520 200 Hor	2524
60 H380 200 STip	2460*
61 Scot 4351 250 Kod	2336
62 H4350 250 Kod	2286
63 RL19 250 Kod	2278*
58 Big Game 250 Kod	2360
60 Big Game 250 Kod	2370

.358 Win, Browning BL-81 TD, 22 in.

Win 200 PwrPt	2445

.35 Whelen, Rem 700, 22 in.

54 3032 180 SP	2736
Rem 200 SP	2574
Rem 250 SP	2390
58.5 H335 200 Sie	2690
56.5 4320 200 Sie	2504*
57 4895 200 Hor	2699*
49 2460 200 Hor	2384
51 3032 220 Spr	2474*
54.5 4064 220 Spr	2466
55 H335 225 Sie	2587
55 4320 225 Sie	2471
54 W748 225 Part	2389
47.5 2520 225 Part	2232*
53 H380-335 250 Part	2455
53 H335 250 Part	2522
56.5 RL15 250 Hor	2523
53.5 4895 250 Hor	2496*

.35 Whelen (Ackley) Imp., Rem. 78, 26 in.

63 4320 180 Spr	2875*
64 W748 180 Spr	2795
60 H380 200 Hor	2617
59 4064 200 Hor	2732*
55 2520 200 Sie	2682
59 4895 200 Hor	2700
58 4320 220 Spr	2626
57 4895 220 Spr	2744
56 4895 225 Sie	2702
56 H335 225 Sie	2760
57 RL15 225 Part	2683
57.5 4064 225 Part	2695
Rem 250 SP	2521
53 H335 250 Spr	2515
54.5 H335 250 Spr	2595
55 H335 250 Hor	2617
56 4895 250 Spr	2635
56.5 4895 250 Spr	2638
59 H380 250 Hor	2500*
60 H380 250 Hor	2473
56 RL15 250 Spr	2560
56 4065 250 Hor	2480*

57.5 4065 250 Hor	2538
58 4064 250 Hor	2640
53 2460 250 Hor	2557
55.5 4320 250 Spr	2453*
63 H414 250 Spr	2476
64 4350 250 Part	2490
54.5 2520 250 Part	2544

.350 Rem. Mag., Rem. 700, 22 in.

Rem 200 CL	2677
58 H335 200 Hor	2722
61 W748 225 Hor	2713
60 W760 250 CL	2345
60 H380 250 CL	2291
56 4320 250 CL	2374
57 4320 250 CL	2385

.350 Rem. Mag., Rem 763 22 in.

Rem 200	2635
58 H335 200 ho	2695
Rem 225 A-Fr	2635
54 H335 225 Part	2755
61 W748 225 Part	2790*
60 W760 250 cl	2410
60 H380 250 cl	2310
56 4320 250 cl	2370
57 4320 250 cl	2420

.358 Norma Mag., Mauser, 25 in.

67 4065 200 Hor	2883
68 RL15 200 Hor	2954
80 RL19 220 Spr	2858
68 432 225 Sie	2812
75 W760 225 BluMt	2934
76 H414 225 Part	3015*
77 4351 225 Sie	2967
74 W760 250 Hor	2760
76 H4350 250 BluMtn	2755
78 RL19 250 Elkh	2807
78 H450 250 Hor	2713
79 AA3100 250 BluMt	2789
80 RL22 250 Hor	2763

.35/404 (.35 Wyatt), Remington 700, 28 in.

96 H4350 200 Sie	3260
98 H4350 200 Hor	3420
99 RL19 200 Sie	3270
100 H4831 200 Sie	3251
98 3100 200 Hor	3219
101 3100 200 Hor	3375
103 WMR 200 Hor	3265
99 H450 200 Hor	3262
95 Big Game 200 Hor	3440
100 H4831 220 Spr	3252
102 RL22 220 Spr	3248
93 H450 225 Part	3086
103 RL22 225 Sie	3320
104.5 RL22 225 Sie	3381
101 H4831 225 BTip	3438
100 3100 225 Sie	3309
100 3100 225 BTip	3378
98 VV N160 225 Swift	3376
100 RL19 225 Swift	3356
101 H450 225 Swift	3280
97 H4350 225 Swift	3321
92 3100 230 BluMtn	3010
102 BigBoy 230 BluMt	2956
94 RL22 230 BluMtn	2925
99 RL22 230 BluMtn	3144
95 H4831 230 BluMtn	3048
97 H4831 230 BluMtn	3100
94 N160 230 BluMtn	3038
96 H450 230 BluMtn	3001
95 RL19 250 Spr	3141
97 RL19 250 Spr	3200
91 RL22 250 Spr	2930
100 RL22 250 Spr	3130
100 H1000 250 Hor	2904
103 H1000 250 Spr	3123
92 H4831 250 Hor	2935
95 H4831 250 Hor	3019
95 3100 250 Spr	3043
97 3100 250 Spr	3126
99 H450 250 Spr	3155
99 WMR 250 Spr	3045
92 N160 250 Spr	3011

9.3x62, Mauser, 25 in.

Norma 286	2760
57 W748 240 TB	2329

58 A2520 240 TB	2450
59 BLC-2 240 TB	2415
57 H380 270 Spr	2104
56 4064 270 Spr	2335
55 H335 270 Spr	2349
52 2230 270 TB	2274
61 W760 270 TB	2195
60 H414 270 Barnes	2100
57 RL15 270 Barnes	2346
61 H4350 285 SP	2048
53 A2460 285 SP	2237
60 Scot 4351 285 SP	2113
59 A2700 293 TUG	2150
61 RL19 300 Barnes	2011
60 H4350 300 Barnes	2007

9.3x62, Kilimanjaro, 21 in.

Hor 286 Spire	2210
53 RL15 286 TSX	2080*
Norma 325 Oryx	2170

9.3x62, Ruger 77 Hawkeye African, 23 in.

Lapua 220 Naturalis	2505
Rem 285 PSP	2260
Hor 286 SP	2210
Norma 325 Oryx	2175

.38-55, Lyman Baby Sharps, 26 in.

BHA 255 CA lead	1317
Win 255 SP	1153

.375 Heavy Express (CCI Magnum primers)

62 VitN135 250 A-Fr	2745
64 4895 250 A-Fr	2820
63 H322 250 A-Fr	2845 Max
62 Benchmk 250 A-Fr	2775
62 H335 260 Part	2688
63 2460 260 Part	2702
66 RL15 260 Part	2785
63 4320 260 Part	2655
61 RamTAC 260 Part	2580
62 2230 260 Part	2695*
67 W760 260 Part	2550*
62 Vit N140 260 Part	2615
61 Varget 260 Part	2580
61 BL-C2 270 Hor	2485
63 2520 270 Hor	2550
60 4064 285 Spr	2445
64 2700 300 Hert	2310
65 H380 300 Hert	2355*
61 RL15 300 Hor	2450
65 H414 300 Hor	2355*
67 Big Game 300 Hor	2420
66 H4350 300 Hor	2335

.375/338 (.375 Chatfield-Taylor), Mausers (Sisk and Dustin), 24 in.

65 4064 250 NorFk	2605
66 RL15 250 NorFk	2635
67 Vit N140 250 NorFk	2680
69 Vit N150 270 Hor	2615
65 4320 270 Hor	2490
66 Varget 270 Hor	2600
72 H4350 300 Hert	2420
71 W760 300 TB	2520

.375 H&H, Win. 70, 25 in.

Speer Nitrex 285	2611
Win 300 STip	2512
81 H4831 300 Hert	2351
81 H4831 300 Hor	2421
77 4350 300 Hor	2488

.375 H&H, Rem. 700, 22 in.

Fed 260 AccBd	2640
Rem 270 SP	2675
Fed 300 TB	2435
77 4350 300 Hor	2440
Hor 300 RN	2595
Win 300 Nos Solid	2415
Norma 350 Wdl	2275

.375 H&H, Sako 85 Kodiak, 24 in.

Fed 260 AccBd	2585*
Hor HM 300 IntBd	2553
Win 300 Nos Solid	2366
77 IMR4350 300 Hor	2369
81 H4831 300 Hor	2306
Nor 350 Wdl	2205

.404 Jeffery, CZ 550 Safari Classic, 24 in.

Hor 400 DGX	2282
Hor 400 DGX	2298
Nor 450 Wdl	2016
Nor 450 Wdl	2007

.411 Hawk, Mauser (Zeglin custom) 24 in.

61 2460 300 Hawk	2391
62 4064 300 Hawk	2388
60 2230 300 Hawk	2377
62 H322 300 Hawk	2541
63 H4895 300 Hawk	2516
61 4064 350 A-Fr	2366
59 H322 350 A-Fr	2393
59 2460 350 A-Fr	2218

.416 Rigby, CZ 550 Safari, 25 in.

Fed 400 Part	2428 1.2 @ 50, irons
Hor 400 DGX	2320 1.1 @ 50, irons
Nor 400 Barnes S	2250 1.0 @ 50, irons

.416 Rigby, Kimber Caprivi, 24 in.

88 4320 335 TB	2369
90 4320 335 TB	2434
91 4320 335 TB	2424
93 4320 335 TB	2564
85 4895 335 TB	2418
87 4895 335 TB	2412
98 w760 335 TB	2466
92 4064 335 TB	2452
94 4064 335 TB	2578
93 2520 335 TB	2657
95 2520 335 TB	2710 Max
94 h380 335 TB	2467
96 h380 335 TB	2470
103 4831 335 TB	2512
105 4831 335 TB	2560
92 W760 400 A-SqDT	2201
97 4831 400 A-SqDT	2169
103 H4831 400 A-SqLL	2310
106 H4831 400 A-SqLL	2431
105 H450 400 A-SqLL	2434
108 H450 400 A-SqLL	2484
96 RL19 400 A-SqDT	2148
99 RL19 400 A-SqDT	2242
115 8700 400 A-SqLL	2105
118 8700 400 A-SqLL	2163
84 4320 400 A-SqLL	2250
86 4320 400 A-SqLL	2297
104 7828 400 A-SqDT	2276
107 7828 400 A-SqDT	2383
110 7828 400 A-SqDT	2436
102 RL22 400 A-SqLL	2250
91 4350 400 A-SqLL	2135
93 4350 400 A-SqLL	2199
115 h570 400 A-SqLL	2155
118 h570 400 A-SqLL	2186
94 3100 400 as dt	2113
97 3100 400 as dt	2237
90 H4831 410 solid	2266

.416/375 Ultra Mag, Rem. 700, 23 in.

95 H380 325 X	2765
98 W760 325 X	2760
100 H414 325 X	2790
103 H4350 325 X	2780
105 N204 325 X	2850
105 RL-19 325 X	2805
105 VitN-160 325 X	2800
105 WMR 400 XLC	2455
105 NorMR 400 XLC	2555
105 RL-2 400 XLC	2570
105 H4831 400 Hor S	2590
105 A3100 400 Hor S	2595
105 RL-25 400 Hor S	2435

.450 Alaskan (in Browning/Win. 71, case-forming loads), 24 in.

66 3032 325 NorPr	2075
68 H322 325 NorPr	2265
69 H4895 325 NorPr	2090*
64 Scot 3032 350 Hor	2049
67 H4895 350 Hor	2052*
63 H322 400 Spr	2086*
65 H4895 400 Spr	1992

.450 Alaskan, Win. 71, 24 in.

58 IMR 4198 300 Sie	2322
67 RamXterm 300 Sie	2320

69 2460 300 Sie	2046
69 3031 300 Sie	2348
69 RamTAC 350 Hor	2274
67 3031 350 Hor	2288
65 RL12 350 Hor	1830
68 H322 350 Hor	2392
70 2460 350 Kod	2108
58 RL7 350 Kod	2120
65 RamXterm 350 Kod	2180
66 H322 350 Kod	2282
68 4064 400 Spr	2130
67 RL15 400 Speer	2076
66 RamTAC 400 Brnes	2120
69 VitN-150 400 Brnes	2066

.45-70, Marlin 1895 (Sisk), 21 in.

Win 300 PtGold	1950
Fed 300 Hi-Shok	1860

(405-gr. factory load listed at 1350. Pressure levels for trapdoor Springfield: 21,000 CUP. Lever-action 1886 Winchester and 1895 Marlin can handle 28,000, bolt-action and single-shot rifles, 35,000 CUP. Top high-velocity load is a 400-gr. bullet at 2000; a safe lethal load for trapdoor rifles drives a 300-gr. bullet 1800 fps.)

.45-70, Browning 1886, 22 in.

Rem 300 SJHP	1632*
Fed 300 HP	1772
Win 405 SP	1360
BHA 405 CA lead	1244*

.450 Marlin, Win 70 (Sisk), 21 in.

Hor 350	1980 (average of 10; 2100 advertised)

.458 Win. Mag., Mauser, 24 in.

Rem	500 mc	2044
Win	500 mc	1973
Rem	510 sp	2014

.500 S&W, Bighorn 89, 24 in.

Hor 350 hp	2140
Hor 350 hp	2070
Win 400 Platinum Tip	1965
Win 400 Platinum Tip	1950
41.5 H110 400 Hor FP	1965
41.5 H110 400 Hor FP	1945

Appendix 2: Product Directory for Handloaders

The shooting sports industry comprises myriad businesses, big and small. Some—even those with enough employees to staff the Department of Homeland Security—operate independently. Others enjoy or endure the umbrellas of corporate parents. ATK owns Federal, RCBS, Weaver, Savage, Bushnell, and other brands. The Freedom Group has corraled Remington, Marlin, Bushmaster, and a heaping handful of companion companies that make guns and related products. This list for handloaders isn't comprehensive, but it's a start. You'll find just about everything you can imagine in tools and components. I've included ammunition firms, as you may want some factory rounds on the shelf too, if only to compare with those from your press. Also on the roster: gunsmithing supply and firearms cleaning and care sources, because you'll need 'em. And manufacturers of hearing protection, because that's important.

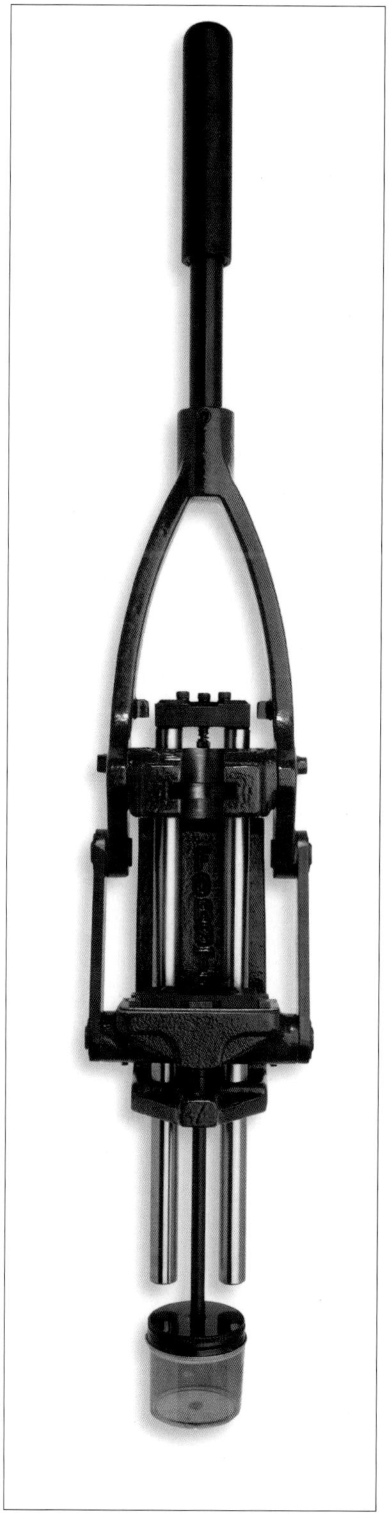

▲ Forster's Co-Ax is one of the most cleverly designed presses. Die change is very quick, case alignment precise.

Alliant Powder
Route 114, Building 229
PO Box 6
Radford, VA 24143
www.alliantpowder.com

Barnes Bullets Inc.
PO Box 620
Mona, UT 84645
www.barnesbullets.com

Battenfeld Technologies Inc.
5885 W. Van Horn Tavern Road
Columbia, MO 65203-9274
www.battenfeldtechnologies.com

Berger Bullets, LLC
4275 North Palm St.
Fullerton, CA 92835
www.bergerbullets.com

Birchwood Casey
7887 Fuller Road
Eden Prairie, MN 55344
www.birchwoodcasey.com

Black Hills Ammunition
PO Box 3090
Rapid City, SD 57709
www.black-hills.com

Black Hills Shooters Supply
2875 Creek Drive
Rapid City, SD 57703
www.bhshooters.com

Break-Free Inc.
13386 International Parkway
Jacksonville, FL 32218
www.safariland.com

Brownells, Inc.
200 South Front St.
Montezuma, IA 50171-1159
www.brownells.com

Butler Creek
9200 Cody St.
Overland Park, KS 66214
www.butlercreek.com

CCI/Speer
2299 Snake River Avenue
Lewiston, ID 83501
www.cci-ammunition.com

Corbon/Glaser
1311 Industry Road
PO Box 369
Sturgis, SD 57785-9123
www.corbon.com

Cutting Edge Bullets
75 Basin Run Road
PO Box 248
Drifting, PA 16834
www.cuttingedgebullets.com

Dillon Precision Products Inc.
8009 East Dillon's Way
Scottsdale, AZ 85260
www.dillonprecision.com

E.A.R., Inc./Insta-Mold Div.
PO Box 18888
Boulder, CO 80308-1888
www.earinc.com

Federal Premium Ammunition
900 Ehlen Drive
Anoka, MN 55303
www.federalpremium.com

Fiocchi, USA
6930 North Fremont Road
Ozark, MO 65721
www.fiocchiusa.com

Flitz International Ltd
821 Mohr Ave.
PO Box 870025
Waterford, WI 53185
www.flitz.com

Forster Products, Inc.
310 East Lanark Ave.
Lanart, IL 61046
www.forsterproducts.com

Freedom Munitions
815 D St.
Lewiston, ID 83501
www.freedommunitions.com

FrogLube
Audemous
1653 Froude St.
San Diego, CA 92107
www.froglube.com

G96 Products Inc.
85-5th Ave., Building 6
Paterson, NJ 07524
www.g96.com

Hodgdon Powder Company
6430 Vista Drive
Shawnee, KS 66218
www.hodgdon.com

Hoppe's
9200 Cody St.
Overland Park, KS 66214
www.hoppes.com

Hornady Mfg. Company
3625 Old Potash Highway
PO Box 1848
Grand Island, NE 68803
www.hornady.com

Howard Leight/Honeywell
900 Douglas Pike
Smithfield, RI 02917
www.honeywellsafety.com

Huntington Die Specialties
601 Oro Dam Boulevard East
PO Box 991
Oroville, CA 95965
www.huntingtons.com

Kleen-Bore Inc.
13386 International Parkway
Jacksonville, FL 32218
www.safariland.com

Lapua
PO Box 2037
Sedalia, MO 65302-2037
www.lapua.com

Lazerroni Arms Company
1415 South Cherry Ave.
Tucson, AZ 85713
www.lazzeroni.com

Les Baer Custom, Inc.
1804 Iowa Drive
LeClaire, IA 52753
www.lesbaer.com

Lightfield Ammunition Corp.
PO Box 162
Adelphia, NJ 07710-0038
www.LightfieldSlugs.com

Lyman Products Corp.
475 Smith St.
Middletown, CT 06457
www.lymanproducts.com

Magtech Ammunition Co., Inc.
248 Apollo Drive, Suite 180
Lino Lakes, MN 55014
www.magtechammunition.com

M-Pro 7 Gun Care
9200 Cody St.
Overland Park, KS 66214
www.mpro7.com

MTM Molded Products Co.
PO Box 13117
Dayton, OH 45413
www.mtmcase-gard.com

Neco Nostalgia Enterprises
108 Ardmore Way
Benicia, CA 94510
www.neconos.com

Norma Precision AB
Jagargatan
Amotfors, S-67040, Sweden
www.norma-usa.com

Nosler, Inc.
107 Southwest Columbia St.
PO Box 671
Bend, OR 97709
www.nosler.com

Oehler Research Inc.
PO Box 9135
Austin, TX 78766
www.oehler-research.com

Otis Technology
6987 Laura St.
PO Box 582
Lyons Falls, NY 13368
www.otisgun.com

Outers Gun Care
1 ATK Way
Anoka, MN 55303
www.outers-guncare.com

Pacific Tool & Gauge
598 Avenue C
PO Box 2549
White City, OR 97503
www.pacifictoolandgauge.com

Peltor
3M Center, Building 223-45-02
St. Paul, MN 55144
www.3M.com

Plano Molding Company
431 East South St.
Plano, IL 60545-1676
www.planomolding.com

PMC Ammunition
23, Chungjeong-ro, Seodaemun-ku
Poongsan Building
Seoul, 120-837 South Korea
www.pmcammo.com

Pro Ears
6893 Sullivan Road
Grawn, MI 49637
www.pro-ears.com

Quality Cartridge
PO Box 445
Hollywood, MD 20636
www.qual-cart.com

Rainier Ballistics
4500 15th St. East
Tacoma, WA 98424
www.rainierballistics.com

Rare Ammo
1609 Highway 90
PO Box 334
Berwick, LA 70342-0334
www.rareammo.com

RCBS
605 Oro Dam Boulevard East
Oroville, CA 95965
www.rcbs.com

Redding Reloading Equipment
1089 Starr Road
Cortland, NY 13045
www.redding-reloading.com

Remington Arms Company, LLC
PO Box 700
Madison, NC 27025
www.remington.com

RUAG Ammotec USA, Inc.
5402 E. Diana St.
Tampa, FL 33610
www.ruag-usa.com

SBR Ammunition
140 Indigo Drive
Brunswick, GA 31525
www.sbrammunition.com

Shooter's Choice Gun Care Products
15050 Berkshire Industrial Parkway
Middlefield, OH 44062
www.shooters-choice.com

Shooting Chrony Inc.
2446 Cawthra Road, Building 1, Unit 10
Mississauga Ontario, L5A 3K6, Canada
www.shootingchrony.com

Sierra Bullets
1400 West Henry St.
Sedalia, MO 65301
www.sierrabullets.com

Silencerco
5511 South 6055 West
West Valley City, UT 84118
www.silencerco.com

Silver State Armory LLC
12913 US Highway 12
PO Box 962
Packwood, WA 98361
www.ssarmory.com

SportEAR
8683 South 700 West, Suite 200
Sandy, UT 84070
www.sportear.com

Stack-On Products Company
1360 North Old Rand Road
PO Box 489
Wauconda, IL 60084
www.stack-on.com

Super Brush LLC
800 Worcester St.
Springfield, MA 01151-1042
www.superbrush.com

Swift Bullet Company
201 Main St.
PO Box 27
Quinter, KS 67752
www.swiftbullets.com

Ten-X Ammunition
8722 Lanyard Court
Rancho Cucamonga, CA 91730
www.tenxammo.com

Tetra© Gun Care
8 Vreeland Road
Florham Park, NJ 07932
www.tetraguncare.com

Top Brass
10325 County Road 120
Salida, CO 81201
www.topbrass-inc.com

Traditions Performance Firearms
1375 Boston Post Road
PO Box 776
Old Saybrook, CT 06475
www.traditionsfirearms.com

Ultramax Ammunition
2112 Elk Vale Road
Rapid City, SD 57701
www.ultramaxammunition.com

Weatherby Inc.
1605 Commerce Way
Paso Robles, CA 93446
www.weatherby.com

Western Powders Inc.
PO Box 158
Miles City, MT 59301
www.westernpowders.com

Winchester Ammunition Corp., Div. Olin
600 Powder Mill Road
East Alton, IL 62024-1174
www.winchester.com

Wolf Performance Ammunition
PO Box 757
Placentia, CA 92871
www.wolfammo.com

Appendix 3: Helps for Handloaders

Most headlines at the annual SHOT (Shooting, Hunting and Outdoor Trade) Show trumpet new firearms. Support products get little press. But they're as important as the dish soap on your kitchen sink and the lug wrench in your automobile. Handloading benches, many of which serve as cleaning stations and repair centers too, collect the paraphernalia that keeps shooters shooting. Here are some worth a look:

4D Reamer Rentals—Want a wildcat chambering, but can't afford the reamer for your gunsmith? Fred Zeglin at 4D Reamers has more than 600 different reamers, ready to rent for that special project. He also markets barrels from McGowan, Criterion/CBI, and Green Mountain. Fred is a wildcat enthusiast and an accomplished gunsmith. I've used rifles he's barreled to Hawk wildcats. His 188-page hardcover book on the Hawk line is loaded with data. Fred has produced DVDs on wildcats. 4D Reamer Rentals, 432 E. Idaho St., Ste C420, Kalispell, MT 59901. 406-752-2520. *4-Dproducts.com*.

Americase Value Series gun cases—Made of .063-inch thick aluminum, Value Series firearms cases can be ordered with "heavy duty" .080-inch sides. Single- and double-rifle cases feature full-length piano hinges, padded spring-loaded handles and dual steel locking rods that secure the hasps. Thick foam inside protects firearm(s); seals keep out dust and moisture. Americase builds more than 130 models of cases, including versions for handguns and .50 BMG rifles. Ballistic Cordura nylon case covers are available too. Americase, 1610 E. Main St., Waxahachie, TX 75165. 800-927-2737. *Americase.com.*

▲ Shooters on the Vortex Challenge rifle course.

Battenfeld Technologies steel targets—As sequels to its popular Magnum Rifle gong, Battenfeld catalogs three additional gong targets. The Kill Zone Magnum Rifle gong, like its predecessor, comes separate or with frame and chains. The Dual Magnum Spinner and Resetting Popper Target include base and spindle. All feature AR 550 steel faces with a Brinell hardness of 550. Targets, chains, and reinforced steel-tube frames include a compartmented carry bag. Tool-free assembly. Battenfeld Technologies, 5885 W. Van Horn Tavern Rd., Columbia, MO 65203. 573-445-9200. *BattenfeldTechnologies.com.*

Brownells field packs—M16/M4 enthusiasts can tap Brownells for a complete firearms maintenance kit in a pouch. All tools and accessories to clean, field-strip, and even make minor repairs are here, in a zippered Cordura case with internal compartments. This armorer-grade hardware includes a brass/nylon hammer, punches and screwdriver with 10 bits, plus M16/M4-specific wrenches. Weight: 5 pounds. You can also choose a Remington 700 field pack, or one for Ruger's Mini-14. There's even one for "foreign weapons" (read: AK-47). Brownells, 200 S. Front St., Montezuma, IA 50171. 800-741-0015. *Brownells.com.*

Caldwell Shootin' Gallery—It's so much fun, you'll forget it makes you a better shot! This 55-pound portable unit brings an endless stream of moving targets in front of your .22 rimfire. Hits topple targets, which reset automatically as the drive chain brings them around again. Of steel construction, the Shootin' Gallery is powered by a 12-volt rechargeable battery. You'll get about five hours of fast-paced rifle or pistol practice from a single charge. I've used this device—it's addicting! Available from MidwayUSA, 5875 W. Van Horn Tavern Rd., Columbia, MO 65203. 800-243-3220. *Midwayusa.com.*

Carson magnifiers—Age reduces your eye's ability to focus up close. Enter Magniview, a 2x handheld magnifier that helps you read fine print, examine primers and cases, and start tiny gun screws. It has a 4.5x spot lens, too. Need more light? The new Magnibrite handheld, pocket-size magnifier has a slide-out 5x aspheric lens with LED (Light-Emitting Diode) assist. These are just two of dozens of visual aids listed in Carson's current catalog for outdoor enthusiasts and gunsmiths. Carson Optical, Inc., 35 Gilpin Ave., Hauppauge, NY 11788. 631-963-5000. *Carsonoptical.com.*

Flambeau Outdoors range bags— Made of tough black nylon, these bags have a big main compartment with additional pouches, mesh and full-fabric. A drop-down work apron keeps parts out of the dust and off concrete. External clips hold earmuffs and shooting glasses. Each bag comes with a Pistol Pack hard case with lockable latches. Choose a 18x10x12 bag with large pistol case and 12x9 ¼ x9 with smaller pistol case. Use these carry-alls for handloads too. Flambeau Outdoors, 15981 Valplast Rd., Middlefield, OH 44062. 440-632-1631. *Flambeauoutdoors.com.*

Forster Precision Plus Bushing Bump Neck Sizing Dies—Neck sizing extends case life. Each of these new dies comes with three cryogenically treated bushings in .002 increments. Use these dies in any press with standard 7/8-14 threads or in Forster's improved B-3 Co-Ax, with additional room for tall micrometer dies. Co-axial alignment of case and die, plus the quickest die change in the industry, have made the Co-Ax press a favorite of veteran handloaders. Forster Precision Products, 310 Lanark Ave., Lanark, IL 61046-9704. 815-493-6360. *Forsterproducts.com.*

Frankford Arsenal calipers—Once in a while you'll find a useful tool at a bargain. Calipers are a must-have for every handloader. Frankford Arsenal stainless steel dial calipers help with cartridge case and bullet measurements to .001 inch. So do FA electronic calipers. Both perform as well as instruments that list for much more (current FA prices: $30 for the dial calipers and $22.50 for the electronic version). An assortment of other economical but durable FA handloading products includes the brand's case tumbler. MidwayUSA, 5875 W. Van Horn Tavern Rd., Columbia, MO 65203. 800-243-3220. *Midwayusa.com.*

Gerber Magna-Tip Multi-Tool—Gerber builds this versatile tool for Brownells, combining a stainless steel multi-plier with straight and serrated knife blades, two-sided wood/metal file, Phillips and small, medium and large flat-blade screwdrivers. Slip the magnetic adapter over the Phillips head, and you can use any of nine included Magna-Tip bits. The adapter will also take dozens of other Magna-Tips, so you can customize your kit. In bright and black versions, this Multi-Tool comes with a ballistic nylon belt pouch. Brownells, 200 S. Front St., Montezuma, IA 50171. 800-741-0015. *Brownells.com.*

HPR Ammunition—A relatively new company, HPR specializes in task-specific handgun and rifle ammo for military, LE, and civilian applications. Top-end components are matched to specific firearms, too. The firm's .380 loads feature lightweight hollowpoints for lethal effect but manageable recoil in pocket autos. Frisky .357 loads presume a stout revolver with recoil-absorbing heft. A plethora of options in 9mm and .45 ACP complement those for the .40 S&W, .44 Magnum, and .45 Colt. Rifle rounds include the .223 (18 loads!), .308, and .300 Blackout. HPR, 1304 W. Red Baron Rd., Payson, AZ 85541. *HPRammo.com.*

Krieger rifle barrels—Custom rifle-makers have relied on John Krieger's single-point cut-rifled barrels for decades. I have several. Lapped after reaming and again after rifling, they have mirror-smooth bores with tolerances of just +.0005 over nominal diameters and .0001 maximum difference within each barrel! In 2002, Rich Desimone used a Krieger barrel to punch a 1.564-inch five-shot group at 1,000 yards! The wide range of contours and bores includes fluted and M1 and M14 Match versions and H-Bar AR-15 barrels. Krieger Barrels, Inc., 2024 Mayfield Rd., Richfield, WI 53076. 262-628-8558. *Kriegerbarrels.com.*

Lyman case cleaners, dies—The new Turbo Sonic 6000 case and gun-parts cleaner has a 6.3-quart tank. That's big enough for 1,300 9mm handgun hulls. Powered by industrial-grade ultrasonic transducers, it has a built-in drain and a large plastic parts basket. Lyman's Turbo Sonic cleaning solution (Orange Turbo, to mix with water) also works in the smaller Turbo Sonic 700, which features oscillation circuitry and digital controls. Lyman, which absorbed the Ideal brand, has served handloaders with tooling since black-powder days. Lyman, 475 Smith St., Middletown, CT 06457. 860-632-2020. *Lymanproducts.com.*

MTM Case-Gard rests, boxes—Plastic boxes are MTM's stock-in-trade. So is innovation. The company also sells rests and cleaning stations. A range box has a padded pistol compartment in the top tray. The Tactical Range Box for ARs has compartmented trays, plus supports to hold the rifle for cleaning. Utility Dry Boxes feature O-ring lid seals. Rifle/pistol loading blocks and ammo wallets come in several colors. Ammo cans have reinforced bottoms and walls, double padlock tabs, and stacking ridges. MTM Molded Products Co., 3370 Obco Ct., POB 13117, Dayton, OH 45414-0117. 800-543-0548. *Mtmcase-gard.com.*

Otis Technology cleaning kits—Known for compact but complete cleaning kits, Otis has AR service kits for .223 rifles. The Wingshooter for smoothbores includes 12-, 20, and 28-gauge brushes. The 3-Gun has brushes for .223, .40 S&W, .45 ACP, and 12 gauge bores. There's also Zombie packaging for the 3-Gun. If you can explain that, you'll probably want it. Kits feature coated cables with brass fittings and slotted tips. You get cut patches and cleaning/lubricating fluid, too. Durable, bagel-size zippered-nylon Otis pouches tuck anywhere. Otis Technology, POB 582, Dept NWS, Lyons Falls, NY 13368. 800-684-7486. *Otisgun.com.*

Redding bullet seating micrometers—When you're chasing top accuracy, eliminating variables is top priority. Co-axial bullet seating to exactly the same depth time after time makes ammo more uniform. Redding's new bullet-seating micrometers with ½x20 threads fit most seating dies, replacing ordinary plugs. In STD and VLD configurations, they ensure .001 precision. Redding forming dies and a National Match die set for the .300 Blackout have also joined Redding's line. Redding Reloading Equipment, 1089 Starr Rd., Cortland, NY 13045. 607-753-3331. *Redding-reloading.com.*

Tetra Gun ProVise gun care vise—This molded plastic accessory belongs on every bench. The padded butt clamp, middle support, and forward V-rest hold long guns securely. Or use the clamp and support for handguns. Recesses in the generous 28-inch base hold cleaning supplies—of which Tetra Gun has all you can imagine. The ProVise rubber feet won't mar table surfaces. Ideal for bore cleaning, this vise helps with scope mounting and other operations that require two free hands. FTI, Inc., 8 Vreeland Rd., Florham Park, NJ 07932-0955. 973-443-0004. *Tetraguncare.com.*

Timney replacement trigger—If your trigger-pull moves the rifle or prompts a twitch in your hand, arm, or shoulder—or delays the shot—you'll miss. Since 1946, Timney has offered affordable, easily installed replacement triggers. The catalog now includes more than 75 triggers for military rifles and sporters from Remington, Ruger, Sako, Savage, Weatherby, Winchester, and others. They're most useful now, given factory triggers with lawyer-proof pulls and limited adjustments. US-made, Timneys carry lifetime warranties. Timney Triggers, 3940 Clarendon Ave., Phoenix, AZ 85019. 866-484-6639. *Timneytriggers.com.*